023256

Publisher
Marie Butler-Knight

Product Manager
Phil Kitchel

Managing Editor
Cari Luna

Senior Acquisitions Editor
Renee Wilmeth

Development Editor
Nancy D. Warner

Production Editor
Billy Fields

Copy Editor
Amy Lepore

Illustrator
Jody P. Schaeffer

Cover Designers
Mike Freeland
Kevin Spear

Book Designers
Scott Cook and Amy Adams of DesignLab

Indexer
Angie Bess

Layout/Proofreading
Svetlana Dominguez
Terri Edwards
Bob LaRoche
Donna Martin
Gloria Schurick

Contents at a Glance

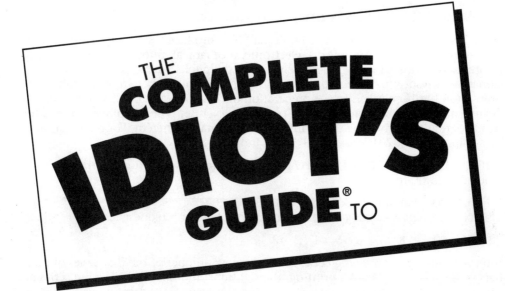

THE **COMPLETE IDIOT'S GUIDE**® TO

Project Management

Second Edition

by Sunny and Kim Baker

alpha
books

Macmillan USA, Inc.
201 West 103rd Street
Indianapolis, IN 46290

A Pearson Education Company

Contents

Part 2: The Project Initiation Processes   45

5 Identifying Stakeholders and Defining Their Roles   47

6 Selecting the Projects That Are Worth Doing   55

7 Scoping Out the Goals for a Project   63

14 The Steps to the Critical Path and a Balanced Schedule 165

15 Budgeting Options for Your Projects 181

Foreword

Project management isn't just for construction engineers and military logistics experts any more.

Consider the case known in my circle as "The Wedding from Hell." Two of my friends—a pair of the most organized managers I've ever met—once catered an out-of-town, afternoon wedding for a colleague. They spent days consulting with the bride and her mother, hiring bartenders and waiters, lining up transportation, and buying and preparing the food, all in addition to handling their busy jobs at a major arts institution. Then, at noon on Friday, the day before the big event, they received a phone call from another colleague. "I have some bad news about the wedding," he said. "It's *today*."

The wedding still took place, with dinner only an hour late. Not bad, considering that when they arrived at what had been promised was a fully stocked kitchen, there wasn't a pot or pan to be found anywhere, and they had to cook the vegetables in coffee percolators. But the moonlighting caterers paid a high price for their failure to manage the project properly. The mistake cost them their friendship with the bride, not to mention their fee. And they had to spend a fortune to dry clean their business suits. (Try making ceviche while driving 70 miles an hour up Interstate 95.)

"The Wedding from Hell" makes a good argument for project management. Like my friends the caterers, you may be taking on a project as a way to launch your own small business. Perhaps you have to organize a conference for your company's hundred biggest clients. Or, your company asked you to open its new store on Madison Avenue or its regional sales office in Sioux Falls. You may even have been charged with reconfiguring your company's whole information system or developing a new product or service.

Top executives like to talk about how their strategy depends on their company's vision, mission, and values. But when pressed, they admit that what really matters is their ability to execute—to get the job done flawlessly, under budget and on time. Without that ability, strategy is just wishful thinking. And great project management skills are essential to anyone who wants to put their strategy into action.

This book will teach you the nuts and bolts of project management, from setting priorities to controlling schedules and expenses to reporting on the results. Using plenty of humor and plain-spoken good sense, Kim and Sunny Baker tell you how to plan a project, set up and lead a team, monitor progress, and bring your project to a satisfying close. Along the way, you'll learn techniques for communicating with team members and anyone else with a stake in the project, resolving the inevitable conflicts, and handling any changes that come your way. Finally, you'll find out how to choose the right computer software to make project management easier.

Don't let all the planning, charting, and reporting that good project management demands scare you off. Even if you don't know a Gantt from a gnu, the tools this book offers will help you succeed in running any project.

You may still end up having to cope with the unexpected, but at least you won't end up with raw seafood all over your suit.

Miriam Leuchter, Managing Editor, U.S. Banker

Miriam Leuchter is the Managing editor of *U.S. Banker,* a monthly magazine for financial services executives published by Thomson Financial Media in New York City. She is the former editor of the *Journal of Business Strategy,* the bimonthly magazine for the corporate strategist, published by Faulkner & Gray in New York City. Before taking the helm at JBS, she served as its consulting editor, while running *Forecast,* the magazine of demographics and market strategy. She has also covered the banking industry and economic development for *Crain's New York Business.*

Introduction

Is rubbing the Magic 8 Ball your best shot at coming up with a project schedule? Does the word "budget" send chills up your spine? When your boss asks for a project status report, do you call the Psychic Network first? Do your project team meetings remind you of clown practice at Barnum and Bailey? Even worse, do you keep a copy of the "Help Wanted" ads in your "Action" file fearing that someone might find out what's really going on with the project? Well, you don't need to resort to psychics, magic, or wizardry to manage projects. And you don't need a genius IQ, or even an MBA, to succeed. What you need is this book, *The Complete Idiot's Guide to Project Management, Second Edition*!

It doesn't take a magician, a soothsayer, or a genius to manage a project, but it does take special skills to bring projects in on time and within budget. Yes, there's some planning and charting involved in getting projects from start to finish, but this book takes the complexity out of the process and puts you in control. The road to successful project management is mapped in the following pages.

The book explains in easy-to-understand language how the power of time-proven project management methods can help your mission-critical projects blast off to bring you and your company to new heights. You'll learn how project teams, in spite of politics and personalities, can be pointed in the same direction; and how changes, no matter how frequent, can be guided to keep projects on track. You'll learn that it's skill, not luck, that makes the difference in reaching your project destination.

How to Use This Book

The book has seven parts, which we recommend you read from beginning to end. Together, the parts demystify the steps and tools behind successful project management and offer practical advice that can be adapted to the needs of today's fast-moving, ever-changing organizations.

Part 1, "Project Management Power," explains how to identify projects that need better management. You'll be introduced to steps that can be used to bring any project to a successful conclusion, on time and within budget, and to the three secrets to success behind any project: the project manager, the team, and the plan.

Part 2, "The Project Initiation Processes," presents techniques to start a project off on the right foot with clear goals and a motivated project team. This part is especially important because the way a project starts off usually defines the way it will end up.

Part 3, "The Project Planning Processes," explains the basic planning processes central to successful project management. You'll observe how tasks are defined, scheduled, and budgeted using powerful charting and analysis tools that can help you scope out projects of all sorts and sizes. This is the most technical part of the book, so you might want to read it twice. Mastering the tools in this part is important because no project is ever better than the plan used to manage the effort.

Part 4, "The Executing Processes," presents proven techniques to transform the plan into action focused toward meeting the project objectives. This is key to successful project management. The end result of a project is always related to the way the plan is translated into actual work in the real world.

Part 5, "The Controlling Processes," talks about ways to monitor, track, and adjust each project so that you can keep everything on schedule and within budget. You'll also find easy-to-follow guidelines for dealing with the most common project problems and for minimizing the impact of the changes and conflicts that are part of almost every project. Using the techniques in this section, you can put even a totally derailed project back on track.

In Part 6, "The Closing Processes," you discover how to finish your project and reap the rewards of a job well done.

In Part 7, "The Organization and Tools to Make Project Management Prosper," you'll learn how to put the discipline of project management to work throughout your organization.

Extras

To add to the material in the main text, a series of boxes throughout the book highlight specific items that can help you understand and implement the material in each chapter:

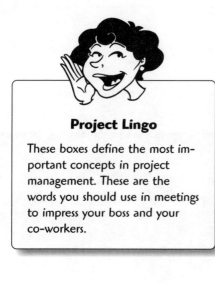

Project Lingo

These boxes define the most important concepts in project management. These are the words you should use in meetings to impress your boss and your co-workers.

High Water!

Sometimes things just go wrong, no matter how well you plan your project. Luckily, there are usually warnings before things get too bad, if you know how to recognize them. In these boxes, you'll learn how to read the danger signs before you get swamped with problems.

Time Is Money

Use the suggestions in these boxes to keep your schedule up-to-date and your budget under control. Hopefully the advice will spare you the embarrassment of running out of money before the project is completed. You'll also pick up on a variety of tips used by veteran project managers to run projects of all sizes and kinds.

Words from the Wise

These quotes and tips include observations from our experience and other experts that may help inspire you to greater achievements, or simply help keep you motivated to do your best, even when the project seems impossible.

Along the Critical Path

Longer stories or information tangentially related to the text appear in these boxes. (You'll learn about critical path—an actual project management term—in Chapters 10 and 11.)

Acknowledgments

Over the years and through countless projects of all sizes, people too numerous to mention have offered advice, shared techniques, and provided examples (good and bad) that have helped us hone our skills as project managers. All of these people deserve our thanks, as they've taught us the ropes and provided us with models to copy (and avoid) as we bring our own projects from idea to fruition.

Regarding this project, the book, and all of the people at Macmillan—editorial paragons, production wizards, and marketing gurus—deserve our special thanks for their professionalism, skill, and good ideas. We appreciate the opportunity to work with such a class act. We also want to express our gratitude to our agent, Mike Snell, who is always smart enough to see an opportunity that makes sense.

Most important, we want to thank you, the reader, for considering the tools and techniques we lay out in these pages. We understand the importance of your projects, and appreciate that you are taking time to consider our ideas for getting them done better, faster, and cheaper.

Special Thanks from the Publisher to the Technical Editor

The Complete Idiot's Guide to Project Management, Second Edition, was reviewed by an expert who not only checked the technical accuracy of what you'll learn in this book, but also provided invaluable insight and suggestions. Our special thanks are extended to James MacIntyre.

Trademarks

All terms mentioned in this book that are known to be or are suspected of being trademarks or service marks have been appropriately capitalized. Alpha Books and Macmillan USA, Inc. cannot attest to the accuracy of this information. Use of a term in this book should not be regarded as affecting the validity of any trademark or service mark.

Part 1
Project Management Power

Meeting the demands of the fast-changing environment of modern business requires a focus on priorities, better management techniques, and effective structures for communication. For these reasons, people like you are turning to project management techniques to meet their goals. The processes and methods of project management provide the structure, focus, flexibility, and control to help guide teams to outstanding results, on time and within budget.

In this section, you'll be introduced to the processes and lifecycle phases of the project management discipline and the success secrets of experienced project managers. You'll also learn how to differentiate between important projects and just plain work, the first step in consistently bringing your projects in on time and within budget. If you can do that, you'll be quite a hero in your organization. That's the power of project management.

Chapter 1

Projects, Projects Everywhere

In This Chapter

➤ Why project management is vital in today's competitive world

➤ Projects versus ordinary work

➤ Project harmony: a balancing act

➤ Six features shared by all projects

➤ Identifying projects that need better management

➤ The common project questions you will learn how to answer

The twenty-first century is here along with tighter budgets, less time to get things done, and fewer resources. Sure, teletransportation and faster-than-light travel are still *Star Trek* fantasies, but rapid change, expanding technologies, and global marketing are real in this, the new millennium.

To compete in the new century, you'll need to do more with less. Competition will continue to pressure you to come up with better ideas. You won't have time to waste on stale methods or wimpy techniques. To captain your business in the future, you'll need to build things faster, cheaper, and better. And you'll need to get things done right the first time.

Project Lingo

A **project** is a sequence of tasks with a beginning and an end that is bounded by time, resources, and desired results. This means that a project has a specific, desired outcome; a deadline or target date when the project must be done; and a budget that limits the amount of people, supplies, and money that can be used to complete the project.

Time is Money

Using project management (PM) techniques to control a project may seem like an additional burden, but it saves time and money in the long term. Properly applied, PM techniques allow you to hold the project in the palm of your hand rather than having it swirling around like a tempest in your brain as you contemplate all the elements involved.

Projects are becoming the way of the working world. Computers and automation have eliminated many types of repetitive work. This has freed people to focus on building new things—new products, new services, and improved organizations. And where there are things that need to be created, there is a need for projects.

But before you can use any of the advice in this book, you need to distinguish the projects in your business from the ordinary, repetitive work. In this chapter, you'll not only learn how to recognize the projects in your business, you'll also see why projects need a special kind of management to get them done right. This will be the first step in taking your projects into the twenty-first century.

Why You Need a New Project-Oriented Outlook

Like most people in business, you are responsible for ordinary work and projects. You probably don't even think about the difference. You just think you have too much to do.

Okay, you're right. There's always too much to do. But people often fail at managing projects not because projects involve too much work, but because the difference between routine work and projects is not clear.

Pretend for a moment that you're a salesperson at Spacely Sprockets. You're already working full-time, day in and day out. Then your boss asks you to open the new sales office in Richmond. Every day you respond to customer requests, make sales presentations, and write trip reports after your client visits. It's pretty easy to figure out that setting up a new sales office is different than your day-to-day sales activities. But what exactly is it that makes the job of opening the sales office a project and the work with your customers just plain work?

Both the project to build a sales office and the everyday work of contacting customers may involve similar activities such as making phone calls, writing reports, and going to meetings, but projects have different goals than ongoing, day-to-day job activities. You do a project only once, and when the project gets done, something exists that never existed before. In this case, you'll have a new sales office.

All Projects Are Work, but Not All Work Is a Project

Here's another example. As the administrative assistant to the CEO, you might be responsible for coordinating the company's annual United Way fund-raising drive, but you'd still be responsible for day-to-day activities including writing minutes of board meetings, scheduling appointments, screening mail, and a myriad of other recurring tasks. The fund-raising drive is a project because it only gets done once a year and it has a clear end result—the deposit of a large sum of donations into the United Way fund account. The ordinary calls, reports, and letters of your job just keep getting done, over and over, every day. There is no end to the process.

To look at assignments as projects as opposed to just plain work or ongoing operations, you need to change your perspective. The goals and deadlines of the business routine are general. Routine work is defined within the scope of a department or functional job description. For example, you probably open your incoming mail every morning and respond to letters. You also might read reports, schedule appointments, attend meetings, screen phone calls, draft letters, or perform numerous other tasks. All this has to be coordinated and completed every day. As much effort as this involves, none of these tasks is a project. They're all just ordinary work.

Most ordinary work is repetitive, process-oriented, and, yes, often boring. Projects usually are defined as specific end-results outside the routine job functions. All projects have a beginning and an end, and every project produces a unique product. Projects have a life of their own, and even though the successful completion and coordination of projects is critical to the success of an organization, projects generally operate outside the normal, repetitive routine of business life.

In today's world, everyone wants to be a project manager. That's because project management skills transcend industry boundaries, resulting in high-paying jobs and self-directed careers. Projects add excitement to an otherwise work-a-day business. They turn office/factory doldrums into new experiences and new opportunities.

Above and Beyond the Ordinary Work

To better understand the differences between ordinary work and projects, consider the following lists that compare the two. Note that the projects all have definable goals. They also have a beginning and an end. Most ordinary work must be done over and over again. Most projects are done only once (if they're done right the first time).

Ordinary Work	Projects
Responding to a customer's request	Producing a monthly customer newsletter for information
Making coffee for the office	Catering the inaugural ceremonies for the president
Writing a letter to a prospect	Writing and publishing a book
Hooking up a printer to your computer	Implementing a company-wide computer network
Meeting with an employee to discuss a new procedure	Hiring a sales team for the new office in Madison
Attending a conference	Promoting your product in a two-week *program* across the country
Ordering office supplies	Opening a new sales office
Writing a progress update memo	Producing the corporate annual report for the stockholders' meeting

Project Lingo

Program is another name for a recurring project. Programs happen over and over again. Good examples include producing the monthly customer newsletter, publishing the annual report, and coordinating the Rose Bowl parade. Recurring projects happen predictably, but each cycle involves a new plan and a unique end product. The plan, resources, and results are what make programs different from other repetitive tasks such as filing.

If It's Not a Project, It's Just Plain Work

As you examine the preceding lists that show differences between ordinary work and projects, you'll see that projects have six important features that make them different from most ordinary work:

➤ A project has a defined beginning and end. Getting from the beginning to the end of a project typically involves a definable sequence of steps or activities.

➤ Projects use *resources* (people, time, money) that have been specifically allocated to the work of the project, as opposed to the ongoing operations of the business.

➤ Every project produces a unique outcome. These project outcomes or end results also have specific goals of quality and performance. Remember: When a project gets done, something new exists that didn't exist before.

➤ Projects (hopefully) follow a planned, organized approach to meet their objectives.

➤ A project usually involves a team of people to get it done.

➤ Projects always have a unique set of stakeholders (including the project team, the customers, the project manager, the corporate executives, the government representatives, or other people who have an interest in the project). Stakeholders almost always bring differing expectations about end results to the project. These expectations must be managed for the completed project to be considered a success.

Project Lingo

Resources are the time, people, money, equipment, and facilities used to complete a project. When you read this word in this book, unless one element such as money is specifically mentioned, you can assume that the reference is to all five of these elements.

Project Success: A Balance Among Time, Resources, Results, and Perceptions

Yes, it may be hard to believe that a project for transporting astronauts to Mars has much in common with opening a new sales office in Richmond, but check it out and you'll see that both of these undertakings meet the criteria to be called projects.

Regardless of their size, both share the six features of projects, and their success is measured in terms of time, resources, and results. Both projects will be deemed successful if they get done on time, use only the resources that have been budgeted or planned, and deliver the results that were agreed upon by the stakeholders.

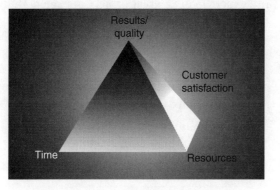

The Universal Project Pyramid

This pyramid demonstrates the balance among time, resources, results, and customer satisfaction that is required to bring a project to a successful conclusion.

7

This brings us to the factors that are essential to the success of all projects. These factors include:

➤ Agreement among the project team and the stakeholders (which include the customers and management) on the goals of the project. Without clear goals and agreement among the stakeholders, the results can be devastating. You'll learn ways to develop clear, agreed-upon goals in this book. No project can be a success unless everybody agrees that they want the same thing produced.

➤ Support from management to supply the resources and to remove organizational obstacles. Without management support, project managers rarely have enough authority of their own to execute the decisions and policies necessary to complete a project. To get that support, you'll need to manage "upward" as well as manage the project team. You'll also learn ways to do this as you read through the book.

➤ Communication that is effective, appropriately delivered, and ongoing throughout the project. Almost every project management technique involves some form of communication. Without clear, concise communication, the people on a project team will never be able to agree on goals and then meet them. The project plan is one major component in this communication, but there are many other components required for project success. This book not only explains how to plan a project, it also examines the ongoing communication necessary to keep a project on focus and on schedule.

Words from the Wise

Project management methods are useful if they can be placed in the context of today's trends, impacts, and technology. If we merely forge ahead and use them as they were used 30 years ago, we will meet with, at most, limited success.

—Bennet P. Lients and Karthryn P. Rea in *Project Management for the 21st Century*

It's Not Magic

Great project managers are often considered magicians, as if their skills were endowed at birth. But, in my experience, all great project managers share skills that can be learned. These skills include the following:

➤ The ability to plan
➤ The ability to gain consensus among diverse groups of people
➤ The ability to communicate effectively
➤ The ability to employ the proven formal techniques of project management

Successful project management involves both art and science. Yes, some of the art of great project managers invokes time-honed political and interpersonal skills, especially the creative ability to make tough decisions and take appropriate risks. But these artful skills can be learned if you observe, listen, and study. And because all projects share similar features and require a balance among time, resources, and results; similar formal project management techniques, the science of the great project managers, is also necessary to bring your projects to successful conclusions. These techniques are what you're going to learn about in the rest of the book.

Whether it's training a team of new employees, creating an ad campaign, developing a new software product, or reorganizing the corporation, the techniques of project management can be used to improve results in meeting the objectives of your projects. Project management tools also can be used to correct midcourse problems that would otherwise go undetected and undermine the success of the project.

They're Not Always Created Equal

Of course, in spite of their similarities, all projects are unique. Projects involve different goals, employ different people with distinctive personalities, take place over varying time frames, and produce different results.

No two projects, even recurring projects with the same general objectives, are ever identical in implementation. People who manage projects successfully quickly learn to become managers of exceptions and risks because there are always plenty of surprises, even in small projects. Thankfully, the project management toolbox offers techniques for identifying and managing the unique attributes and risks as well as the similar aspects of projects. You will learn about these techniques throughout the book.

When you master the techniques of project management, you'll see that the project of opening a sales office and the project of building a spaceship to fly to Mars depend on many of the same project management tools, even though the projects require disparate implementation skills and dissimilar technical resources. You'll also learn that the project management techniques best used in general business projects are the same ones applied by engineers to develop complex new technologies.

How Many Projects Are You Responsible For?

Projects are the means by which companies change and adapt to meet the needs of changing markets, new technologies, and expanding opportunities. Given that business is becoming more project oriented, almost everyone will benefit from learning the project management skills in this book.

As you start reviewing the activities in your business, you'll see that the business endeavors that meet the project criteria are endless, varying from small to large and from simple to complex. If you try listing all the projects in your area of responsibility, you may discover a lot more on the list than you anticipated.

All Projects Great and Small

It's usually easy to identify the most complex projects in business, such as developing a new model automobile, designing a new data-processing system, or building an overseas manufacturing facility. But smaller and more mundane business endeavors can also be projects, even though they may not be called projects.

Consider the job of hiring a new marketing manager for your company. Most experienced managers wouldn't consider this a project because they know how to plan and schedule all the steps in their head. You simply put an ad in the paper, interview some people, and make a choice. But hiring a new marketing manager involves deadlines, people, money, and time—and hopefully, you only have to do it once. You'll probably use a team of people to interview the candidates as well. And when you're done with the project, you'll also have something you didn't have before—a new marketing manager.

When viewed this way, hiring a marketing manager is a project and deserves to be treated with the respect of a project. Good project management will help you hire the right marketing manager in the shortest period of time—and that could make a big difference to your company.

Sure, it won't take as long to plan the project of hiring a marketing manager as it will to plan how to build a new bridge across the Potomac. You probably won't have to use a computer program to create the schedule or to manage the budget (although you might). But using good project management techniques from this book is still important because the choice of the marketing manager is important to your business.

You can't afford to treat even a small project, such as hiring a new employee, like ordinary work. Now would be a good time to identify two small but important projects, one from your work and one personal project that you have been postponing. For practice, you can apply to them the techniques you learn in this book.

Project List

*Today's Date*_____

Project Name	Does it have a beginning and end?	Does it use resources?	Does it have specific goals?	Does it need a plan?

Use this form to list all the projects in your business.

The Next Step

In the following pages, you'll be taken step-by-step through the fundamentals of planning, scheduling, tracking, and controlling the costs and resources of any project—whether the project is mundane or technical or multifaceted and complex. These practical techniques are applicable to the projects that people in sales, marketing, human resources, finance, and general management positions are responsible for—yet they are based on the same general, accepted methods employed by engineering project managers in building skyscrapers, satellites, or software systems.

Words from the Wise

"No project is too small to not be taken seriously."

—An Intel project manager

After learning about project management techniques, you'll be able to answer questions like these:

➤ How can I best define the work that needs to be done to make the project a success?

➤ How can I gain ongoing consensus about the goals and scope of the project?

➤ How long should the project really take to complete, and how much should it cost?

➤ How will I attain enough authority to get things done?

➤ Who should I put on my project team?

➤ How much work can be expected of each person on the project?

➤ How can I control cost overruns?

➤ Where is the project in danger of failure?

If you can answer all these questions, who knows? Maybe with good project management you really could build that teletransporter.

Beam me up, Scotty! We're ready to go.

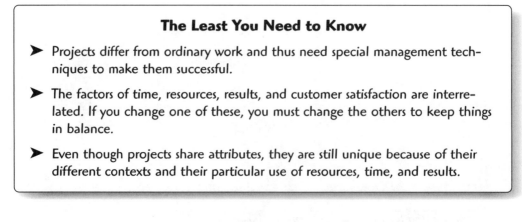

The Least You Need to Know

➤ Projects differ from ordinary work and thus need special management techniques to make them successful.

➤ The factors of time, resources, results, and customer satisfaction are interrelated. If you change one of these, you must change the others to keep things in balance.

➤ Even though projects share attributes, they are still unique because of their different contexts and their particular use of resources, time, and results.

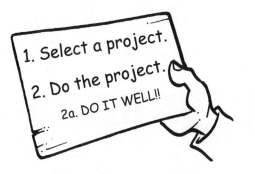

The Processes That Work

The pressure is on. Like most people in business, you have more projects to manage than ever before. Whether you're responsible for major projects, such as bringing new products to market, or smaller projects, such as producing a customer newsletter, you need to get your projects done on time and within budget. Even worse, you're expected to get your projects done faster, better, cheaper, and with fewer resources.

Don't panic. You're not doomed—yet. You just need a new method and the right tools to sort things out. The new method is called project management, and the tools are the procedures, strategies, and tips that can be used during the project management processes to keep things focused on the project objectives. Together, the project management tools you'll learn about in this book can help you bring sanity to the chaos of managing wide-ranging projects, diverse personalities, and the constant change associated with modern business.

Why Do You Need to Learn About Project Management?

The cost-reduction programs and management approaches of the past are not enough to meet today's corporate challenges. Meeting the demands of the fast-changing environment of modern business requires a focus on priorities, better tracking techniques, and effective structures for communication. Companies need to streamline operations, reduce risks, and improve overall productivity. Project management techniques are one part of a solution to adapt and prosper.

Time Is Money

Good project management saves money. Providing effective control of expensive resources (people, money, equipment) involved in projects not only helps the bottom line but also delivers the "goods" when they need to be delivered.

Project management is simply a combination of steps and techniques for keeping the ol' goals, budget, and schedule in line. Project management tools offer a way to avoid the frustration of missed deadlines, unclear expectations, and budget overruns. By clearly defining responsibilities for activities, focusing resources on specific objectives, and providing a structure for communicating within and across organizational boundaries, the project management processes can help anyone meet project goals better and with less frustration.

What Is Project Management All About?

The *project management* toolbox for business includes manual and computerized processes that are directly applicable to improving performance and efficiency in today's organizations. Project management techniques offer proven methods for working with project teams formed across traditional, functional, and organizational boundaries.

Putting You In Charge

Project Lingo

Project management is a discipline of combining systems, techniques, and people to complete a project within established goals of time, budget, and quality.

Ideally, in a project-driven business, work is managed and controlled by the people doing the work—not by an executive two or three levels removed from the tasks. People in project groups are able to assume responsibility for and derive satisfaction from their own objectives while continuing to contribute to the larger objectives of the organization as a whole.

Okay, but Does It Really Work?

At this point, you're probably thinking that project management tools may be useful for engineers who need to structure and focus their efforts for building bridges and dams, but if you're not in engineering, you may wonder if the techniques are relevant to your needs and those of your modern business?

Along the Critical Path

The first modern application of project management is often attributed to the building of the first nuclear submarine in the 1950s. Hyman Rickover was the project manager for this undertaking. The admiral was faced with coordinating hundreds of contractors who kept asking for more resources. Everything had to be done by hand, and there were few methods available for coordinating all the complexity. Out of this need came the technique now known as the Program Evaluation and Review Technique (PERT) and the critical path method. (You'll learn a version of these methods later in this book.) Over the years, the techniques continued to be used on large-scale aerospace, military, and construction projects. Project management really took off in the 1960s when computer programs for project management were made commercially available. (For the record, those early programs cost hundreds of thousands of dollars and ran on computers the size of a house. Today, equally powerful programs cost only a few hundred dollars and run on ordinary personal computers.)

As a skeptic, you may ask how massive projects such as the Pyramids in Egypt or even the Great Wall of China were completed without the aid of project management tools. And given that projects obviously got done long before anyone came up with project management techniques, why should you bother learning how to plan, schedule, track, and control your projects with anything more than you've used in the past? After all, most of your work gets done eventually—and it doesn't go over budget too often.

Sure, just like the engineers in Egypt with thousands of slaves and unlimited resources at their disposal, it is still possible to get projects done today without using proven project management techniques. But why work harder than you have to? Project management can help you reduce risk and can make it easier to get more done with less effort. If you don't believe us, try it out. You'll see that the project management process will really help you achieve more predictable results.

This is not to say that project management techniques will make managing projects a perfect science. Projects always involve people, and getting people to work together to accomplish defined goals is always complex. The techniques and discipline of project management just make it easier to coordinate things and can help you secure more predictable results. The techniques also help in getting you out of trouble when things go wrong.

Tools for Modern Times

The project management process offers you clear steps and powerful tools that can be employed to get projects done on time and within budget—this is something from which everyone can benefit.

Many organizations have already introduced project management processes into their everyday operations. For this reason, some tools may already be familiar to you including teams, charted schedules, matrixed management, zero-based budgeting, and streamlined reports.

All Projects Mundane and Marvelous

If you're still thinking that your projects are too small or too ordinary to benefit from project management, think again. The project management process can be used with all sorts of projects, whether they are onetime endeavors, recurring projects (often called programs), or product-oriented undertakings. The project management process supplies the necessary structure, organization, focus, and control to drive any project from concept to successful completion.

Can Project Management Help You?

To decide whether you or your organization would benefit from the project management processes, even for your small projects, take a few minutes to answer the questions on the worksheet in the following section. Like most people, you can probably improve your ability to get things done on time and within budget—and the project management processes can help.

The Five Processes of Project Management

It's important to remember that the project management processes work for projects of all kinds because of the project similarities discussed in Chapter 1, "Projects, Projects Everywhere." Like living beings, all projects have predictable stages that start with an idea to do something and end (hopefully) with the delivery of a complete project that meets its goals for quality or performance.

In total, there are five general processes in every project: initiating, planning, executing, controlling, and closing. These five processes parallel the project management processes as defined in the *Project Management Institute (PMI)* Project Management Body of Knowledge (PMBOK). The PMBOK is PMI's reference document describing core project management functions, processes, and techniques.

Project Lingo

PMI is an acronym for the Project Management Institute, a professional organization that studies and promotes project management techniques. If you want to join PMI to learn more about project management, contact information is provided at the back of this book in Appendix B.

Each of the five general processes includes different tasks, behaviors, and skills that are necessary to be successful. You'll learn about these in subsequent chapters. For now, take a look at the five general processes to understand how project management proceeds from beginning to end.

Project Initiating Process

The initiating process stresses the selection of a project worth doing and then the development of a vision and the establishment of goals for the project. During project initiation, some key individuals will be brought together to form a core project team (often called the management team) to start the planning process. The general steps in initiating a project include:

➤ Recognizing that a project should be done.

➤ Determining what the project should accomplish.

➤ Defining the overall project goals.

➤ Defining general expectations of customers, management, or other *stakeholders* as appropriate.

➤ Defining the general project scope.

➤ Selecting initial members of the project team.

➤ Writing and agreeing on the statement of work or contract for the project.

➤ Establishing the "rules" for the project including levels of authority, communication channels, and the chain of command.

Complete this worksheet to determine whether you and your enterprise could benefit from employing the power of project management in your projects.

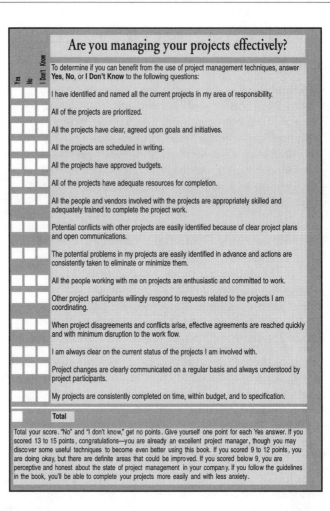

Are you managing your projects effectively?

To determine if you can benefit from the use of project management techniques, answer **Yes, No,** or **I Don't Know** to the following questions:

Yes	No	I Don't Know	
			I have identified and named all the current projects in my area of responsibility.
			All of the projects are prioritized.
			All the projects have clear, agreed upon goals and initiatives.
			All the projects are scheduled in writing.
			All the projects have approved budgets.
			All of the projects have adequate resources for completion.
			All the people and vendors involved with the projects are appropriately skilled and adequately trained to complete the project work.
			Potential conflicts with other projects are easily identified because of clear project plans and open communications.
			The potential problems in my projects are easily identified in advance and actions are consistently taken to eliminate or minimize them.
			All the people working with me on projects are enthusiastic and committed to work.
			Other project participants willingly respond to requests related to the projects I am coordinating.
			When project disagreements and conflicts arise, effective agreements are reached quickly and with minimum disruption to the work flow.
			I am always clear on the current status of the projects I am involved with.
			Project changes are clearly communicated on a regular basis and always understood by project participants.
			My projects are consistently completed on time, within budget, and to specification.
			Total

Total your score. "No" and "I don't know," get no points. Give yourself one point for each Yes answer. If you scored 13 to 15 points, congratulations—you are already an excellent project manager, though you may discover some useful techniques to become even better using this book. If you scored 9 to 12 points, you are doing okay, but there are definite areas that could be improved. If you scored below 9, you are perceptive and honest about the state of project management in your company. If you follow the guidelines in the book, you'll be able to complete your projects more easily and with less anxiety.

Project Planning Process

The planning process involves defining the work necessary for completion of the project, identifying the resources required to complete the project, devising a schedule, and developing a budget for the project. Planning also involves identifying objectives for *stakeholders* and team members involved in the project and establishing the means to achieve those objectives. Some of the typical activities involved in the planning phase include:

➤ Refining the project *scope*, which includes identifying the balance required among results, time, and resources.

➤ Listing tasks and activities that will lead to achieving the project goals.

➤ Sequencing activities in the most efficient manner possible.

➤ Developing a workable schedule and budget for assigning resources to the activities required to complete the project.

➤ Getting the plan agreed to and approved by the appropriate stakeholders.

The five phases of project management can be used to manage any project to a successful conclusion.

Project Executing Process

The executing process involves coordinating and guiding project team members to get the work done as laid out in the approved project plan. Executing processes, also known as implementation processes in other books, concentrate on keeping resources and people focused on the work. Some of the executing tasks include:

➤ Procuring necessary resources (money, people, equipment, time) to carry out the project plan.

➤ Leading the team.

➤ Meeting with team members.

➤ Securing the special talent and expertise required to implement the tasks.

➤ Communicating with stakeholders (an ongoing process).

Project Controlling Process

The controlling process is about watching over the project. Controlling a project involves measuring progress toward the objectives and taking action to ensure that deviations from the plan do not adversely affect the end results of the project. The controlling processes stress your understanding of unexpected delays, cost overruns, or changes in scope. When controlling a project, the project manager must decide between alternatives for solving problems. Controlling activities may include:

19

➤ Monitoring deviation from the plan.

➤ Taking corrective action to match actual progress on the plan.

➤ Receiving and evaluating project changes requested from stakeholders and team members.

➤ Rescheduling the project as necessary.

➤ Adapting resource levels as necessary.

➤ Changing (usually cutting) the project scope.

➤ Returning to the planning stage when necessary to make adjustments to the project goals and then getting them approved by the stakeholders.

➤ Fire-fighting (also known as conflict resolution) to resolve problems that always arise during a project.

Project Closing Process

The closing process is the final process in project management. The closing process involves time for both celebration and reflection. The closing process includes keeping people involved in bringing the project to fruition, even when their thoughts may be moving on to new enterprises. The closing process stresses gaining acceptance of the end-product and bringing the project to an orderly conclusion. The activities at this phase may include:

➤ Acknowledging achievement and results.

➤ Shutting down the operations and disbanding the team.

➤ Learning from the project experience.

➤ Reviewing the project process and its outcomes with team members and stakeholders.

➤ Writing a final project report.

A Rose by Any Other Name

Many project managers boil the five project management processes down to only three general functions: defining, planning, and controlling. This is another general, useful way to look at project management processes—although for the purposes of this book, we've decided to take the five-process view of project management, which has worked better for us in describing how projects work through time. Whichever view you take, you'll see that some processes are repeated throughout the *product development lifecycle,* and some are used less frequently at specific stages in the project.

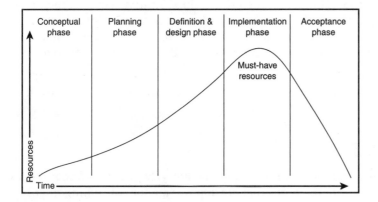

This diagram of a typical project lifecycle shows how most projects use resources over time.

How the Project Processes Work Together Over Time

As you study the diagram of the five processes of project management, note that processes two through four (planning, executing, and controlling) are in a circle. This is because these three processes are interdependent and are cyclical throughout the project. For example, plans may need to be revised due to things learned during executing and controlling the project. Execution changes because the plans change, and controlling is important throughout the project to keep things on track.

As you notice this, it's important to distinguish the lifecycle of the project through time from the processes of project management, remembering that similar words (such as "planning") are often used to mean different things. (For example, the term "planning" might be used to describe both the phase of a project and the processes used throughout the project to plan and replan aspects of the work.)

Project Lingo

A **product development lifecycle** is a specific set of phases and steps to bring a product to market within an industry or company. Most product development lifecycles comprise multiple projects as well as ongoing operations.

The Lifecycle of a Project

Every project has a lifecycle that takes it through time from beginning to end. The lifecycle starts with deciding to do the project (the project is "born" or "initiated") and ends when the project is either completed or terminated in some other way.

Projects have lifecycles because they always create something that didn't exist before—so projects themselves are not cyclic (although many of the techniques and processes in project management are, as you've just learned).

The most common product lifecycle is defined by four phases: project definition, project planning, project execution, and the project close. At first glance, it might seem that the project phases are the same as the project management processes or functions. But even though similar defining words are used, the lifecycle is linear through time—the project management processes recur throughout the lifecycle.

At the end of each phase of a project lifecycle, there is an implied decision point; often, the decision point is when the stakeholders decide either to proceed with the project or to terminate the work and cut their losses.

Different Names, Same Idea

Be aware that companies and industries may give the lifecycle phases different names or may break a project into more phases that are appropriate for controlling important end-points in a project. For example, in software-development projects, the lifecycle phases might be defined as project conception, software requirements, top-level design, detailed design, implementation, integration, testing, and product review. In this lifecycle model, the project-conception phase is roughly equivalent to the project-initiation phase; top-level design and detailed design are equivalent to the planning phase; implementation, integration, and testing are all part of the implementation phase; and product review is similar to the closing phase.

Regardless of the lifecycle phase names, the functions and processes of project management are generally the same, no matter the industry or project size. Be aware, however, that even though project management techniques are industry-independent, the talent and skills used by the people who work on project implementations must still match the specific project objectives.

Project Lifecycles Versus Product Lifecycles

Project management is becoming increasingly important as a way to bring better products to market in less time. Of course, not all projects bring new products to market. However, because project management is so important in product development, people new to the field often confuse the product development lifecycle with the general lifecycle of a project.

Product development has many of the same characteristics as a project. Product development, like a project, produces a unique product. Also like a project, product development has a beginning and an end. Thus, developing products such as a new type of toothpaste, a new drug, or a new model of an automobile offers the opportunity to apply project management processes. However, the product development lifecycles for these products are industry-specific. The specific steps for bringing a product to market in the auto industry are quite different from those for bringing a new pharmaceutical to market with FDA approval.

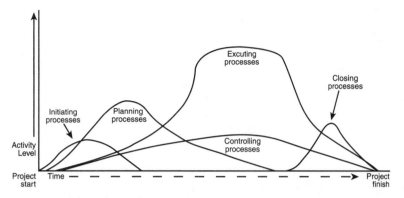

This chart illustrates how the various activities may be used throughout a project lifecycle.

Even with the differences among specific industries, most product development lifecycles fall into four general phases. The phases, which may include many different projects, include:

➤ Requirements planning

➤ Product design

➤ Product construction

➤ Product operations

This simplified model of a product lifecycle is useful for general discussion, but most companies use a far more detailed product lifecycle model, which can contain as many as 100 to 1000 discrete steps or more.

The important thing to remember is that the product development lifecycle focuses on creating and managing the development and then the sales or operation of a new product over time. A project management lifecycle focuses on actually managing the work for completing a defined objective. Thus, a product development lifecycle may contain many projects (as the diagram shows), each with a definition, planning, implementation, and closing phase.

Not Just the Same Old Routine

Whether you're developing a new product or completing some other type of project, the five processes of project management and the phases of the project lifecycle may seem pretty ordinary—but they're not. Yes, many management methods used in business today follow a similar pattern based on planning the work and developing schedules and budgets, implementing the work with teams of people and other resources, and controlling the work through tracking and monitoring progress against a plan. The reason so many methods use the same processes is simple: The processes work.

23

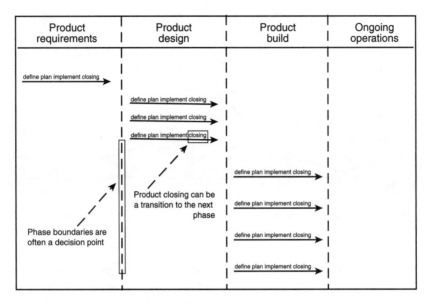

Most product lifecycles are made up of multiple projects, as shown here.

The Least You Need to Know

➤ The constraints of time, resources, results (or quality), and customer satisfaction are interrelated. If you change one of these, the others must change to keep things in balance.

➤ The five processes used in project management include initiating, planning, executing, controlling, and closing activities. These processes are also summarized as embodying the three general functions of project management, which are definition, planning, and control functions.

➤ Different skills, steps, and techniques are applicable to managing each phase of the project lifecycle effectively.

➤ As things change on a project, the processes involved in planning, executing, and controlling may need to be repeated again and again.

➤ A project management lifecycle and a product development lifecycle are different things, although all product development lifecycles include projects within them.

Chapter 3

The Rules of the Project Game

In This Chapter

➤ Universal project success criteria revisited

➤ Standard reasons for project failure (and how to avoid them most of the time)

➤ The 12 golden rules of project management success

➤ Simple ways to help you follow the rules for success

We know you're just chomping at the bit to get started managing your projects. But before you become convinced that project management is more about process than substance, you need to know that all the ingredients that make up the project management recipe for success boil down to only 12 rules you need to follow.

These 12 golden rules have been honed from years of experience by all kinds of project managers responsible for all types of projects in diverse managerial and political environments. So, whether your projects involve building spaceships or building ships in bottles, you'll get better results by paying attention to these rules from the initiation phase to the closing phase of every project.

Universal Project Success Criteria

You may recall from Chapter 2, "The Processes That Work," that, for almost all projects, project success is defined as meeting three simple states:

1. Getting the project done within a specified schedule.

2. Completing the project within the guidelines of an approved budget.

3. Meeting quality outcomes (or goals) that have been agreed upon by the project team and the project stakeholders.

Quality may be difficult to define in some cases, but in project management, the quality of outcomes almost always refers to producing a project that does what it is supposed to do (functionality) and making sure that all the functionality works (performance). Thus, if you're building a spaceship to transport 100 people to Mars, but it can only take 50 people to the moon, you've missed both the functionality and performance goals for project quality.

Project Failure—The Reasons Are Simple

If the universal success criteria are agreed upon (and they should be), there are really only five reasons why an otherwise viable project can fail:

➤ Not enough resources are made available to complete the project.

➤ Not enough time is approved to complete the project.

➤ Unclear project expectations lead to inappropriate or incomplete results.

Words from the Wise

"He enunciated no rules for success but offered a sure formula for failure: Just try to please everyone."

—E. J. Kahn Jr.

➤ Necessary changes in the scope of the project are not understood or agreed upon by the stakeholders, leading to varying views of the quality, budget, or time frame expected for the project. This means that stakeholder expectations have been poorly managed, which is a failure of the project manager as well as the project.

➤ Disagreements among stakeholders regarding the expectations for the project lead to dissatisfaction with the end results.

People don't start a project hoping it will fail, yet projects fail all too often because project managers disregard the 12 basic project management rules that can help avoid the five reasons for failure.

12 Golden Rules of Project Management Success

The 12 basic rules of project management define the focus needed to get things done on time, within budget, and to the expectations of the stakeholders. As you read this book, you'll see how project management techniques are designed to help project managers put the 12 golden rules into action over and over again.

In the sections that follow, you'll be guided to the chapters of this book that offer specific advice related to the rule being discussed. Of course, if you consistently break or ignore the rules of project management, regardless of your diligent use of charts, plans, and reports recommended in the rest of this book, you'll probably doom your project to failure or at least cause a lot of problems that otherwise could have been avoided.

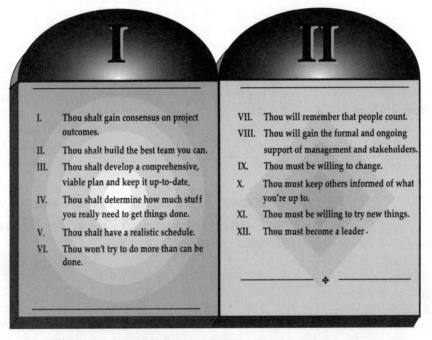

I.   Thou shalt gain consensus on project outcomes.

II.   Thou shalt build the best team you can.

III.   Thou shalt develop a comprehensive, viable plan and keep it up-to-date.

IV.   Thou shalt determine how much stuff you really need to get things done.

V.   Thou shalt have a realistic schedule.

VI.   Thou won't try to do more than can be done.

VII.   Thou will remember that people count.

VIII. Thou will gain the formal and ongoing support of management and stakeholders.

IX.   Thou must be willing to change.

X.   Thou must keep others informed of what you're up to.

XI.   Thou must be willing to try new things.

XII.   Thou must become a leader.

The 12 Rules of Project Management

You'd be wise to keep this list of rules in front of you throughout your projects.

Rule 1: Thou Shalt Gain Consensus on Project Outcomes

If you don't know what you intend to accomplish, it's not likely that you'll accomplish anything of value. A project without clear expectations is really just a bunch of work without a purpose. To be considered a success, a project must have clearly defined goals that specify what the project looks like when it's done.

It's not enough, however, for you to know exactly what you want to do. You also have to reach consensus with the stakeholders and team members on the project that the goals and expectations are the right ones. In Chapter 7, "Scoping Out the Goals for a Project," you'll learn how to set clear project goals and expectations, and you'll get tips for gaining the consensus required to ensure that the project you finally finish is the project people wanted to get done.

Rule 2: Thou Shalt Build the Best Team You Can

A willing, skilled, appropriately organized project team is the key to success. This is a group of people you'll have to develop because the perfect team almost never starts out that way. A good team starts with good choices on your part; however, sometimes the people you pick may turn out to be total dummies or uncooperative blockheads.

Time Is Money

Review the 12 golden rules at least once a week, and you'll have a much better chance of getting things done the right way, on time, within budget, and to the specifications agreed upon by customers, management, or other stakeholders. Of course, the schedule and budget may change over time, but as long as people agree on the changes, you're still getting things done the right way. A review of the rules will remind you of that.

It's your challenge to make sure the project team gets smart really quick and stays ambitious in spite of inadequate experience and training, family problems, or conflicting priorities. If people must be trained to get things done right, that's one of your responsibilities as project manager. Of course, the people must also be willing to work on the project and learn the new skills. That means you'll have to use your best management skills and motivational tactics to guide them in the right direction. (That's the direction you want them to go.)

Rule 3: Thou Shalt Develop a Comprehensive, Viable Plan and Keep It Up-to-Date

A complete, appropriately detailed project plan is central to successful completion of any project. The plan helps you guide the project. It is the document that communicates the overall intentions, tasks, resource requirements, and schedule for the project. Without a plan, its almost impossible to lead a group to achieve a common goal. You'll learn about creating the various parts of the project plan in Chapters 9 through 16.

Of course, creating a plan isn't enough. Because you can't see into the future any better than a fortune teller with a broken crystal ball, the plan you develop and get approved will probably change many times from project initiation to project closing. As you gain more information about the realities of the project and as the stakeholders change their minds about what they need done, your plan will have to be reevaluated. Be forewarned (you'll hear about this again in Chapter 24, "Changes, Changes, More Changes"), if you don't update the project plan—and negotiate these changes with the stakeholders—you're going to be responsible for the budget and schedule of the original plan.

Along the Critical Path

Think about all the really smart people who use project management techniques, develop detailed plans, and still seem to fail in getting projects done on time and within budget—like the engineers and rocket scientists at NASA who designed the space shuttle. According to the news media, that project was out of control and over budget. But if you think about it, even the space shuttle got off the ground eventually. If you remember that the space shuttle was a high-risk project with lots of speculative technologies, it's unlikely that the original budget or schedule could ever have been met with certainty. From the perspective of the original plan, the space shuttle might seem like a failure. But from another perspective, the space shuttle flights ultimately succeeded on many levels. In spite of the accomplishments, the news media and the taxpayers still held NASA to the original (and highly speculative) plans. Don't let this happen to you. Make sure the changes in the plan get communicated to everyone as they are made—even to the news media.

Rule 4: Thou Shalt Determine How Much Stuff You Really Need to Get Things Done

No matter what your boss says, you can't squeeze blood from a turnip. Without adequate people, capital, and equipment to complete a project, there is no way you can make it happen. You must get sufficient resources allocated to the project, or you must renegotiate what is going to be done so that fewer resources are required (refer to Rule 1). Getting sufficient resources (including equipment, people, and supplies) for a project is an ongoing problem in most companies—and one of the most important responsibilities for all project managers. In Chapter 11, "Getting What You Need: Supplies, Equipment, and Other Stuff," you'll learn how to scope out what you really need to get a project done. In Chapter 25, "When Push Comes to Shove, You Can Always Negotiate," you'll discover some techniques for negotiating when you don't get everything you need the first time around.

Rule 5: Thou Shalt Have a Realistic Schedule

Without a realistic schedule, you'll never succeed—and you'll run out of time before you get to try again. You can get more people and buy more supplies, but you can't produce more time no matter what you do. (Of course, if your last name is Wells and your initials are H. G., you might be the exception.)

Words from the Wise

"Time waits for no one, and nowhere is that more true than when managing a project."

—Project manager and PM teacher Jim MacIntyre

Time Is Money

Learning to work with people takes a lifetime—and at the end, you'll still be wondering how people really work. Even with all the good advice in this book, people will surprise you in mysterious and wonderful ways. That's what keeps project management interesting.

There's no faster way to lose credibility as a project manager than to change the schedule without a really good reason. Then again, if you follow Rules 1 and 8, you can get more time for yourself by getting a new schedule approved. In Chapters 11 and 12, "Building a Winning Implementation Team," you'll learn how to develop a schedule you can meet (and how to change it when necessary).

Rule 6: Thou Won't Try to Do More than Can Be Done

You must have an appropriate scope for the project. The scope of the project involves more than goals. For example, the goal could be to build a two-story building on the location of the back parking lot by next December. But the scope of the project could range from putting up a prefabricated metal building with a cement floor to building a miniature Taj Mahal for the chairman of the board. While the first scope is feasible, the second is not. Make sure the objectives and the scope of the project are clear to everyone if you want to be considered a success when the project is done.

Rule 7: Thou Will Remember that People Count

Sometimes, in focusing on the process of project management, you may forget that projects are mostly about people. Project success depends on people, not on reports or charts or even computers. To be a successful project manager, you must accommodate people's needs and priorities. People manage the project. People do most of the work. People enjoy (or curse) the end results. Projects also put stresses on these people because projects almost always involve new group structures, deadlines, and extra work. If a project's end results don't serve people, then the project has failed.

Another way of stating this rule is: Do no damage to the people on the project! Don't overwork the staff; don't demand the impossible; never lie to anyone (even if it seems like a way out of a tight situation).

Projects almost always incorporate built-in priority conflicts between ordinary work and project work. The bad news is that you must eventually satisfy people's needs, priorities, and conflicts for the project to come to a happy ending. The good news is that, in Chapter 23, "Conflicts: Resolving and Benefiting from Them," you'll learn some techniques to help you deal with the inevitable conflicts among the people and the priorities in your projects.

Rule 8: Thou Will Gain the Formal and Ongoing Support of Management and Stakeholders

It's obvious (or at least it should be) that you must have approval from management and the key stakeholders before you initiate a project. This involves not only communication skills but also negotiation skills. This rule is a lot like Rule 1, except that it means you must add a formal approval stage to the general consensus you gained in keeping Rule 1. You need to get all the people who have to contribute resources (time or money) or who may be impacted by a project (if it will change their job or life) to formally endorse your project and to agree that the project is worth doing. You also need to get formal agreement on some basic rules from the stakeholders for dealing with issues of authority, changes in project scope, and handling basic communications.

For many of the stakeholders, support requires signed approval, but it doesn't stop with a signature. Keeping this rule also demands that you ensure the stakeholders' ongoing interest in your project. If you start a project for your boss and your boss has no real interest in the project even after he's signed on the dotted line, it's unlikely you'll get any praise for finishing the feat. Remember to read Chapters 23 and 24 whenever support wanes for your projects.

Rule 9: Thou Must Be Willing to Change

This rule goes along with Rule 3. You must be willing to adapt the project plan and implementation to guide the project where it needs to go. Sometimes things change for justifiable reasons, such as a rain storm that stops the work on a construction project. Sometimes things change because you get new information, like the time researchers in Utah discovered cold fusion in a test tube, which changed the whole perspective on building fusion reactors and stopped projects worldwide (for a while at least—the whole experiment was found to be erroneous and unscientific). As one researcher put it, "It was like we were trying to invent the biplane and someone shows us up with a 747." Sometimes changes are simply the result of peoples' whims, like the advertising agency's customer who now wants a videotape instead of a brochure to promote a new product—even though the brochure is almost ready to go to the printer.

You'll also learn in Chapter 24 that change is an important part of controlling a project. Thus, good project managers need to identify when changes are needed, learn how to introduce changes, and know how to measure the impact of change.

Words from the Wise

Graham's Law: "If they know nothing of what you are doing, they suspect you are doing nothing."

—Robert J. Graham in *Understanding Project Management*

High Water

Cost, schedule, and quality (also called results) are the three primary variables in a project that can be changed. If you change one of these variables, the remaining ones will also change. Thus, if time runs out, the quality of the project will likely be reduced, or it will not be completed at all. Similarly, if you need to deliver the quality in a shorter amount of time, it will likely cost more to get it done. To avoid this quandary, your challenge is to maintain and communicate the ongoing equilibrium among the variables of cost, schedule, and quality. If you don't, the water of stakeholders' discontentment will rise to overtake your project's success.

Rule 10: Thou Must Keep Others Informed of What You're Up To

You must keep all the relevant stakeholders informed of your progress, problems, and changes. The way to obey this rule is simple: communicate, communicate, communicate. As things change on the project (and they always do), you'll find through your communications that the stakeholders may want or need to introduce their own changes into the project. You'll have to frequently refer to Rule 9 while adhering to Rule 10.

Rule 11: Thou Must Be Willing to Try New Things

Because every project is different, with different people, goals, and challenges involved, it would simply be inappropriate to use the exact same methods, software, charts, graphs, or other aids on every project. The standard methods and tools can be used with all projects, but not all projects involve the same risk or complexity. Thus, not all the techniques in this book should be used on all of your projects.

Large, complex projects will likely use more methods or tools than smaller projects. Both too many methods and too few tools can doom a project. You must adapt the processes, technologies, tools, and techniques to the needs of the project at hand. For example, you obviously need to put more detail into the network diagram (see Chapter 10, "The Network Diagram: A Map for Your Project,") for building a new corporate headquarters from scratch than you would for setting up a new sales office in a rented building. And some recurring projects, such as managing the monthly production of a newsletter, might not need a network diagram at all.

Rule 12: Thou Must Become a Leader

Leadership is an art that comes naturally to some, but the rest of us have to work at it. Chances are, you have to work on your leadership role, too. Reading management books won't be enough to bring your projects in on time and within budget. As a project manager, you must put what you read into action. You need to become a leader as well as a team member. You must not only plan, track, and control the project, you must also be a source of wisdom and motivation for the team members and stakeholders. Without leadership, even a well-coordinated project can fail to meet its goals—the people in the project won't feel they have the support or guidance they need to make things happen. That's your job as the project manager. In Chapter 4, "You? A Project Manager?" you'll learn a lot more about being a good project manager.

Keep Your Eyes on the Prize

Projects help further personal goals as well as those of companies and organizations. If you keep the 12 golden rules of project management in front of you throughout the project phases, project failures can be minimized if not eliminated.

Yes, there will be times when fate plays a role, and you can't do everything to everyone's satisfaction. But if you remember the 12 golden rules throughout the five phases of the project management process, you'll succeed more times than you fail. Keep working at it. The prize for your effort will be projects done on time, within budget, and with less stress on mind and body.

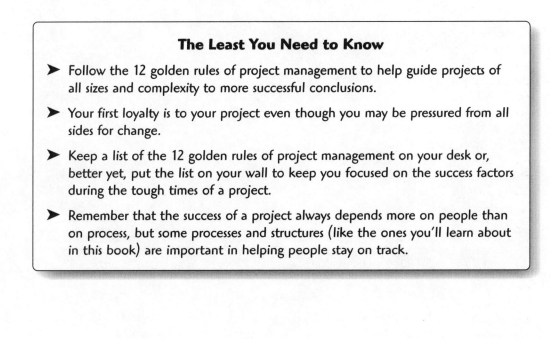

The Least You Need to Know

➤ Follow the 12 golden rules of project management to help guide projects of all sizes and complexity to more successful conclusions.

➤ Your first loyalty is to your project even though you may be pressured from all sides for change.

➤ Keep a list of the 12 golden rules of project management on your desk or, better yet, put the list on your wall to keep you focused on the success factors during the tough times of a project.

➤ Remember that the success of a project always depends more on people than on process, but some processes and structures (like the ones you'll learn about in this book) are important in helping people stay on track.

You? A Project Manager?

Your business card may not say "Manager" or "Executive" or even "Supervisor," but when you are responsible for any project, large or small, you are a project manager—albeit an accidental one. In this chapter, you'll learn what it takes to be a good project manager because project success depends on good project managers.

The Accidental Project Manager

Pretend for a moment that you work at NASA. You are responsible for developing a new space shuttle that will transport astronauts to Mars and back. To succeed, you must schedule all the tasks for building the vehicle as well as hire and coordinate the best people and right suppliers for each job. Throughout the five phases of the project, you will manage complex interrelationships among staff, vendors, and the government. You must also track the budget and control costs.

You need special project management skills for planning, executing, and controlling a project of this scope, which involves hundreds of people, tons of supplies, thousands of tasks, and millions of dollars. As the capable person responsible for this complex mission, you deserve a special title, and you have one: You are the *project manager*.

In product- and program-oriented companies, there are usually people with primary responsibility for managing large projects. These people, like the project managers at NASA, have titles and authority to match their project responsibilities. You might be one of these project managers that enjoy primary responsibility for a project. But in many enterprises, people are project managers by accident, not by design. These part-time project managers have other jobs to do besides managing the project, making it even more important to know the tricks of the project management trade.

Words from the Wise

"Be not afraid of greatness: Some are born great, some achieve greatness, and some have greatness thrust upon them."

—William Shakespeare, *Twelfth Night*

Project Lingo

The **project manager** is the person who takes overall responsibility for coordinating a project, regardless of its size, to make sure the desired end result comes in on time and within budget.

Dealing with Dual Responsibilities

In some ways, full-time project managers have it a lot easier than accidental ones. Full-time project managers, like the person at NASA responsible for the Mars shuttle, have only one major responsibility: the project. The majority of the job involves managing the project, and other priorities rarely interfere with this work. Thus, everything the full-time project manager at NASA does revolves around the planning, coordination, and monitoring of the Mars shuttle. Most people in business, however, have responsibilities outside their project goals—and these responsibilities may conflict with project priorities.

People in business must competently finish their ordinary work and their projects. In this chapter, you'll learn what it takes to be a good project manager, even if you may have been thrust into the role by accident.

As a project manager (accidental or otherwise), you are the one person assigned to lead the project management process, and in most cases, you alone are ultimately responsible for the project's success. (The exception is when a project management team is chartered with the ultimate responsibility for a project's success.) Even if you have other work to do or if you manage the project as part of a project team, you need to make sure the project gets done as specified.

The responsibility of being a project manager can be a heavy load, even for the superheroes among us. As an accidental project manager, your dual responsibility for projects and ordinary work makes the skillful use of project management techniques vital to the success of your projects (and your career, we might add). Through effective communication, scheduling, and prioritization of tasks, the project management process can make it easier to maintain control of projects while continuing to meet the priorities of everyday life.

What Do You Need to Do?

Bringing a project to fruition is a creative process with a focus on the "management" of the process. To be effective, whether you're a full-time or accidental project manager, you need to employ technologies, charting techniques, and budgeting tools to define the project. But to be truly successful, you must first establish yourself as a competent manager.

Learn to Plan and Act

Project management as a discipline evolved because of a need to coordinate resources and technology to secure predictable results. The common project management tasks include establishing objectives, breaking work into well-defined tasks, charting the work sequences, scheduling, budgeting, coordinating a team, reporting, and communicating throughout the project. These tasks involve two general types of activities: planning and definition activities and implementation and control activities.

Because of these two types of activities, people who manage projects effectively, no matter what the size, must know how to plan effectively and act efficiently. In fact, balancing the interplay between planning and acting may be the most important skill a person must learn to be effective at managing projects. Planning benefits from tools, charts, and techniques, and the ability to take action requires the skills of a leader.

High Water!

If your boss or someone else asks you to add projects to an already overloaded work schedule, you'll need to politely employ the most important word in the project manager's vocabulary. That word is "No!" You can cloak it in friendlier terms, but you must stand your ground. Agreeing to do the impossible still leaves whatever you agreed to as, well, impossible! Negotiate later.

Time Is Money

According to the Project Management Institute (PMI), project managers must coordinate nine areas of expertise: cost, time, scope, quality, communications, human resources, contracts, supplies, and risk management. Whew! That's a lot of stuff to handle. No wonder project management was invented.

You Must Be a Manager and a Leader

Good project managers command both the authority and the responsibility to guide the project. Management of the project and leadership go hand in hand. As a leader, your team will expect you to be honest, competent, and inspirational as well as competent in the use of project management techniques. But most of all, to be an effective project manager, you need to lead the project with an energy and a positive attitude that make you the catalyst for moving your project forward. Never put the techniques of project management above your attitude—it's your attitude that gives you power.

It is possible to complete the management part of the project—the meetings, assignments, audits, reports, and other communications—and not attain the status and influence of a leader. To be a successful project manager, however, you must be both a manager and a leader. You must develop administrative procedures for ensuring that work is getting done on time and within budget, but more importantly, you must gain the trust and respect of the project team so that people feel comfortable taking your direction.

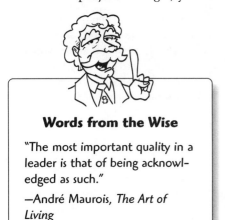

Words from the Wise

"The most important quality in a leader is that of being acknowledged as such."

—André Maurois, *The Art of Living*

Focus on the Project's End

In the 1970s, a popular management fad was to look through tasks of all sorts as though they were already complete. Only the work in the middle remained. For example, a salesperson, instead of focusing on the unlikelihood of a sale, would look through to the close as though it was already in hand. Although this fad largely died (fortunately), you should use part of it in managing projects. Instead of looking at a project as 50 tasks, always keep the end in mind. That way, the project is less likely to stall midstream. It also makes you a stronger project leader. Like General Patton, you have your goal firmly set in your mind, and nothing can deter your success in reaching it!

The Leadership Roles of the Project Manager

You'll need to develop your people skills to be regarded as a leader. As part of your responsibility for leading the various phases of the project, you'll need to assume a variety of roles with other people including interpersonal, informational, and decisional roles. Accomplished leaders move effortlessly among these roles as required.

Along the Critical Path

After a seminar on project management, one of the attendees (a wag obviously) ran up to us and told us that, after listening to our presentation, she had finally figured out how to be a perfect project manager. "All you have to do is have the intelligence of Einstein, the patience of Job, the integrity of a Supreme Court judge, the negotiating skills of a Mongolian horse trader, the savvy of James Bond, the appeal of Marilyn Monroe, the charisma of Sir Ralph Richardson, the communication skills of Tom Peters, the ideas of Stephen King, the planning skills of Colin Powell, the personal drive of Bill Gates, the financial acumen of Alan Greenspan, the skin of an armadillo, and the ego of Mother Teresa." Maybe she's right. Maybe we should shorten our seminars to give attendees less time to think up stuff like this...

Interpersonal Roles

To be perceived as a leader, you must be regarded as honest, capable, and dependable—as well as personable. In your interpersonal roles, you'll need to do these kinds of things:

➤ Deal effectively with people from various professional backgrounds and create team unity.

➤ Solve team disputes.

➤ Focus and motivate team members to achieve milestones on the way to achieving the project goal.

➤ Build positive relationships with project stakeholders.

Informational Roles

You need to assume informational roles to keep people up-to-date and on track. When you do so, you'll need to accomplish these sorts of tasks:

➤ Arrange and lead team meetings.

➤ Create and maintain work schedules for other people.

➤ Communicate project vision to upper management.

➤ Provide feedback regarding results, quality, and project deliverables.

Time Is Money

A project manager who views the responsibility of managing a project as one of guiding, facilitating, negotiating, and coordinating will do better than will one who views the project management responsibility as one of ordering, dictating, and coercing.

Decisional Roles

To move forward, projects demand that countless decisions be made, ranging from trivial to critical, at every phase of the project. When a decisional role is required, you'll need the expertise to do the following without alienating the people who may be affected by your choices:

➤ Distinguish between features and benefits.

➤ Appropriately allocate resources if a project falls behind schedule.

➤ Strike a balance between cost, time, and results.

➤ Prevent scope "creep" (when the project keeps getting bigger and more complex) and budget "slippage" (when the money starts running out).

The Other Business Management Roles

In addition to the roles detailed already, project managers will often have to assume roles in financial management, customer recruitment (also called sales), and human resources management including both employee recruitment and employee development. Thus, being a good project manager involves all the general skills required of any skilled manager in business.

The Seven Traits of Good Project Managers

In addition to having knowledge of project management processes and an understanding of your various roles as a project manager and leader, research and experience point to seven additional traits that can help you become a successful project manager. These seven success traits are shown in the following figure, and we will discuss each of them in turn.

Trait 1: Enthusiasm for the Project

Good project managers want to do a good job. Your enthusiasm for the project permeates to other people on the team, making it easier to keep people motivated and involved.

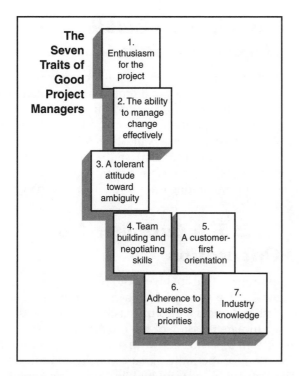

As project managers gain experience, the successful ones develop these traits to make their work easier and more satisfying.

Trait 2: The Ability to Manage Change Effectively

Change is inevitable in projects. Customers change their minds about the end results. Managers decide to make changes to the scope of the project. Team members need to change their schedules. People who manage projects successfully learn to become managers of exceptions because there are always plenty of surprises, even in small projects.

Trait 3: A Tolerant Attitude Toward Ambiguity

Project managers often have ambiguous authority. This means that people may have other bosses to report to during the project and may not consider you a manager (unless you earn their respect as a leader). In fact, many of the roles in large projects are not clear cut.

Some of the team members may make more money or have more senior jobs than the project manager; customers may get involved as team members; other departments may have a stake in the project. A good project manager must feel comfortable with these ambiguous roles and expectations and must learn how to manage them to see the project to a successful conclusion. If you need clear authority and an absolute plan, your project management days are numbered.

Time Is Money

Talk to experienced project managers. They'll tell you (if they admit it) that at least one of their first projects was a dismal failure. If this happens to you, don't kick yourself. Instead, pick up the pieces, learn from your mistakes, and move on.

Trait 4: Team Building and Negotiating Skills

A project manager needs to build coalitions among the various stakeholders in a project: management, customers, the project team, and suppliers. Power is only granted to a project manager who builds these relationships. Project managers must negotiate authority to move the project forward, so the success of any project depends on the project manager's ability to build a strong team among internal and external players.

Trait 5: A Customer-First Orientation

In projects that involve customers or clients (and most do), a good project manager puts the customer first and understands the customer's perspective regarding the project. After all, the ultimate measure of the project's success is the customer's satisfaction with the results. In a partnership with a customer or client, a skilled project manager crafts a vision for the project that can be communicated to the rest of the project team. Through alliances, team building, and empathy with the customer or client, the project manager is ultimately able to turn changing expectations into satisfaction with the completed project.

Trait 6: Adherence to the Priorities of Business

Even though projects often focus on people, project managers need to keep the business aspects of the work in mind. Because most projects need to turn a profit, the project manager also needs to keep the larger organizational and profit-making goals in focus when making decisions about the project. Even when projects don't involve a specific profit goal, successful project managers must control the cost, time, and quality of their projects, and that's a business orientation no matter how you look at it. You'll also hear this called a "bottom-line" orientation, but paying attention to the budget and costs is only part of the business equation. The other business priorities involve maintaining competitive advantage, integrating the project into the culture of the organization, managing stakeholder issues, and ensuring both productivity and excellence as the project proceeds.

Trait 7: Knowledge of the Industry or Technology

Even though most project management skills are industry-independent, as a project manager, you'll need to have both project management skills and some experience or specific knowledge relevant to the industry you're working in. For example, if you're managing software projects, you'll need experience with programming concepts. If you're managing the development of a new shopping mall, you'll need a background in construction. You may not be an expert in the field and may not be capable of actually doing the work, but to lead your team, you'll definitely need some information on the specific industry issues and technologies that are important to the project you'll be managing.

Be the Best Leader You Can Be

Of course, there are other traits that project managers would be wise to develop such as written and verbal communication skills, computer literacy, and above all, dependability. If you aren't dependable, you can't expect the rest of the team to be dependable.

If you work at being all the things talked about in this chapter, you'll reap the rewards of your labor with the help of project teams that respect your efforts as a leader. As a result, your projects will meet their goals more often than not.

Words from the Wise

"Every man is the son of his own works."

—Miguel de Cervantes

The Least You Need to Know

➤ You need to coordinate and prioritize your ordinary work along with your projects so that both get done effectively.

➤ To be successful as a project manager, your team must perceive you as a leader.

➤ You need people skills, communication skills, business skills, and technical skills to be an effective project manager.

➤ As a project manager, you'll need to assume interpersonal, informational, decisional, and business management roles, depending on the phase and the needs of the project.

➤ Being a good project manager takes ongoing, enthusiastic effort.

Part 2

The Project Initiation Processes

You may think it's easy to get a project started, but starting a project off right takes some hard thinking and involves some tough decisions.

First, you need to identify who the players are—these people are the stakeholders who'll help you define the project. Then, one of your initial tough choices is deciding which project to do first. After that, you need to define the specific goals for your project and identify all the risks and constraints that may cause problems for the project after it is started. You'll then need to get a statement of work approved that defines the project you're going to plan and the rules by which you're going to play. Only then will you be ready to start planning the work, the schedule, and the budget for the project plan (which you'll learn to produce in Part 3).

Okay, this seems like a lot to do just to get to the planning phase. But that's what you need to do to start your projects off on the right foot—and that's what this part is going to help you do.

Chapter 5

Identifying Stakeholders and Defining Their Roles

Always remember that projects are successes because the stakeholders on the project are satisfied. Thus, identifying the right and complete list of stakeholders is the first step in getting your project moving and an on-going responsibility as the project proceeds through its lifecycle. These key stakeholders will make all of the important decisions during the project. In this chapter, you'll learn how to identify the key stakeholders: those people who will have the greatest influence and authority as you proceed in defining and planning your project.

Start by Identifying the Stakeholders

The stakeholders include all those who will make a meaningful contribution to a project. Thus, the stakeholder list includes:

➤ You (as the project manager)

➤ The managers in your company who are involved with approvals

➤ The customer

➤ The project implementation team

There may be other stakeholders as well—such as government overseers or agency representatives.

Key Stakeholders and Their Contributions

Project Manager	Leads the project; plans, monitors, tracks, controls, documents, and reports project activities.
Sponsor (may be a customer representative or functional manager)	Provides authority for project to proceed; guides and monitors the project in partnership with the project manager; key organizational advocate for the project.
Core Implementation Team	Provides skills, expertise, and effort to perform the tasks defined for the project; assist with planning and estimating project tasks.
Customer (may be internal or external)	Establishes the requirements for the project; provides funding; reviews the project as milestones and deliverables are met.
Functional Managers	Establish company policy; provide resources; some will provide review and approval authority.

It's your job to manage the stakeholders by including only those people on the list who have a need to influence your project or other requirement to contribute. Not every customer representative or manager in the company is or should be a stakeholder. Keeping the list of stakeholders down to the truly involved will help keep the project doable.

The Stakeholder Roles

Obviously, the project manager is a key stakeholder in any project. We've already talked about your role as a project manager in detail in Chapter 4, "You? A Project Manager." The following sections list the other stakeholder roles you'll need to be familiar with on most projects.

The Customer

This is the person or entity that pays for the project. In some cases the customer may be a department or division or your own company. In other cases, the customer is the one who orders the project. In either case, the customer contributes both funding and project requirements. When defining the customer stakeholders, be careful to distinguish between the people with final authority for project approvals and changes, and those who must simply be kept informed.

Stakeholder	Roles	Approvals
Project Manager: Joel Baker	Defines, plans, controls, monitors, and leads the project.	Makes recommendations for approval; signature authority for any purchase under $1500.
Sponsor: Joe Macdonald, Director of Engineering	Authority for most operational project decisions; helps guide the project; assists project manager with planning and approvals by other stakeholders.	Approves personnel requests and hiring decisions; signs off on SOW and project plans before submitting to the customer; signature authority for any purchase under $15,000.
Customer: Managers Sarah Goodwin, Vice President Fred Catwalk, Director of Finance	Helps define the project; authority for all major project plans and changes; budget approvals.	Final approval for SOW and all project plans; initial budget approval; signatures required for any non-planned purchase of $5000 or more.
Customer: Experts Allen Strange Jell Elsewhere	Experts who help define the project and develop product specifications.	Works with project manager and team; makes recommendations; not formal signature authorities.

A simple chart like this can help you identify the roles and authorities of the key stakeholders on your project.

The Project Sponsor

The project sponsor is your most important ally in the project; this is the person who shares responsibility for project success and helps everyone on the project team be successful. The sponsor doesn't usually have the title of sponsor—but it's important that you identify the person who has the role. It is usually a key manager or customer representative who provides the authority for the project to proceed.

This authority, and the person's support of the project, are the person's primary contributions to the project. The sponsor supports the project through issuing the project charter, advising you as the project manager, assisting you in the development of the statement of work (SOW), and consulting on the development of other project documentation.

A good sponsor will also assist you in overcoming organizational and political obstacles. Many times the sponsor will be your direct manager, but other times it will be a person from another department or a customer representative with a primary interest and assigned authority for the project. Developing and maintaining your relationship with the project sponsor is key to making the overall project and its implementation successful—in many ways it's a partnership. The sponsor will always be the first person you should confide in when you need help or think you're in trouble.

49

Functional Management

Functional management, also known as line manage-ment, are the company officials with an interest in your project. These may consist of department supervi-sors, managers, or vice presidents. With the exception of organizations that are organized based on projects, these managers are responsible for organizational units within the company, such as "engineering," "market-ing," or "finance." They are the managers that have long-term management responsibility for the people who will be working on your project team. You must work closely with these people to ensure that you get the best people for your project.

As the project proceeds, you must keep the relevant functional managers informed of project progress and personnel performance issues. These managers can help you out of personnel jams if you let them; but if you don't keep them informed, they can derail a pro-ject from underneath you.

After identifying the obvious functional authorities for your project, you'll need to identify those people who will have informal veto authority on decisions that will affect the project. Many of these managers will be involved in approval processes even if they don't have a formal stake (for example, required signatures) in the project; it's your job to identify these people to make sure they are included at strategic points in the project initiation and development.

The Review and Approval Team

The Review and Approval Team (sometimes called a management team) is the group of stakeholders who must approve and agree on project definitions, budg-ets, plans, and changes.

Obviously, one or more key customer representatives will be included in this group, but it will likely in-clude functional managers and executives from your own organization who must approve aspects of the project. The key is to keep this team limited in size and scope to those people who really do need to ap-prove project documents.

On a large project you'll need to develop an approval matrix that describes the people who will have a say in, review, and approve each type of document and project change.

The Core Project Implementation Team

Choosing the core implementation team could be the single most important decision you make as a project manager. Strong team leaders effectively combined with knowledgeable experts (where necessary) build the momentum required for successful project planning—and good planning is paramount to a successful implementation of the project.

The core implementation project team usually consists of the most important players, who will be associated with the project implementation from start to finish. On small projects, the core implementation team might be only you and another key person who will be working with you on the project.

Time Is Money

As part of your choice of supervisors and managers, look for people who can work within an ordered system of checks and balances. Prima donnas may seem to perform admirably on the surface, but if they impose their own agendas on your project, you could lose control. If you have a choice in the matter, choose someone who will accept your role as manager without resentment or hostility.

Rank is not always a consideration in forming the core project team; for a larger project—sometimes skill or experience are more important factors. The core members work on the project from start to finish while other workers come and go as their tasks are completed. Your core implementation team will most likely consist of:

➤ You (the project manager)

➤ Two or three managers, coordinators, and supervisory personnel in the project hierarchy

➤ A couple of expert players, such as engineers, design specialists, scientists, advisors, and other experienced folks who have important roles in the project

The core implementation team doesn't usually have signature authority for the project, but this group of people is directly responsible for the overall success of the project planning and implementation phases. The membership of the core implementation team may shift as segments of the project are completed and new ones open up the need for different skills and expertise. Throughout the project, however, your core implementation team should consist of your most trusted employees and central advisors.

High Water!

When taking over an on-going project and its staff, check out the team before you accept the job. Make sure you have the authority to make changes to the team as necessary. There might be good reasons why there's an opening for a project manager. Forced inheritance of a poor team could make you the project scapegoat instead of its savior.

Words from the Wise

"Groups of two or more people are political entities."

—Kim Baker, explaining graphic design realities at an Apple Computer-sponsored seminar in 1991

The Other Implementation Team Members—Who Are They?

All the implementation team members are stakeholders in the project—they'll all make a contribution of one sort or another toward project completion. In addition to your core implementation team, on a large project you will likely have many other staff working on the project. In addition, you might need outside consultants and specialists. Generally, these people perform a role during one part of a project and then are phased out once their work is completed. In addition to these players, administrators and other staff play a role in most projects, but because their roles are generic and they are replaceable, they are not considered to be core team members. Nonetheless, even team members with minor and replaceable roles should be kept informed as progress on the project proceeds—just like all the other stakeholders will be. You'll learn more about building your implementation team in Chapter 12, "Building a Winning Implementation Team," and discover ways to organize the people during the implementation process.

Working Together: The Magic Success Formula

The project manager (that's you) will have responsibility for assuring that the stakeholders on the project work together and gain consensus on project decisions.

Not only at the beginning of the project, but as it continues through the phases, the project manager must continue to clarify who the key stakeholders are and the roles they will play.

Many of the stakeholders, including the sponsor, the functional managers in your company, and the customers will have more formal authority than you—but even so, you need to lead them. Your leadership will be embodied in the tough questions you ask, the facts you provide, the ideas you inspire, and the enthusiasm you convey for the project. You'll need to coordinate the stakeholders and guide them through the various project stages. Some experts call this "managing upward." Your ability to do this is at the heart of successful project management.

The Least You Need to Know

➤ The identification of key stakeholders on your project is an ongoing process that is key to the implementation, planning, and execution of the project.

➤ At the very least, the project stakeholders include you (the project manager), the customer, the project sponsor, company functional managers, and the implementation team members.

➤ Coordinating and communicating with the stakeholders is a primary role of the project manager.

➤ As a project manager, you'll need to "manage upward," to guide the key stakeholders through the project phases.

Chapter 6

Selecting the Projects That Are Worth Doing

In This Chapter

➤ Prioritize the projects in your business.

➤ Some projects aren't worth bothering with.

➤ Is it worth it? Eight steps for making this decision.

➤ A project charter should be created to initiate a project after it's been selected as a priority.

Some projects simply shouldn't be started. They might not have enough priority as compared to other work, or they might suffer from fatal flaws that are not evident when the idea first pops into your head. It may seem silly to say this at all, but in most cases, the most important projects should be started first. So, it isn't enough just to identify the projects in your business. You also need to prioritize them before you start them. Why waste your time managing projects that don't really need to be done?

Sometimes, as the project manager, you might be brought in after the project prioritization step. For example, you might be assigned a project by your boss, or you might be chosen as the project manager after other people have been considered. For other projects, you will be responsible for project selections on your own or as part of a project team. Whether your project is selected by management or you are asked to evaluate a project, you need to carry out the steps in this chapter to ensure that you're not taking on an unachievable project.

The First Step in Project Initiation: Deciding What to Do

Project prioritization and selection is the first of many decisions in the initiation phase. In this chapter, you will learn how to prioritize the projects in your area of responsibility into those that need to be done now, those that should be started later, and those that simply should be scratched off the list and forgotten.

Selection and prioritization of projects is one of the first steps in the project initiation phase of the management process. In some companies, this will be called the conceptualization phase of the project lifecycle. Remember the processes and lifecycles of project management that you read about in Chapter 2, "The Processes That Work"? To remind you what they are, keep the reference card provided at the front of the book handy as you read through the book. You're going to have a lot to keep ordered in your mind; the reference card will help keep your memory fresh.

In Chapter 1, "Projects, Projects Everywhere," you learned how to tell the difference between projects and ordinary work. Simply knowing this difference is an important first step in taking advantage of the power of the project management processes you learned about in Chapter 2.

Words from the Wise

"A job not worth doing is not worth doing well."

—Jerry Pournelle, Pournelle's Fifth Law

Telling Good from Bad

All projects start as ideas or concepts. There are always more ideas in a business than there is time and resources to implement them. And we all know that not all ideas are good ideas. Some ideas turn out to be inappropriate or unfeasible; others don't have enough importance to take up your valuable time or the company's resources. Still others are better shelved for completion at a later date when the timing is more appropriate.

Eight Steps to Determine the Most Important Projects

Whether prioritizing projects for a major corporation or as an individual, eight basic steps can help you choose the most important projects to work on. These steps are:

1. List all current projects and project ideas in your area of responsibility. This is often called the idea-generation phase. It will likely generate more product ideas or proposals than can realistically be pursued. The next point is pretty obvious, but we're going to emphasize it because too many businesses spend time on the wrong projects: Just because a project is on your list doesn't mean it's worth doing.

	Profitability[1]	Time to market[1]	Development[2]	Commercial viability[1]	
Guestimate score:	1 2 3 4 5	1 2 3 4 5	1 2 3 4 5	1 2 3 4 5	Totals
Project name:					
Fix last year's interface boards	✓	✓	✓	✓	13
New computer/TV interface	✓	✓	✓	✓	16
New hi-rez color board that works	✓	✓	✓	✓	12
Open Cucamonga sales office	✓	✓	✓	✓	11
	([1]higher is better)		([2]higher is better)		

This type of checklist can be useful in identifying the relative importance of projects on your list.

2. Determine the need or opportunity for each project on your list.

3. Establish rough delivery dates and budgets for each project. These can be very rough at this point; you're just determining the relative cost and time required to complete one project compared to another.

4. Judge the overall feasibility of each project. This may take some guesswork. For example, if one of the projects on your list is to discover a cure for cancer, you have to make some (hopefully) educated guesses about your team's ability to bring the prize home at the end of the day. Sometimes, usually in large, high-impact projects, the feasibility analysis is a complete phase in the project lifecycle that involves its own project plan.

5. Establish the risk (the possibility of failure) associated with each project. This step goes hand in hand with step 4. High feasibility means relatively low risk in most cases, but there can be a high feasibility and high risk when lots of money is involved.

6. Review the project list, objectives, feasibility studies, and risks with your manager or boss (and the customer, if appropriate) and other members of the potential project team to gain consensus on the projects. The more

High Water!

Watch out for pet projects! People often rank the projects they want to do higher than the projects that really should get done. There often is a "pet" project that is personally interesting, that promises new career challenges, or that holds possibilities for promotion. If a project is selected for personal reasons instead of enterprise objectives, watch out! Pet projects can dilute resources and negatively affect the results of the business.

complex the projects, the more important it is to get the opinion of other people before you prioritize the work.

7. Eliminate from the list projects that are inappropriate or unfeasible and prioritize the rest. If the decision about prioritizing a project is not yours alone, this process may take a few meetings with your boss, customer, or other members of the project team. Read Chapter 25, "When Push Comes to Shove, You Can Always Negotiate," on negotiation and Chapter 23, "Conflicts: Resolving and Benefiting from Them," on conflict resolution before you come up with the final priorities.

Reasons for eliminating projects from your priority list include:

➤ Lack of money, people, skills, time, or other resources that are required to make the project successful.

➤ Goals that are in conflict with the long-term goals of the organization or enterprise.

➤ Lack of support and strong sponsorship within the organization.

➤ Outcomes that will violate existing policies or laws or otherwise negatively affect the position or public image of the organization. Even government or corporate officials have pet projects, and your evaluation techniques can help them to see the bottom-line effect of their projects. If they insist on going ahead anyway, find your way out as diplomatically as possible.

➤ Inability to act quickly enough, even if the project is otherwise feasible. Who wants to be the second man on the moon?

➤ Conflict with other projects in progress or planned that have a higher priority and are grabbing key resources.

➤ Risk that jeopardizes the possibility for success. High-risk projects should be eliminated early. All projects have risk, but the risk should be both reasonable and worth the investment. (See Chapter 8, "Understanding Risks and Constraints," for more information on risk assessment.)

Some projects that ultimately need to be done may be rejected because of low priority or bad timing. These projects should be considered again in the next project-selection review. Their priority may change as other projects get done.

Words from the Wise

"All sciences are now under the obligation to prepare the ground for the future task of the philosopher, which is to solve the problem of value, to determine the true hierarchy of values."

—Friedrich Nietzsche, *The Genealogy of Morals*, "First Essay," sct. 17 (1887).

Sometimes a screening or rating checklist, like the example provided here, is a simple way to determine project priorities. This method is expedient but doesn't provide a great deal of depth to the analysis. Keep this caveat in mind when you use this technique. In constructing a checklist like the example provided, you need to define the criteria that are important for selecting one project over another. In the sample product-selection checklist, we've established the criteria of profitability, time to market, development risks, and commercial potential. Each criterion is equally weighted and is scored using a five-point scale. The total scores for each project are shown in the rightmost column. Typically, a cutoff point or threshold is specified below which the project idea is abandoned. Ideas exceeding the threshold are held for further analysis. Some of the abandoned ideas may be shelved for future reviews. Others may be eliminated altogether.

You can also use this list technique with weighted scores, giving different weights to the criteria that are most important to your business. For example, you might give the score for profitability a weight of 1.5 and the score for time to market a weight of 1.0. This means that you'd multiply the score times the weight to determine the weighted score for each criterion. The weightings, as well as the selection criteria and cutoff point, should be agreed upon by the key stakeholders in the project selection process.

8. Select the most important projects and act on them now. Get going (as soon as you read the rest of this book, that is).

Try the eight steps on your own project list. The high-priority projects on your list should be the most important projects in your area of responsibility. The priority projects should also be the first ones you manage with the tools and techniques described in the rest of this book. If you do this, you'll have a much better chance of getting them done on time, within budget, and to everybody's satisfaction.

High Water!

If you're managing your first project, select one of limited scope, limited time, and limited impact to try out the process. For example, choose a project of less than 12 weeks, a team size of less than 4, and a project with a positive impact if it succeeds—but something that won't kill the business if it does not. Of course, some of you won't have this option; you'll simply get shoved into managing a megaproject without a thought. If this is the case, you'll need to really pay attention to this book and other sources of project management insight (including the PMI Institute, other books on project management, and most importantly, the advice of experienced mentors).

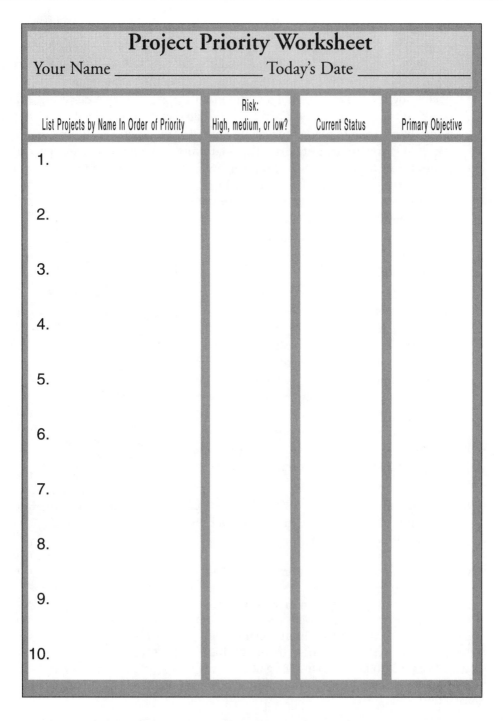

Use this worksheet to prioritize the projects in your enterprise.

The Project Charter Gets Things Going

Once a project has been selected as something worth doing, it's always a good idea to have a manager or customer produce a project charter to announce the establishment of the project. The purpose of the project charter is to publicize both the new project and the role of the new project manager (or project management team, if a team management approach is used). A good project charter is usually no more than a page (maybe two) in length, and it should be sent to everyone associated with the project as far as this is practical. This powerful yet simple document should accomplish the following:

➤ Acknowledge the support of the issuer; the person who produces the charter is most often the "sponsor" for the project, a manager or executive who has formal authority but who acts independently of this or other projects. Other times the charter document may be issued by the customer. The sponsor or customer provides authority for the project that the project manager may lack. (You read about the role of the project sponsor and other stakeholders in Chapter 5, "Identifying Stakeholders and Defining Their Roles.")

➤ Establish referent authority for the project manager. The expert authority a project manager has is earned through his or her own performance on the job, but referent authority is only granted by other managers or stakeholders. Because project managers rely on both referent authority and expert authority, the establishment of referent authority is important in the overall operation of the project. (But don't think the charter solves all the authority problems; project managers lead best when they have established expert authority to complement the referent authority.)

➤ Enable further work on the project to commence. This allows the project manager to begin further planning the project.

Even on small projects, a simple announcement of the initiation of the project and the project manager should be made to clearly establish the project manager's right to make decisions and lead the project. On large projects, this initial project document, the charter, has even larger ramifications—it gives fair warning that the project manager has the power to begin assembling the significant organizational resources necessary to meet the project's goals.

Words from the Wise

"Much of our American progress has been the product of the individual who had an idea; pursued it; fashioned it; tenaciously clung to it against all odds; and then produced it, sold it, and profited from it."

—Hubert H. Humphrey

So, How Will It All Get Done?

Once you've accepted authority to manage a selected priority project, you may wonder how you are going to coordinate this with all the other work you have to do. Without some tricks up your sleeve, it's pretty tough to schedule, budget, and coordinate a project while still getting ordinary work done—and getting everything completed to everyone's satisfaction. It may sound like an impossible challenge, but the project management tools and techniques you'll learn about in the upcoming chapters can help you sort things out.

Don't panic if it seems like more than you can handle. The project management processes take time and practice to learn, but they're not impossible to master. The responsibility that goes along with managing projects doesn't need to be stressful because the project management toolbox offers a structured approach for handling projects that makes them easier to control. Project management reduces the surprises and makes it possible to bring work in on time and within budget, even when large numbers of people and strict deadlines are involved. The project management processes include both manual and computerized techniques that can help improve performance and efficiency in today's fast-paced, objective-driven businesses.

The project management processes have proven value in getting things done on time and within budget in any organization. These proven tools and techniques are commonly used by engineers and scientists in complex projects with huge budgets, thousands of tasks, and hundreds of people, but the power of project management is not limited to large-scale scientific, engineering, and construction applications. The techniques and advantages of project management concepts can be applied to any project in any business—if you know how to recognize a project when you see one. (You should have a pretty good handle on that by now.)

The Least You Need to Know

➤ Projects should be prioritized so the most important projects get done first.

➤ The projects selected as appropriate for further effort must conform to agreed-upon criteria including general feasibility, prudent timing, adequate resources, and acceptable risk.

➤ Projects worth doing should have appropriate agreed-upon objectives, adequate time available to meet the objectives, and enough resources available to commit to the project.

➤ Once a project is selected for further action, a project charter should be issued by the project sponsor or the customer.

Chapter 7

Scoping Out the Goals for a Project

> **In This Chapter**
>
> ➤ Why specific goals (also known as objectives) are important to project success
>
> ➤ Six criteria of all good project goals
>
> ➤ Steps for establishing project goals
>
> ➤ Choosing a scope for a project that meets the project goals
>
> ➤ Creating the statement of work (SOW) to establish clear expectations among all project stakeholders

Even a good idea can be a bad idea if the goals and scope of a project are not clearly defined before major resources are committed to it. Smart goals are project end results that are specific, measurable, agreed upon, realistic, and timely. Fuzzy goals can be interpreted differently; thus, people may never agree on whether you're done or whether you've succeeded or failed. It's not enough to say you're going to build the next version of a software product; you need to establish what the new version will do, how much it will cost to build it, and how long it will take to design it, among other goals for the project.

In this chapter, you'll learn why you need to get very specific about what you expect to accomplish on your projects. You'll also learn how to set goals for your project that no one can argue with.

Why Bother with the Goals? I Know What I Want to Do!

Okay, okay. Patience is not always a project manager's best virtue, and lots of projects get started without clear goals. Please don't let this happen to you. Slow down. Don't rush into further planning until you have consensus on the goals. The time you spend on setting goals will help ensure that the project you deliver is really something worth crowing about.

Words from the Wise

"A project is different from usual work. It has a single focus ... It is a child in the midst of a family of adolescent and adult tasks."

—Bennet Lientz and Kathryn Rea in Project Management for the 20th Century

The fate of the people-mover project that a major American city invested in years ago may help you understand the importance of setting clear goals. The project seemed like a good idea at the time. Just like the Jetsons, people would be transported to where they wanted to go within the downtown area. The city council that approved the project wanted to be progressive and modern, and maybe they thought the project would help solve downtown congestion—or maybe they'd watched too many cartoons.

You see, the goal of the project was to move people around the downtown area in carts on a conveyor belt. The approach worked at Disneyland, so they figured it must be viable for a real city. No one asked these critical questions about the project before it got started: How many people would need to be moved around? Would people pay to take a people-mover? How long would it take to use the people-mover as opposed to walking to and from the same place? What about all the health-conscious types who prefer to walk anyway? And most important of all, did anyone really need or want a people-mover?

Millions of dollars were spent on studies, on property for building the ramps, and on engineering the people-mover components. Then, at about the same time that researchers determined that most people wouldn't pay to take the people-mover, the engineers discovered that it would take as much time to get on and off the moving ramp as it would take to walk the distance between locations. The project was killed. Sadly, more useful projects for solving the problems of downtown congestion would have to wait because of the funds wasted on the people-mover fiasco. Perhaps a new version of the people-moving idea could be viable today—with a new design and a justifiable goal—but the project as conceived should never have been started. Rushing ahead with a good idea isn't always the same as reaching consensus on the viability of a good idea. Consensus takes more time.

The lesson to be learned here is that you want to be clear on some things before you commit to a project: the goals (including the need for the project and the measurable benefits to the stakeholders and users), the scope, the time to carry out the project, and a rough estimate of resources and costs. Doing this work up front gives your project more credibility and manageability.

Clear Project Goals Make Sense to Everyone

Goals are the heart, mission, and purpose for initiating a project. In the most simple view, goals are the specification of what you hope to achieve at the end of the project. But the people-mover story illustrated some important concepts to know about setting appropriate goals for your projects:

Words from the Wise

"It concerns us to know the purpose we seek in life, for then, like archers aiming at a definite mark, we shall be more likely to attain what we want."

—Aristotle

➤ Any project you undertake must make sense in terms of an overall goal that benefits people in some way. If a project doesn't have a benefit for someone, why bother? Another way to look at this is to make sure the goals for the project specify how completing the project will make things better than they would be without the project. You should be able to clearly describe the outcomes, deliverables, and benefits to stakeholders and end users.

➤ Project goals must be carefully thought out; even the most obvious questions should be considered to make sure the idea is really as good as people think it is.

➤ Project goals should provide the criteria you need to evaluate your success in completing a project. These criteria include measures of the time, costs, and resources required to achieve your desired outcomes.

➤ The project goals need to be reviewed with the core team, and consensus must be reached before you move into the next phase of the project.

Of course, you can use project management techniques on projects with inappropriate goals and still accomplish something, but you may fail to do anything useful. For example, if your goal is simply to build a bridge over the River Kwai, as the project manager, you might feel quite proud when the bridge joins the two banks of the river. But if that same bridge collapses under the weight of rush-hour traffic, your project isn't really a success. Or, what if your goal is to build a better mousetrap to rid your city of rats—but after you build it, no one comes rushing to your door to buy it. Has the project succeeded? Not really. Even if the rat trap works, people have to want to use it to get rid of the vermin.

The Primary Goals of Every Project

Every project has three primary goals:

➤ To create something (such as a product, procedure, organization, building, or other deliverable)

➤ To complete it within a specific budgetary framework

➤ To finish it within an agreed-upon schedule.

Beyond these goals are the other goals that must be specified that actually define the project. For example, it's not enough to have the goal of building a mid-priced sports car. A more appropriate set of goals would be to build a mid-priced, convertible sports car that will

➤ Use both gas and electric power.

➤ Be of a quality comparable to the Jaguar XK8.

➤ Sell for 10 percent less than all comparable competitive cars.

➤ Offer specific features to meet competitive demand, such as antilock brakes, a geo-navigational system, on-board Internet access, and an electrically powered convertible top.

➤ Be available for the 2004 season.

➤ Be manufactured by the factory in Dublin but designed by the engineers in the United States.

To differentiate primary goals from other project goals, these other goals are often referred to as "objectives" in other books—but "goals" and "objectives" are really different words for the same thing. Whether they're called goals or objectives, they should meet the criteria outlined in the following section.

High Water!

Taking over someone else's goals can be difficult. If you aren't in on the goal-setting process, carefully review the goals before you assume the project. Make sure the goals are complete and well-formed. If they are off base, ask to review and revise them with the key stakeholders. If you're not given that opportunity, consider looking elsewhere. It's better to decline the offer to be responsible for an ill-defined project than to be blamed for it later.

Six Criteria for Setting Great Goals

As you and the key project stakeholders begin setting goals, you should be aware that there are six general criteria that most project goals should meet to ensure that the project will accomplish something of perceived value.

The Six Criteria for Good Project Goals

If you write goals for your projects that always meet these six criteria, you'll be working on projects with a purpose.

Criterion 1: Goals Must Be Specific

Your goals are adequately clear if another, equally competent manager can take over your responsibilities and guide the project to completion. If your goals meet this criteria, you're pointed in the right direction. Ask co-workers to read your goals and determine what has been stated and what the project will look like when it's done. Confused, surprising, or conflicting responses mean more refinement is required.

Criterion 2: Goals Must Be Realistic

Your goals must be possible or at least be within the realm of possiblity. For example, if you have a project to build a house on land that costs $1 million and you only have $100,000 available in cash and credit, you obviously have little chance of getting the house done. In this case, perhaps you should consider a preliminary project to build up your cash reserves before you draw up plans for the house.

Criterion 3: Goals Must Have a Time Component

Projects must have a definite finish date, or they may never be completed. Projects with no terminus never terminate, so to speak. Projects with unrealistically short dates blow up like an overloaded fuse.

Criterion 4: Goals Must Be Measurable

You must be able to measure your success at meeting your goals, whether you use a powerful computer or a chart full of colored push-pins tacked up on the wall. These results are called *deliverables*—the results of the project. Quality is a vital part of this criterion.

Projects can have interim deliverables that don't reflect the final product. For example, a part might need to be machined early in the project cycle so that more work can be completed downstream. The part required is a deliverable.

Deliverables, like projects, are evaluated not only by the fact that something is produced but by their quality as well. A perfect example is the more than 1,000 pairs of shoes that were delivered on time by a work group in the former Soviet Union. As required in the plan, the shoes were stitched all the way down to the mounting for the soles; however, no one specified soles in the plans. The shoes were delivered but the results weren't too useful. The shoes lacked that subtle edge of quality (a sole) that most buyers would prefer for the demands of the Soviet winter.

Criterion 5: Goals Must Be Agreed Upon

At the onset of a project, you as the project manager and the other initiators of the project (your boss, for example, or the customer or the city council in the case of a city project) must agree on the goals before you take any further steps toward planning the project. If you don't reach consensus, there's no point in beginning the project; it's doomed from the start because the stakeholders can't agree on the outcomes that will make the project a success. In a large project that crosses many departments or other organizations, gaining consensus can be a long and thankless process. (Refer to the section "Seeing Eye to Eye" later in this chapter.)

Eventually, all the team members as well as the stakeholders must buy into the project goals if you're going to manage the project effectively. Without consensus on the goals, the project faces a bumpy road to completion. Projects started with misunderstood goals often have team members working at cross purposes or occasionally duplicating each other's efforts.

Criterion 6: Responsibility for Achieving the Goals Must Be Identified

Although you, the project manager, bear the brunt of responsibility for the overall success of the project, others may be responsible for pieces of the goals. Like agreeing on the goals, the people responsible for the goals must be identified and be willing to accept responsibility before the project proceeds further.

If you can identify all the major players who will be making decisions and contributing major pieces to the project, it is best to get their sign-off up front. For example, if your project is to choose and implement a new piece of software to allow field personnel to input customer requests from the field, you need to get an agreement from your hardware and software groups that the communications hardware and extended computing power will be there to support the software.

Establishing Goals Step-by-Step

It's easy to establish goals for your project. In fact, it's so easy that you'll find yourself with more goals than you can handle. The establishment of goals and objectives takes time to ensure that you aren't, well, biting off more than you can chew. The trick at this point is to limit goals to those of priority to the overall project. (You'll have time to develop objectives for specific activities later in the planning cycle.)

Here's what to do to establish good overall project goals:

1. Make a list of the project's goals. At this point, don't rule anything out. Just make a list and check it twice.

2. Study the list and zap anything that has no direct bearing on the project.

3. Eliminate anything that is really a step in meeting the goals and is not a goal for the end result of the project.

   You should now have a "pure" list of project goals. It's now time for the final step in goal setting.

4. Study the list again. Make sure each goal meets all the relevant six criteria. Now determine whether all these goals are doable within one project. Look for goals that really belong to a separate project or are not directly germane to the project at hand. Cross them out. They may be really important and should not be forgotten, however, so don't forget to consider them again when planning another project. But leaving them in your current project confuses team members and eats resources you need for this project to succeed.

If the items you yanked from the list are important, you should consider alerting your management to them so they can decide what, if any, action to take. This may require explanation on your part as to why you can't take on the extra work and how each item really deserves a project world of its own.

High Water!

Goals and objectives must be established and agreed upon by other team members and managers before project execution. You can't expect team members to hit invisible targets, although the more loyal or uninformed ones may make a go of it.

Project Lingo

The **statement of work** (SOW—nice acronym, huh?) is an integrated set of purposes, goal descriptions, resource requirements, conflicts, assumptions, and authorities that define a project and accompany the evolving master project plan during its development throughout the project.

Successful projects must meet their goals with a minimum of changes and without disturbing the main workflow of the organization. If a project derails for one reason or another, additional resources may be used in an attempt to meet dates. This can cause serious organizational problems as other important work is put aside to accommodate the problem project. Your task is to run the project as smoothly as possible with no requirement for additional time, bodies, or money that interferes with other projects or day-to-day operations.

The best goals are spelled out in writing. Written goals are a powerful consensus builder, especially in a large, complex, or multilayered project. When you and other decision makers need to make changes to a project, the goals help you decide whether each change fits the confines of the goals. If it doesn't, the change may be unnecessary or detrimental to the project. It may indicate that a problem needs further research, which could require approval from other teams' managers and possibly senior management or whoever is paying the bill.

The goals document (usually a part of the *statement of work*, which you'll learn about in this chapter) becomes the vehicle for discussion and consensus building. In its agreed-upon form, it gives you the frame-work to proceed with detailed planning of the project.

Project Scope

No, it's not a mouthwash development project. The scope is the size of the project. When looking at any project, you always look at its scope. Some project managers specialize solely in projects of a certain scope, considering small ones to be too petty for their talents or massive ones to be too long-lived or problematic to get involved.

Project scope can include one or more of the following considerations:

➤ How much is to be achieved in the project?

➤ What is the length of the project window? (When must it be started and when should it be completed?)

➤ What is the obligation of resources (the usual: money, people, supplies, equipment)?

Complexity versus Scope

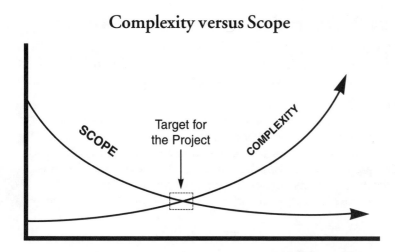

As scope "width" increases, the project has fewer tasks. As it decreases, more projects may spin off. Where the lines meet in this simple model is the ideal point— a balance of complexity versus simplicity.

With the exception of the simplest projects, squeezing the scope often spins off additional subprojects. Making it too broad adds complexity because too many disparate elements must be managed simultaneously. As mentioned in Chapter 2, "The Processes That Work," scope is project management lingo for project size. As you would rightly assume, the project scope for assembling a marketing plan for a minor new product is much smaller than for building an attack jet. As a project manager might explain, "It's a small-scope project."

When establishing a new project, the scope must be clearly defined and agreed upon, just like the goals for the project. It's the scope that defines the assumptions for making all the cost, schedule, and resource projections in your planning of the project. The scope established for a project puts some boundaries on the planning process and the deliverables. In defining scope, the specific outcomes or deliverables of the project should be delineated along with those activities and deliverables outside the scope of the project.

Scope "creep" is the process of adding work to a project, little by little, until the original schedule and cost estimates are completely meaningless. Always make sure that any creep in the SOW or project plan is agreed to in writing—along with the schedule and budget changes.

The terms "project charter" and "SOW" are often used interchangeably. Many companies use the term "charter" to refer to the document that is actually the SOW. That's okay as long as you understand the difference. The charter is a simple announcement that recognizes the authority of the project manager. This is the way the Project Management Institute (PMI) uses the term. The SOW, on the other hand, is the formal project definition document. Both uses of the term "charter" will likely continue, just to confuse things.

Putting It Down in Writing: The Statement of Work

The statement of work is a formal project management document that establishes expectations and agreements about the project. It is not a contract, but a tool for clarifying responsibilities and working relationships among project stakeholders.

The audience for a SOW includes all the project stakeholders including the customer. When a project is produced for the company alone (the customer and the project team work for the same company), the SOW is the only project agreement required. When outside customers are involved, both a contract and a SOW are advisable because the SOW specifies project details typically outside the scope of a contract and the contract specifies legal agreements outside the scope of the SOW. In some cases, a SOW will be referred to in the contract as the official definition of the work to be completed.

The Components of the SOW

A SOW lists and defines the goals, constraints, scope, communication guidelines, and success criteria for a project. The initial SOW, once written, becomes a document subject to negotiation and modification by the stakeholders. When the SOW is finally approved, it becomes the "official rules" for the project.

In size, the SOW can range from a one- or two-page memo on a small project to a 100-page document of understandings for a major technical endeavor.

The usual minimum content of a SOW includes:

1. **The purpose statement:** The basic question of "Why are we doing this project?" should be clearly answered in this section. In addition, the business case for the project is referenced but not necessarily detailed. (If a detailed business case for a project is required, this typically is done in a separate document, often called a cost-benefit analysis.)

2. **The scope statement:** The scope statement clearly defines what the project will and won't do. The relationship of the project to other priorities or business endeavors should be mentioned here as well, especially when the project is a subproject of a much larger project.

3. **The project deliverables:** This section defines what the project is supposed to produce. This helps focus the team on producing outcomes. The intermediate deliverables as well as the final deliverables should be listed by name. For example, "tilled soil" is an intermediate deliverable on the way to a final deliverable of "a fully planted field." Even regular status reports, change requests, and other reports should be specified as part of the deliverables of the project, along with the frequency and audience for each report. It's important for the project management deliverables as well as the project deliverables to be written into the SOW; this ensures that the basic communications within the project are clearly understood.

4. **The goals and objectives:** This section defines the criteria for success. Not only will the on-time and within-budget criteria be specified, all the other goals that were derived for the project should be listed here. Some of the goals may include those that protect the customer's business ("We will install the software without disrupting current operations.") or that measure specific outcomes ("New customer sales will increase by 25 percent within four months of introducing the new e-commerce Web site.")

5. **The cost and schedule estimates:** This section provides the rough but well-researched estimates of both the cost and the schedule for the project. The questions of "How was the budget arrived at?" and "How was the deadline determined?" should be answered in this section. On large projects, most of the complete project planning process (refer to Part 3, "The Project Planning Processes," of this book) might need to be completed to produce adequate numbers. In other cases, reasonable budgets and schedules will be set with specific variances that will be detailed further in the next stages of project planning. In either case, the rule is to set realistic expectations for project stakeholders; thus, the figures must be reasonable if not yet set in stone.

6. **The list of stakeholders:** This is the section in which all the key influencers, managers, and sponsors for a project should be introduced. At a minimum, the names and roles of the project manager, key project team members, the sponsor, managers with an interest in the project, and the customer contacts should be identified.

7. **The chain of command:** This section defines who reports to whom on this project. A project organization chart is required here. Another useful tool is the written responsibility matrix—a table that defines the important roles and responsibilities on a project. This section of the SOW is particularly important because projects often cross organizational boundaries; thus, projects have their own reporting structure that is outside the functional reporting structure of the overall organization. If project roles and reporting requirements aren't defined and agreed to in the SOW, conflicts about decision-making roles and authority can often derail a project midcourse.

8. **Assumptions and agreements:** Any assumptions that limit the project or agreements that form the basis of interactions should be detailed here. Don't leave anything out that could affect the future management of the project. If you want the project to be considered a success, all "side" or "off-line" agreements must be agreed to in the SOW. This is the section in which to document them.

9. **The communication plan:** This section details the basic reports that will be produced and any meetings that will be held during the detailed planning phase of the project. At this point, the frequency and audience of the status reports and basic meetings for the project planning phase should be specified. On large projects, a more detailed communication plan will likely be produced later in

the planning cycle or during the project implementation phase(s). These later communication plans will add more information about the author, content, and frequency of reports to be produced and meetings to be held during the later phases of the project. On small projects, these more detailed communication plans probably won't be required if the SOW is sufficiently detailed.

The responsibility matrix is a useful tool in defining roles and responsibilities in a project.

RESPONSIBILITY	VP Customer Co.	General Manager	Project Manager	Software Manager	Network Support MGR.	Database Programmer	Director, Finance	Customer Service MGR.	Quality Assurance MGR.
Establish statement of work	6	2	1	4	4	4	4	4	4
Define WBS	6	2	1	3	3	3	4	3	3
Hardware specs	3	4	1	4, 5	4, 5	4, 5			4, 5
Software specs	6	6, 4	2	1	3	3		4	4
Interface specs	3	6	2, 3	1		3		4	4
Define documentation	3	6	2, 3	4	4	4		1	
Material costs	5	2	1				3		
Labor estimates	5	2	1				3		
Establish schedules	5	6	1, 2	3	3	3	4	3	3
Final plan for implementation	6	6	1, 2	3	3	3	4,5	5	5

Legend
1 Primary responsibility
2 General supervision
3 Must be consulted
4 May be consulted
5 Must be notified

High Water!

Too many goals and objectives are like too many cooks in the kitchen—they spoil the broth. When considering a project, look for tasks or sets of tasks that should really remain as separate projects. Split them off as such. A word of warning: Management may attempt to add objectives to your project that don't belong there in order to meet other political agendas. Make sure this doesn't happen.

Seeing Eye to Eye

Consensus has been mentioned several times in this book already, and it will be used many times to come. Gaining consensus is the all-important process of getting honest buy-in from the people involved that all aspects of the project are understood and agreed upon. Further, consensus implies that people chosen for certain roles will accept them eagerly and that the goals are smart (meaning they're specific, measurable, agreed upon, realistic, and timely). Before you proceed with the project, consensus must be reached on the SOW. Give the stakeholders plenty of time to give their input. It may take multiple meetings and multiple iterations of the SOW to get it right.

Once the SOW is agreed upon by all the key stakeholders, the final step in initial consensus is getting signed agreement on the SOW from the stakeholders. The signatures provide evidence in the future that everyone agreed to the project as defined in the SOW. At this point, the SOW establishes the baseline for the detailed planning activities and establishes a detailed schedule and budget for the project.

As time goes on in the project, the SOW will likely need to be amended and agreed to again. Making changes to the SOW becomes an important way to manage stakeholders throughout the project lifecycle. The SOW at the end of a large project might be quite different from the SOW you agree to at the beginning of the endeavor. The difference is not important. The only things that matter are that everyone has been informed and all changes have been agreed to by key stakeholders—and always in writing. Thus, consensus building will be an ongoing activity during the project—especially when project changes are necessary. You'll learn more about consensus building and change management in Part 5, "The Controlling Processes," of this book.

The Least You Need to Know

➤ Project goal number 1 is to complete the project on time.

➤ Project goal number 2 is to complete the project within budget and using available resources.

➤ Project goal number 3 is to complete the project by achieving the desired quality in the final result.

➤ Goals (also called objectives by some project managers) consist of specific, measurable, agreed-upon, realistic, and timely aims.

➤ Goals require clear, concise writing so that project participants understand each one.

➤ When planning a project, its size (scope) must be specified and agreed upon by the stakeholders.

➤ The statement of work (SOW) should be written and approved to document the goals, scope, deliverables, cost and schedule estimates, stakeholder roles, chain of command, and communication guidelines for a project.

➤ The SOW becomes the basis for the rest of the formal, detailed project plan and is a tool for managing stakeholders throughout the project.

Chapter 8

Understanding Risks and Constraints

In This Chapter

➤ Understanding that risk involves uncertainty and loss

➤ Dealing with risky business projects

➤ Constraints that bind you

➤ Trouble with a capital T right here in River City

➤ Managing risks and constraints

A good project manager measures risks in advance. Even with clear goals, you need to establish the feasibility of what you have set out to do. On a small project, this step may only take a moment to ponder, but on larger projects, risk assessment can be a complete project in its own right. The goal of the risk and constraint analysis is to establish the feasibility of the project within the constraints of economy, politics, laws, and organizational structure that limit your business. This risk and constraint analysis establishes whether the project goals you just defined in Chapter 7, "Scoping Out the Goals for a Project," are really feasible. These risks and constraints should also be documented in the statement of work (SOW) you just learned about.

A project that moves beyond initiation without taking into account risks and constraints, including the organizational and business environment for a project, becomes much like a silver ball in a pinball machine: It gets bounced with abandon from bumper to bumper by elements beyond its control. Bad weather? A delay. Your main supplier goes bankrupt? A delay. A strike? A delay. Waffling among senior management? A delay and maybe even project termination! Maybe even your job ... well, we won't say it. You get the idea.

Risk Management Is Part of Your Job

There are a number of definitions and uses for the term "risk," but there is no universally accepted definition. What all definitions have in common is agreement that risk has two characteristics:

Uncertainty: An event may or may not happen.

Loss: An event has unwanted consequences or losses.

Therefore, risk involves the likelihood that an undesirable event will occur as well as the severity of the consequences of the event should it occur.

Many risks can be planned for in advance. The likelihood of some risks is unknown, but by identifying potential risks in advance, their impact is often reduced. This is called risk management, and as a good project manager, it's part of your job.

Risk management is a continuous process that starts during the initiation of the project and proceeds until the project is completed. Risk management can help you accomplish the following:

➤ Identify potential problems and confront them when it is easier and cheaper to do so—before they are problems and before a crisis exists.

➤ Focus on the project's goals and consciously look for things that may affect quality throughout the project lifecycle.

➤ Identify potential problems early in the planning cycle (the proactive approach) and provide input into management decisions regarding resource allocation.

➤ Involve personnel at all levels of the project, focus their attention on a shared project (or product) vision, and provide a mechanism for achieving it.

➤ Increase the overall chances of project success.

Constraints Versus Risks on the Project

Constraints, unlike risks, are known in advance. If you have only $10,000 to buy a car, that's a constraint. No matter how much you want that new Mercedes, $10,000 won't buy it for you. Constraints are the real-world limits on the possibilities for your projects. If you violate the constraints in defining your project, the project will fail in some way. Your job as project manager is to make sure you understand the constraints of your project and work within their limits.

Look at the Upside and the Downside

Instead of looking at everything you can/should do, look at everything that will get in your way or become a potential roadblock. Although motivational speakers may try to convince you otherwise, looking at the downside of a project is the best way to anticipate events that might slow down or even kill the project. Because you, as project manager, are directly responsible for the success or failure of your project, you

78

must look at both the positive and negative sides of the equation before making a commitment to the project. It could be a relatively risk-free venture, or you could be handed the task of captaining the equivalent of the maiden voyage of the Titanic.

Risky Business

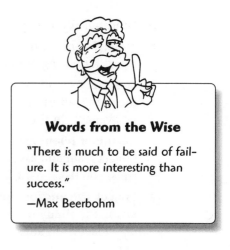

Words from the Wise

"There is much to be said of failure. It is more interesting than success."

—Max Beerbohm

As project manager, you're responsible for all aspects of the project including those that, while a part of the project, are largely out of your control. Projects may involve risks in any one of a hundred areas beyond your direct control, but as project manager, the finger of responsibility will point directly at you.

Identifying risks and constraints beforehand provides you with time to mitigate those that can be fixed or to notify the stakeholders (both verbally and in writing) that the project may be in jeopardy before it even begins. A critical analysis of the project is crucial to get it off to an acceptable and workable start. It is not unheard of for a would-be project manager to be handed a project that has languished for a period of time because no one in his or her right mind would touch it. This is especially typical of a new employee handed an obvious boondoggle. Although the people delegating the job may congratulate the person on getting off to a good start with an important piece of work, once the poor soul has left the room, they sigh with relief, all pleased with themselves that somebody was foolish enough to take on the work.

Going into a project with a "We can do anything" attitude may support team spirit at the onset, but when things come unglued and reality sets in, your team will become frustrated, management will complain, and you will kick yourself for not fixing the up-front problems up front. Plus, budget and schedule problems will blow any possibility of getting things done within the constraints of the original plan, and this means asking for more time and more money. You need to learn to communicate and negotiate change (see Chapters 24 and 25).

If you're lucky, you'll get a new lease on life and resources to revive and revise the project. If not, you'll have to read Chapter 28 to learn how to bring such a project quickly to its termination—it's not the most pleasant process in project management, although we must admit we've been forced to that stage once or twice through the years.

The Common Project Risks

As the project proceeds, a number of risk areas may have an impact on delivery of the defined product or service. The primary among these include:

➤ **Funding:** You may not get the full amount of capital that your project needs.

➤ **Time:** You may find that things are taking longer than originally planned. Thus, you risk running out of time.

➤ **Staffing:** As work on the project begins, you might realize that you can't find the right staff in the marketplace or don't have the requisite experience or skill set available in the company to meet the project objectives.

➤ **Customer relations:** If your customer does not have the time to work with the project team and assist in defining the attributes of the solution to project problems, you risk having a dissatisfied customer as the project proceeds.

➤ **Project size and/or complexity:** The project is large or complex to the point of taxing the ability to complete it on time or within budget. There are just too many factors to attempt to control, especially given the time or budget restrictions.

➤ **Overall structure:** As a result of political decisions, responsibility is fractured between competing work groups or organizations.

➤ **External factors:** There are external risk factors outside of your control such as new government regulations or shifting technologies.

Don't Forget the Business Risks

Business risks also may have an impact on the acceptance of a product or service. These risks include:

➤ **Market acceptance:** The product is a good one, but customers won't want to buy it.

➤ **Time-to-market:** It will be a good product, customers will want it, but only if you can deliver it six months earlier than projected.

➤ **Incompatible product fit:** It will be a good product, customers will want it, but due to the cost of producing it, customers won't be able to afford it.

➤ **Difficult-to-sell:** It's a great product, but who's going to sell it? It will be too expensive for retail outlets but won't cost enough to provide dealers with incentives for selling it.

➤ **Loss of political support:** If a project loses support from executive management, the whole project could be jeopardized. This might happen when a new manager is brought on board. This also could mean loss of financial support.

The Ultimate Risk: Acts of God

As humans, we can do little to prevent acts of God from affecting projects, but we can take steps to avoid the most likely. Don't build precision models in San Francisco under concrete freeway ramps, for example, and avoid vibration-sensitive experiments near the runways of Dallas-Fort Worth airport.

Otherwise, with this in mind, your project should be insured. It's the best, well, insurance against hurricanes, floods, earthquakes, and other unpredictable acts of God. (Check the policy to verify that such events are covered and are not exclusively prohibited, as is common in most commercial policies.)

The Three Types of Risk

As you might assume, the nature of risks varies with the project. Team members may fail at their tasks, sunspots may blow away your satellite uplink in the middle of an important transmission, and the concrete rebar used in your new corporate headquarters may turn to rust about one month after installation.

Ultimately, all the risks in a project boil down to these:

➤ **The known risks.** These are the risks that we can identify after reviewing the project definition within the context of the business and/or technical environment. You must draw on your experience and that of the stakeholders in defining risks of this nature.

➤ **The predictable risks.** These are risks that might occur. They also are anticipated risks based on work on other similar projects. These risks have to do with things such as staff turnover or economic changes that can have an anticipated impact. Instinct rather than something concrete tells us to be wary of these risks.

➤ **The unpredictable risks.** These are the things that go bump in the night or the "stuff that just happens" beyond the control of the project manager or team. You simply can't predict everything!

Constraints to Consider

Project constraints, along with risks, are a major factor when establishing the project plan and when the project is underway. You may want to add a third tower to New York's twin trade towers, but you may be constrained to assembling little more than a tin-roofed shack with tar-paper windows. The constraints that bring a high-flying project to earth include answers to questions like these:

➤ How much money is really available and when?

➤ By when must the project be completed?

➤ What inside resources are required?

➤ What outside resources are required and can you afford them?

➤ Can you get consensus among project members, executives, and stakeholders that the project is important and deserves your time and effort?

➤ What are you willing to settle for that will still meet your needs?

➤ Is there a way to do it using less expensive or fewer resources? (If there is, your problem may be solved.)

Words from the Wise

"Laws and regulations can be constraints, sometimes acting in strange ways. For example, a project might be planned to implement a new accounting procedure to meet new laws or regulations. In that case, the constraint is that, if the project is not completed by that date, the organization might be breaking some law. So, perhaps the scope might be pared back in other ways: for example, deciding to implement a manual procedure first and then later integrate it into computerized systems."

—James MacIntyre, project management expert

The process of answering these questions permanently grounds some projects as the real world intrudes on what's really little more than an energetic pipe dream. Constraints are a modicum of reality. Use them as a tool to fine-tune a project as well as to brush off grandiose suggestions.

Project constraints are quite broad. Similar to the restrictions every manager faces when confronted with any task, constraints, like risks, must be identified beforehand or an expensive project may hit the skids (along with its manager) after bogging down in an avoidable quagmire.

Constraint 1: The Budget

The budget is both a constraint and a risk. Most projects suck up money faster than you may realize. Whether you're opening a new sales office or developing a new product, the budget will constrain your efforts. Most organizations will also charge your project budget for the employees you borrow and any company-provided services you may require. Depending on the charge-back service, you may find it less expensive to bring in outsiders because you can choose exactly the skill set you require without the corporate baggage that comes with insiders from some organizations. You should be aware of the danger of agreeing to a budget to please the boss, management, or the customer when you know in advance the funds will be inadequate. See Chapter 15 for more information on project budgeting.

Constraint 2: The Schedule

Time waits for no one, especially not the manager of a faltering project built around impossible dates. In addition to being a risk for failure, the schedule is always a constraint, even if a project's due date is not that critical. If it rambles on after the predicted end date, the budget will expand, and team members may be pulled off to handle other responsibilities. Missing an end date may cause serious marketing consequences. A new but late-to-market product may arrive at the market window only to find it closed and firmly locked.

Constraint 3: The People

We'll explain how to build a team in Chapter 12 and how to deal with people conflicts in Chapter 23. For now, keep in mind that people skills, as well as their conflicts, are always a project manager's most pressing concern. You can argue for more money and time, but it's the people who really make the project. If the right ones are not available or are unaffordable, you will have to make do with the team that's available—no matter how inexperienced. The availability of the right people is both a risk to anticipate and a constraint that must be dealt with as the project proceeds.

Constraint 4: The Real World

Once a project is underway, reality has an ugly habit of settling in. Inadequate budgets, impossible schedules, and team members with more spirit than skills make for a project that's late, under-funded, and difficult to complete. Getting a project underway is like breaking in a new car. It takes time to get all the parts accustomed to working with each other. On a project, this synchronization may require fine-tuning. Some people may not get along with their supervisors, or a brilliant engineer may quit and join a competitive company. Communication is the best vehicle for keeping the watch fine-tuned. The first milestone, positioned at about 10 percent of the project (5 percent on large projects), is the time to review relationships, progress, and the effects that the actual project is having on your workforce, the project budget, and the schedule.

Time Is Money

A project that has more than one manager controlling it is likely to be unsuccessful no matter how hard you work. Pass on such opportunities unless you can (politely) demand that you have only one boss running you and the project. On the other hand, many projects require the approval of managers in more than one department. Your skill as a project manager may be measured by your ability to form a schedule and budget that they agree on. Just make sure you're the one to control things after consensus is achieved.

Constraint 5: Facilities and Equipment

Every project assumes that required equipment will be available within the project's time. Whether it's a 20-ton grader, an electron microscope, or a simple freight elevator, the right tools must be available for their period in the spotlight. Just like people, equipment resources are key to completion. If a project slips its dates, that slush drink machine you ordered for the big party may be tied up at another get-together.

The constraints for your project should be well-documented in the SOW as part of the scope statement (refer to the preceding chapter for more information on the SOW). These constraints limit what can be done in the project.

The Basics of Risk Management

You can't do too much about constraints except negotiate for what you need in terms of time and resources, but you can reduce the risks on your project through risk management. Some folks even refer to project management as "the practice of risk management."

In basic risk management, you plan for the possibility that a problem will occur by estimating the probability that the problem will arise during the project, evaluating the impact if the problem does arise, and preparing solutions in advance. Here are the steps we use on our projects:

1. All risk management starts with identifying the risks. We do this by making a list of the risks and describing their potential impact on the project. Identifying risks involves careful analysis. Assume that anything can go wrong. Learn from past projects. The failures of the past are often the best source of risk-control information. You can also anticipate problems by looking at critical relationships or resources in the project and anticipating what could occur if these change. It also helps to look at deliverables from different points of view including those of the staff, subcontractors, vendors, suppliers, service providers, management, and customers. You should also evaluate the environment, labor practices, and the availability of raw materials or technologies.

2. Analyze the probability that the risk will occur and the potential impact of the risk. One way to do this is to assign a number on a scale from 1 (lowest probability or impact) to 10 (highest probability or impact) to quantify the probability and potential impact of the risk.

3. Determine the overall severity or importance of the risk. We do this by multiplying the probability number by the impact number to come up with a measure of severity.

4. Determine which risks are the most important for further action. We usually establish a "risk threshold," which is a severity number of 40 or higher. Risks with less severity than this are not considered for further analysis. You can use whatever number seems appropriate for your industry; the key is to come up with a risk threshold that establishes the risks that require further attention throughout the project.

5. Document a response plan for the risks. This plan should be approved by the stakeholders as part of the SOW or project plan. You have four basic options for dealing with the risks on your list:

   ➤ Accept the risk. This means you intend to do nothing special at this point. If and when the risk emerges, the team will deal with it. This is an appropriate strategy when the consequences for the risk are cheaper than a program to eliminate or reduce the risk.

➤ Avoid the risk. This means you'll delete the part of the project that contains the risk or break the project into smaller subprojects that reduce the risk overall. Be aware that reducing or avoiding the risk in this way may also change the business case for the project. Sometimes you'll want to take on more risk to earn more return. This option is similar to the sentiment of "no pain, no gain" in the athletic world.

Risk Management Worksheet							
Type of Risk	Jeopardy	Description of the Risk	Expectation of the Risk (1 to 10)	Impact of the Risk (1 to 10)	Severity of the Risk (Expectation X Impact)	Contingencies Plan of Action
Critical Resource Delay	Budget, schedule	Crane not available due to other project	7	9	63	Increase funding for lease from another vendor
Permit delay	Schedule	Building permit not approved	3	7	21	Focus on the task, not additional contingency required
Project staffing	Schedule, resources	Can't hire enough carpenters	2	5	10	Not necessary to monitor; low risk

Use a form like this one to analyze and respond to the risks in your projects.

➤ Monitor the risk and develop a contingency plan in case the risk becomes imminent. If the best offense is a good defense, then when problems are encountered, having a contingency plan in place is vital to ensure continued success of the project. Developing contingency plans for key risks is one of the most important aspects of risk management. These contingencies are alternative plans and strategies to be put into place when necessary, often referred to as Plan B. The whole concept of contingency planning is based on the assumption that you can develop more effective and efficient scenarios if you do so proactively before things happen rather than reactively when you are under the stress of a slipping schedule or a cash shortage.

➤ Transfer the risk. Insurance is the most obvious, although often expensive, way of transferring risk. The risk is effectively transferred to the insurance company for risks including theft, fire, and floods. Another way of transferring risk involves hiring someone else to implement a part of the project. For example, with a fixed-price contract with a vendor, you transfer the risk of cost increases to the vendor. Of course, fixed price contracts aren't always possible—but when they are, they can reduce a substantial amount of budgetary risk on a project.

85

Remember that risk management and response planning are ongoing processes. Risk must be regularly reevaluated. Every project encounters problems neither planned for nor desired, and they require some type of resolution or action before the project can continue. Depending on the size and type of problem, various types of resources may be required to solve it. Note that, in some cases, no action is required! Project managers get to live long, productive lives by properly recognizing which is which.

Keep a Weather Eye

Ultimately, the key to managing risk is to be aware of everything that can negatively affect the project. Be suspicious. Look for problems. Persistence in analysis reveals risk, and new risks bring new plans for dealing with them. Although risk management starts at the beginning of the project by identifying the problems and constraints that are known, it will continue as you identify and contend with the unanticipated sources of risk that inevitably emerge until the project is finished.

The Least You Need to Know

➤ Project risks and constraints are known roadblocks that should be accounted for before the project is underway.

➤ Some projects should simply be avoided. Be especially careful of "inherited" problem projects.

➤ The impossible remains impossible no matter how enthusiastic your team.

➤ Rome wasn't built in a day, and project management won't let you do it either.

➤ The risk management process can help you identify, quantify, and ultimately reduce the risks (problems) that may affect your project.

Part 3

The Project Planning Processes

Congratulations! You've made it through the initiation steps, have selected the right project to work on, and have identified a core team to work with you. Now you can start planning the work, schedule, and budget for your project.

The plan is a template for your project that helps you guide the work from start to finish. It not only details the work that will be done, but it also serves as a tool for communicating with stakeholders and the project team.

In addition to the goals and objectives for your project, the risks and constraints, and the core project-implementation team that you identified in the initiation phase, there are three standard components in most project plans: the task list or work breakdown structure (WBS)—which may or may not be put into a network diagram or another charting format—the schedule, and the budget. Even a plan for the simplest project should contain these three parts. In this section, you'll learn how to put them together as a complete plan for projects both large and small.

Chapter 9

The Breakdown of Tasks: What Really Needs to Be Done?

In This Chapter

➤ Starting at the top and working down to the details

➤ Why breaking a project into tasks is a good idea

➤ Subprojects as milestones and milestones as groups of tasks

➤ Understanding the work breakdown structure (WBS)

➤ The right WBS levels for your project

➤ Measuring the quality of task completion

Okay, you've earned it—a complete breakdown—a work breakdown, that is. And you're ready for it! With the goals and objectives agreed upon, the risks understood, and the stakeholders identified, you need to figure out the specific work required to achieve the project's objectives. You need to break the project into manageable tasks that can be assigned, scheduled, tracked, and organized. This isn't always an easy chore, but someone has to do it—and as project manager, you're the most likely candidate.

Of course, you can call on the individual expertise of your core implementation team and the other stakeholders to help you break the work into manageable, trackable segments, but as project manager, you ultimately are the person who will put all these segments together into a workable plan of action.

The All-Important Task

Why break your project into tasks? This is a good question. There are five reasons for organizing your project into smaller work packages called tasks:

➤ When breaking work into tasks, you can put the work in your project in the most logical sequence for completion. This can help you determine the best schedule for your project. By wrapping up related elements into units called tasks, it's much easier to see how things fit together in a project, how work overlaps, and how one task may interfere with another if its not done on time.

➤ Tasks are a way of modularizing the project into manageable segments. Thus, tracking the progress of tasks is a way to assess and control the work done on a project.

➤ By breaking work into tasks, you can determine the skills you need to complete the work on a project, and you can quantify how many people will be required to do the work.

➤ Tasks allow you to communicate the work that needs to be done to other team members without getting into too much detail. A task list also can be used to negotiate necessary changes to the work sequences during the project.

➤ Breaking the work into tasks ensures that all the work sequences are identified and understood.

The bottom line is this: Tasks help you organize the hundreds of small work elements that go into completing a project. Without tasks, the amount of work to track would make your head spin. You would have no way to keep track of things or prioritize work.

Tasks: What Exactly Are They?

Each *task* represents some related package of work completed to help get the project done. Tasks are also called activities by some project managers, but in this book, we call them tasks. Tasks can be combined to become subprojects or *milestones*.

Project Lingo

A **task** is a cohesive unit of work on a project—one that's not too big or too small to be tracked.

As you'll see in the following pages, building a task list for a complex project takes time. Tasks are listed so the overall amount of work can be assessed and the work can be sequenced in the most logical fashion. A list of tasks can be short and simple or long and detailed, depending on the size and goals of the project. Don't try to sequence the tasks or estimate time and budget during task definition. Those steps come later (see Chapters 10 through 15).

The task list makes communication among core project team members easier. And, as mentioned (nay, harped on) throughout this book, forgetting to list an important task can have a very negative effect on the project's bottom line and its schedule. Therefore, it's a good idea to have someone else, or maybe even a few people, review the task list before you complete the rest of the project plan—or before you start working on the project, for that matter. The tasks should account for the production of every deliverable on the statement of work (SOW) that was approved for the project. Use the goals and *deliverables* in the SOW as a starting point for developing the tasks.

Project Lingo

A **milestone** summarizes the completion of an important set of tasks or the completion of an important event in a project such as a subproject.

A Tisket, a Task ...

Developing task-sense (something like horse-sense) takes time. "Do I lump all these procedures into one task? Or are they actually two, five, or nine separate ones?" Correctly defining the level of tasks in a project provides an easier way to control the project and keep it in the groove.

Given that you're only going to write a sentence or two about each task, here are some hints for helping you define the right level of tasks within your projects:

Project Lingo

Deliverables are the clearly defined results, goods, or services produced during the project or at its outcome. Deliverables and goals are often synonymous. Deliverables, like goals, may include organizational attributes, reports and plans, and physical products or objects.

➤ A task should be unambiguous. The "design the button layout on the hand-held remote control" task is much clearer than the "design the TV control system" task, which is really five to ten separate tasks. The latter is so unclear that you can't schedule it because there are too many elements; team members won't know where the "task" starts or stops. ("Do we complete the remote control and the TV's receiver side of the system as well as the power controls? Or do we just do the remote control?") But the "design the TV control system" task could be a milestone—one that includes tasks for the remote control, primary power system, and television receiver.

➤ All work within the same task should occur within a sequential or parallel time frame without gaps for possible other tasks in between. Thus, "framing and plumbing the bathroom" is not a well-formed task in your bathroom remodeling project because plumbing the bathroom is not necessarily related to framing the bathroom—and other tasks, such as adding insulation, also could come after the framing task. It's better to define the tasks as separate units, "framing" and "plumbing," in the project plan rather than to risk confusion about the sequence or priority of events. Also, don't confuse tasks with milestones, which are a logical combination of tasks or a subproject.

➤ A task should only include related work elements. When washing your car, for example, the task "get soapy water" wouldn't fit with "polish the car" because there's no relationship between the procedures and they occur at different times in the project cycle. (At least they do when I wash my car!) Therefore, a task called "get soapy water and polish the car" is not a well-formed task because it involves unlike steps.

➤ Most (but not necessarily all) steps in a task should use the same team members. Within a complex task, this improves communication and makes scheduling easier. Should something go wrong somewhere, the responsibility for the task will also be clear, which makes fixing the problem easier as well.

➤ While not always possible, a task that involves multiple people goes smoothly if all the people working on the task work at the same site or within walking proximity of each other.

➤ In scoping out the size of a task, you can use the 8/80 rule and the reporting period rule. The 8/80 rule means that you keep your tasks between 8 hours (1 work day) and 80 hours (10 work days). The reporting period rule states that no task should be longer than a standard reporting period. Thus, if you make weekly status reports, no task should be longer than a week in length. This helps eliminate task statuses that are 73 percent or 38 percent done; tasks will only be reported as started (50 percent done), not started, or complete (100 percent). If a task using this rule is started and is on the not-complete list for more than two reporting periods, there is a problem to solve. Both of these rules are guidelines, not dictates.

As an example of a task list for a small project, we've provided a list of tasks to produce a customer newsletter. Note the active aspect of each task description. Do this, do that. Tasks are also known as activities for good reason! Dates are eventually assigned to each of these tasks to further clarify the work plan. Thus, each task must be something that can be scheduled and measured. On a larger project, the scheduling step may not occur until after the network diagram is assembled. (You'll learn how to do this in the next chapter.) On a small project, however, the schedule can be put right next to the tasks, as shown in the illustration of the newsletter project.

Project Lingo

An element of work (also known as a subtask) is an activity required to complete a project that's too small to be elevated to the rank of task. Elements are the steps to complete a task. Remember, tasks are tracked in the plan, but elements are not; elements still need to be accounted for, however, in the overall time allocated for the tasks.

Task List Worksheet		
Project: January Newsletter	**Produced by:** Gail Murphy	**Date:** 12/14/01
Task Ideas:	**Comments:**	
Complete focus research	Actually a separate project, schedule separately	
Meeting to identify stores and editorial for the first issue	Check with department about other assignments	
Final draft of stories		
Final draft approved	Get Sam to do final approvals.	
Layout stories with computer		
Layout approved		
Final changes for proofreading		
Final sign-off	Get Eleanor to do this for complete newsletter.	
Send output to Linotronic typesetter	Find source for this service	
Camera-ready film to the printer		
Review "blueline" proof at printer's shop and approve	I'll do this.	
Finished newsletter delivered to office	Get them to courier these over.	
Distribution of the newsletter	George can handle this.	

A simple task list for a newsletter project.

Also note that some work on the example list is more complex. For example, the task called "complete focus research" is really a small subproject that involves designing the focus research, finding subjects for the research, initiating the focus sessions, and summarizing the results. Tasks that involve a plan or task list of their own are often called "subprojects" or "summary tasks" or "milestones."

Milestones or subprojects should get a task list of their own within the larger project plan. On a small project, we usually note the milestones with an asterisk or a different typeface. On a larger project, each milestone will get its own set of tasks—called a work breakdown structure (WBS). (We'll talk more about this later in the chapter.)

Over and Over Again

If you manage projects in which many of the same kinds of tasks are duplicated over and over again, you may want to create a *standard task unit* for these common tasks. This technique is used often in construction and engineering, where the time to complete a standard operation has been established and proven over time. It is important to remember that standard task units may change over time. Building a suburb with four house models used to build 100 homes? Standardization is a great (and maybe the only) alternative to individual house plans. You wouldn't want to plan each house from scratch because you'll be building at least 24 others exactly like it.

Project Lingo

A **standard task unit** is an agreed-upon description of a common task performed in multiple projects and the amount of effort used for that task.

Standardized task units should be measured and evaluated on a regular basis. As technology and culture evolve, a standard task unit that took two days back in 1979 might take less time today because of new tools and techniques. And it's always possible that the standard task unit was established based on faulty information. If in actual practice the task takes longer or shorter than the standard task unit, you'll waste time (money) or add a crimp to your schedule when a supposed two-day task really takes a week. Thus, you need to track actual task times and adjust the standard task units as necessary over time.

Also, be careful not to assign a standard task unit to a task that sounds similar but in practice is really quite different. In language study, words that sound the same in English as they do in another language may mean something very different in the foreign tongue. The same is true in project management. A marketing report produced for X division may be a much shorter document than the one required by Y division. When planning, however, the tasks of "writing the marketing plan" sound identical. Make sure you research the requirements for an ordinary-sounding task before you assign a schedule or budget to it.

Some kinds of tasks are not easily standardized. You may perform the function once on a unique project and never use anything like it again. That's not to say you can't keep a library of tasks and timetables on a computer and modify them as needed, but sometimes changing the tasks is more work than figuring the work out from scratch. Only standardize tasks that are really repeated on a regular basis in multiple projects.

The Work Plan and Your Project

The work plan is the document that organizes and summarizes the tasks necessary to complete the project. Every work plan starts with a summary of project tasks and milestones. A work plan can be as simple as a sequential list of tasks like the one shown previously for the newsletter project. For most larger projects, however, the tasks you list for a project should be organized into some kind of hierarchy (which you'll learn about here) and then translated into a network diagram (explained in Chapter 10, "The Network Diagram: A Map for Your Project"). The complete work plan ultimately will include a schedule (see Chapters 13, "Project Start to Finish—Establishing the Time to Get Things Done," and 14, "The Steps to the Critical Path and a Balanced Schedule") and a list of resources required to complete each task (see Chapter 11, "Getting What You Need: Supplies, Equipment, and Other Stuff").

The work plan you create should be able to help you do all of the following:

➤ Identify the major tasks in the project so that all the work needing to be done is clearly indicated.

➤ Organize tasks in the most logical sequence so the tasks can be efficiently scheduled.

➤ Identify tasks that need to be assigned to various team members.

➤ Identify the resources necessary to complete each task so a budget can be developed.

➤ Communicate the work to be done in an unambiguous way so that team members understand their assigned jobs and responsibilities for completing the project.

➤ Organize related tasks into logical milestones.

> **High Water!**
>
> Sometimes it makes sense to break tasks into very small increments, maybe even into tasks of one hour or less. This is especially common on complex projects with a short duration. When doing this, there are three questions to consider when breaking tasks into smaller units: Is the task easier to assign? Is the task easier to estimate? Is the task easier to track? If the answer is "no" to all three, then it's probably not worth doing.

Task organization is crucial in the work plan. On a large project, related tasks should be organized into milestones or subprojects. This makes it easier to visualize the overall project without getting into the details.

Your work plan is the underpinning of a successful project because the need for resources and the schedule come from your task list and work sequences. On larger projects, the task list will likely undergo several revisions before you get it right. If you are new to project management, you should have the core team members or

other key stakeholders review your task lists and sequences until you include all the work necessary to get things done.

Five Steps to the Work Plan

You must complete five steps to develop a work plan that meets all of its goals:

1. Define the work as independent tasks that can be sequenced, assigned, scheduled, and monitored.

2. Define the tasks at a level of detail appropriate for the length and complexity of the project.

3. Integrate the tasks into a total system with a beginning and an end. This may involve combining tasks into milestones (also called subprojects).

4. Present the sequence of tasks in a format that can be easily communicated to people involved in the project.

5. Verify that completion of the tasks will result in attainment of all the project goals and objectives.

For most large projects, assembling and organizing a work plan takes time, but a carefully assembled tasks list goes a long way towards streamlining a project after the work begins.

The WBS

The most important method of organizing tasks for a project is called the *work breakdown structure (WBS)*. The WBS is a sort of organizational chart for a project. We've provided some examples of WBS charts to give you an idea of the different ways the same project can be organized.

High Water!

When you believe you have a credible draft of a work plan, put it away for a week and then revisit it. This gives you a chance to get an objective view of the various elements. You might see something you forgot to consider, or you might notice a better way to organize the tasks.

Project Lingo

A **work breakdown structure (WBS)** is a hierarchical chart used to organize the tasks of a project into related areas. It often is completed as a tree diagram or as an outline. In the WBS, milestones and tasks are clearly defined. The completed WBS can be used for budgeting and personnel-selection purposes as well as scheduling and network diagramming.

The WBS uses a top-down planning methodology: You build a structured view of your project starting at the top from the overall project objective, moving to the clarification of goals and milestones, and then planning the details of activities, resources, and assignments. This enables you to manage the present and plan the future.

The WBS can be used to assign project task responsibilities, to build the budget, and to look for money "sinks" (tasks that require excessive amounts of capital). You also can use it to rough out the schedule and time required, but scheduling for large projects is more accurate when precedence is identified and a network diagram is used, as explained in Chapter 10.

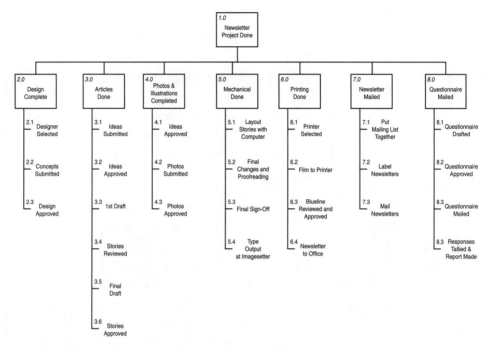

A work breakdown structure for the newsletter project.

Levels and the WBS

The idea behind the WBS is to break larger tasks (or milestones) into individual components. In the newsletter example, you want to separate disparate functions, such as separating writing stories and shooting photos from printing and production.

Once the milestone structure of the project is created, the real work breakdown begins. You can have as many summary levels as befit your needs. In a complex project, such as building a new ride for Disney World, the first level in the master work breakdown is actually a list of smaller projects that are themselves projects within projects. Without this type of organization, large projects are simply too complex to manage.

Some projects need as few as three layers in a WBS. Others require as many as five levels (our unwritten limit in a WBS, although some managers employ more layers) or require a WBS for each subproject or milestone within the WBS. You might set three levels for the comparatively simple newsletter project versus seven or more for creating a new division in a corporation or five or more for building a 600-unit apartment complex. Here is a list of the levels in breaking down the work in any example project:

1. The total project

2. Subprojects or major milestones

3. Milestones

4. Major activities—also called summary tasks

5. Tasks (also called activities, work elements, or work packages)

An outline-style WBS. If the tree method doesn't appeal to you or doesn't work for your project, you can accomplish a similar result using the outline method shown here. This method works best for projects with too many layers to conveniently lay out in the tree format.

Outline of the WBS for the Newsletter Project

1.0 NEWSLETTER PROJECT DONE

   2.0 Masthead and Design Complete

      2.1 Designer Selected

      2.2 Concepts Submitted

      2.3 Design Approved

   3.0 Stories and Photos Complete

      2.1 Articles Done

         2.1.1 Ideas Assembled

         2.1.2 Ideas Approved

         2.1.3 First Draft of Articles

         2.1.4 Stories Reviewed

         2.1.5 Final Draft

         2.1.6 Stories Approved

     2.2 Photos and Illustrations Completed

        2.2.1 Ideas Approved

You can choose to focus on whatever level of the project is germane to your current management needs. Remember, the smallest unit in your WBS should be the smallest unit of work you must track in your project—this is the task level. It is only the task level (work package) that is actually assigned an estimate and a cost—everything else in the WBS is simply an organizational tool for summarizing how the tasks combine to complete components of the project.

As a project manager, the levels in your project plan will help you control work at each level. An appropriately organized task list or WBS can help identify the right time to ask and answer resource and staffing questions.

The lowest level in your WBS should not reach the level of absurdity, but you should track everything that could affect something else in the plan. While doing this, you must remember that not everything in life can be planned down to the minute; if it could, nothing would ever go wrong. Unless you're omniscient or equipped with a time machine, you'll need to make your best guess about the detail and sequence of most project tasks.

Plumbing the Depths

We already talked about using the 8/80 and reporting period rules for scoping out tasks. Another way to judge the lowest-level task you should accommodate in your WBS is to consider budget or time criteria. The lowest-level task should require at least .25 to 2 percent of the total budget or project time. You also can use segments, such as half or full days, to define the smallest task levels. These approaches may appear initially imprecise, but they establish a general guideline for the lowest-level tasks in your project.

Including too many elements in the WBS amounts to micromanaging in the extreme. Again, this may miff your staff; they might think you're attempting to manage their lives as well as the project—an impossible and thankless task.

Dividing the WBS

There's no magic formula for organizing a WBS. In the newsletter example, the WBS is based on the category of tasks. Alternately, you could base it on any of the following (and I'm sure you can think of other ways, too):

➤ **Functional or technological disciplines.** What is required in each phase of the project? Schedule the machine tool operators separately from the marketing specialists.

➤ **Organizational structure.** In a clearly divided organization or a cooperating set of separate organizations, choose to establish the WBS according to reporting structure. If outside vendors are involved, they can be included in this kind of planning.

➤ **Physical location.** Working with separate facilities? Build the WBS based on the geographical locations instead of the people.

➤ **Systems and subsystems.** If there is clear demarcation between several aspects of a project, the WBS can be assembled to reflect this.

Words from the Wise

"If a defect caused by incorrect requirements is fixed in the construction or maintenance phase, it can cost 50 to 200 times as much to fix as it would have in the requirements phase. Each hour spent on quality assurance activities such as design reviews saves three to ten hours on downstream costs."

—Steve McConnell in *Rapid Development*

High Water!

Don't forget to put the project management tasks into the WBS. These tasks take time, too. These tasks might be grouped under a summary task called "Managing the project," which would include time for developing reports, holding meetings, and gaining approvals from stakeholders.

You can use the "wrap-up" approach as well. In a wrap-up, you start at the bottom, listing each element, and work up. Each layer as you move up contains a wrap-up of all the elements of the layer underneath it. The detailed newsletter WBS example works like this, although you may want to draw lines across the chart to ensure that all applicable levels are addressed for each level in the chart.

There are a few other suggestions for creating a WBS that you might want to consider. They are especially important for assembling a complex WBS.

➤ Each element of work should be assigned to only one level of effort. Never repeat an element in another part of the tree.

➤ Narrative must accompany the WBS. You may want to label each box with a number that references a page in an overview narrative document to provide more detail than "Get CEO approval for expansion plan."

➤ Related tasks should be clearly identified in the WBS. A color printer can help with this.

➤ At all levels, the WBS should provide measurable deliverables for each aspect of the project. At a low level, the selection of the masthead designer for the newsletter is a deliverable. At a high level on the same project, the completion and approval of the masthead is also a deliverable.

➤ Assemble the WBS in a format that allows changes if and when the project shifts slightly in direction. Computers are ideal, but a carefully protected whiteboard (wrap it loosely with plastic wrap) can fill the bill for a simple project. Lots of sticky notes can be used as well so that things are easy to move around as you make changes.

Along the Critical Path

When maintaining a WBS for a large project, you need version control in place. This means that each version, no matter how preliminary or final, should be date- and time-stamped. That way, older plans can be relegated to the file, and everyone works only with the most current document. Even if you work on a computer and don't print all versions of the WBS, each iteration should be saved separately by date so you can be sure you're using the latest and greatest plan. Also, the older versions should be saved so they can be used to track project history and to serve as a learning tool to evaluate what (if anything) went wrong.

Criteria for Ensuring Quality Work

As you develop the WBS, you need to have some way of determining whether a task is done and that it was done correctly. You can do this through establishing measurable quality levels based on the standards in your industry. You can also do this by establishing standard quality checklists and formal testing procedures, which are often done on engineering projects. Another way to ensure quality is through identifying peer review or stakeholder acceptance reviews as tasks on the project.

One way to document these criteria is to develop an outline of the WBS with the quality criteria and review process noted next to each appropriate task or milestone. An example of such an annotated WBS is shown for the newsletter project.

Completion and evaluation criteria improve the understanding of each task and ultimately the quality of the project plan. This is important because it's a lot cheaper to fix a problem or task description during the planning stage than during implementation.

So that's a wrap! Now you know how the work breaks down in your project. You've taken all the goals of the project that were developed in the SOW and have broken them into specific work units. But that's just one important step in planning. Now, let's take a look at sequencing the work in a network diagram.

The Least You Need to Know

➤ A single task is a cohesive package of work that can be monitored and tracked.

➤ A work breakdown structure (WBS) organizes the tasks of a project into hierarchies and milestones.

➤ Milestones divide the project into logical, measurable segments. When all the milestones are completed, the project should be done.

➤ When a complete task list and WBS are done, the schedule and resources for the project can be planned.

➤ Criteria for measuring the quality and completion of tasks should be built into the WBS and the project plan.

Step One:
Begin
Project

Step Two:
Complete
Project

Chapter 10

The Network Diagram: A Map for Your Project

> ### In This Chapter
>
> ➤ The *network diagram*—your project's roadmap
>
> ➤ Why network diagrams are a lot of work but a good idea
>
> ➤ Symbols and conventions in network diagramming
>
> ➤ Five steps to create a network diagram
>
> ➤ Major network diagramming systems

You may be thinking that this is going to be the cool chapter in which you get to use networks and computers to plan and control your project from the depths of cyberspace. Forget it. This is a book about project management. Even though you could put information about your project plans and status on the Net or the Web to keep team members up-to-date, when most project managers talk about the network, they're not talking about an information superhighway or even a slow road.

The network, in project management terms, is a tried and proven way to organize and sequence the tasks of a project. Anything but the simplest project should have a network diagram. Yes, the network diagram is a roadmap of sorts, but you won't find mondo sites on weird cults by following the links like you would on the Web—you'll just get your project done a lot easier. In fact, you don't even need a computer to create a network diagram (but it sure helps on big projects).

In this chapter, you'll learn how to create a network diagram by hand using pencil and paper, although we mention how computers can help throughout the text. In Chapter 30, we talk a lot more about the computer tools you can use to do the same thing (and do it a lot faster). It's important that you understand how to create your own network diagram before you start letting the computer do your thinking for you. For small projects, doing it by hand is often easier and faster. (Don't tell our friends at Microsoft and Intel about this heresy—they think everything is better and faster with a computer.)

What's a Network Diagram?

The *network diagram* shows the path of the project, lists starting and completion dates, and names the responsible party for each task. For people not already familiar with your project, such as management and new team members, the network diagram explains at a glance (well, it might take more than a glance) how the work on the project goes together.

If properly sequenced, a network diagram will:

➤ Show the sequences and relationships among tasks necessary to complete a project.

➤ Identify relationships of milestones in the project that can be used for monitoring progress and completion.

➤ Show the interrelationships of tasks in different parts of the task list and work breakdown structure (WBS) hierarchy.

➤ Establish a vehicle for scheduling tasks (covered in Chapters 13 and 14).

➤ Help reduce uncertainty in the project by breaking it into many small phases that have been analyzed and sequenced in advance of starting the work.

If you put the network diagram on a wall where the whole project team can see it (especially your boss) and then use a bright color to mark off the tasks as they are completed, the network diagram can be a powerful way to communicate what has been done on the project and what remains to be accomplished. Of course, if the project gets stalled and the tasks don't get done, it also can be a sure way to let people know you're in trouble. (Hopefully, this won't happen to you.)

Project Lingo

A **network diagram** is the logical representation of tasks that defines the sequence of work in a project. A network for a simple project might consist of one or two pages. On a large project, several network diagrams might exist: one for the overall project based on the project milestones and one for each subproject that leads to the completion of a milestone.

Why Do I Need a Network Diagram?

For simple projects of fewer than 30 tasks, the list of tasks is often all you need to schedule a project. If you're the only person working on a small project, you'll likely complete the work one task after the other until the project gets done. If this is the case, simply list the tasks in your project in the proper order, and you can move on to Chapters 13 and 14 right now to learn about project scheduling.

Before you start scheduling, be aware that if your project involves more than one person or more than a handful of tasks, the sequence of tasks is probably not a simple matter of working on one task after another. Project work also happens in parallel because people may be working on different tasks at the same time. To make things more complicated, the tasks may be related to other tasks that depend on them. All these relationships and interdependencies can be tough to figure out in your head—and impossible to understand from a list of tasks.

This is why you need a network diagram: to help you understand how the work should really go together. Only then can you develop a somewhat reliable schedule for your project.

The WBS and the Network Diagram

Detailed task lists and a WBS are a great first step in identifying the work packages or tasks in a project. However, WBS representations don't graphically display the sequencing relationships between various parts of the project. A WBS only shows hierarchical relationships—you can't schedule a hierarchy as easily as a sequence. Therefore, it cannot be used to create a schedule or to coordinate work done by different people or resources unless all the tasks in a project are sequential (and they rarely are).

There are complex Gantt charts that can display relationships among the tasks, but these are best produced by computer programs. Network diagrams are an easier way to identify and plan task sequences.

Network diagrams reveal the workflow, not just the work. Networks are usually drawn from left to right with lines drawn between tasks to indicate the precedence among tasks. Arrowheads are placed on the lines to indicate the direction of the workflow through time. Though it is possible to create a network diagram for a small project without first developing a WBS, there are some limitations to network diagramming that make this undesirable. Network diagrams simply sequence the work tasks and identify their relationships in time. Networks are not as good as a WBS at demonstrating hierarchical relationships (milestones) in a project, but they can be used to demonstrate the sequence of tasks and relationships among tasks in different milestones in the WBS.

A Network diagram is awkward for managing budgets and personnel assignments. A WBS is awkward for scheduling. Thus, the use of both a WBS and a network to describe and control a project offers more powerful options.

If a task list or a WBS is done first (and it should be), completing the network for a project is easy because the tasks used to create the network have already been identified. Because tasks and milestones must be identified for a project to create a network, first create a WBS to identify the tasks in a project and then create the network diagram to show the sequence and relationships between tasks.

To review, a properly sequenced network diagram will:

➤ Show the sequence of tasks in completing a project.

➤ Identify milestones in the project that can be used for monitoring progress and accomplishments.

➤ Show the interrelationships of tasks in different parts of the WBS hierarchy.

➤ Establish a framework for scheduling tasks (covered in Chapters 13 and 14).

➤ Help reduce uncertainty in the project by breaking it into many small phases that have been analyzed and sequenced in advance of starting the work.

Two central concepts must be understood before a network diagram can be created for a project: the concept of precedence and the concept of concurrent (or parallel) tasks.

Precedence Relationships in a Project Network

Precedence defines task-sequencing order and how tasks are related to one another in the plan. If one task must be completed before the next task can be started, the first one has precedence over the second. In the newsletter project, for example, the articles must first be written before they can be reviewed. In a network diagram, this precedence is illustrated by drawing one task after another. There is other precedence in the project as well. For example, the newsletter must be designed before it can be assembled, and it must be assembled before it can be printed.

Though some tasks must precede others, many tasks can be started parallel to other tasks. This leads to the other important diagramming: the concept of simultaneous activities. Many project tasks can be worked on simultaneously as long as suitable resources are available. For example, it is possible to begin writing the newsletter articles before the format and masthead have been designed. However, both completing the

Project Lingo

When one task must be completed before another task can be started, the first task is said to have **precedence** over the other.

articles and designing the format have precedence over assembling the newsletter. In a network diagram, it is possible to identify concurrent activities by drawing them parallel to each other in the same plane.

The concepts of precedence and simultaneous work are important because the relationships between tasks ultimately will establish the basis for scheduling a project. (You will learn about this in Chapters 13 and 14.) That's why these network diagrams are usually called *precedence diagrams*. Adjusting the parallel activities and the precedence alters the time and resources required to complete a project. The goal in developing the network diagram is to identify activities that can occur in a parallel manner and to specify the precedence that exists among the activities. This leads to the development of an optimum sequence of tasks for scheduling purposes.

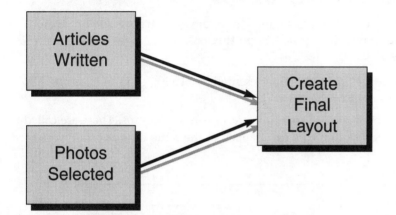

Two simultaneous tasks that have precedence over the same task.

How It Works: Symbols and Conventions

We have found that simple is better in most project management situations. Therefore, the network diagramming techniques we recommend are simple ones. Still, in every networking method, specific symbols used in the charts can seem complicated if you're new to the idea of a network diagram. But stay with us. The system we recommend is based on a simplification of a diagramming technique called precedence diagramming. If you work through the steps, you'll see that it isn't as difficult as it looks at first glance. It's really just lots of lines and boxes—and most people learn to draw those in kindergarten.

Boxes hold the description of each task. Lines connect the tasks to one another, as you can see in the

Time Is Money

If a task does not have a clear precedent (that is, if it is unrelated to any tasks performed previously), it can stand alone with an arrow pointing to it from the Start Project task. Such tasks might have significant float (explained in Chapter 14) and can provide you with additional scheduling flexibility.

diagram in the following section. The tasks are laid out horizontally from left to right to coincide with the time sequence in which the tasks will be completed. Groups of tasks that lead to specific deliverables are identified by boxes with rounded corners. These mark the milestones in the chart.

Network diagrams are really only a simple matter of linking tasks in boxes with lines. Just put the tasks in the right order, draw lines between them, and you have a network diagram. Of course, where you put the boxes and how you draw the lines both mean something—so make sure you get it right. Otherwise, you'll have the truck pouring concrete before the carpenters build the frame to hold it.

Diagramming the Relationships

So that everyone who uses network diagrams can figure out what's going on, there are a number of basic conventions (rules) in putting tasks into a network diagram. Here are some of them:

➤ The defined sequences of tasks are represented by placing tasks in horizontal order from left to right in the network.

➤ Tasks that can happen at the same time are shown in columns. These are called "parallel tasks" because the work can happen at the same time as other work in different rows.

Standard conventions for network diagrams.

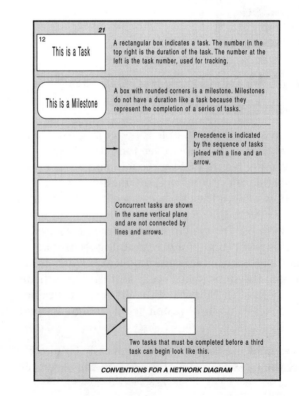

108

➤ The precedence between tasks and milestones is shown by drawing lines from task to task, indicating that the task on the left must be completed before the task on the right can begin. The task that must be completed first is called the precedent task. The task that starts after the precedent task is called the dependent task. That's why the network diagram is said to reveal the dependencies among tasks. (Getting pretty technical? Don't worry. This is as hard as it gets.)

➤ Lines among tasks can cross the rows to show how tasks in the various sequences relate to each other.

Other relationships among tasks also should be clearly explained in a network diagram. Here are some of them:

➤ One task may depend on the completion of multiple tasks or milestones. The precedence for all of these tasks must be shown by drawing lines from the precedent tasks to the dependent task.

➤ A task may start independently of some tasks but still be dependent on others. Lines are only drawn between tasks with dependency.

➤ A task without a precedent task or milestone can logically be started at any time after the initial "Start Project" task because it has no other dependent relationships. Put such a task in its own row.

If you look at the complete network diagram earlier in this chapter, you can see most of these conventions put into action. You'll also notice that it's pretty easy to figure out what's going on when you follow the rules.

Five Steps to Create a Network Diagram

By convention, most network diagrams start with a box labeled "Start Project" and end with a box labeled "Project Finished." All you have to do is fill in the tasks in between. But as you may have guessed, there's probably more to it than that. Actually, there are five steps (explained in the next sections) that can be followed to produce a network diagram for any project. Before you start, however, get lots of scratch paper, sharp pencils, and a good eraser. These tools can help as you try to figure out the sequences and relationships.

Don't expect to get things right the first time. Network diagramming takes practice. Even after you get it all put together, you should have some other folks from the project review your efforts. Now, with all that in mind, the following sections describe the steps to follow.

Words from the Wise

"Begin at the beginning," the King said gravely, "and go until you come to the end; then stop."

—Lewis Carroll, *Alice's Adventures in Wonderland* (1865)

Step 1: List the Tasks Using the Task List or the WBS

You have already learned how to create a task list and a WBS (refer to Chapter 9, "The Breakdown of Tasks: What Really Needs to Be Done?"). For a network diagram, each task should have a unique identifying number or other code. A network diagram will lay out the work units or individual task level in your WBS. Higher WBS levels will be identified as milestones (see step 3).

Step 2: Establish the Interrelationships Between Tasks

To determine the sequences and precedence to be diagrammed for the tasks, ask the following questions about each task:

➤ What tasks must precede this task? That is, what other tasks must be completed before this one can be started?

➤ What tasks follow this task? That is, what tasks cannot be started until this task is complete?

➤ What tasks can take place concurrently with this one? Or more simply, what tasks can be worked on while this one is being completed?

The precedence and dependencies should be noted in a simple list. Some of the precedence won't become apparent until step 4, however, when you actually draw the tasks and link them. If you don't identify all the precedence now, it's fine. Just list them as you discover them to form a record. This list of task numbers and their precedence is especially useful if you use computerized project management programs.

Step 3: Identify the Milestones You Want to Specify

Milestones summarize a sequence of tasks or specify a key accomplishment during the project (refer to Chapter 9). Milestones are not tasks. Milestones do not take effort; they are just convenient markers for summarizing work that has been performed to that point on the network diagram. The top levels in the WBS are a good source of milestones for the project. Milestones also have defined precedence and sequences. You can draw a network of only milestones, or you can combine milestones with activities to display a complete project—or you can leave the milestones out of your project altogether (recommended only on small projects).

Step 4: Lay Out the Tasks and Milestones as a Network

Some experienced project managers start from the last task in the project and work backward when charting the project. Many people find it easier to identify preceding tasks than successive ones. However, there are many arguments for starting with the first task and working forward because this is how the work will actually be done. The outcome is the same—the approach used is a matter of preference.

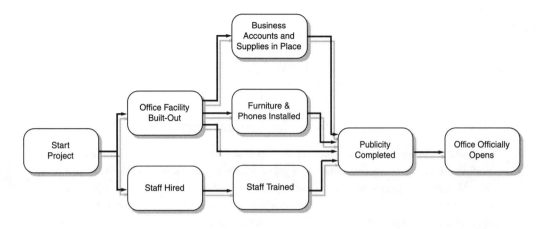

Milestone Network for San Francisco Sales Office Project

Here you see a milestone network for a project to open a new sales office.

Step 5: Review the Logic of the Network

The network review process is important because it is through adapting sequences and precedence that an optimum order of project tasks can be identified. To review the logic of the network, look at each task and each connection and ask yourself the following questions:

➤ Are the tasks properly sequenced?

➤ Is all necessary precedence identified?

➤ Is there any precedence that isn't really required? That is, are there tasks that can be completed concurrently (in parallel) that are incorrectly shown as sequences?

➤ Are all of the tasks really necessary?

➤ Are any tasks missing?

➤ Does the completion of the tasks in the network represent the accomplishment of everything necessary to meet the project goals that have been specified?

Time Is Money

When establishing a network diagram using a computer, before using the software's demand for start, duration, and finish dates, take some time to roughly diagram the basic network on paper. This will help you understand the basic precedence and will assist you in building the chart correctly once you begin the computer entry procedure.

Along the Critical Path

To make tasks and sequences easier to find in your network, be sure to identify each task and milestone with unique numbers or other identification labels. In computerized project management programs, tasks are always numbered as well as being identified by task description. The same method of identification or numbering used in the WBS is usually appropriate; however, it is common in networks to skip numbers between tasks to allow flexibility in the network when requirements for new or different tasks may become apparent later in the project. For example, instead of numbering tasks as 1, 2, 3, and so on, it might be better to number tasks as 10, 20, 30, 40, and so on. Then, when you need to add new tasks between task 10 and task 20, you can number them 10.1 and 10.2 without disturbing the logical numbering sequence of the original tasks. The numbering system should be flexible because projects almost always have changes that need to be represented in the network.

The sequences of tasks you put in your network are not absolute. Experienced project managers often revise and adjust the networks until they are optimized. People often find when they begin mapping precedence that tasks have been left out of the WBS. Add these new tasks and make sure to note them in the appropriate places in the WBS. The network and the WBS should always match. In reverse, if you find that some tasks are redundant, remove them.

Be careful not to sequence tasks in an arbitrary order. Just because you've always done something a certain way does not mean it is the best way to do it. Try to look at the network from a new point of view; find better ways to get the work done. A network diagram provides a great opportunity to do this. Can the tasks be sequenced differently for better use of resources? Can some tasks be split into two or more tasks to make the organization of work more flexible? It is usually a good idea to have objective outsiders review the sequences, in addition to the project team, to avoid bias in the sequence of work. Sometimes a person outside the politics of a project can identify a better way to complete the work.

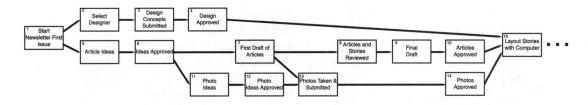

Even a relatively simple project, such as developing a newsletter, has parallel tasks and dependencies that are best understood through the development of a network diagram.

Complex Time Relationships for Critical Projects

For the most accurate scheduling, there are some advanced concepts in network and precedence diagramming that are important for some project managers to consider—especially for construction and engineering projects.

The optimum way to represent precedence in projects is not always a simple matter of completing one task and then starting another (called a finish-to-start precedence). Your precedence diagrams also can specify complex timing relationships between tasks. By overlapping tasks in the diagram and using arrows to represent specific timing, relationships can be shown in which tasks must be started at a certain point after another task is started. This is especially important in complex projects. For example, using precedence diagramming techniques, you can show complex task-sequencing requirements such as:

High Water!

If a task defined in the WBS doesn't seem to fit in the network diagram, this usually means it's out of place. The task could be too small to include in the network diagram, or it could be too large and require further breakdown into more elemental tasks. If you change a task's status, make the change in your WBS so that it and the network diagram match.

➤ A task that should start at the same time as another task because they're logically related. For example, preparing the soil and planting the seeds in the garden can be done at the same time, even though planting the seeds will take longer to complete. Overlapping tasks like this reduces the total project duration.

➤ A task that must be completed at least five days before another can begin. For example, the pouring of foundation must be done five days earlier to allow the cement to cure before any more work can be done on the building.

➤ A task that must finish before another task can finish. For example, the planning of a product can start before the design approvals are started, but the planning cannot be completed until the design approvals are done.

113

For most simple business projects, it is not necessary to define these types of complex *lead* and *lag* times at the subtask level. Simple precedence relationships (finish-to-start relationships) are adequate for all but the most complex scientific and construction projects. The terms are mentioned here, however, because they are often referred to in computerized project management systems or in other project management literature. You should know what the terms mean even if you don't use them. As a project manager, it's a matter of pride (and being knowledgeable). These advanced techniques can also come in handy when you need to adjust tasks to meet a deadline.

Complex precedence diagramming conventions for showing lead and lag times between tasks.

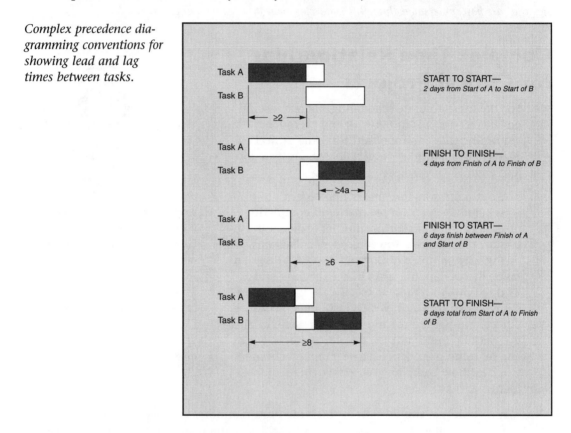

When Is Enough Enough?

Goals and constraints establish the scope for your project. (You learned about this in Chapter 7, "Scoping Out the Goals for a Project.") In creating a network, as in creating the WBS, the project goals and scope establish the level of detail for defining the work that must be completed. Even so, the question arises in developing every network as to how many tasks should be included. There are no hard and fast rules, but the experiences of early project management practitioners revealed that, after a certain point, the marginal return in control offered by more detail is far outweighed by the additional work required to develop and maintain the network. At some point in every plan, more detail becomes a negative rather than a positive attribute. The best advice is to use your judgment.

Slaying the Goliaths of Project Networks

Some giant networks for major construction or engineering projects may have 25,000 or more tasks that really need to be tracked. It obviously is impossible for any one person to understand all the relationships between these 25,000 individual tasks—and the network diagram would take up an entire wall or more of a large conference room.

One way to make such a large network more manageable is to create network diagrams for each major subproject or milestone of a project based on the WBS. These milestones can then be summarized in another diagram. If there are dependencies between the milestones, they can be noted in the milestone network. This approach also allows people responsible for specific milestones within a project to be responsible for a detailed network of his or her own subproject.

Project Lingo

Lag is the amount of time after one task is started or finished before the next task can be started or finished. **Lead** is the amount of time that precedes the start of work on another task.

When Is a Network a Waste of Time?

The more complex a project is, the greater the value of network diagram in developing a schedule and a budget. Though there is a cost associated with implementing network management of a project using network diagrams, this cost is relatively low when compared to the potential advantages. Typically, the cost in time and money for implementing a network-based planning system is somewhere between .1 to 1 percent of the total project—the percentage gets smaller as the project becomes larger.

The value of using network diagrams is not universally accepted, however. Wags often argue that taking time to develop a network is a waste of time. And some research indicates that the use of PERT/CPM (see the following section) or other related methods has no significant effect on the technological performance or final deliverables of projects. In other words, projects that were managed without the use of network systems in these studies seemed to get the same amount and quality of work done.

Most studies, however, indicate a significantly lower probability of cost and schedule overruns when network diagrams are used. In a business world concerned with profitability and performance, this seems like a pretty good reason to employ the network technique for organizing and scheduling work—it reduces the risk of going over budget or running late.

115

Three Major Network Methods and Others You May Encounter

We've discussed the basic precedence diagram because we think it is the easiest, most effective networking diagram for most small to mid-size projects—the projects most people manage in everyday business. But even if it's just to impress your boss by using nifty acronyms, you should know that related systems of network diagramming and scheduling techniques are used in industry today.

The two most common forms of networking systems are the Performance Evaluation and Review Technique (PERT) and the Critical Path Method (CPM). The techniques are similar in principal to what you've already learned. The differences lie in how the projects display information and deal with scheduling uncertainties. And given that these techniques were developed by engineers for engineering projects, a lot more symbols are used to represent the relationships between tasks in a network.

Until PERT/CPM techniques were developed, simple Gantt charts or other bar charts were the best tools available to represent project sequences. Gantt charts show a graphic representation of work on a time scale. You will learn more about Gantt charts as a useful way to represent the overall project schedule in Chapter 13. Gantt charts are really just timelines that show tasks in parallel. The complex versions produced by today's project management software can even show the dependencies between tasks represented in networks, work in progress, and comparisons between the current status and the planned status (baseline) of the project.

Along the Critical Path

One of the first pioneering efforts to show the interrelationships among tasks on a project was undertaken by the science management team of Morgan R. Walker and James E. Kelly in the mid-1950s at the E. I. Du Pont Company. Their joint efforts resulted in the Kelly-Walker network technique. However, in later publications of their work, they referred to the method as the Critical Path Method. Du Pont tested the CPM method in the construction of a major chemical plant and in several maintenance projects that were completed by the middle of 1958. It is claimed that Du Pont credited more than $1 million in savings to this technique in the first year it was used.

During the same period of 1957–58, the management scientists of the Special Projects Office of the U.S. Navy, along with the firms of Lockheed and Booz, Allen, and Hamilton, developed a similar network system called PERT, which stands for Program Evaluation and Review Technique. The system was developed to help coordinate more than 3,000 people involved in the development of the Polaris missile. The use of PERT is credited with reducing the time required to complete the project by two years.

CPM is often cited as better for construction-type projects. It is argued that PERT is more appropriate for research-oriented projects. The primary reason for this is the different approaches the two systems use for scheduling, not because of the networks, which are largely the same in terms of sequencing possibilities. In CPM, one time estimate is used for creating the schedule; PERT uses a more complex system based on three time estimates that are used to determine the most probable time for completion.

This more complex time-estimating approach is deemed by some to be more appropriate for research projects with high degrees of uncertainty and risk. For most general business projects, these differences are not critical, and some people call all network systems by the name PERT/CPM because of their similarities.

Circles or Boxes? Who Cares?

Okay, this next part is for people who just want to know more about the PERT/CPM differences. It might get a bit technical—you can opt out now if you just want to get your project plan done. See you in the next chapter.

Still with us? Curious? Glutton for punishment? Well, in any case, here's the scoop on PERT and CPM.

Traditionally, PERT/CPM networks use circles and arrows to describe work in a project. The two systems use the same basic diagramming conventions you've already learned as a way to link tasks, except that the arrows represent tasks (called "activities" in PERT/CPM) and the circles represent something similar to milestones (called "events" in PERT/CPM). These two concepts, activities and events, are central to the traditional PERT/CPM diagrams. An activity is a specific project task that requires resources and time to complete. An event is a specific end state for one or more activities that occurs at a specific point in time. An event occurs as a result of completing one or more activities.

AOA and AON

There are two methods of representing activities and events in PERT/CPM networks: activity on arc (AOA), also called activity on arrow, and activity on node (AON). The method used is largely a matter of preference. In AOA, the arrows are the activities, and the circles (called "nodes" in PERT/CPM) are the events. In the AON method, the

117

activities are the circles, and the lines demonstrate the precedence between activities. Some of the traditional ways of diagramming tasks in a PERT/CPM chart are shown in the following diagram.

Simple precedence networks using boxes, as shown here, are really just another version of an AON PERT/CPM network. We think the boxes are a lot easier to use. (Bet you do too at this point.) We've found that most mid-size business projects are easier to describe and understand using the boxes than by creating complex number, circle, and arc networks. In fact, most computerized project management programs now offer boxes to replace the circle/arc format.

Pert/CPM Activities.

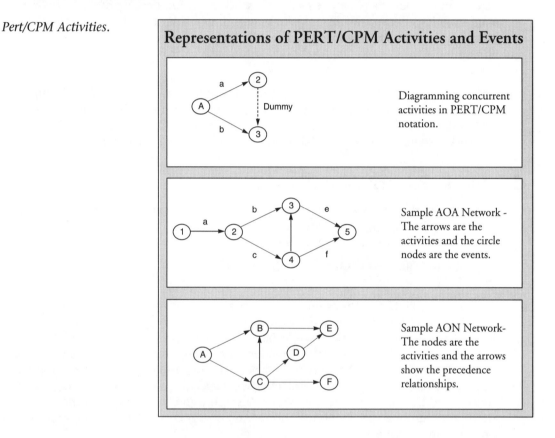

Representations of PERT/CPM Activities and Events

Diagramming concurrent activities in PERT/CPM notation.

Sample AOA Network - The arrows are the activities and the circle nodes are the events.

Sample AON Network- The nodes are the activities and the arrows show the precedence relationships.

We're glad you made it through all this because it's important for an informed project manager like you to be familiar with some of the other diagramming options in project management. As you get more experience, you might want to experiment with these other diagramming techniques for your networks. (We suggest you get a comprehensive book on PERT/CPM techniques before you do.)

Tried and True Networks

Over the years, with the advancements in computer software, some of the representational techniques in PERT/CPM and precedence diagramming have been improved or modified and expanded. Still, the simplicity of the original system has withstood the tests of time and application, and no truly substantive changes have been made in the original methods.

Some computer systems for project management combine the advantages of the various network methodologies into programs that give project planners the option to represent projects at various levels of detail and complexity using modified and/or expanded network representations. However, the true innovation of putting the tasks together in precedence and showing how all the tasks relate to one another through time is still the most important thing to know about creating a network diagram—even if you use a computer program.

As long as the logic and precedence relationships remain intact, it doesn't matter whether you use circles, boxes, or any other shape for representing tasks and milestones. The important thing is to understand how all the tasks in a project fit together—only then can you create a viable schedule.

In Chapters 13 and 14, you'll learn how to turn your network diagram into a schedule you can be proud (and confident) to present to management for approval. But before you get to scheduling, it's important to figure out exactly who and what you need to do all the work you've drawn in the WBS and the network. This is what you're going to learn in the next chapter.

The Least You Need to Know

➤ The network diagram is not always necessary for small projects, but it's a good tool for most projects to establish the order of steps and the relationships among the various tasks in a project.

➤ As a project manager, you predict the future. The tough part is making the future match your predictions! A network diagram can help.

➤ The task-in-box method is supported by most project management software and is relatively easy to use.

Chapter 11

Getting What You Need: Supplies, Equipment, and Other Stuff

In This Chapter

➤ Establishing exactly what you need

➤ Getting bids from outside vendors and suppliers

➤ Choosing the best vendors and suppliers

➤ Checking price and availability

After the tasks have been defined and a basic network established, a complete list of resources required for your project can be developed. Why wait until you have the list of tasks? Because before listing the tasks, you might not have realized that you need an electron microscope and an electron microscope operator to clone sheep. But with all the tasks identified, you can choose exactly what you need to get all the work done on your project—even the sheep.

After you determine all the resources you need and how to get them, you have to schedule all this to be in the right place at the right time. That's what the network diagram described in Chapter 10, "The Network Diagram: A Map for Your Project," helps you do. It shows you how to assign dates to tasks so you get the resources you need at the time you need them. Before you can do that, however, you need to know exactly what needs to be scheduled.

The Seven Resources You Need

As you proceed to figure out what you need to complete the project, you'll have to consider the seven fundamental resources required to implement almost any project:

➤ People (We'll talk about them in Chapter 12, "Building a Winning Implementation Team"; they're the project team members you need to find and assign.)

➤ Money

➤ Equipment

➤ Facilities

➤ Materials and supplies

➤ Information

➤ Technology

These are the seven things that you and the core project team need to identify for the entire project. There are two basic questions you and the core project team need to answer before a complete project plan can be approved:

➤ What people, materials, equipment, and other resources are needed to complete each task on the project? You answer this question by determining the needs for each task on the project network or WBS and then developing a list of everything you need. Determining the requirements for personnel is an important task that we'll hold off on for now. You'll learn how to do this in the next chapter. In this chapter, you'll learn to figure out what other resources (materials, supplies, facilities, and equipment) you'll need.

➤ What resources are already available for the project? We often use a resource inventory to list everything available for the project (including equipment, facilities, and supplies).

Three More Things to Consider

After you (and the core team) answer the questions in the preceding section, you still need to know three things before you can complete your plan for project resources. Those things are:

➤ The cost estimates for each resource, including the overhead assigned to your project for each resource during the course of the project, if applicable. For people, this could be the hourly rate and any overhead costs associated with them. For outside resources, it's a good idea to get bids and estimates for services, supplies, and equipment before approving the plan. (You'll learn more about cost estimates and budgeting in Chapter 15, "Budgeting Options for Your Project.")

➤ The availability of each resource. For people, this means knowing their work availability, holiday schedules, and commitments to other projects. For other resources, this means verifying the general availability of the supplies or equipment during the timeframe of your project.

➤ The estimated quality and output of people and equipment resources. This is important because it allows you to make a trade-off analysis between similar resources. If time is most important, choose the fastest resource. But if a slower resource really saves money in the long run, and if you have the time to spare in the project, then a slower but cheaper resource might be a better selection. If you don't make these estimates in advance, you won't be able to put the best budget and schedule together for your project.

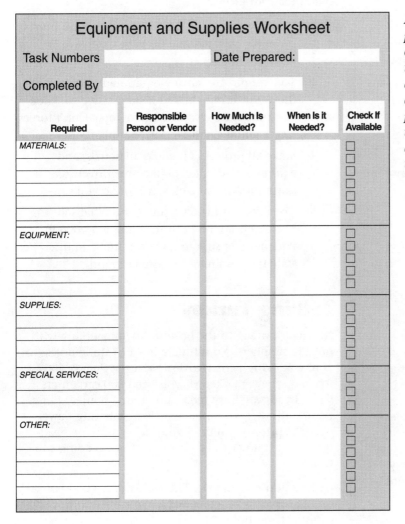

An equipment and supplies worksheet like this one can be used to identify things that are needed and those that already are available for your project. Be specific. We usually list equipment and supplies based on the tasks in the WBS.

Planning for Outside Vendors, Contractors, and Suppliers

During the planning phase (where you are now), you need to determine a list of probable vendors, suppliers, and contractors for your project and get estimates of cost and availability. Before you talk to vendors, you need to be crystal clear about the materials, equipment, and/or work you want from them. You'll usually make your final vendor selections based on these estimates after the plan is approved.

Words from the Wise

"For art and science cannot exist but in minutely organized particulars."

—William Blake, Jerusalem, 1818–20

High Water!

You've probably seen the old film footage of the Tacoma Narrows Bridge in Washington State. It started swaying in the wind on completion day and quickly crashed to the river below. Someone learned an expensive lesson in checking out vendors before counting on their performance. Don't wait for your own disaster to make the same discovery.

You want to know that the estimates are good ones—and that the eventual commitments will be met. You should follow these guidelines for getting the best estimates for your project:

➤ Whenever possible, get written estimates from suppliers with whom you have extensive and positive experience.

➤ Save money by renting equipment required for the short term, whether it's a massive backhoe or a miniature electron microscope. Don't forget to get rental estimates for your plan.

➤ Make all providers (people, materials, and equipment suppliers) bid competitively. Get a minimum of three bids or more if you can.

➤ Consider out-of-town suppliers. What sells for $12,500 in Manhattan may go for $3,000 in Phoenix. (Be sure to take shipping and interstate tax requirements into account!)

Talking Turkey

Now you can get to the bottom line of working with outside suppliers. No estimate is set in stone unless you're working with a government provider or looking at a seller's market. (If you need 500 carpenters who already are busy rebuilding frame homes after a natural disaster, you'll have little negotiating power over the price of building your new corporate headquarters. Timing can be everything in a bidding situation.)

Negotiation is a fine art. There are many good books on the topic. Read a few. For a complete and free education, spend time at a flea market. Watch as expert negotiators go up against the most set-in-concrete pricing scheme and drive the prices down. Or even better, watch your organization's best salespeople at work. They wouldn't make those big salaries if they didn't know how to negotiate.

Choosing the Outside Sources and Suppliers

You need good estimates for your plans and good working relationships with your vendors to get these estimates. Work with suppliers, study the goods or services they sell, and check up on their reputations. Never let a powerfully persuasive salesperson push you into a commitment before the plan is approved. It may be harder to resist than you think when a honey-voiced merchant visits and applies rose-colored glasses to the top of your nose.

If you follow these simple steps, you'll get more accurate estimates from suppliers of all sorts of goods and services:

1. Get written estimates for your service, supply, material, and equipment needs. On large projects, you may want to put together a formal request for proposal (RFP) to attract the maximum number of potential suppliers. Advertise the RFP if that's what it takes to get good estimates and quality vendors. Offer detailed specifications of your project and its needs by return mail, fax, or e-mail. Vendors will assume bidding is competitive, although the words "Competitive Bid" stamped (in heavy red ink, of course) on the RFP will help get the point across.

2. Fully explain, demonstrate, and document your requirements for equipment, materials, and supplies for the estimate or in the RFP. Be as precise as the following sample bid request for copy paper: "Bid required for bright white copy paper suitable for laser printing, 20 pound bond, 8½" by 11", quantity 100,000 sheets packaged in 500 sheet reams, 10 to a box. Recycled paper consisting of at least 40 percent recycled paper is preferred. Please indicate the percentage of recycled paper used in your paper. Enclose a sample please."

3. Include delivery mandates in the description of your needs. (Ordinary but unavailable materials have sunk more than one project.) These specifications must indicate when the goods must be delivered and to where; otherwise, the contract is void. If the company turns out to be a no-show, you're still in

Time Is Money

Keep in mind that, as you develop the rest of the plan, your resource choices will affect the quality, schedule, and budget for your project. If you aren't able to get the resources you planned to use, you'll have to adapt the objectives, schedule, and budget accordingly. It's a good idea to verify the availability of as many resources as possible before the project plan is approved.

trouble project-wise, but at least you won't owe a bill for a shipment that arrives three weeks too late. (You won't be able to specify dates, however, until you complete the schedule in Chapters 12 and 13.)

4. Make sure the vendors know that acceptance clauses will be inserted in the final order for goods. This means goods that don't meet specified standards will be returned and replaced at no cost to you. Also, make sure the vendor will be responsible for picking up the shipping tab for return freight if materials or supplies are inappropriate or substandard upon delivery.

5. When getting estimates from consultants or other service providers, ask for a formal proposal for their services. When hiring a packaging expert, for example, you might ask competing designers to create rough illustrations of how they would package your project.

6. When hiring consultants or service providers, also ask for a description of their current workload. Many will boast about current projects without realizing that what you're looking for is a person with the time to take on your tasks. Although it's true that the busiest may be the best, when it comes to managing a project, you need adequate share-of-mind for your work and committed schedules from the vendors. Thus, a vendor who is a close second in quality but who has fewer commitments may be a better choice.

7. Check references, compare estimates, and use the estimate from the most likely choice of vendors for the rest of your planning purposes.

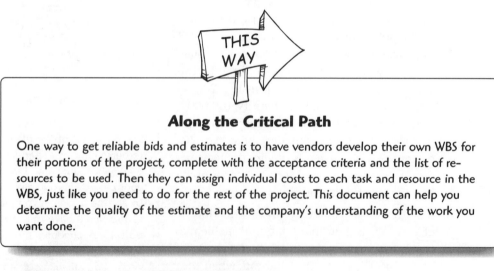

Along the Critical Path

One way to get reliable bids and estimates is to have vendors develop their own WBS for their portions of the project, complete with the acceptance criteria and the list of resources to be used. Then they can assign individual costs to each task and resource in the WBS, just like you need to do for the rest of the project. This document can help you determine the quality of the estimate and the company's understanding of the work you want done.

The Ghost in the Machine

Sometimes you won't be given the opportunity to get estimates or to order resources without going through the purchasing department. This can be a relief—it takes the work out of your hands. But the purchasing department is the bane of projects (and project managers) more often than not.

If you're lucky, you'll find a professionally run organization with experienced purchasing agents who take the time to understand your needs and to handle your bid requests with aplomb. Be aware, however, that you may be faced with the uphill task of (literally) fighting with your organization's purchasing personnel to place an order.

The only way to know what you'll be up against during a project is to test the waters. Begin by ordering something simple such as a desk for a team member. The resulting cooperation of the purchasing department—or lack thereof—will let you know whether you need to add tasks to your project that read: "Work with purchasing to explain need, secure bid, and gain approvals to order desks."

Sadly, in our 25 years of experience with purchasing departments, many are run by bureaucrats who slow the estimating-buying cycle to a crawl as six signatures of approval are required to order a new light bulb for an overhead projector. Too many purchasing departments work with favored vendors who make the purchasing process easy for the purchasing department but costly for your project. The department may choose vendors based on who buys the best lunch in town rather than price, timely delivery, and a workable approach to handling problems. Remember, it's not their project they're purchasing for—it's yours.

The best way to solve problems with a recalcitrant purchasing organization is to learn its procedures, follow its processes, and make friends in the department. If the department causes more problems than it solves, try to work around it when you can and learn to work within the process when you must. The test of the project manager's mettle is to make it all work, easy and hard.

Don't Skimp on the Team's Needs

Your project demands the best equipment you can afford. Before you rent bargain Pentium I desktop computers for $9.95 each per week, consider your hard-working (and well-chosen) project team. With inferior equipment, less work will get done, and staff members might become alienated because they assume no one cares about their productivity. Is this saving money? We don't think so.

Give your people the right tools for the job. Provide them with modern equipment, a comfortable and safe place to work, and quality supplies as necessary. For special needs, ask project participants what they need and do your best to furnish that high-powered workstation or linear accelerator

Time Is Money

A database program on a personal computer can be used to maintain the equipment inventory for your project. The equipment categories can be assigned codes for easy sorting. Some of the more sophisticated project management programs allow you to include equipment inventories as part of the project data.

if necessary. Obviously, people might ask for more than they really need, so give the choices some thought. Still, giving people the right tools is essential to completing a project on time and within budget. You need to sort out wants from requirements and then make sure your project gets all of the latter.

From the Plan to the Stuff

For planning purposes, getting the bids for people, supplies, materials, and equipment may be enough to establish a budget for your project. After the plan is approved and you have the go-ahead to proceed with the project, however, you'll have to choose the specific vendors you want to use on the project.

At that point, you'll need to check references (if you haven't already), compare bids, verify delivery dates, and then choose the best vendor (probably in conjunction with the core project team). Then, by all means, get an attorney or the corporate legal counsel to draft the actual work agreements with any suppliers or outsider vendors. Require vendor signatures on the agreements before work commences or money is exchanged. All these procedures are part of the procurement process, and procurement is a major portion of your job as the project manager.

For now, with the resources completely documented, you're ready to move on and look at the staff for your project. Then you'll be ready to draft a schedule and a budget for your project. The saga of the plan continues …

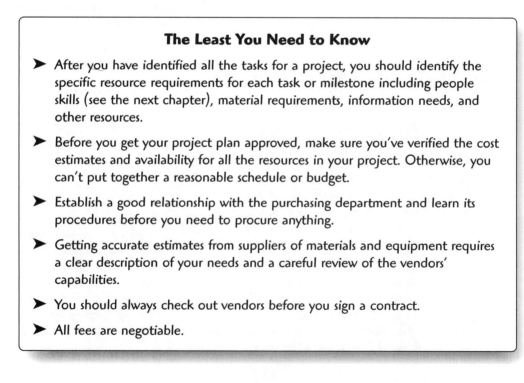

The Least You Need to Know

➤ After you have identified all the tasks for a project, you should identify the specific resource requirements for each task or milestone including people skills (see the next chapter), material requirements, information needs, and other resources.

➤ Before you get your project plan approved, make sure you've verified the cost estimates and availability for all the resources in your project. Otherwise, you can't put together a reasonable schedule or budget.

➤ Establish a good relationship with the purchasing department and learn its procedures before you need to procure anything.

➤ Getting accurate estimates from suppliers of materials and equipment requires a clear description of your needs and a careful review of the vendors' capabilities.

➤ You should always check out vendors before you sign a contract.

➤ All fees are negotiable.

Building a Winning Implementation Team

A single person doesn't win a basketball game—a team does. The same is true of projects. Thus, as in sports, project success depends largely on the team members. The ideal project implementation team completes the work on time and within budget with little micromanagement on your part. A weak or misaligned team requires substantial management on your part to limp past the finish line days, weeks, or for a major project, even years late. San Francisco's Bay Area Rapid Transit (BART) project and Los Angeles' unfortunate subway are prime examples of projects gone awry in part due to bumbling project teams as well as the ill winds of fate.

This chapter explains how to scope out required skills, assess current talent, and develop a list of people required to complete each task on your project. In addition, this chapter offers guidelines for filling the gap in people skills when adequately trained resources are not readily available.

You'll actually be doing most of your hiring after the plan is approved and you move into the project execution phase (that starts with Chapter 17, "Getting Started on the Right Track"), but you need to verify personnel costs and resource availability before the plan can be put into effect.

From Core Team to Complete Team

Remember, at this point, you are only planning the project staff and resources. You're probably already working with a subset of the project team, often called the core project team, which includes the managers, stakeholders, and key personnel. The core implementation team is the group you identified to help initiate and plan the project. (Do you remember doing this in Chapter 5, "Identifying Stakeholders and Defining Their Roles"?) But not all of the resources for your project can be identified during the project initiation phase. You just don't have enough details about the project to know who and what you need until you have listed the tasks.

Words from the Wise

"There is no substitute for talent. Industry and all the virtues are of no avail."

—Aldous Huxley

Only when you have the tasks and the work breakdown structure (WBS) in hand can you identify all the resources required to complete the project. The project sponsor and the core project team may help you do this; however, it isn't until after the project plan is approved and the execution phase begins that you'll actually start working as a fully functioning project organization. (You'll learn how to organize the project team during the execution phases in Chapter 19, "What an Organization!".)

The Complete Implementation Team: The Worker Bees on the Project

The project implementation team includes the people who will actually do the work to develop the project end results. On almost any project, this team is made up of people with differing personalities, skills, ability, knowledge, and temperament. Your mission is to evaluate the project prior to choosing implementation personnel and to build an implementation team that takes advantage of each team member's skills without taxing their weaknesses.

Unfortunately, this is not as easy as it sounds. Building the team and keeping it together are two of the most difficult tasks for any project manager. Whether through neglect or confusion, it's easy to let the team spirit slip away—and a spiritless project comes in with a bang and leaves with a whimper. Don't let this happen to you and your project! Read this chapter and learn how to find the right people for your project to reap implementation success.

People First, Please

Even on a small or routine project, choosing the right people to successfully complete the work can be difficult, risky, and potentially time-consuming. The effort is worth it, however, because without people, the project will never happen—regardless of the cost and the availability of equipment and supplies. Thus, it's important to seriously consider the needs of personnel, even on the smallest project. People are, after all, the common denominator in making projects successful.

In any project, three major questions must be answered regarding the people used to complete the work on a project:

➤ What skills are required to complete the tasks on the project?

➤ Where will the people come from to complete the tasks?

➤ How should the people working on the project be organized?

Words from the Wise

"A man's labor is not only his capital but his life. When it passes, it returns nevermore. To utilize it, to prevent its wasteful squandering, to enable the poor man to bank it up for use hereafter, this surely is one of the most urgent tasks before civilization."

—William Booth (1829–1912)

The first two questions are the most important at this stage because the answers affect the number and cost of people required for the project. In Chapter 19, you'll learn a lot more about the organization of the project; however, some general thinking about the organization is necessary because the organization of the project can impact the need for supervisory personnel and other support people. It's a good idea to have some general organizational strategies while you're planning for resource requirements.

Matching Skills to Tasks on the WBS

The questions about the people skills you need for your project can be answered with confidence using a structured approach that starts with the project's WBS. For each task in the project, answer questions similar to the following:

➤ Is there a specific technical skill or combination of skills required to complete this task?

➤ How much experience should the person or people have to complete this task?

➤ Does a person need to have specific experience doing this task or can general experience be applied? If so, what general experience is required?

➤ In addition to technical skills, are any specific interpersonal skills required to complete this task effectively such as good written or verbal communication skills, diplomacy or negotiating skills, or management ability?

➤ How many of these skilled people will be needed for each task and how would they be organized by job title and job function?

List the skills and experience next to each WBS level or use a worksheet like the example shown for the newsletter project. With a form like the example shown here (often called a Skills Requirement Document or Skills Matrix), you can list the actual skills you'll need to complete your project on a task-by-task or milestone basis.

With a form similar to this one, you can list the skills required for each component of the project. We usually use the WBS as a basis for this document.

Skills Requirement Worksheet			
Project: January Newsletter	**Produced by:** Gail Murphy		**Date:** 12/16/01
WBS:	**Tasks:**	**Skills Required:**	**Experience and/or Degrees:**
2.0 4.0	Design of newsletter, Concepts Produce mechanical artwork	-Graphic design -Use of InDesign program -Illustration skills with Illustrator -Experience in our industry	-BS/BA Graphic design preferred -3 years experience preferred -Strong portfolio of similar projects
3.0	Article ideas, First draft, Final drafts	-Experience writing for corporate publications -Strong research skills -Experience in the industry -Strong editing skills -Proofreading skill	-BS/BA in Journalism or similar training in writing and editing -Portfolio of writing samples
3.2	Photography	-Experience in brochure photography -Use of scanning technologies -Use of PhotoShop for retouching	-2-3 years experience in professional photography -Portfolio of professional photos

More Questions About Whom to Choose

In addition to completing the Skills Requirement Document, to decide on the team members you need, you'll also have to answer questions like these:

➤ If you could choose anyone you wanted for your team, who would these people be and why? (Hint: Your answers should involve both skills and personality for each person you choose.)

➤ Given the team that you actually get to work with, what levels of supervision will be required? You must be brutally honest here, especially if you're evaluating the skills of people who also happen to be friends or colleagues. Regardless of the talent involved, there's no sense in pretending that your team members will be self-sufficient. Some people simply need more direction than others—and these people will need some of your time.

➤ Where will the people come from? Do you have the talent in your own department (assuming these people have the time to be assigned to your project) or must you hire outsiders or raid another department for talent? (You'll learn about many of the sources for obtaining people later in this chapter.) The source of the people will affect their cost and availability—maybe even the quality of their output. These are all things that will affect the schedule and budget you have yet to create and get approved.

Answering these questions will allow you to compare the talent required for the project to the people actually available. Are the people you need ready, willing, and able? If so, are they affordable? Will your project demand that already overburdened co-workers take on yet another responsibility? How much will outside resources, such as consultants, experts, and grunt labor, really cost?

Wow! This whole thing is sure interrelated. That's why you need to put your thinking cap on while you're planning. The better you understand your choices, the better chance you'll have to make good ones.

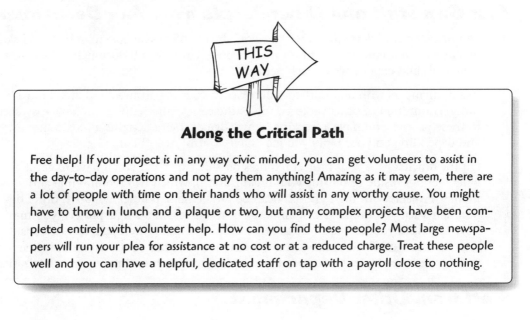

Along the Critical Path

Free help! If your project is in any way civic minded, you can get volunteers to assist in the day-to-day operations and not pay them anything! Amazing as it may seem, there are a lot of people with time on their hands who will assist in any worthy cause. You might have to throw in lunch and a plaque or two, but many complex projects have been completed entirely with volunteer help. How can you find these people? Most large newspapers will run your plea for assistance at no cost or at a reduced charge. Treat these people well and you can have a helpful, dedicated staff on tap with a payroll close to nothing.

Where Will the People Come From?

Manning (or womaning) a project can be difficult because co-workers are already buried in their own work and hiring outsiders is expensive. Typically, your options are limited by manpower availability and the cost of hiring staff. But an organization that wants or needs to complete a project must make staff available, even if it means pulling people off other projects or bringing in outside help. Staffing options include:

➤ Using your own staff and other people from your department.

➤ Using staff from other departments.

➤ Contracting with consultants, outside vendors, or temporary agencies.

➤ Hiring and training new staff.

As with business options, each of these choices has an upside and a downside. Just working with unfamiliar faces can mean a few surprises. You might have to adjust the project to accommodate each personality and productivity level while keeping a weather eye on the project dollars and timing.

Your Own Staff and Other People from Your Department

The first step is to determine the skills you already have available to you. A staff skills inventory is a useful document for this purpose. On it, you'll document all the relevant skills and experience of each person.

If staff members with appropriate skills exist in your department and aren't already (fully) committed to other projects, this is the easiest alternative. You have easy access to these people, you have a working knowledge of their strengths and weaknesses, and depending on your rank, you may have control over them.

On the downside, if your project requires outside expertise, you'll have to get it elsewhere (either inside or outside your organization), which will require time and money. Projects with high visibility can be problematic politically, too. If other departments see you utilizing vast amounts of resources on a single project, you may have to justify your resource use as other projects slip. Further, you may be considered hard to work with because you use only people from your own group when more experienced talent is known to exist elsewhere in the company or organization.

Staff from Other Departments

Working with others in your organization makes for good communication and camaraderie among those involved. In a large organization, this might get you the technical or specialized staff you need, or it might allow you to bring in a competent project manager whom you watch with awe as he keeps the gears oiled. For example, you might need a financial wizard from the finance department to track your budget and streamline purchase orders.

On the downside, the main difficulty you will encounter is convincing someone's manager to allow him or her to join your project. Down the line, you also might discover that your outside staff member is late on his tasks because his boss agreed to let him join your project without reducing his current workload.

Contracting with Consultants and Temporary Agencies

Outsiders are always available—for a price. With careful selection, you can fully man a project with exactly the right mix of people. Hire them when you need them and let them go when they're done. This is a flexible arrangement in that you have no responsibility (other than paying the bill) to keep them on or even to provide office space because all but some temp agency employees will already have space of their own.

On the downside, outsiders can be expensive. The key to using outside consultants and temporary labor is to schedule their work carefully. The cost for a highly trained welder priced at $100 per hour by his agency is mitigated if, with careful scheduling, he comes in, welds using his own equipment, and leaves in five hours. But should the work fall behind, he may spend three weeks cooling his heals while the clock is running. He'll become an expensive liability, regardless of his admirable skills.

Along the Critical Path

Be careful of using the word "headcount" when you talk about additions to your project team. Headcount is the term used to describe the fixed number of internal employees approved to work in an organization or on a project. Hiring a new person "increases headcount." On many projects, using an outside consultant or other temporary worker only increases costs. Sometimes it's easier to increase costs than to raise headcount because headcount enlargement shifts the permanent overhead costs. Expenses for office space, furniture, tools, benefits, and even additional management time must be accounted for. Thus, if you need a person for a project and you don't have a job for that person after the project is done, it's usually easier to propose an outside team member than to propose additional headcount.

Snakes and Consultants

You may have to get estimates for service providers or consultants for your project because you don't have all the people you need within your own company. Choosing the consultants and service providers for a project can be a tough call. Experts, consultants, and even temporary labor can hide behind a salesperson's persona.

Good consultants are masters at selling themselves; otherwise, they would be out of business. Remember, just because someone proclaims himself an expert doesn't necessarily mean he has a track record to back up the claim. Make sure the vendors you choose have been around the block a couple of times.

Words from the Wise

"Knowing what you *cannot* do is more important than knowing what you can do. In fact, that's good taste."

—Lucille Ball

Even hiring low-level labor must be handled carefully. The temporary agency's polished salesperson may overwhelm you with smooth promises and glossy brochures, but eventually, you'll just need grizzly old ditch diggers to dig those ditches. Remember, the gloss and polish you paid extra for probably won't make any difference if you just need good ditch diggers.

Because talk really is cheap, you must be careful of whomever you hire. Unfortunately, you won't really know what you have in hand until the person performs—or fails to perform. Check the person's references and get performance guarantees in the contract before you sign on the dotted line.

Hiring and Training New Staff

If the project is a long-term commitment or is ongoing with a finish date far enough out, you might find that adding to the headcount is the most expedient method for bringing in the manpower and expertise required. Of course, you noted the word "training" in the title of this section. You must be fully prepared with time and money to train your new bodies in everything from their task requirements to the culture of your organization. But adding new workers often brings a fresh point of view, takes some pressure off other staff members, and is an easy way to add a much needed skill set not available elsewhere in the company.

On the downside (yes, you've heard those words before), headcount increases are enormously difficult to justify in most organizations, especially those furloughing long-time employees while you are looking to add. You may be told "no way" or be asked to take on an employee otherwise slated for a one-way trip out the back door. The latter could force you to choose someone with no appropriate skills for the task at hand. Avoid this potential nightmare by being very specific in your description of the job. If no one with a pink slip exactly fills the bill, you'll have an opportunity to choose from fresh stock.

If you don't have experience in hiring personnel, you should do some reading about this subject. This first task is to become familiar with the hiring procedures in your company. (Almost every company has documented guidelines to help you and copious rules that you must follow.) And be sure to enlist the help of an experienced human resources manager before you make any decisions about who will be on your team and how much they'll be paid.

Individual Contributors Versus Team Players

Not everyone you hire will like being a part of the team or will be good at playing the role of a team player. Team players function like members of a football team: They work together and build on each other's strengths and accomplishments. They make for great project supervisors, and you'll see them having a beer with other team members after work on Fridays. But there are also the invaluable individual contributors in many projects.

Those with specialized creative skills, such as engineers, designers, writers, and (for lack of a better phrase) project visionaries, may appear to you and other team members as downright hostile. That's okay if their expertise is a must-have for the project. Although you should avoid mercurial personalities with no people skills whatsoever, a genius with a compelling vision might make the difference between a mediocre project and a great one. Just keep him or her out of supervisory roles wherever possible.

You must structure the project team to work like a clock. Appropriate matches of worker to co-worker, manager to worker, and manager to manager are crucial. Assuming you are the team leader, you must also be comfortable working with the parties with which you have direct interaction.

In a long project, this team assembly becomes more important. Someone who gets along with a colleague for a five-week project may grate on the person's nerves during a project spanning a longer period of time. Conflicts are inevitable, but you should do your best to assemble a team that's prone to cooperation rather than discord.

Assigning People and Skills to a Job Description

"Go team!" "That's the spirit!" "Onward and upward." "Let's review the plan and make things happen." Most projects begin on these positive cries. As project manager, you should strive to sustain this positive "We can do it" attitude among the team members.

As you would assume, staffing and motivating a small, closely held project team is less complicated than building a finely honed organization for a major project. A really large project involves more risk and goes through large sums of money quickly. To help make your choices better than the luck of the draw, a skills inventory is required—along with the help of your human resources department if you have one.

For most projects, the staff assignment involves two steps: developing the job descriptions and then matching people to the jobs. You can create job descriptions by referring to the skills requirement document you develop. (Your human resources manager or someone with this experience can probably help you with the job descriptions as well.) Some of the job descriptions and related job titles will be obvious; for others, you'll need to group like skills together into a job description that makes sense. These descriptions should be complete, to the point, and realistic. (If one of the job descriptions requires the skills of a supreme being, you need to revisit Chapter 7, "Scoping Out the Goals for a Project," and work on the project's goals and scope prior to this step.)

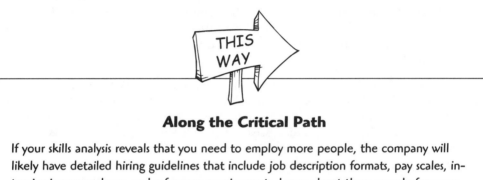

Along the Critical Path

If your skills analysis reveals that you need to employ more people, the company will likely have detailed hiring guidelines that include job description formats, pay scales, interviewing procedures, and reference requirements. Learn about these now before you have to start recruiting people. And don't forget to establish a good relationship with your human resources manager. This person can be a lifesaver when you need to get people on board in a short period of time.

Create a Skills Inventory

Before you decide whether to use existing staff, hire new people, or use outside vendors in your project to fill the job titles, you should develop a skills inventory of people in your own organization. Such an inventory in a large organization often is maintained by the personnel or human resources department, although this normally lists only the technological skill levels and formal educational backgrounds of people in the company.

Managerial and communications skills should be listed if your information is credible, but only if you have direct experience working with a person or reliable feedback from people who have such experience.

Developing a skills inventory can be an informal process or part of a formal personnel review system. The end result of completing a skills inventory will be a listing of the technological, management, administrative, and human skills for each staff member in your organization. If you have a complete, up-to-date skills inventory, you can easily match the skills required on your project to the people who have those skills.

A skills inventory is something that must be kept up-to-date to be useful. It is also something that can be used for many projects, so developing a regular procedure for keeping it up-to-date is worth the effort. Skills inventories also can help you identify people for your project whom you might overlook if you rely on memory or intuition to establish your project team. A simple form can be used to create a skills inventory and cost analysis of people available for your project. We have provided an example in the next section.

Matching People to the Jobs

Using the skills inventory and your other personnel options, you need to identify someone to fill the shoes of the person you described in each job description.

Work in pencil! You might find that you can handle the project using people already on staff, or you might find that expensive (or maybe even cheap) outside resources are required because the time available simply won't allow you to train existing staff to do the job. At this point, it's a "We can do it" or an "It's too expensive" decision. The exercise of developing a skills inventory points out the degree of resource drain and quantifies the use of people not available on staff or in other departments.

Skills Inventory				
Produced by: Gail Murphy				**Date:** 12/17/01
Name:	**Category:**	**Current Job:**	**Skills:**	**Experience and/or Degrees:**
Fred Sands	Software Engineer 1A	Sr. Systems Analyst	-C++ -Oracle Database Programming -Human Resources Applications -Systems design using CASE	-BSEE Computer Science, UCLA -15 years in MIS, various positions
Sarah Wilkins	Software Engineer 2B	Application Programmer	-Java Certification -Some C++ -Web programming/HTML	-AA, CS Whittier College -3 years Web programming
Sam Garcia	Software Engineer 2A	Supervisor, Web Group	-Java -C++ -Perl -Web programming/HTML -XML -ASP -Management training	-BA, Sociology SJSU -MSCSE,1999 -4 years programming, 2 years on Web

Use a skills inventory like the one shown here to quantify the talent you already have available for your project.

Choose Me!

After you identify the jobs and pencil in the names, you must move people around for the best fit. If there are too many question marks instead of names next to the job descriptions, you might need to take a longer look at the project and its scope. Maybe the project really isn't viable after all, or maybe you're trying to do something too ambitious with your existing talent pool.

If, after matching people to jobs, it still looks like you have the right talent available for the project, it's time to study the political ramifications of your choice of project team members. (You'll learn more about organizing people in the next chapter.) If the people are under your direct management, it's usually no problem. Simply have a meeting and explain the project and individual responsibilities to your staff. If you need to put a team together with resources from other departments, you need to answer these questions before you go any further:

High Water!

There are times when an individual has a unique technical skill and must be given a supervisory or leadership role, regardless of how difficult this person is to work with. You (and the rest of the team) will just have to learn to work with the difficult personality to get the job done. This is one of the standard challenges project managers must handle with aplomb.

➤ Who will you have to deal with in other parts of the organization to get approval for a prospective team member's participation? Is this politically workable?

➤ How much will outside services cost? Plop the Yellow Pages on your desk and make calls to get quotes. Would it be easier to use outside resources than to get approval to use the inside people?

➤ How much training is required for each team member? Is it worth it?

➤ Will team members come willingly or are you imposing your agenda on workers who would prefer to have no part in the project?

➤ Is another manager offering you a team member because he or she wants to get rid of the person? (Beware!)

What If You Need Someone Else?

Sometimes you don't have or can't find the person you really need to build your project team—even if you've done all the people-planning suggested in this chapter and the next. Other times, you'll find that the team simply isn't working out because the people aren't as skilled as you originally believed. In these situations, don't underestimate the role that training can play in solving your people needs. Also, it may take time for people who aren't used to working together to build a relationship toward maximum efficiency. In this situation, training can hasten the process (and possibly avoid conflicts).

When developing a team for a project, it may be possible to train or retrain existing people instead of hiring new ones. Existing employees are already familiar with the project policies and culture, a distinct advantage. Existing employees are also known quantities, so you avoid the risk of hiring someone who doesn't fit in. Besides, training people is often cheaper than hiring new employees when all the costs and time are added together. And if you encourage the development of existing staff, the entire organization will benefit from the resultant knowledge gain and the atmosphere of support and encouragement. If people are given an opportunity to advance, they are much more likely to be consistently productive and loyal. When considering training as an option to meeting organizational requirements, the following choices are available:

➤ Mentoring relationships with existing experts in the organization. Mentoring programs are excellent for developing management skills. Books on mentoring are available in the business sections of most well-stocked bookstores.

➤ These programs are best for general technical training or basic skills training. Because these programs can be costly, check their quality before you enroll people.

➤ Internal training programs developed by in-house specialists. These programs are good for company-specific technologies and procedures. Internal training programs may be time-consuming to produce, but if there is a continual need for new skills in specific topics, then a project to create these training programs is in order.

Call on Your Contacts and Supplier Networks, Too

If you will be working on many projects, build and maintain a network of contacts and suppliers as well as an inventory of your own organization's skills. If you will be producing different kinds of printed projects, for example, interview a variety of printing companies in your area and become familiar with their pricing structures and quality of work. If you will be hiring a large number of temporary manufacturing services, keep a list of temporary agencies that supply these types of services.

You can develop your own skills inventories and ratings for these contacts and vendors, just as you would describe your own internal staff. Then, when a project comes up, you are ready with a list of people and vendors that can fill your project's needs. This extra time up front on your first project may pay off in later projects.

A Survival Resource After the Project Starts

Skills inventories and contact lists also are useful after the project starts. What happens if a key staff member assigned to your project quits or gets sick? Pull out your skills inventory to identify potential replacements. If you don't have a network and skills inventory ready, you will waste valuable time trying to find someone who can take over for the lost resource, and the project may suffer delays or other problems as a result.

Words from the Wise

"In order that people may be happy in their work, these three things are needed: they must be fit for it; they must not do too much of it; and they must have a sense of success in it—not a doubtful sense, such as needs some testimony of others for its confirmation, but a sure sense, or rather knowledge, that so much work has been done well, and fruitfully done, whatever the world may say or think about it."

—W. H. Auden

The Best of the Best: Making Your Selections

After you've considered your options and the talent available to you, create a list of possible people and vendors for each task on your list. This list should include the alternatives available. For large, complex projects, the alternatives should be ranked in priority order, and the strengths and weaknesses of each choice should be well understood. A worksheet like the one shown previously can be useful in identifying people and their strengths and weaknesses for a project team. (Don't publish this list!)

If you depend on your skills inventories, you will discover that there are almost no perfect matches of people and project requirements on your list. Because no one can perfectly fit your needs, the selection process usually involves trade-offs. For planning purposes, identify people with the closest match of required skills and ask yourself whether the skills deficiencies are workable. Can you use two people who complement each other's skills on the project? Can you make up for the lack of skills in other ways? The more critical the tasks, the more important the match of skill requirements to people becomes.

Sometimes You Have to Compromise

Obviously, you want the best people possible for your project, but even after making compromises and trade-offs, it is not always appropriate to use your first choice for every task, especially if another person's skills are adequate.

For example, there might be two designers who could be hired to create a newsletter. The first designer is truly exceptional in creativity and works fast. The downside is that this person is also very expensive. Another designer has adequate creative skills and is much less expensive.

Because your newsletter project requires a relatively straightforward design, the use of the first person would not be a good choice because the project budget would be exceeded. Thus, the most technically qualified person in this case is not a good choice because of the budget constraints on the project. Every choice involves risks and trade-offs.

Why is this so complex? Because people are involved. Things are almost never easy when people are involved, and they're never totally predictable. You'll have to make choices based on your own interpretation of the most important needs and your best guess of what you expect to happen with these people. It's the best you can do. With experience, you'll get closer to getting the right people for your jobs (but you'll still get surprises on occasion—that's why things never get boring in project management).

The Problem of Imposed Team Members

You won't always have the advantage of being able to choose and organize every member of the team for your project. The team and its structure may be imposed on you by other managers within your own organization. Sometimes people are selected because they are available and not because of their skills or talent. Imposed team members are common in every business for a variety of practical and not-so-practical reasons.

Before you decide that someone on your team is incompetent, give the person a chance. People can often do more than you think. Remember the self-fulfilling prophecy: If you believe people have talent, they will exhibit talent. If you believe they will fail, that's likely to happen. Be realistic about your team's ability, but don't charge the project with unnecessary negative energy before it even starts.

In dealing with imposed team members, there are a number of alternatives you can consider to make things work:

➤ Do the best you can with the people you have, but make sure resulting problems are documented as they occur (otherwise known as covering your rear end).

➤ If your team doesn't have all the skills necessary, build training into the project.

➤ If your team is not qualified in all required skills and training takes too long, consider hiring a consultant or an outside vendor to fill in the gaps (if you have the budget to do this).

➤ Compromise and negotiate for the team members you really need. Don't just complain—be constructive. If some of the team members are not appropriate, suggest a different team to the people who made the original selections. Always discuss the alternatives with the appropriate decision-makers. These people may be able to offer explanations for the staff selections that you never considered, making the choices more reasonable than you thought. If you have documented your own case with task requirements and skill inventories as suggested earlier in this book, a rational manager will usually listen. You may not get everyone you want, but if you identify the priorities, you might be able to negotiate for the people you really need.

As an alternative, you may attempt to approach the manager with specific alternatives in mind and a convincing argument as to why your proposed changes would result in a more efficient project team that's better able to deliver the project on time and within budget.

➤ Suggest an alternative team-selection process for the next project. Though this may not help this time, it may be that the other managers never considered having you involved in the selection process. Explain the advantages of having the project manager involved and offer a structured approach to the staff-selection process. You may meet with political resistance if people are afraid of giving up their authority for making project decisions, but you can explain to your bosses that they can make the final selections—you just want to be involved.

Putting Your Best Foot Forward

Because there is no perfect project team, what do you do with the intangibly less-than-perfect set of players? First, try to avoid the imposed team whenever possible. Always negotiate for the right team members, even when your choices must be approved and/or paid for by the stakeholders and managers who approve your project budget. Suggest alternatives and justify why your recommendations make economic sense. "Well, sir, Jenkins is an accomplished microprocessor designer, but I'd rather see Biggles take the job. He can do it in half the time, according to the research I've done, and that saves the company money ...."

Second, whether the team is imposed or not, you should interview possible team members as if they were taking a new job. (They are unless the project is ongoing—and even then, if you are interviewing them, they're getting a new boss.) In the interview, try to get a reading on their enthusiasm for the project and ask for a resumé before the interview if you hadn't already done so. This gives you basic details on their backgrounds and interests so you can ask probing questions about specific skills.

Finally, when you find that you really are stuck with certain team members, training is almost always an alternative. Pair a novice team member with an experienced one. Working together to learn new skills has long been a standard educational practice. It usually works (unless the two team members kill each other in the process). If you match the two players appropriately, you might have the joy of watching an immature team member graduate to the status of important contributor once he or she sees how the "pros" do it.

There are many reasons why the project manager should be involved in personnel selection, such as becoming familiar with the strengths and weaknesses of the team as early as possible. This insight leads to better schedules and the development of monitoring and control systems that are geared toward the needs of the various staff abilities.

What About Next Time?

In a project-oriented workplace, it's rare that the same exact group of people works over and over again on the same kinds of projects. Projects usually bring unique groups of people together—groups of people from different departments or companies or points of view. Thus, it's important that you not be married to working with your favorite project members. You need to be willing to work with new people and be willing to take on different roles in other projects. It's all part of the project management style.

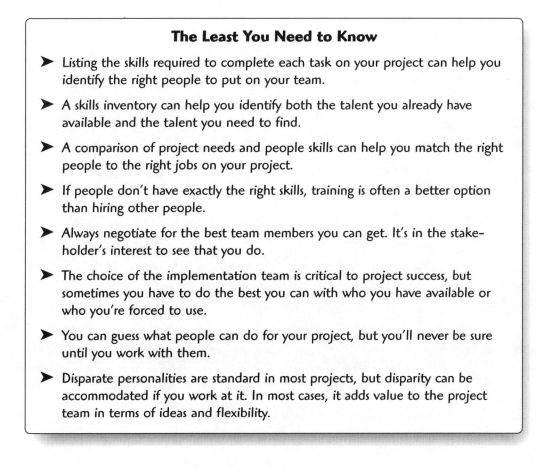

The Least You Need to Know

➤ Listing the skills required to complete each task on your project can help you identify the right people to put on your team.

➤ A skills inventory can help you identify both the talent you already have available and the talent you need to find.

➤ A comparison of project needs and people skills can help you match the right people to the right jobs on your project.

➤ If people don't have exactly the right skills, training is often a better option than hiring other people.

➤ Always negotiate for the best team members you can get. It's in the stakeholder's interest to see that you do.

➤ The choice of the implementation team is critical to project success, but sometimes you have to do the best you can with who you have available or who you're forced to use.

➤ You can guess what people can do for your project, but you'll never be sure until you work with them.

➤ Disparate personalities are standard in most projects, but disparity can be accommodated if you work at it. In most cases, it adds value to the project team in terms of ideas and flexibility.

Chapter 13

Project Start to Finish— Establishing the Time to Get Things Done

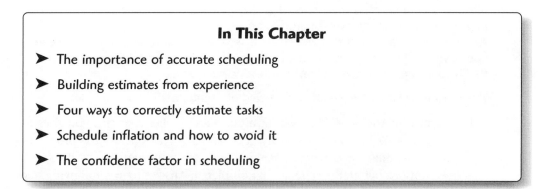

In This Chapter

➤ The importance of accurate scheduling

➤ Building estimates from experience

➤ Four ways to correctly estimate tasks

➤ Schedule inflation and how to avoid it

➤ The confidence factor in scheduling

As you would assume from reading earlier chapters in this book, the schedule is intertwined with the task list, the network diagram, and eventually, the budget. Change one and you invariably influence the others. We have separated the schedule and the budget in the next few chapters, but in reality, you should work on both at the same time. The schedule and the budget work together to float a project or sink it.

The Schedule or the Budget: Which Is First?

Some naive project managers are inclined to start with the budget first, but we don't recommend it. Because time is money, the schedule will affect the final budget in many ways. That's why we talk about scheduling first. The best project managers establish the schedule before finalizing the budget, even if everyone thinks they're nuts. It's best to try to determine how much time is really required to complete a project before you let your (lack of) money get in the way of your thinking.

The experienced project manager can look at a task, understand what's required, and provide a reasonably realistic guesstimate of the time requirement as if pulling the number from the air. You will get to that point someday with the help of this book and with a few projects under your belt. But until you get that experience, you can establish a reasonable schedule using this and the subsequent chapter's advice as a procedural guide. And maybe more importantly, in the following pages, you also will learn how to deal with external pressures (such as bosses and customers) that demand unrealistic dates. No matter what your manager says, you can't build Rome in a day.

Building a schedule also verifies the project's viability. If, when assembling the schedule, time is not on your side, you may need to work out an extension with management or an increase in resources. Working on the schedule might also reveal missing tasks. Remember: It's all interrelated, so expect to adjust the network, task list, and budget as you adapt the schedule.

The Schedule Synchronizes the Project

Accurate, realistic, and workable scheduling is what makes a project tick. The schedule shows who is doing what and when they are supposed to be doing it. Scheduling involves converting the well-organized and sequenced tasks in your work breakdown structure (WBS) and network diagram—as well as the list of resources and vendors you developed in Chapters 11 and 12—into an achievable timetable with start dates, finish dates, and assigned responsibilities for each task.

The steps in creating a schedule are carried out sequentially and include:

1. Establishing the scheduling assumptions. From earlier chapters, you already know why it's important to clarify goals and objectives before the project plan reaches its final stages. For the same reasons, it's important to specify scheduling assumptions before the schedule is completed. Answering the following questions should help in this process. We've also included a simple worksheet (see Chapter 14, section "How to Determine the Critical Path on Any Project") that will assist you in determining the assumptions germane to your project.

   ➤ Are there a fixed number of resources to be used on the project? Or, can you add them to meet the schedule priorities?

   ➤ Is there an absolute date by which the project must be completed so that it doesn't become worthless? (An example would be designing a new trade-show booth for the big July show. If the booth is a no-show, then the time and money used to design and build it as well as the cost of the tradeshow floor space gets flushed down the toilet.)

   ➤ Can the completion date be negotiated based on a realistic schedule of when all the deliverables (goals) can be met?

   ➤ Will people work standard workdays or will overtime be allowed or expected? Watch for holidays and expect to pay extra for resources working on Christmas Day!

➤ Are all resources currently trained and available? Or, will your project require hiring additional people and acquiring new equipment? If training or hiring is required, it should be scheduled.

Here are some examples of assumptions: A network expert from the organization will be available from August through October; new milling machinery will be operational as planned by January 25th; there will be no major changes in procedures for tracking inventory within the next six months. Assumptions protect the project from being severely impacted by planned change in other parts of the organization, change that the project manager may not be aware of. Assumptions can also reveal risks and limitations, and then enable you to build contingencies for them into your plan.

Large projects require that you document your assumptions in writing. That way, you are less likely to forget something. Simple projects don't always require documentation of the assumptions, but you should have a verbal agreement on them among your team and outside resources.

2. Estimating the number of resources, the task effort, and the task duration (the time to complete each task on the network diagram) based on the resources you have on hand or can afford. Remember that these estimates are all constrained by the resources. The more resources, the less time required (in most but not all cases). Here you need to estimate the duration of a task over a number of days.

Sometimes duration and effort are the same. If it takes seven hours of effort for a secretary to stuff envelopes during the course of one day, then the effort is one workday, and the duration of the task is one workday. Sometimes duration and effort are very different. It may take only four hours of meeting time to get the building inspector's approval of a building's wiring, but these meetings happen over a period of two weeks. Thus, the effort for getting the wiring approved is four hours, but the duration of the task is two weeks.

It is important to know both the effort (also called labor estimates) and the duration required to complete a task to create both an accurate schedule and a detailed budget for a project. Note that some books refer to estimating the duration of work packages instead of tasks—but the concept is the same. It's important to know that you can often, but not always, shorten the duration of a task by adding more people to complete the labor. Thus, estimating the number of people and resources that will perform a task is an important consideration in estimating duration.

Duration stands out in project management terms because the accumulated duration of tasks along the critical path in the project plan directly affects all the subsequent tasks in the project. (You'll learn about the critical path in Chapter 14.) It is the duration (the total time span, usually noted as a number of days) of

149

the tasks that, when added together, establish the time required to complete the project. Enter each task duration into the scheduling worksheet provided in the next chapter. For now, just know that you need to estimate the effort (work), the number of resources to perform the work, and the duration (time span) of each task in your network diagram or work breakdown structure (WBS).

To complete this estimating process, it's necessary to work with the network diagram and task list developed for the project. You will need to revise your plan when you combine two tasks into one or split one into two or more. You also might think of tasks that were forgotten earlier in the planning stage. Should you modify the plan, include your changes in all associated documents such as the work breakdown structure (WBS).

3. Determining calendar dates for each task and creating a master schedule. For a complex project network, you also will need to determine the critical path and float for each task on the project. (You'll learn how to do this in Chapter 14.)

4. Adjusting the individual resource assignments as necessary to optimize the schedule. This is called the resource-leveling phase. (You'll learn about this in Chapter 14.)

5. Charting the final schedule. (Note: In most cases, all of these scheduling steps arc casicr with a computcr program unlcss thc projcct is vcry small.)

Estimating Time: Your Best Guess at Effort and Duration

Of all the steps in scheduling, estimating the duration of tasks is the most important. Unfortunately, this is like trying to predict the future. You can only guess, but there are better ways to guess than others. Estimating the duration of tasks is the most important aspect of the project scheduling process. Without accurate task-duration estimates, the entire plan and project might crumble around you.

When estimating the duration of tasks, there are five options you can use to make the estimates (guesses) as good as possible:

➤ Ask the people who will actually do the work, but have them estimate the work they'll be doing—not the durations. You'll have to extrapolate the durations based on their workload, their other commitments, and their experience with similar tasks.

➤ Get an objective expert's opinion (for example, from someone who isn't working on the project).

➤ Find a similar task in a completed project plan to see how long it took to get done.

➤ If you have the time and the task lends itself to this type of verification, perform a test session of the task to see how long it really takes using your resources.

➤ Make your best educated guess. This is the last resort when you're under pressure, so make sure the guess is more educated than it is arbitrary. If possible, instead of guessing, try the preceding options instead.

Who You Gonna Call?

To get reliable estimates on the duration of tasks and the effort required, you will likely need to ask other people about the time it will take them to get things done (unless you're completing the entire project on your own, of course). The following sections describe some of the people you can ask to help determine the task duration and the effort estimates for your schedule.

Representative Team Members for Each Part of the Project

Seek out the most experienced team members who will be completing work on your project. Have them estimate the task durations in their areas of expertise; then, adjust the estimates based on your own experience. Remember, some team members will pad their estimates a little or a lot, and some will be overconfident about their abilities to accomplish miracles. You must adjust the duration in the final plan to account for these idiosyncrasies if you want to come up with the optimum schedule.

It's often useful to sit down with all the team members to estimate task durations. Even if nothing useful (to you) comes of the sessions, they still serve to build camaraderie and to give you a better understanding of the project from the team members' points of view. It's also an excellent technique for assembling a rough-cut schedule in a hurry.

Outside Vendors and Service Agencies

You must get estimates directly from any outside service providers and consultants who will work on your project. Never estimate their time for them. You can negotiate their estimates, but if you dictate a vendor's schedule without their input, you'll never get the schedule you demand. You should politely demand a written estimate that fixes the cost and commits them to a schedule (unless the project runs off the rails or changes in nature, of course). Shop price! Shop time! (You already read about this timely topic in Chapter 11.)

Experienced Managers or Experts

People in your organization who have handled similar projects can provide excellent advice and can study cost estimates for problems. They also might be able to provide exact estimates if a project they worked on had elements common to yours. Or, they

151

may be much more experienced project managers and be willing to help. If no such experts exist within your company, you could get advice from a consultant or a colleague in another company who can help verify your work and duration estimates.

Management and Other Project Stakeholders

If you want your managers and stakeholders to buy into your schedule, you need to give them an opportunity to help plan the schedule (or at least review it before you submit the project plan for approval). By bringing stakeholders into the process, they'll see that you will efficiently use your time and wisely spend their money. Their involvement will assist you in getting the final plan approved because they'll already have a grasp on the realities of the schedule.

Weighing the Risk

After getting information on the labor requirements and task durations from various sources, you'll need to use your judgment to determine the duration you'll actually assign to the schedule. Each of these durations will have a risk associated with it. It's often useful to come up with a best-case schedule and a worst-case schedule based on these risks.

Best Case and Worst Case—Compromising Between the Two

In estimating every task, assume that the actual time required will fall somewhere between flawless execution and major disaster. The best approach is to establish a compromise between the two. Some project management methodologies, such as PERT (refer to Chapter 11), provide the mechanics for estimating all three. These include:

➤ The optimistic estimate. Everything goes like clockwork and without problems.

➤ The realistic estimate. A few problems crop up, and subsequent delays compromise the optimistic estimate.

➤ The pessimistic estimate. Allowances are made for many elements to go wrong, substantially delaying or jeopardizing the task. Note: The pessimistic estimate assumes that the project is going ahead. A complete disaster could still occur that would sink the project's timetable and budget.

Ultimately, these three estimates will be used in combination with each other to come up with a "most likely" schedule based on your confidence in the estimates. Sometimes people just go with the pessimistic estimate; other times, the realistic estimate wins out. If you use the optimistic estimate, you're just looking for trouble.

Many managers of large, high-risk, big-money projects use fancy algorithms and weighting factors (like PERT techniques) to determine the most likely duration. The approach that's best for you will depend on the project, your experience with similar work, and your organization's culture.

152

Along the Critical Path

In the standard PERT methodology, the accepted algorithm for coming up with the "most likely" estimate of a task's duration is:

Expected duration = (OD × OWF) + (MD × MWF) + (PD × PWF) ÷ (OWF + MWF + PWF)

OD = Optimistic duration
OWF = Optimistic weighting factor
MD = Most likely duration
MWF = Most likely weighting factor
PD = Pessimistic duration
PWF = Pessimistic weighting factor

The weighting factors indicate the relative likelihood of each duration occurring in a real project like yours. Traditionally, the optimistic and pessimistic weighting factors are set to 1, and the most likely weighting factor is set to 4. Most project management systems will allow you to set the weighting factors for PERT estimates and can then assign the resource durations based on these calculations.

The Confidence Factor

Just how reliable are your estimates? You might be comfortable with the timetable for delivery of a photocopier and other office equipment to a new company headquarters but be unsure how long it will take to complete the electrical wiring for the building. You're even more uncertain about the task to design a new logo, which takes lots of creativity and political approvals.

For each task duration on your list, you'll have varying degrees of confidence. The tasks with the highest degree of confidence are usually those you've performed previously or those you'll do yourself. The tasks you aren't sure of usually are those with which you have no direct experience. A task with complete confidence might rate at 99 percent. (Remember, no estimate can be perfect in scheduling; there is always the risk of the unknown, unexpected event.)

The degree of confidence is also influenced by the complexity (or simplicity) of the task and how much the task is dependent on the completion of preceding (and possibly complex) tasks.

153

Remember that, if you do the estimates alone, your team members may not buy into them. You might create and sell a schedule to management that team members cannot support (or deliver). Make sure team members are involved in task estimating.

An "iffy" task that has risk associated with it may have a confidence rating of 10 percent or less. Use your confidence in tasks to determine the best- and worst-case scheduling scenarios described in the previous section.

If many of the estimates have low confidence associated with them, move your schedule dates toward the worst-case scenario. If most of the estimates are high confidence, a schedule closer to the best-case estimate is the best choice. Further, the more complex (and interdependent) the tasks, the more you might want to lean toward a worst-case scenario.

If you do add a little protection to your schedule for risky tasks, never make your padded time estimates too obvious. ("Trip to grocery store for product rollout party supplies: seven days.") This tactic won't win you any popularity contests with management. Such obvious protection schemes will have management sniffing through the entire project for inflationary tactics at all levels including in the budget. Ultimately, you'll lose not only credibility, but the real resources and time you need to get things done.

If your schedule starts looking like it will take too long to get things done, try adding more people or resources to the plan. This impacts the budget, however, and some tasks could suffer from the too-many-cooks-in-the-kitchen syndrome. More people doesn't always mean you'll get things done faster. More people always has unforeseen costs in management time and coordination, so make sure that adding people is really a good solution to adjusting the schedule.

Details, Details ...

After estimating the task durations and making a judgment on the estimates, you must decide on the level of detail you want to put in the initial schedule. Usually, the scheduling level should relate to the levels in your WBS or network diagram. For example, you can probably schedule a small project down to the day or even the hour on the first go-around, but you won't be able to schedule a megaproject any finer than by the month or week.

For planning purposes, the schedule may be produced at the weekly or monthly level—or maybe even at the yearly level—for a megaproject. As work on the project proceeds, you can schedule the work at finer levels. Many large projects are scheduled phase by phase instead of scheduling the entire project from the beginning. Obviously, scheduling a megaproject to the hour from the beginning of the project would produce silly schedules and mounds of useless paper. On the other hand, inadequate schedule detail at the beginning of a small project might leave team members thinking they have more time to get things done than they really have. It takes practice—you'll get the hang of it.

Applying Calendars to a Resource

Every resource will have dates and times when it will be available for use on your project. These dates and times are called the "calendar" for that resource. For people resources, you need to create calendars that include their work hours, workdays, and vacation days. You also need to specify how many overtime hours will be allowed if any. Sometimes you may want to assign a different person to a task based on his or her calendar availability.

For equipment resources, you need to indicate any special restrictions on the availability of a resource. For example, if you only have one electron microscope available and it is being used by three different research projects, you'll need to specify when this resource will be available for your project (or vice versa, you'll need to tell the other projects when you'll need it—if your project has priority, that is.) As you develop the schedule for tasks, you'll need to take the calendar into consideration as you write out the dates.

On a complex project, dealing with the calendars of all the resources can get very complex. Thank heavens for computerized project management programs that enable you to define calendars for all the resources including working days, hours, and non-working periods such as holidays and vacations. The computer can then do the complex scheduling for you.

Putting It Down on Paper

Once the assumptions for the schedule (that is, the number of people and the task sequences) and the *durations* are nailed down, you can begin assembling a reasonable schedule. For a simple project with few dependencies, you can simply list durations on the project task list. For more complex projects, use the WBS and the network diagram to schedule your project. You'll need to note the labor for the tasks as well as the durations as you work on the schedule. You may find that you need to adjust durations but not in a way that will affect the actual labor needed to complete a task.

Scheduling with a network diagram is conceptually simple. Plug in the estimated task durations for each task on the network and then add the durations to get the total time required to complete the

> **Project Lingo**
>
> **Duration** (as opposed to task duration) is the time, usually in days, that it takes to complete the *entire* project, from starting the first task to finishing the last one. Task duration is the total time span for all the labor and effort to complete a task. Task duration and task labor are usually different—labor is usually estimated in hours, where task duration is typically measured in days.

155

project. Just lay the days out on a calendar and—voila!—you have a schedule. To show you how it's done, we've provided the following example of a network diagram with task durations and dates added.

Of course, nothing is ever as simple as it sounds. You need to take into account workdays, holidays, vacations, parallel tasks, and other special circumstances. That's why scheduling a large project is easier with a software program designed for the job. (See Chapter 30, "Software for All Projects Great and Small," for more information about project management computer programs.) You'll also need to level the resource utilization on a large project if you're overworking some of the resources (or underworking others). You'll learn more about making these schedule adjustments in the next chapter.

Schedule Charting Pros and Cons

There are several schedule-charting formats of which you should be aware. The trick is choosing the format that best suits your project. Here are some of your options for displaying the schedule:

➤ **Listings.** Schedules that follow the formats in the sample forms are useful for most projects and are necessary for keeping track of progress as the project proceeds. For manageability and control, break these schedule listings into subprojects if the project is extremely large and combine them with a milestone schedule.

➤ **Calendar charts.** Annotated calendars can be extremely useful for keeping track of schedules for many small projects. Multiple projects or different team member tasks can be entered in various colors on the calendar. Calendars are a good communication tool when displayed in a central location where many team members can see the dates. Large display calendars with reusable, washable surfaces are available at many business supply stores for this purpose.

➤ **Gantt charts.** Gantt charts are best used as a visual overview of project timelines; however, they should not substitute for a network diagram or master schedule listing. Gantt charts can be very useful in initial schedule planning, for simple projects, or for individual timelines on a complex project involving many people. These charts also are good for comparing project progress to the original schedule.

➤ **Milestone schedules.** In Chapter 11, you learned that milestones can be assigned to summarize major paths on a network. Milestones also can be used to chart an overall project schedule. A milestone schedule doesn't have enough information to help you manage a project, but it can be useful for communicating an overall schedule on a large project to upper management or other people who need an overview of the project without task details.

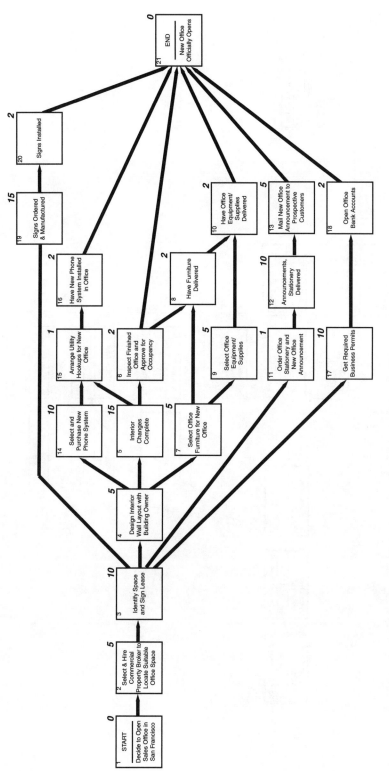

San Francisco Sales Office Project showing task duration estimates in "workdays."

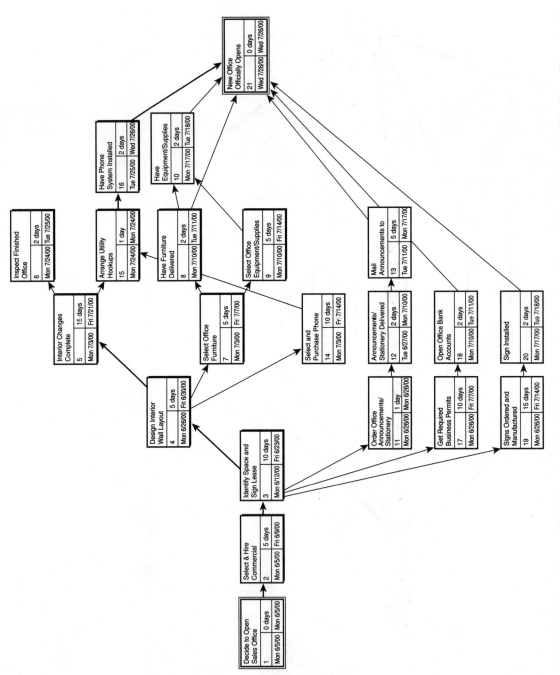

Here is the precedence diagram for the Sales Office Project completed in Microsoft Project 98, showing the earliest start and finish dates.

For complex projects, most project managers use more than one schedule format because it allows them to view and communicate the project in different ways. Even on small projects you might want to use two or more charting options to represent a project schedule.

More on Gantt Charts

Simple Gantt charts—sometimes referred to as project timelines—are the most commonly used scheduling charts in business because they're easy to produce and easy to understand. Gantt charts, named after Henry Gantt who developed them in the early 1900s, ordinarily have a list of dates at the top and a list of tasks down the left side. A line on the Gantt chart shows the date each task begins and ends based on its precedence and duration. The level of scheduling detail you display in your Gantt charts will be determined by the time periods you use on the top: daily, weekly, hourly, monthly, or whatever is appropriate for your project. If a project takes a year or more to complete, you may want to use a monthly or weekly Gantt chart. If your project takes 30 days or less, a daily Gantt chart will provide more useful information. Gantt charts are most effective if you can present the whole chart on one document such as on 8½" by 14" or 11" by 17" paper.

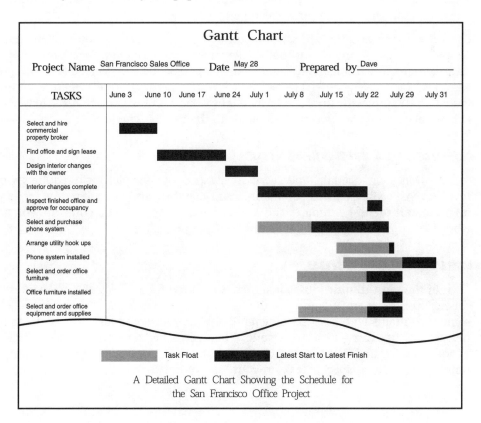

A Detailed Gantt Chart Showing the Schedule for the San Francisco Office Project

Gantt charts are useful for envisioning the entire project through time.

Be aware that simple Gantt charts don't show the interrelationships among tasks. You need a network diagram for this or a project management program that produces complex Gantt charts that indicate summary tasks and task relationships. Also, a Gantt chart alone may not provide enough detail to communicate schedules to individual team members in a complex project. For this, you'll want a project task list that includes task assignments and schedule dates. The following Gantt chart shows general float time among tasks and even task precedence.

Scheduling on the Network Diagram

In addition to creating a Gantt chart, some people like to annotate the schedule dates directly on the network diagram. Although this is a good reference tool for reviewing the entire project, it is awkward to use as a working schedule when assigning responsibilities to individual team members. Therefore, you should again use a schedule listing in addition to the network diagram to display and communicate the schedule details.

Another schedule format that is seen more frequently, thanks to computer programs, is the time-scaled network. This combines the timeline approach of the traditional Gantt chart with the precedence relationships of the network diagram. We've provided a sample of a simple time-scaled network here.

Of course, many variations of schedule formats can be used to accommodate individual preferences. It is important that the key information, including task descriptions, start dates, expected finish dates, and assigned people, be easy to read and interpret. As project manager, you need to be able to create a personal timetable for each individual on the project team. Each individual working on the project also needs to be able to relate his or her personal timetable to the master schedule.

Revisions and the Schedule

Assume that your schedule (and every other aspect of your plan) will require several revisions. As feedback arrives from both team members and outside resources, you might redraft the task estimates and dates several times until you come up with a workable, approvable timeline (schedule) for the project.

Learning Takes Time

Even in the most routine jobs, some time is required for learning the procedures in the new company and adapting to the new work environment. This also is true of some consultants who must become familiar with your company's way of doing business before they can get down to work. When you schedule a project, allow for these various training and development requirements. You might even want to identify training activities as specific tasks in your WBS or network.

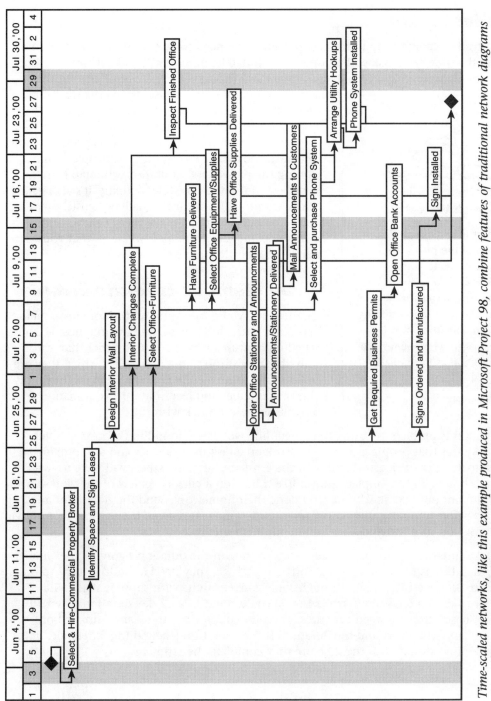

Time-scaled networks, like this example produced in Microsoft Project 98, combine features of traditional network diagrams and Gantt charts to help you visualize both the precedence and the timeline for a project.

The Heat Is On

Instead of caving in to unrealistic pressure, you need to be comfortable with estimating the time each task will require. Unfortunately, no one will make it easy for you. Team members may pull a date or time block (hours required) out of a hat at the same time senior management wants the work completed the day before yesterday. Every project is a rush. With that in mind, how do you, as project manager, avoid succumbing to unrealistic expectations and unrealistic goals? Assuming that the people commissioning the project are semirational human beings, your best tool is the schedule. Actually, it's all a game. Management will constantly challenge costs, time, and resources. You must make them believe—through a well-documented schedule and plan—that your estimates are realistic and not unduly padded.

High Water!

If you must share your preliminary drafts of the plan with management, stamp "DRAFT" or "INCOMPLETE" in bright red letters on each page. That way, you won't be held to the shifting sands of an unfinished plan by senior managers who assume that an early version of the project plan is final.

Team Member Estimate Errors

Chances are, you're counting on the core team members and experts to provide the best and most accurate scheduling estimates possible. But rather than carefully thinking through the process for which they are responsible, some members of the team might simply choose a number and feed that into your plan. If it's unrealistic, you're stuck with it.

Avoid this problem by using the scheduling worksheet found in the next chapter. It requires that people estimate the work on a task-by-task basis and also provide an estimate of the risk associated with the estimate. Team members will have to turn their brains on to complete a form like this. Even a cursory review of the worksheet will point out people who haven't done their homework. Send them back for another pass before adopting their effort and duration estimates. Even then, you'll likely have to use you own judgment for coming up with the final figures.

Make sure the estimators consider elapsed time in the duration figures. For example, if their task is to evaluate a new software package, they need to build in time to order it, install it, test it, and go through some conversations with support staff. What looks like four days of effort (32 hours) could result in a 12-day duration when all the "dead" time between activities is accounted for. Have the team estimate both numbers—the effort and the duration. If they don't understand the difference, have a training session with them before they complete the estimates.

Along the Critical Path

A new technique we started using to cope with uncertainty in a schedule involves simply putting the "padding" for the project into a final task called "Schedule Contingency" with a duration that's based on a percentage of the total duration of the project. For most projects, a schedule contingency of 2 to 7 percent of the total duration should be adequate, with the larger percentages going to the longer projects. If you use this approach, you should keep the padding out of the individual task estimates—use the estimates you think will be most likely. This keeps the team focused on the real time they have to complete a task, not an inflated estimate. Then the "padding" at the end becomes a sort of savings account for contingencies that you can use as needed when real schedule changes are required. Using this "padding" account will still add cost to the project in most cases, but it won't mess up expectations about the delivery date you've promised to the stakeholders.

The Just-In-Time Strategy for Scheduling Resources

The just-in-time strategy for getting materials and supplies is credited to the Japanese, but the technique is now common practice worldwide. Just-in-time delivery depends on accurate scheduling and project coordination. With an accurate schedule in place, you can order just what you need and get it delivered exactly when you need it. This means that supplies, equipment, and even people arrive only when the project is ready for them.

By having goods delivered (or people hired) exactly when they're needed, you save money for storage, reduce up-front costs for ordering materials, and are assured that you don't have extra stuff on hand that is costing you extra money.

The key to making this approach work is, you guessed it, communication. Having a contract with suppliers that lets you adjust dates is the essence of just-in-time delivery. That way, you don't have to warehouse 1,000,000,000 chicken feathers when the tacky straw hats you planned to adorn haven't arrive from the supplier. You need to make just-in-time delivery a mandatory contract clause: no delivery until a written request is made and guaranteed delivery within a set number of days or hours after you put the order in.

The window for just-in-time delivery must be agreed upon in advance; otherwise, the whole schedule falls apart. A temp agency hiring 20 people for your project will want enough time to hire the needed people, but you should notify them if the project goes late. The maker of 6,000 bicycle seats won't want to wait three extra months because the frames are coming in late from France. They'll want them out of the way and will expect payment as well. You, as project manager, must ensure that people and supplies arrive appropriately according to the original or revised schedule.

Dictate Doesn't Mean Doable

At some time, you'll be asked (actually told) to shorten the schedule—even though you know it's impossible to get the work done any faster. Before you cave in to dictate, sit down with everyone pressuring you and go over the schedule day by day if necessary. Be friendly and cooperative and explain each task and the assumptions about your time allotments represented in the schedule. Bring in expert project managers or technical team members to explain the more opaque tasks.

Your goal for this process is to communicate why the project requires a certain amount of time. In a truly impossible situation, you might need someone senior to you (usually the project sponsor) to go to bat when others attempt to force an unworkable adjustment to the plan on your shoulders.

Now you're ready to learn about how to fine-tune a schedule to meet your stakeholder's objectives. You've only just begun to understand the scheduling complexities.

The Least You Need to Know

➤ Scheduling involves estimating the task durations for the project and plotting the dates on a calendar. You need to account for holidays, special events, and unknown circumstances.

➤ No schedule is ever perfect, but the goal is to make the best estimate possible. You do this by using your own judgment and the experience of others to help you make your estimates.

➤ A Gantt chart is an excellent tool for studying overall schedules, but it doesn't show the interdependencies among tasks shown on the network diagram. Thus, using both in a project plan is a good idea.

➤ Time estimates should be based on best-case/worst-case scenarios. Your degree of confidence in the accuracy of these estimates should dictate the ultimate schedule, which should be a compromise somewhere between the two extremes.

Chapter 14

The Steps to the Critical Path and a Balanced Schedule

In This Chapter

➤ Understanding the critical path

➤ All about float and slack in a project

➤ Important adjustments necessary in complex project schedules

➤ Leveling the resource utilization

➤ Ways to adapt a project to meet a forced schedule

In Chapter 13, you learned the good news: Scheduling is a simple matter of estimating durations for tasks and then plotting the dates on a calendar. Now here's the bad news: Even using computer-based project management software, scheduling a complex project is, well, complex. Because an accurate schedule is essential to managing projects of all sizes, the process is not one in which you should attempt to cut corners. You need to consider some of the complexities of scheduling before you finalize your project plan. That's what this chapter is all about—the complexities of project scheduling.

For complex projects, computers have a significant advantage over manual scheduling. Yes, you learn how to calculate the critical path and *float* in a complex project schedule in this chapter, but you should get a computer program to help on projects of more than 25 or 30 tasks (see Chapter 30). Then you can easily change and revise the schedule as you work through the issues and changes in a project.

Here is an example of the step-by-step scheduling process.

The Scheduling Process Step by Step

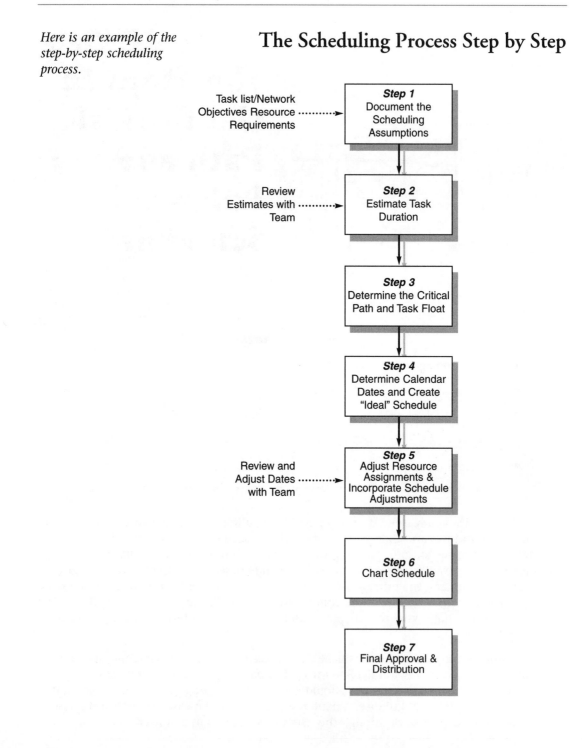

Task list/Network Objectives Resource Requirements ·········▶ **Step 1** Document the Scheduling Assumptions

Review Estimates with Team ·········▶ **Step 2** Estimate Task Duration

Step 3 Determine the Critical Path and Task Float

Step 4 Determine Calendar Dates and Create "Ideal" Schedule

Review and Adjust Dates with Team ·········▶ **Step 5** Adjust Resource Assignments & Incorporate Schedule Adjustments

Step 6 Chart Schedule

Step 7 Final Approval & Distribution

How to Determine the Critical Path on Any Project

When you have determined task durations and are confident in your estimates, it's time to assemble a schedule using real dates. On a large/complex project, however, one more step remains in the way of assembling a working schedule. On projects with multiple parallel tasks and subprojects, a critical path must be determined to identify the time required to complete the project. (Most small projects with few tasks can skip this step.)

Scheduling Assumptions Worksheet

Project Name: San Francisco Office Project   Date: May 22

1. Are all the resources currently available for this project?
If no, list the resources required that are not available:
People: Leasing Agent Needs to Be Found
Equipment: _____

☐ YES   ☒ NO

2. Is there a due date when the project absolutely must be complete?
If yes, enter date: _____
Reason: _____

☐ YES   ☒ NO

3. Will overtime be allowed?
If yes, how much? _____

☐ YES   ☒ NO

4. Are there any holidays or other breaks during this project?
If yes, list dates: July 4

☒ YES   ☐ NO

5. Have additional resources and people been approved for this project?

☒ YES   ☐ NO

6. Have the work schedules and availabilities of all resources been documented?

☒ YES   ☐ NO

Notes: Follow the Phildelphia Office Plan as Reference

Use a worksheet like this one to help detail the assumptions about the schedule for your project. Don't forget to refer to the statement of work (SOW) for additional scheduling criteria and constraints.

The critical path is a sequence of tasks that forms the longest duration of the project. If a task is delayed on the critical path, the project is delayed. For example, when opening a new sales office, the interior build-out can't begin until you've negotiated and signed the lease.

Tasks not lying on the critical path are more flexible. You can install the telephones at any time from the completion of the build-out to the office's first day in operation. That's assuming you have enough time to accommodate the install between build-out completion and an opening day party for customers.

Adding together the duration of tasks on the critical path determines the total time the project will take. Because each task on the critical path must follow its predecessor in order, any task that is late on the critical path will cause the project to be late—and all tasks following a late task on the critical path will be late. Yes, the delay will hold up the entire project. That's why the critical path is, well, critical.

Not Just Floating Around

Tasks not on the critical path also must be completed. You can't build a house and ask someone to move in before the water and sewer are connected, but such tasks can occur later in the project's timeframe without substantially delaying other tasks downstream. This gives them a flexible start and finish date, which in project management lingo is called *float*.

The Different Views of Critical in Project Management

The term critical chain is used to describe a concept that is quite different from the schedule-based definition of tasks on the critical path. The concept of the critical chain is one of the ideas preferred by Dr. Eliyahu M. Goldratt's Theory of Constraints (TOC). The TOC states that any system has at least one constraint. Otherwise, it would be generating an infinite amount of output. Bearing this in mind, the TOC in project management is explained through use of the chain analogy: "A chain is only as strong as its weakest link."

If you look at your project as a chain in which each department, task, or resource is a link in the chain, what constrains your project from achieving its goals? Only through identifying and focusing on the weakest link, the critical link in the chain, can substantial improvements be made. In other words, if the weakest link dictates the pace of an organization's ability to achieve it's goal, it makes sense that attending to this critical link will allow the organization to achieve a substantial rate of throughput faster.

To illustrate how the TOC can be applied without getting into too much theoretical detail, the critical chain concept illustrates that project control and scheduling can be improved through identifying the critical links in the chain of a project and then focusing creatively on reducing these problems. The objective is to develop solutions of compromise based on fresh thinking that can help you continuously improve project performance through time. The performance is improved continuously because, as you fix one weakest link in the chain, a new weakest link emerges through focusing on the project again. Since project performance is never perfect, there will always be a weakest link to work on.

If you're interested in the application of the critical chain concept and the Theory of Constraints on project management, get a copy of Dr. Goldratt's books on the subject, including *The Goal, It's Not Luck,* and *Critical Chain,* or visit the Avraham Y. Goldratt Institute on the Web at www.goldratt.com. An adequate presentation of TOC is beyond the scope of the book, but for people interested in continuous quality improvement, there's a lot of substance in Goldratt's work.

Establishing the Critical Path

The critical path is easy to determine in a project that has been documented with a good network diagram. Simply add each parallel path's tasks together, and the path requiring the most time to complete is the critical path. In the example shown for building a sales office, the longest path requires 41 days. That makes it the critical path. Critical tasks—those on this path—not completed on time will delay the project unless you can make up the time further down the critical path or an on-the-path task finishes ahead of schedule.

Critical Path: Myth or Reality?

The concept behind critical path is simple: If you delay a task on the critical path, the project is delayed. This seems to make perfect sense to most people new to project management. The path on the project has to go from beginning to end.

Unfortunately, as in all things involving people and plans, there are complexities. First, some tasks on the critical path may be less important than others. Some of the tasks may be there for mathematical reasons (which you'll learn about in a bit), not managerial priorities. For this reason, many managers also create a priority task list,

High Water!

When its tasks go late, the critical path becomes the roadblock to project completion. That's why you should put extra effort into estimating these tasks. If you lack confidence in the task schedule or resource availability, delay the project until everything fits into place. If the project is already underway, put your best people on the tasks and focus your energies on catching up. Use this worksheet to calculate the critical path and float for the tasks on your project. If you have more tasks than will fit on a page, look into getting a computer program (see Chapter 30). Use this worksheet to help you schedule your projects.

which is a list of the most important tasks on the project. This managerial list of priority tasks, along with the mathematical list of tasks on the critical path, can be used to focus attention on the important work of the project.

Always remember that regardless of the mathematics of it—or the managerial importance—when you change task dependencies, duration estimates, and other network details, you need to reevaluate the critical path and reassess the schedule. There's no way around it. You can't change the sequences without impacting the schedule.

Use the Critical Path Worksheet to Calculate Path and Float

If you're new to project management, the calculation of the critical path initially sounds complicated. It's really simple, however, assuming you've done your homework by correctly listing, estimating duration, and assigning precedence to each task. If you're using a computer-based program, it will probably identify the critical path automatically. Otherwise, the steps are as follows (refer to the network diagram in Chapter 13 as you work through this example):

1. List the tasks and estimated task durations on the worksheet.

2. Calculate the earliest starting number for each task. This is called the forward pass through the project schedule. The earliest start is the number of duration days at the point at which all precedent activities before it in the path have been satisfied. The first task begins on day zero—a D-day of sorts for the start of any project. Assume that each subsequent task begins after the finish of the preceding activity. It works like this:

    Earliest start = least number of days from the beginning of a project before it can begin

   In the example, the earliest start for task #14 "Select and purchase phone system" becomes 0 + 5 + 10 + 5 = 20 because 20 is the total of all durations that immediately precede the beginning of that task on the network diagram.

3. Calculate the earliest finish number for each task. To do this, add the task duration (as a number of days) to the earliest start number.

    Earliest finish = earliest start number + task duration number

The earliest number to start "Select and purchase phone system" is calculated as 20 + 10 = 30. Thus, this task can't be done before day 30 in the project.

Critical Path Worksheet

Project Name: Philadelphia Sales Office Project   Date: January 25

Task	Duration	Earliest Start	Earliest Finish	Latest Start	Latest Finish	Total Float
Select and hire commercial property broker	5	0	5	0	5	0
Find office and sign lease	10	5	15	5	5	0
Design interior changes with the owner	5	15	20	15	20	0
Interior changes complete	15	20	35	20	35	0
Inspect finished office and approve for occupancy	2	35	37	35	37	0
Select and purchase phone system	10	20	30	28	38	8
Arrange utility hook ups	1	30	31	38	39	8
Phone system installed	2	31	33	39	41	8
Select and order office furniture	5	20	25	29	34	9
Office furniture installed	2	37	39	37	39	0
Select and order office equipment and supplies	5	25	30	34	39	9
Office equipment delivered and set up	2	39	41	39	41	0
Order and manufacture signs for new office	15	15	30	24	39	9
Signs installed	2	30	32	39	41	9
Order stationery and announcements	1	15	16	25	26	10
Stationery and announcements delivered	10	16	26	26	36	10
Announcements mailed	5	26	31	36	41	10
Get business permits	10	15	25	29	39	14
Open bank accounts	2	25	27	39	41	14

ALL TASKS WITH ZERO FLOAT ARE ON THE CRITICAL PATH

Refer to the network diagram in Chapter 13 as you review this worksheet. Use the worksheet to calculate the critical path and float for the tasks on your project. If you have more tasks than will fit on a page, look into getting a computer program (see Chapter 30).

4. Calculate the latest finish number for each task. This is often called the backward pass through the project schedule. The latest finish is the last day a task can be performed without changing the end date of the project. The latest finish is calculated by first noting the largest number in the earliest finish column. This number is the total number of days in the project. Assign this number to the last task in the project and subtract the duration from the number of duration days in the path. To calculate latest finish, you work backward from the last day of the project—it's like calculating the earliest start from day zero but in reverse. So the latest finish for the "Select and purchase phone system" task becomes 41 – 2 – 1 = 38 because this is the total number of durations between the task subtracted from the number of the last day in the project.

171

5. Calculate the latest start number for each task. The latest start is the last day in a project that a task can begin and still be completed without affecting the end date of the project. In other words, if a task hasn't begun by this date, the project will be late. Determining the latest start date is simply a matter of making the following calculation:

> Latest finish – duration = latest start number

For the "Select and purchase phone system" task, this becomes 38 - 10 = 28. Thus, if this task begins after workday 28 in the project, the project will be late if all the other task durations are correct.

6. Determine the total float for each task. Total float is determined by the following calculation:

> Total float = latest finish – earliest start – duration

The tasks with zero float are on the critical path. Check this with the network diagram illustrating the critical path shown earlier. Tasks with float have some flexibility. In the "Select and purchase phone system" task, the total float calculation is 38 – 20 – 10 = 8. Thus, there are eight days of scheduling flexibility associated with this task.

Even if you use a computer to help you with your network diagrams and critical path calculations, it's important that you master the basic scheduling principles presented here. If you don't understand the basic principles of float, start dates, finish dates, and critical path, you won't understand how the computer derives the schedules it produces. And if you don't understand these concepts, you won't be able to appropriately modify the schedules to suit your project's priorities.

Calculate the Dates on the Calendar

With the tasks, durations, and start and finish calculations complete, it's time to assemble the actual schedule with dates on a calendar. Use the form included and make copies to accommodate all of your project's tasks.

The starting date of the project is determined by you, management, and your team. Using a calendar with room for notes, number each day in sequence. Days you don't plan to work, such as weekends and holidays, shouldn't be numbered. Remember, too, that tasks on the critical path should have the same earliest start date and latest start date as well as the same earliest finish date and latest finish date.

Once all the dates are entered on the schedule worksheet, you will have assembled the ideal schedule. The ideal schedule is just that: the best-case schedule if all resources are available and ready when planned.

Ideal Schedule Worksheet

Project Name: Philidelphia Sales Office Project
Scheduled Start: June 3   Calculated Finish: July 31

ID	Task	Precedences	Responsible People	Duration	Earliest Start	Earliest Finish	Latest Start	Latest Finish
1	Decide to open office in San Francisco		John	0	June 3			
2	Select and hire commercial property broker	1	John, Dave	5	June 3	June 10	June 3	June 10
3	Find office and sign lease	2	Agent, Dave	10	June 10	June 24	June 10	June 24
4	Design interior changes with the owner	3	John, Dave, Agent	5	June 24	July 1	June 24	July 1
5	Interior changes complete	4	Owner	15	July 1	July 23	July 1	July 23
6	Inspect finished office and approve for occupancy	5	John, Dave	2	July 23	July 25	July 23	July 25
14	Select and purchase phone system	4	John	10	July1	July16	July12	July26
15	Arrange utility hook up	5,14	Jennifer	1	July 16	July 17	July 26	July 27
16	Phone system installed	15	Phone Co.	2	July 17	July 19	July 29	July 31
7	Select and order office furniture	4	Jennifer	5	July 1	July 9	July 15	July 22
8	Office furniture delivered	7	Jennifer	2	July 25	July 29	July 25	July 29
9	Select and order office equipment and supplies	7	Jennifer	5	July 9	July 16	July 22	July 29
10	Office equipment delivered and set up	8,9	Jennifer	2	July 29	July 31	July 29	July 31
19	Order and manufacture signs for new office	3	Dave	15	June 24	June 16	July9	July29
20	Signs installed	19	Dave	2	July 18	July 18	July 10	July 31
11	Order stationery and announcements	3	Jennifer	1	June 24	June 25	July 24	July 10
12	Stationery and announcements delivered	11	Jennifer, Printer	10	June 25	July 10	July 10	July 24
13	Announcements mailed	12	Jennifer	5	July 10	July 17	July 24	July 31
17	Get business permits	3	John, Jennifer	10	June 24	June 9	July 29	July 31
18	Open bank accounts	17	John	2	July 9	July 11	July 29	July 31

Use this worksheet to help you schedule your projects.

Normalizing the Schedule

You must review the schedule to determine whether the resources you assigned are actually available within each task's schedule window. After individual assignments are finalized and reviewed by the team, the schedule must be adjusted to accommodate any other necessary changes. It needs review and approval by senior management as well, as part of the project plan.

When you use the critical path in a project, the tasks that are not on the path (called noncritical) can be scheduled in a number of ways to accommodate various needs of the organization. Three strategies are ...

➤ Schedule all noncritical tasks at the earliest date possible. This offers a way to free up resources earlier for other projects or the later critical tasks.

Time Is Money

If one unique resource commands the premier place in the project, you must wrap your schedule around its availability. For example, you can find plenty of typists, and you can rent a crane from another company, but locating a qualified biomechanical engineer or getting time on a linear accelerator may limit your scheduling options.

➤ Schedule all noncritical tasks as late as possible. This shows how much work can be delayed without causing the critical tasks (and thus the project schedule) to slip.

➤ Schedule a subset of noncritical tasks. As milestones are met, complete the rest of the schedule. This gives the manager scheduling flexibility and a way to assign resources to critical activities without causing political problems.

When assigning resources, the rules are simple:

➤ Make sure you know the specific availability of all resources (as much as humanly possible).

➤ Assign the best-suited available people to each task.

➤ Use resources efficiently to ensure the smallest gaps in working schedules.

➤ Redo the schedule over and over until you get it balanced. (Get help in terms of experts or computer programs if it takes more than three tries.)

Loading Up and Leveling Out

Many ideal schedules forget to deal with conflicting availability of resources, potential overuse of key resources, and the needs of other projects and priorities. For example, the ideal employee to supervise the alarm installation and testing may be unavailable the week you need her due to mandatory booth duty at a trade show in another city. If the task can't be rescheduled until her return, you'll have to choose someone else.

After working on your schedule, you will likely find that some team members have too much work—more than they can accomplish in a work week. Others may not have enough. The amount of work each team member or other resource is assigned is called resource loading. As you would expect, it's easy to overwhelm important resources with an impossible workload while underloading others.

To compensate for overloaded workers, scheduled work should be redistributed from resources with too much responsibility to those not fully booked. This is called resource leveling. As you level resources, skills and availability must be considered. If Shendyl, your computer network expert, has an unreasonable 164 hours of work scheduled per week, you can't redistribute the extra workload to three or four other team members who lack experience with computer networks. Instead, you need to acquire additional experienced resources or adjust the schedule and ultimately the budget to accommodate the necessary changes.

The Reallocation Questions

Before you reallocate and level the resource commitments, you need to ask yourself these questions:

➤ How many hours per day is each resource available? Can we expect employees to works 8 hours a day? They do—but all that time is not necessarily applied to the project. After all, they do have to go to the bathroom, take phone calls (some personal, most legitimate business calls), get coffee, talk to other project team members informally (sometimes personal, but more often it's discussion about work on the project), and talk to other employees in the company (sometimes personal, but frequently it's important networking with other team members or peers). As a manager, you should completely support these activities. Comfortable employees who feel they have control over their work life are that much more productive. As a manager, however, you also need to recognize that a work day usually consists of only 6.5 hours of productive work time as a result.

➤ Is an assigned resource allocated to multiple projects for multiple project managers? Depending on shared resources is not an optimum state for a project manager, but frequently we have limited control over the resources we get on a project and have to take their other responsibilities into consideration. Too many times in the past, we have had teams composed of individuals who have a minimal time allocation to another project. ("No more than a couple of hours a week, I promise.") Then, during project execution, we don't see him or her for a couple of weeks due to legitimate problems on the other project. ("Sorry, Sally is the only one who understands payroll, and we lost the ability to create payroll checks—we need her to help us figure out the problem.") Make sure you have a contingency built in for these people.

➤ Have you factored in time lost to anticipated interruptions? You can expect downtime due to weather, holidays, vacation and sick time, doctor's visits, and other personal requirements.

➤ Have you factored in sufficient time for administrative overhead? This means allowing time for company meetings, company travel time, completing time reports, completing weekly status reports, and project team meetings. This may also include reviewing team deliverables as well as internal reviews of prototypes or documents.

➤ Are you using specialized skill sets appropriately? Are team member assignments accurate in terms of matching skills and task requirements? Is there a need to reallocate resources or reassign work? Have you considered the productivity of the resources as well as their relative skills?

➤ Are you scheduling resources without appropriate skill sets? Frequently, we send team members out to be trained on a new skill and expect them to come back fully proficient in that skill. Depending on the skill, you should assume reduced productivity for a limited period of time to allow that resource to become fully proficient after applying the new skills in the project environment. The period of time should be directly related to the complexity of the new skills.

➤ Have you planned for the time required to acquire additional resources? Depending on the environment you work in, it will be more or less difficult to get the authorization to bring in additional staff regardless of whether they are full-time employees or temporary contract staff. In some organizations, that may take as little as a week or as long as two months. Once you have the authorization, there is the time required for getting applicants, interviewing them, checking references, making an offer, and waiting for the prospective employees to finish commitments at their current place of employment. Then, once they do come on board, there will be the time required to get up-to-speed on what the project is about, the project's goals, and their job. If you are moving really fast in all of this, allow at least six weeks to bring on a new project team member (on top of the time required to get the authorization). During all of this time, remember that your project is supposedly making progress.

Ready for Leveling Out

After making adjustments in response to all the preceding questions regarding the resource schedules, you're ready to do the final leveling of resource commitments. One of the tools to help you do this is the resource histogram, a visual tool that allows you to chart resource task allocation for each period through the project. In the example, notice how the histograms chart the availability of the resource and the effort of that resource through the life of the project.

In period 1, the resource is overallocated but is underallocated in the following periods. In this example, you would want to smooth out the peaks and valleys as best as you can by moving work out of period 1 into period 2 or 3 as time is available. You can move the task within the available float for that task (remember critical path?).

You can extend the duration of a task within the available float. You also could reassign some or all of the work to underallocated resources (if they have the right skills for the job—you'll have to refer to your skills inventory to do that).

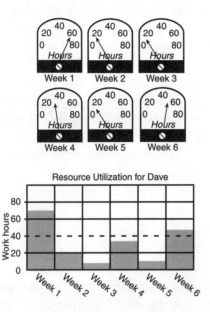

The resource histogram can help you visualize resource utilization during phases of a project. Here you see that Dave is overutilized during Week 1 and Week 6.

You can also use the leveling technique to smooth out the work allocation for a single department. Add up all of the department's project commitments. Identify the appropriate department workload. Visually demonstrate the difference between the department projection and the actual work in the department's work queue. Present this information to the department manager, who then has the ability to make the decisions as to what work should get done (and not done) or to approve the acquisition of additional resources.

Options for Adjusting the Schedule

In total, here are your options for reworking an impossible schedule with excessive resource loading:

➤ Change the scope (size) of the project or add resources, keeping in mind that more people and materials will impact the budget. Obviously, this has to be done with approval of the Review and Approval Team of stakeholders.

➤ Give a task more time or spilt it in two, modifying resource utilization to make the process work. You can also adjust the basic finish-to-start precedence relationships (but only when appropriate) by adding lead or lag time to tasks that enable some of the work to occur in parallel. (Refer to Chapter 10 if you've forgotten how this works.)

➤ Move a task to a time when more resources are free. This will mean calculating the entire schedule again to make sure the moved task doesn't impact the critical path.

➤ Outsource the work. Remember that outsourcing work, while reducing work done by the implementation team, also adds new tasks for vendor management. Outsourcing also assumes that the required resource expertise is available and uncommitted.

➤ Negotiate for additional time in the schedule with a later completion date and a budget increase. You'll obviously (we hope by now) need stakeholder agreement to do this. Don't negotiate the time required to complete the tasks (these should be good numbers if you've done your homework). Instead, negotiate the balance among the time, resources, and results (goals) of the project.

➤ Reprioritize the goal and scope of the project. (Reduce the number of project deliverables and goals.) Again, this will depend on the consensus of your stakeholders.

➤ Deliver components of the project in a phased approach, thereby extending the total project schedule but still giving the customer acceptable products or services.

➤ Find resources that are more productive (better trained, more experience). This choice may increase the budget, but you might get most of the added employee expense back in terms of increased productivity—if you choose wisely.

Adjusting a Schedule to Meet a Forced Deadline

Many projects have a forced or dictated deadline. A customer may need a project completed by a specific date. An event must take place on the day it's scheduled; otherwise, the effort will be a useless write-off. In the office project, a preannounced opening party for customers won't be much fun if crews are still cutting and installing dusty drywall.

Such a project should commence as early as possible in case unforeseen delays slow completion. If your careful scheduling shows that a project due date is impossible, you have three alternatives:

➤ Reduce the scope of the project.

➤ Add additional resources.

➤ Work out some way to extend the completion date (not always possible).

There are also projects with externally imposed finish dates that allow more than enough time to complete the project. Be wary of these because the time slips away faster than you think. At the beginning of these projects, there is actually no critical path at all because all the tasks have float.

Unfortunately, when the float has been used up (on any project), a new form of float emerges: *negative float*. When there is negative float on a task, adjustments need to be made to keep the schedule in line with the critical path (and to ensure completion on the approved end date for the project). A project with negative float will have a new critical path that is longer than the approved schedule. If it isn't possible to make adjustments to realign the tasks to the schedule, you'll need to renegotiate the cost-schedule-results equilibrium with the key stakeholders.

Project Lingo

Negative float is the state at which all the float in a project is used up and any imposed or approved schedule dates are impossible to meet. In essence, a project with negative float is another description for a project that will come in late (unless you do something about it).

Chart the Final Schedule and See If It Works

When the final schedule is in place and approved (along with the rest of the project plan), it should be distributed to all team members and posted in a common area so that team members can measure progress. This helps you maintain a healthy competitive attitude as the various team members rush to meet or exceed their scheduled delivery dates. At that point, you cease to be a project planner and take on your role as project manager. Of course, you still need a budget before you have an approved plan. With the schedule in hand, the budget should be no problem. Read on. It's time to play with the money. It's not just politicians who love to do that. We will discuss how to use the schedule for tracking in Chapter 23.

The Least You Need to Know

➤ Understanding the concept of critical path is important in keeping a project schedule on track.

➤ When assembling a project, you must document your assumptions. Can you assume that Grand Central Station will be deserted at noon for your restoration and painting project?

➤ Holidays slow projects because team members' minds may be on family matters rather than work.

➤ For noncritical tasks, there's float—the extra time between the earliest date a task must start and the latest date it is possible to start the task and still meet the rest of the project schedule.

Chapter 15

Budgeting Options for Your Projects

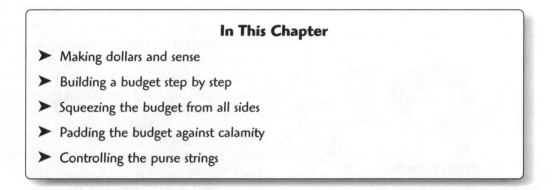

In This Chapter

➤ Making dollars and sense

➤ Building a budget step by step

➤ Squeezing the budget from all sides

➤ Padding the budget against calamity

➤ Controlling the purse strings

Having a robust budget allows you to fix almost anything that goes wrong. In the real world, however, most projects run on a tight budget. Funding is often inadequate for reasons we'll discuss in this and later chapters. Managers want blood from turnips. Things go wrong. Project delays waste budget dollars you can't afford to lose. Inflation takes its toll as the project takes longer than planned. Every minute a project is delayed because of a sick participant, equipment failure, or a blizzard cooling delivery of vital project components, money is wasted. Project budgets have something in common with storing radioactive elements—they lose strength over time, even when not in use.

The Five Horsemen of the Project Apocalypse

Budget pressure comes at you from five directions (sometimes all at once):

➤ **Problem 1:** Your vendor's estimates are all over the spectrum. Do you have three quotes from expensive services but they're 50 percent apart? Are you getting a bargain or is the vendor taking the job at a loss to build cash flow (called *buying the job*) in hopes of gaining repeat business charged at higher prices? You'll need to figure out why the bids differ. Are the assumptions different? The quality? The materials?

Time Is Money

The conceptual budget process is as follows:

People + Resources + Time = Budget.

Project Lingo

Vendors who are low on cash or are looking to soak you on future jobs might bid at a loss to blow away the competition and get the work. This is called **buying the job.**

➤ **Problem 2:** The occasional alligator among senior management will attempt to compress costs. He will do his damnedest to badger down your carefully calculated budget figure. Even if you know that the decreased budget is wholly inadequate, it's politically difficult to stand up to the big cheese. A misinformed senior manager might take the attitude that "I'm going to cut this budget in half!"

Such an attitude may bring short-term glory to that senior manager, but it courts long-term disaster. It may be especially problematic if you are dealing with a senior manager who sees himself retiring (in glory, complete with golden handshake and stock options) before your long-term project is completed and the folly of his ways has been revealed.

➤ **Problem 3:** Suppliers, consultants, and even department heads lending you people will demand as much money as they can get. Negotiation is the key to keeping these people's hopes on the earthly plane. Remember that, for all but the most esoteric services, someone else can be found to do it cheaper. Remind your would-be prima donna of this vital underpinning concept of capitalism. Just say, "That's more than I can afford to spend. I guess I'll have to look around for someone else who is less expensive." That should do it if anything does!

➤ **Problem 4:** The twilight zone. Have you forgotten something? What key tasks have been left out of the project plan? This is common in every project, but a really expensive task can eat the budget of other project tasks. (If you see Rod Serling lurking in the shadows nearby, carefully review your task list!)

➤ **Problem 5:** Not enough time to do it right. When a project manager has to turn out a budget quickly, he or she often does not calculate or estimate in a sufficient level of detail to permit correct tracking later.

All in all, budgets are affected by pressures from outside, within, and above projects. As project manager, you need to resist pressures that will negatively affect your plans.

These project caveats might seem difficult to deal with. Further complicating project budgeting is the fact that problems might rear their ugly heads simultaneously. For example, Chansen's, a now-defunct department store in Wyoming, simultaneously ran into three of the five horsemen. During major remodeling to update an aging store, the budget first was set adrift and then ran aground. Here's what happened:

➤ Management squeezed too much money from the project budget. Demanding a complete remodel, funds were squeezed from a realistic project budget to make the firm's stockholders happier with the store's profitability (Problem 2).

➤ The architect refused to deliver the final plans until she received a substantially larger fee. Already unhappy with the number of changes she was forced to make gratis, she took a negative attitude. Holding the blueprints hostage, she demanded more money for her labors (Problem 3).

➤ The store's escalators were not inspected before the budgeting and were later found to be in need of an expensive overhaul. No permit would be forthcoming from the city until they were repaired and brought up to modern code (Problem 4).

At about this time, a desperate project manager was last seen thumbing a ride to points south. Can you blame him?

High Water!

You must understand that, once a budget is established, it becomes sacrosanct. You are stuck with it. Changing an entrenched (note this word) project budget is like trying to modify the Ten Commandments—if you could find the original stones and do a little chisel (again, note the word) work.

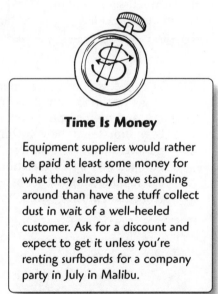

Time Is Money

Equipment suppliers would rather be paid at least some money for what they already have standing around than have the stuff collect dust in wait of a well-heeled customer. Ask for a discount and expect to get it unless you're renting surfboards for a company party in July in Malibu.

Developing Budgeting Skills

How do you establish a budget? It's initially easy. You follow the yellow brick road or, as in *All the President's Men,* "Follow the money!" Instead of hassling the Wicked Witch of the West or Charles Colson (remember him from the Watergate fiasco), you acquire the requisite estimates and then, fingers crossed, look at the project's totals. This is done task by task, step-by-step. Doing the budget for a small project, such as establishing an internal copy center, might take an afternoon. For large projects, a team might take months to bring expenses into line and to remember forgotten tasks.

The budget should help the project manager control the project; however, it's common for the project manager to find the budget controlling him or her. A realistic budget is central to keeping control of the project. It's okay to have one that's a little too conservative, but you can't turn lead into gold.

Time Is Money

"Money talks" is one of life's truisms. (We'll skip the second part—you already know the sentiment.) You'll find that this is especially true when you control a project budget of which outside providers want a share. Avoid taking money, gifts, or vacations of any kind on a vendor's tab. This keeps the bids on the level and the lawyers out of your life.

Building a Budget

The budgeting process can be intimidating to project managers. How much will it really cost? What if the price of widgets doubles on the Chicago Mercantile Exchange? How can I control an important staff member who demands a salary increase? What if I make a mistake? (If you see someone at the office with the shakes, it's probably because he or she either has recently given up coffee or is assembling a project budget for the first time.)

The process of building a budget should be an orderly one; otherwise, it's impossible to get reasonable numbers. You must carefully understand the components of each task and then cost out each one. Yes, you might make an error, underestimate (or overestimate), or blow it completely, but all you can do is try, using your best estimating capabilities. Even so, business conditions might change, the project might get bumped into a new direction, or a task might fail. So, what you are making in your astute budgeting is a set of assumptions that might change. Rub a lucky rabbit's foot while remembering the following:

➤ Costs are tied to project goals. Is your company's plan to build the cheapest notebook computer possible, even risking a 25 percent out-of-the-box failure rate? Or is it planning on a top-of-the-line model offering every feature and built to take a five-story drop without so much as dinging the case? Obviously, one is going to cost more to build than the other, and you must account for that in the budget. (Refer to Chapter 7 for more information on setting project goals.)

➤ Costs are tied to timeframes and schedules, and doing things faster usually costs more money. Need a swanky $48,000 tradeshow booth for an important show next week? It can be done, but if you're using an outside booth builder, you'll have to come up with 200-percent *rush charges* to motivate them. (Rush charges are substantial extra costs tacked on when people have to sacrifice their nights and weekends because of your bad planning.) Substantial rush charges make a sizable dent in your project budget.

➤ Costs require expert input. With specific tasks at the ready, query the people who will be doing the work about their charges for time and materials (refer to Chapter 11). It's important for each contributor to understand exactly what you want. For example, if you run a winery, your 1,000-pound order of cork for the latest vintage might turn into two 500-pound pigs because the rep heard "pork" instead of "cork." That's why written information, sketches, and models from the rep, showing his interpretation of your requirements, are vital to ensuring that what you ordered is what's delivered. This is called the *answer-back process*.

Project Lingo

Rush charges are applied by outside vendors when you rush them. If a task normally takes a film lab 24 hours, the lab may as much as quadruple the original charge if you must have your job done in two hours. So, a $150 charge could become a whopping $600. Imagine the rush charges on a $48,000 tradeshow booth like the one previously mentioned!

You also will need budget input from …

➤ **Staff.** You need firm estimates for the time required for task completion as well as all supplies and equipment. These estimates must be specific. Do not assume, for example, that five company Macintosh workstations will be idle and available March 4 to 24. They might not be, and you'll have to pay a fortune to rent them.

➤ **Outside service vendors.** You must have hard numbers from outside service providers and consultants. Demand (politely, of course) a written estimate that fixes the cost unless the project runs off the rails or changes nature. The latter might force the consultant to redo his work, and he should be compensated for it. As mentioned in Chapter 11, always shop price!

➤ **Other managers or experts.** People in your organization who have handled projects can provide excellent advice and study cost estimates for problems. They also might be able to provide exact estimates if a project they worked on had elements common to yours. Or, they might be much more experienced project managers and be willing to help out.

This type of project summary helps you see the costs and resource usage for the project at a glance.

Project Summary with Schedule, Costs, Deliverables, and Resource Assignments

WBS	Task Name	Type	Duration in Days	Start Date
	HELP DESK INTRANET PROJECT			13-Dec-99
	Project End Date			
1	Specification Development	Phase	5	13-Dec-99
1.1	Functional Specification	Task	5	13-Dec-99
1.2	GUI Specification	Task	3	13-Dec-99
2	Testing Documentation Development	Phase	11	20-Dec-99
2.1	Test Plan Development	Task	3	20-Dec-99
2.2	Test Case Development	Task	5	23-Dec-99
2.3	Documentation Review	Task	3	30-Dec-99
	Documentation Completed	Milestone	0	5-Jan-00
3	Development	Phase	23	5-Jan-00
3.1	Knowledge Base Development	Phase	23	5-Jan-00
3.1.1	Coding	Task	10	5-Jan-00
3.1.2	Unit Tests	Task	4	19-Jan-00
3.1.3	Function Test	Task	4	25-Jan-00
3.1.4	Data Input	Task	5	31-Jan-00
3.2	Discussion Forum Development	Phase	4	5-Jan-00
3.2.1	Coding		2	5-Jan-00
3.2.2	Unit Test	Task	1	7-Jan-00
3.3.3	Function test	Task	1	10-Jan-00
3.3	HTML Development	Phase	20	5-Jan-00
3.3.1	Coding	Task	10	5-Jan-00
.3.32	Unit Test	Task	5	19-Jan-00
3.3.3	Function Test	Task	5	26-Jan-00
	Development Complete	Milestone	0	4-Feb-00
4	Testing	Phase	69	13-Dec-99
4.1	Test Case Execution	Task	5	13-Dec-99
4.2	SW Defect Fixes	Task	10	20-Dec-99
4.3	Test Case Execution	Task	5	3-Jan-00
4.4	SW Defect Fixes	Task	5	7-Mar-00
4.5	Final Testing	Task	3	14-Mar-00
	Final System Signoff	Milestone/Deliverable	0	16-Mar-00
Totals				

➤ **Your managers or owners.** Although sometimes unhappy about a project's bottom line, they might be able to provide advice from their own years managing projects. Plus, by bringing them in early, they'll see that you're carefully covering your bases and are spending their money in an equitable manner. That observation will assist you in getting the final budget approved because management already will have a strong grasp on the realities of the project and its budget requirements—not to mention faith in you and your abilities.

End Date	Labor in Hours	Deliverable	Cost	Resource
16-Mar-00				
21-Mar-00				
17-Mar-00	**64**		**$3,840.00**	
17-Dec-99	40	Functional Spec	$2,400.00	Technical Architect
15-Dec-99	24	GUI Spec	$1,400.00	Design Architect
3-Jan-00	**76**		**$3,040.00**	
22-Dec-99	24	Test Plan	$960.00	Test Lead
29-Dec-99	40	Test Cases	$1,600.00	Test Lead
3-Jan-99	12		$480.00	Test Lead[50%]
5-Jan-00				
4-Feb-00	**310**		**$15,500.00**	
4-Feb-00	**168**		**$8,400.00**	
18-Jan-00	80	KB Code	$4,00.00	DB Developer
24-Jan-00	32		$1,600.00	DB Developer
28-Jan-00	16		$800.00	DB Developer[50%]
4-Feb-00	40		$2,000.00	DB Developer
10-Jan-00	**12**		**$600.00**	
6-Jan-00	4		$200.00	Java Developer[25%]
7-Jan-00	4		$200.00	Java Developer[50%]
10-Jan-00	4		$200.00	Java Developer[50%]
1-Feb-00	**130**		**$6,500.00**	
18Jan-00	80	HTML Code	$4,000.00	HTML Developer
25-Jan-00	30		$1,500.00	HTML Developer[75%]
1-Feb-00	20		$1,000.00	HTML Developer[50%]
4-Feb-00				
16-Mar-00	**448**		**$17,200.00**	
17-Dec-99	80	Test Report	$2,000.00	Tester #1, Tester #2
31-Dec-99	240	Defect Fixes	$12,000.00	DB Developer, HTML Developer, Java
7-Jan-00	40	Test Report	$1,000.00	Tester #1
13-Mar-00	40	Defect Fixes	$1,000.00	Tester #2
16-Mar-00	40	Test Report	1,200.00	Tester #1, Tester#2
16-Mar-00		**Signed FSS**		
	1208		$55,080.00	

Expert project managers estimate budgets accurately not because they have years of experience, but because they look at the budget and final costs of similar tasks on related projects. You can do it, too. If you furnished an elementary school last year and have a similar one to equip this year, base at least part of your estimate—accounting for inflation—on last year's costs.

➤ **Suppliers/service providers.** You must have supplies and equipment commensurate with your project's requirements. Shop price but be careful about taking the least expensive option if quality is an issue. Building a neighborhood police station as a charity project? Supplier A might provide clean two-by-fours for the same price as supplier B's knotty, warped, and generally misshapen lumber. Ask for samples.

187

This worksheet can help you determine the costs associated with your project.

		Budgeting Worksheet						
Project			**Date**		**Completed By**			
Task Number	**Responsible Person or Vendor**	**Dates**		**Estimated Costs**				**Actual**
		Start	**End**	**Equipment**	**Materials**	**Labor**	**Total**	

➤ **Purchasing department staff.** The purchasing department may or may not save you money. Purchasing is a department that may help you in your quest for success or may stand in your way at every turn. Use them if they've proved helpful in a timely manner in the past. Avoid or work around them if they are difficult to deal with. You might need an order from senior management to avoid working with them. This tactic is a slap in the face to the purchasing people. Don't expect to win any popularity contests with them next time you order a box of number two pencils.

Project Lingo

If a process is highly technical, large, or complex in scale, ask for an answer back. In the **answerback process,** the vendor takes your specs and builds a simple model that allows your experts to ensure that a clear understanding exists and that no significant parts or systems were neglected.

➤ **Experts.** Completely lost? Request (probably expensive) a budget from someone with budgeting skills to assist you through a sticky project. Hire experts after carefully explaining their duties and setting a firm budget for their time. The best and least expensive experts are often people who have retired from a field after a lifetime of experience. You also can hire an expert project manager—not to take the reins but to review results and proffer advice.

➤ **Standard pricing guides.** Many government-regulated organizations and some private companies offer standard pricing in printed-guide format. Need to know how much Federal Express charges to move an elephant from Zoo A to Zoo B? Just look it up in the free user guide (assuming you have the current version!).

Once these cost estimates have been gleaned and carefully listed along with the names of the contributors, it's time to do a task budget roundup. In this process, you take all the estimates for Task A and combine them. (Use a worksheet like the one included in this chapter or enter the numbers in your project management software.) After you wrap up costs for all the tasks separately, you can add the total of the entire plan to ascertain the project's total cost. Costs that are not available because Joanna in research is out of town must be guesstimated with a large highlighter used to indicate that the total is possibly fictitious. With a computer, most unknown/unverified estimates can be indicated separately. Your manager and most stakeholders will want to see the budget in two formats—by cost center and by month—to assess cash flow and cost allocations. Some project managers will also want to present the budget by project milestones, WBS summary levels, or project phases.

Direct and Indirect Costs

Before you put any numbers to paper, you must learn the difference between direct and indirect costs on a project. Your budget must account for both of these types of costs, although how this is done will vary from organization to organization.

Direct costs are those specifically required by the project. Indirect costs are those not specific to the project; their value can be shared among many projects. You'll need to find out (usually from the finance officer for your project or from the accounting department) how indirect costs are allocated for projects. Then you'll need to establish the appropriate line items for indirect costs as part of the overall budget.

Direct costs include the following:

➤ **Labor:** The cost of the people working on the project. Benefits for the employees may be charged as direct costs or as a percentage of all overhead for housing the employee (which might include the cost of facilities, benefits, and so on).

➤ **Supplies and raw materials:** The cost of materials consumed by the project.

➤ **Equipment:** The cost of tools and machinery.

➤ **Travel:** The cost of travel associated with the project.

➤ **Legal fees:** Direct legal expenses charged specifically for work on your project.

➤ **Training:** Training for project team members and for the project end users and customers during project installation or implementation.

➤ **Marketing/advertising:** The cost of project introductions, announcements, promotions, and public relations; these costs can be quite large on a project to introduce a new product.

Indirect costs include the following:

➤ **Facilities:** The physical location required for the project participants and shared resources, such as the company intranet or communications network. The exception is when facilities are purchased or leased specifically and exclusively for the use of the project.

189

➤ **Site-specific requirements:** State- or county-specific charges for business operations.

➤ **Management and administrative overhead:** This is the cost of paying for the managers and support staff (such as human resources people) used by your project but that don't directly report to you.

Indirect costs may be allocated on a percentage basis from some central accounting or management organization such as a corporate office or the department responsible for the project. Don't forget to include these costs because it could doom your project to budget overruns before it even starts.

Types of Budgeting Methods

There are two established methods for budgeting: top-down and bottom-up. Which is best for your project depends on your organization's standard approach to decision-making. Does management dictate most mandates? Or, is the staff expected to produce ideas and decisions that percolate up to management for final analysis? Your answer to this question will determine the most likely budgeting approach for the project.

Bottom-Up Budgeting

In bottom-up budgeting, staff members get together and attempt to hammer out a budget from the task-level detail. As a group, they can speak frankly. One member might have a solution that's superior to another. It's also a good way to avoid missing a subtask. If one group member forgets it, another (hopefully) will remember it. This helps avoid budget-gobbling tasks appearing midproject and throwing everything off down the line.

Time Is Money

Make an extra copy of a draft network diagram and write the budget for each task next to its box. In a glance, you will see where most of the money is being spent.

Top-Down Budgeting

More difficult than bottom-up management, the top-down approach has senior managers estimating budgets from their experience and then allocating funds to lower-level managers for execution. Top-down budgeting works if managers carefully allocate costs and possess significant project management experience.

In many progressive organizations, a combination of top-down and bottom-up budgeting is used to ensure that the top-down numbers (which establish general expectations) are grounded in the reality of the workers' experience.

Phased Budgeting

Phased budgeting, like phased scheduling, can use either top-down or bottom-up estimates or both, but it estimates only one phase of the project at a time. On very large projects, this is a commonly employed methodology because it limits risk and uncertainty in the approved operational budget.

Refining the Budget

When the budget numbers are in, although subject to correction, the next step is to fine-tune the numbers. You might have to go through this process several times as new estimates arrive and are revised or as tasks enter the project that were forgotten or ignored in the initial estimating pass.

Here are the steps (all required) in refining the estimates:

Time Is Money

Are you assembling a budget using a spreadsheet program such as Excel? Don't accept the final numbers without calculating them separately using a calculator. Otherwise, an error in an underlying formula might be invisible until the money prematurely runs out. Or, the numbers might come in so high that management scraps it as impossibly expensive.

1. **A rough cut.** This is a number pulled out of a hat, and it might have little to do with the final number. "Ed, I think we're looking at $50,000 for the Forbin Project." (If you missed this movie, keep it that way.) "Tammy, will $200,000 open the new office?" On a megaproject with subprojects, "Sally, how much will Interchange 195 cost with the art deco toll booths?"

   Rough cuts should never become the actual budget numbers. This will kill a project manager and project faster than anything. Rough cuts are remembered as real budget quotations. Run like hell if you're asked to stop budgeting at this step.

2. **A second cut.** The resources required for each task estimate are reviewed carefully. These include the cost of labor, supplies and materials, equipment, overhead, and fix-priced bids from vendors (which account for all the vendor costs). This estimating process might demand the use of outside providers or might require more than one take as a complex subset of work is reliably broken down. You should also look at historical project costs to help guide your estimates. All estimating should involve the relevant stakeholders.

3. **Getting it right.** The third pass is the one in which you (and the team, of course) do the fine-tuning. For example, you might reveal that your initial $2,400 guesstimate is more realistic at $15,243.23. This process accomplishes two things: It turns guesstimates into something close to reality, and it provides an overall estimate of the project's real scope. This might not please the bill payer, but it must be done. Again, the relevant stakeholders need to be involved in these refined estimates.

191

4. **Wrapping it up.** If the budget appears to be workable (that is, affordable), it gets wrapped into the project plan while simultaneously heading for the front office for approval or at least groans. (Bring a bottle of aspirin to these initial stakeholder meetings.)

5. **Presentation for approval.** At this point, the budget shouldn't be a surprise to anyone on the approval cycle. Your complete cut at the budget is presented for approval. Even though people have seen it before, they may still ask you to find ways to cut it, to modify the project, or to scrap the project as not worth the money (more common than you might think). If you're lucky, it gets approved right there. If not, continue to revise and present until you get consensus and signatures on the bottom line.

Stuffing the Pillow with Money

Are you uncertain of the level of risk in a project? Want to provide a buffer of extra money? Add 10 to 100 percent to the budget to ensure completion and treat it as an insurance policy. *Padding* is a standard procedure in managing any project. There's no way that every risk can be fully calculated or anticipated. Everything from lightning blowing out your computer network to an outbreak of Legionnaire's disease might increase the budget as progress decreases. Padding, however, can get you into trouble; a small amount is reasonable and expected, but too much padding can distort the real requirements for a project. Instead of overpadding the budget, negotiate for the money you really need—or adjust the project scope and objectives to be less expensive.

At the same time, you need to remember that it's often easier to get required money at the beginning of the project than to keep coming back for more because your estimates were bad.

Project Lingo

Padding means adding extra money to a budget for overruns. This is a standard project management tactic (also known as a contingency plan) used to combat sloppy estimating or unexpected cost overruns.

Master Budget Control

Who holds the purse strings? You? Your management? A combination of both? Whatever the arrangement, you want as easy access to the money as possible. That way, you can pay bills and purchase supplies in a timely manner. In one kind of arrangement, you theoretically own the budget but must get multiple signatures from senior management each time you need to spend a chunk of it. This slows projects to a crawl because some members of the executive suite might be out of town and unable to sign. Besides, executives often let authorizations requiring their signatures sit in their in-boxes because they're too busy with their own projects.

Removing the Lid from the Pressure Cooker

Here are two techniques that won't make the problem go away but might at least ease the pressure:

➤ Get as much signing authority for yourself as possible; anywhere from $500 to $5,000 is appropriate. This allows you to pay the majority of expenses without the multiple-signature process.

➤ Establish (and closely monitor) a $500 petty-cash box. It's a resource for quick payoffs for small parts, day laborers, or taking the gang out for pizza after reaching a major milestone. All cash that comes from the box must be replaced with a receipt. Replenish the petty cash when it reaches the $100 level. Regularly count the remaining cash and receipts to ensure that no $20 bills have grown legs and walked out the door.

All in all, if you estimate carefully and document your assumptions thoroughly, you'll get a good budget approved—one that gives you enough money to get things done on time.

The Least You Need to Know

➤ Establishing a reliable budget is likely the most difficult task a project manager faces—for political as well as logistical reasons.

➤ Management personnel will rarely accept your budget as reasonable; they will attempt to squeeze money from it, even if it means putting the project at risk. You'll need to document and negotiate what you really need.

➤ Your budgeting skills will improve after successful completion of several projects.

➤ You want as much direct control of your budget as possible if you're going to be held accountable for the project outcome.

Chapter 16

Putting It All Together: The Approved Plan

Okay, you've assembled a statement of work (SOW), a work breakdown structure (WBS), a network diagram, a schedule, a description of team requirements, and a budget. You understand the tasks for the plan and the resources required. After all this effort, you may feel too tired to start working on the project, but don't throw in the towel. Besides, you haven't even finished the plan. You still need to integrate, evaluate, and get approval for the fruits of your planning labors. Yes, it's nearing ground zero in your plan, but you need your plan approved before you can start working on your project.

This chapter reminds you of all the good reasons for planning in the first place and provides advice for getting your project plan approved so you can get to work. Don't fret. D-Day is almost here! With an approved plan in hand, you'll be ready to start working on the project. Finally!

Reasons to Plan in the First Place

Sometimes people complain that plans take too much time. People would rather start working on the project than think about the plan. Some plans are created only because other people want to see them. Your boss asks for a plan and you write one. The customers want a plan so you draft something to make them happy. Plans prepared slavishly rather than thoughtfully are a waste of time for the reader as well as the writer. Plans written only for the benefit of someone else rarely meet their goals of guiding the project to a successful conclusion.

If you're not going to take planning seriously, don't bother. Without a good plan, you're like a surgeon who decides to remove his appendix with a can opener. You'll likely get the offending organ out, but you'll also make a mess of things in the process.

A good plan can help avoid most problems (but not all). Even so, you should know that no amount of planning will make your project go exactly as planned. Your plan will go off course because of things you didn't know in advance—and every project will encounter some things that cause you to deviate from the plan. Of course, if there are too many deviations, you might never reach your destination. So the better the plan, the more likely you'll get where you want to go. And the better you keep the plan up-to-date, the more likely you'll be able to make the best adjustments to keep the project on course.

Putting It All Together

The diagram shows how all the pieces of the plan you've learned about in this book so far are interrelated. Ultimately, all of these pieces should be put together in an integrated document called "the plan."

Project plans can vary from fairly simple documents that list the tasks, budget, and resources on a single page with a cover memo to detailed books with overwhelmingly intricate levels of detail. Typically, the plan will include additional narrative and organizing information to help readers (and team members) understand how the entire project fits together. The complete project plan for a large project might include a table of contents like the following:

1. Executive Summary of the Project (or Project Overview)
2. Project Objectives
3. Project Assumptions and Risks
4. Project Milestones
5. Work Breakdown Structure
6. Network Diagram

7. Resource Details

> Human Resources
>
> Equipment
>
> Materials and Supplies

8. Budget Details

9. Project Organization

10. Operating Procedures

11. Assessment and Review Standards

12. Contact Points and Information Sources (if relevant)

13. Project Approvals

There is no magic formula for the right level of detail in the plan. We use this rule of thumb in our own planning efforts: Never spend more time on the plan than it would take to fix the project if there were no plan. Thus, if your project is only a week in length, it doesn't make sense to spend two weeks on the plan. On the other hand, if your project involves hundreds of people and millions of dollars, you'll want to put detail in the plan that allows the myriad resources to be coordinated.

The project planning stage dominates almost one-third of this book, but the actual time required to complete the plan (including the work plan, resource assignments, schedule, and budget) might only be a few hours for a very short project. It might take a month or more for a very large project. But it is the quality and thought that goes into a plan—not the time—that determines its value in the project management process. This is why it's so important to understand the issues in creating each component of the plan as we've explained them in previous chapters.

Who Should Write the Project Plan?

When you have completed the OW, a WBS, a network diagram, a resource list, a schedule, and a budget, you have all the elements necessary to put together the plan. But who does all this work? And who should put the plan together in final form?

You generally have three alternatives in preparing the final plan. Your choice of approach will depend on your organization, your personal experience and expertise, and the complexity of the project.

Create the Plan Yourself and Have It Reviewed

Creating the plan on your own is a good approach for small projects that have only a few participants or if you have expertise in a project that makes you especially well-qualified to draft the major sections of the plan. Also, if you are basing your project on a plan used successfully for a previous project, this approach can work because you will only be making adjustments to an existing plan that has worked before.

The project planning documents are interrelated. If you make a change to one, you need to adapt the rest. If you don't keep the plan up to date, it doesn't matter how good the initial plan was. An out-of-date plan is a statement of what didn't happen—not a guide for the future.

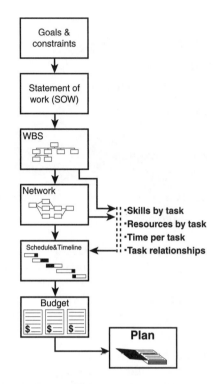

The downsides of completing the final plan on your own include:

➤ It is more difficult to identify errors in the logic of a network diagram or WBS.

➤ You might not identify missing tasks or incomplete activities.

➤ You might not have all the information you need to create an accurate schedule or budget.

➤ It is often difficult to see your plan objectively when you do it yourself. Even when other people review it, they might not be familiar enough with the logic of your plan to offer alternatives.

➤ On a complex project, it is rare for one person to have the expertise and experience to detail all the tasks at the same level with great accuracy.

➤ People might feel left out, thus creating a negative political environment that affects your ability to manage the project through the next stages.

The two primary advantages of doing the plan on your own are ...

➤ It is faster. If you are familiar with the steps and logic in a project, you can usually create a WBS and a network diagram with little input. It takes less time than asking opinions and having meetings to discuss the options.

➤ You can complete a plan on your own before the team members are identified. Of course, when you do identify other people who will be working on the project, they will need to review your work and offer suggestions for modifying the work sequences and tasks.

On a project with a short deadline, these advantages can be critical to getting a plan done on time, but the disadvantages usually outweigh using this approach.

Construct the Plan with the Key Players

Getting the key players and stakeholders involved in project planning requires one or more structured meetings and advance preparation by each of the team members. Of course, if you haven't yet identified the key players in the project, this is not practical. Instead, you might identify a team of people who have had responsibilities similar to those on your project to help you create the plan, even though these people won't necessarily be involved in your project. In any case, it always helps if you provide some initial planning information (such as a milestone network) and some overall project objectives to get the planning started in the right direction.

The disadvantages of the team approach to detailed planning include:

➤ It can be time-consuming. Meetings take time, and a complex project might take multiple meetings to plan down to the task level.

➤ Unless you handpick the participants, different levels of planning expertise will be evident, making it difficult to establish consistency in each component of the plan.

➤ Conflicts will need to be resolved, and compromises in the plan might be necessary to keep the project team cohesive and focused on the project goals.

➤ To be successful using this approach, the project manager will need to spend a significant amount of time in preplanning activities to coordinate, structure, and lead the meetings.

The potential benefits of the team approach include:

➤ It can create shared responsibility among team members for planning the project.

➤ Team members will benefit from a better understanding of the work required of others.

➤ It can identify potential conflicts and inconsistencies early in the project planning cycle, so they can be dealt with before they affect the project outcome.

➤ It can be used to create camaraderie among team members who have not worked together before.

199

➤ The process provides a way to verify and clarify the team's understanding of the project scope and goals.

For completing the plan for an entire project, this approach works bests if there are 10 or fewer people on the project team and if the total project network involves 200 tasks or less. Otherwise, bring the team members in after some of the planning has been done.

Break the Project Into Subprojects and Plan Accordingly

For large projects, you can assign small groups to develop the subplans for the individual subprojects and then meet to put all the subplans together. Then, a few selected people from each of the groups will be assigned to integrate the subplans into a project plan, using a methodology similar to the team approach described earlier.

The disadvantages of this approach include:

➤ The coordination of the various groups can be difficult and time-consuming.

➤ The different groups might define tasks with inconsistent levels of complexity. This can be minimized if the project manager is involved with each of the groups to help ensure consistency.

➤ Each group must have a manager trained in project management techniques. This is not necessarily a disadvantage, but it can be a constraint in some organizations.

For a large or complex project, this approach can have all the advantages of the team approach, and for an extremely large project, it is mandatory. No single project manager can define the work for something large and complex without making mistakes or omissions in the plan.

No matter which of the alternatives you choose to develop the plan, you will need to have the plan approved and reviewed by the appropriate people in your organization. Even after the plan is approved, as you bring new people into the project later in implementation, changes might be necessary if the new team members offer better or more appropriate alternatives for completing their assigned tasks and reaching milestones. (When you start thinking about changing and modifying a network diagram with hundreds of activities during the life of a project and communicating these changes to multiple people, the rationale behind using computerized project management tools becomes apparent.)

From Plan to Approval

In the real world, the plan for a large project (or even a small one) will go through multiple versions on its way to approval. First, project objectives are established.

Next, a rough work plan, schedule, and budget will be produced. These will be debated, discussed, enhanced, expanded, and revised until the project plan is complete and approved.

When the Planning Phase Terminates a Project

Of course, some projects collapse before the project plan gets approved. Here are some standard scenarios for projects that never make it out of the planning stage:

➤ Inadequate planning. You rush a plan together, and it's tearing at its seams under the weight of reality. If the stakeholders see the plan as inadequate, it's not going to get the go-ahead.

➤ Incomplete plans. You or your team provide uncertain estimates for scheduling and budgeting or fail to bring in the expertise to quantify the technical tasks.

➤ The mission of the organization changes during the planning process. Many organizations change their priorities like people change clothes. A project must fit into the current political, economic, and business priorities of the company to gain approval. The truth is that many organizations are trying to react to a rapidly changing marketplace—this is more of a reality than a fault.

➤ The project is no longer relevant, seems too risky, or has little chance of completion before the target date. Who wants to support a project going down in flames in front of his or her management peers? After all, part of your work as project manager is to evaluate and present the feasibility of a project to stakeholders and senior management. You are helping management decide whether to proceed with the project as defined.

> **High Water!**
>
> While you work on a plan, your project might change in relevance, and you might be plugging away at something currently as important as yesterday's newspaper. Avoid this problem by continually feeding progress reports to management and other stakeholders during planning. And learn to take the company's pulse on a regular basis to see how the political health might be changing.

Sometimes the plan demonstrates to the stakeholders that the project is not viable. If you get stuck with one of these, just be happy that the project got stopped at the planning stage before you got stuck with trying to manage an impossible feat.

Other Issues That Can Sink a Plan

Upon integrating the various components of the project plan, you might find issues that have not been addressed in your other planning efforts. Not all of these are worthy of a task in the plan, but if you ignore them or don't address them somewhere in the schedule, the project will suffer. Typical things that get left out of the plan (but shouldn't) include:

➤ **Space and facilities**   Do you have basic office, manufacturing, and sleeping accommodations arranged that are suitable for your team? Do these costs appear in the budget?

➤ **Transportation**   Should your team need transportation above and beyond normal commuting, you must locate effective transport and budget for it.

➤ **Permissions**   Do you require written or at least verbal permission to use specialized equipment, to trespass on private property, to cross international borders, or something similar?

➤ **Licenses, permits, and clearances**   Do you need official permission to use hazardous chemicals, to block access to a structure or roadway, to enter restricted government facilities, to move confidential equipment or materials, or something similar?

➤ **Insurance**   Are your team and other resources underwritten for accidents and infringements that might occur? If insurance is required, what existing policies protect you and how can you fill the gaps with additional coverage?

➤ **Weather**   How will the weather impact your plan? Can you hold the dates together if rain or snow delay construction, hinder delivery of materials and equipment, or impact team member performance?

➤ **Unavailable resources**   Is a strike possible within your organization or a major vendor? Is a key material in short supply? How will you address the problem and resolve it?

These are just some of the more common risk factors that might impact your project's timely completion. When reviewing your plan, you might find others that must also be addressed with contingency plans or specific tasks and schedules.

Uncertainty and Risk—What Level Is Acceptable?

When you submit your plan for approval and discuss it in review meetings, the reviewing managers or stakeholders will judge the risk factors associated with each aspect of your plan.

Remember that tasks with less than 50 percent certainty reflect a need for better planning or the assumption that the plan is more of a guideline than a real project plan. In many projects, pivotal points with low certainty become high risks. Designing a new appliance? What happens if, during a too-brief testing prior to production, the sample units catch fire and melt?

Most projects have potential weak points. You should study your plan to identify each one if you want to get the plan approved. If you don't want to be blamed for your failure to predict the future when things don't go as planned, be honest about the risks by documenting them in the plan and by coming up with ways to reduce them if possible.

The Reality Check Before Approval

Before submitting the plan for final approval, you need to perform one last *cross-check* of your planning efforts. This involves a line-by-line matching up of the WBS, schedule, budget, and network diagram, assuming you created these pieces. Computer-based planning software can help by finding impossible dates and durations on the critical path, missing network links (only if they're obvious), and missing task data. Even when you use a computer, however, you should check the logistics and flow of your project personally and by hand.

Here are the steps for cross-checking a project plan:

1. From the network diagram, match the tasks, durations, and dates to the scheduling worksheet.

2. From the network diagram, match the resources to the scheduling worksheet.

3. From the network diagram, match the task to the activities shown in the WBS.

4. Verify the numbers on the budgeting worksheet and retotal them to make sure they match your existing estimate.

5. Study the tasks on the critical path. Is the right path selected? Are there any tasks that require more time? Have you separated the labor required from the duration on each task?

6. Verify that the milestones (if you chose any) make sense as a means of summarizing the main activities in a project.

7. Check to see if the start and finish dates are still reasonable. Also verify that you have accounted for all holidays and vacations in the schedule.

Project Lingo

One of the best tests of completion, whether for the doors on an airliner or the workability of a project plan, is **cross-checking.** To cross-check a plan, one person lists a procedure and another verifies it. With two independent bodies carefully verifying the plan, chances for error greatly diminish.

If you didn't assemble either a network diagram or a WBS, it's almost impossible to cross-check a project. Reread earlier chapters on why the components are important. If you're unwilling to prepare this level of detail in plans, whether formal or informal, consider another type of job. A plan is an absolute requirement of success in project management.

203

Time Is Money

All steps of the plan should be run past your core team members before approval. The final fine-tuning of the project plan is no exception. After all, if you missed something, they might be able to fill in the gaps. If you've asked the impossible of a team member, you'll have an opportunity to hear about it before the work starts.

Checking It Twice

Inevitably, discrepancies will appear in the cross-checking process. As you might expect, larger projects tend to have more mistakes than smaller, simple ones. After finding the errors, you must modify the plan to correct them. If more than 3 percent of the plan requires modifications due to your changes, perform the cross-check from scratch one more time after the changes are made. It's always possible to "fix" errors by introducing new ones. For that reason, review your notes from the previous procedure and do it again.

One way to encourage review is to have a dedicated wall or cubicle where the latest project data is displayed. Team members can check it and flag changes or problems. Team meetings take up a lot of time and should be limited. In today's networked world, you might consider additional "groupware" tools to share project information, but don't let tools replace your involvement as project manager.

A plan that changes more than 10 percent during the cross-check demonstrates a plan that needs further work. Look at the errors to establish where they lie: schedule, budget, resources? If a definite pattern to the mistakes appears mostly in one part of the plan, consider redoing that part of the plan from the beginning.

Getting the Plan Approved

The final step before the ship sails, so to speak, is getting the project and its cross-checked plan approved by the people paying the bills. The people who approve the plan will vary by company, project, and assignment. As mentioned in Chapter 5 when we discussed the stakeholders on the project, make sure you know who will approve the work and the budget for the project. Sometimes multiple departments will be involved. Sometimes you'll get to sign the approval sheet on your own. In any case, the most important aspect of the approval is getting the money freed up (the budget) so that you can start work on the project.

You'll need to package a large plan in an organized way. Using tabbed dividers is a good idea. Don't forget to put in summary sheets and narrative explanations about the assumptions you made when planning the project as part of the appendixes.

Most projects require a presentation by you to sell the project to the person with the money (the manager, customer, VP of finance, or whoever is "it" for your project). Your presentation might be little more than a brief chalk-talk with a whiteboard; for a large, big-budget project, the presentation of the plan might be a project in its own right involving an interactive multimedia extravaganza that wows and amazes the stakeholders into utter submission.

A Presentation of Project Priorities

Before you present your project for final approval, study the presentation of the plan from an outsider's viewpoint. Do the tasks explain themselves or is additional notation required? Are the tasks equal in scope (or almost)? Is the presentation clear and organized? Is the level of presentation appropriate for the scope of the project? Make sure the project sponsor reviews the project plan before you have any other decision-makers on the approval team look at it.

If you present your plan to a manager, customer, or review committee, you must be prepared to justify your choices, dates, and budgets. You'll need a compelling reason why each task is required and the associated budget justified. (Even if the reviewers don't ask, you should be prepared.) You also need to be prepared to talk about risks and contingencies if things go wrong.

> **Time Is Money**
>
> An efficient way to present a plan is with a summary presentation backed up by hard copies of the plan's WBS, worksheets, and network diagram. Presenting a management overview hopefully will avoid a line-item review of each task, its schedule, and its budget. If it comes to that, however, the backup data you've provided will do the trick.

Use judgment in what you present from the plan. Always start with an overview of the plan and then move on to details. Remember, the people who approve the plan will have a copy of the complete document to review anyway; you don't need to go over every detail in the presentation. The goals of the presentation are to present the overall structure and objectives of the project, to answer questions, and to establish your credibility as the project planner (and project manager).

Too much detail in the presentation can be as devastating as too little. With too many tasks in your presentation, you'll be bombarded with questions and arguments from management about the details. Managers might grandstand their opinions and try to save money on things they don't really understand. Avoid this by using milestone summaries of tasks so that managers don't fail to see the big picture during your presentation. Keep the meeting short (one hour) and focused. Senior managers dislike meeting for longer than an hour. Keep it crisp, but make time for their searching questions and time to get their approval.

The result of your presentation will be either the approval (by signature) of the project (which is unlikely on the first presentation of a large project) or a request to make revisions. Changes should be made to the general plan (scope and strategy) first and then to the details of the plan (the tasks, network, resources, and so on). Remember, you must change both. You can't just adapt the schedule because the stakeholders don't like it. If you've done a good job of planning, you'll have to communicate this fact to the people who approve (and sign off on) the plans.

If real objections crop up, stop the presentation and reschedule the meeting after the plan has been modified. If more than three revision meetings are required, then either your plan has serious problems or the political agenda of the people approving it is likely to prove impossible to circumvent. Without full management commitment to your project, successful completion is unlikely at best.

If you get caught in a political situation, have one-on-one discussions with individual stakeholders to understand their concerns and then come up with a strategy for circumventing (or reducing) the politics from the process so you can go forward with the plan.

Presenting Your Plan as an Outsider

As an outside project management consultant or vendor, you might be required to present your plan and sell it in a competitive bid. Although management will be focusing on costs, try to emphasize the quality of your proposal as well. If you're not the lowest bidder, convince the potential customer that your organization delivers consistently high-quality work, on time and within budget. (Hopefully, this will be the truth.) As for a group sold solely on schedule and/or budgetary concerns that turns down your carefully honed estimates, you probably wouldn't have liked working for them anyway.

Approval at Last

Finally, there's great news: Your plan is approved. They've signed on the dotted line. The accounting department has assigned a budget number and account codes for the project. You're ready to go.

The plan you created and got approved is not the only plan you'll use during your project. During a project, you'll typically have three or more versions of the plan active at one time. First, there is the original approved plan. This is sometimes called the baseline plan. Second, there is the actual plan, which reflects the actual work done to date. Third, there is the future schedule based on work done to date. Finally, there could be a number of contingency plans developed for a complex project over time.

Just remember to keep the plans numbered and keep them up-to-date. A big filing cabinet is a good idea if you'll be managing big or frequent projects. A good computer program should be able to manage more than one version of the project at a time so you can compare various stages of the project as you proceed.

Bringing a Delayed Plan Back to Life

In too many organizations, your carefully constructed project plan might be shelved if organizational and market changes alter management priorities. Then, vampire-like, the project rises from its grave to haunt you.

Before you seek the approval of such a plan, make sure you verify all the tasks, assumptions, and budgets. Don't just blow the dust off yellowing pages. Make sure the old plan still makes sense.

If a plan slips a month past its starting date, a new schedule is mandated. If it slips more than one month, the entire plan must be scrutinized. A new schedule is in order, but you must also verify resource availability and make changes to the plan to reflect management dictates. Even equipment and supply lists must be updated. Last year's order of 48 top-of-the-line computers might be superseded by newer, cheaper models. Suppliers might have closed up shop, moved, or been unable to deliver a brand they carried 365 days ago. You'll have to modify the budget to reflect the improvements in technology, market changes, and the effects of time.

Words from the Wise

When the company archives your plan because it's so important, it's a goner. You won't ever see it again. And it will never ever serve its purpose as a plan.

—A project manager for a multi-national company

From Plan to Action, Finally

After getting a plan approved, it might seem like you've done an awful lot of work and still not gotten anything done.

The central role of the plan in the project management process often leads people to the mistaken conclusion that the creation of the plan is project management. It's not. Most of the time spent in project management involves management. As you've already surmised, project management involves much more than just a plan.

Words from the Wise

The longer a project's duration, the less likely that changes in organizational priorities and happenstance will allow it to reach completion.

—A standard project manager's axiom

Still, don't be surprised if people identify your project management skills with your ability to create a nifty network diagram and an impressive-looking planning binder. Worse things could happen, and as long as they pay you for it, well, you don't have to tell them that it wasn't really that hard.

You'll soon get to work and put your approved plan into action. Forward and onward! The executing or implementation phase is about to begin. In the next phase, you'll learn how to take the baseline and create both plans that reflect work done and schedules for remaining work. But that's to come. For now, just enjoy your completion of a demanding phase of project management.

The Least You Need to Know

➤ You need to cover all your bases in planning. A brilliantly scheduled research project in Switzerland will come in over budget if you don't remember to include the team's travel, food, and lodging expenses.

➤ Projects with a degree of significant risk might require a second look from the bottom to the top.

➤ Risky tasks should be analyzed. If a less risky approach is possible, the plan should be modified to accommodate it.

➤ All planning documents from the WBS to the network diagram should be scrutinized to ensure that they match and work together.

➤ Aging or delayed project plans require revamping before going for approval.

➤ You'll probably have to present your plan to management and customers before it gets approved—and it probably won't get approved the first time around.

➤ You must sell your plan to the stakeholders and get their commitment to the plan, its schedule, and its budget before starting work on the project.

Part 4
The Executing Processes

Well, you've done it now—you've initiated a project and have gotten the plan approved. You're ready to begin, and the beginning is a very delicate time in any project. How you begin the executing phase (also commonly called the implementation phase) of the project will establish your likelihood for success—or failure.

To start toward the finish line of a project, you establish your leadership, organize the team for optimum performance, institute operating guidelines, and yes, figure out what kind of reports and other paperwork you'll need to get things going and keep them headed in the right direction.

These are the things you'll learn how to do in this section. Always remember that the right direction is spelled out in the plan—but only if you keep the plan up-to-date will this direction continue to be the right one. Keeping things on track is one of the controlling processes. You can't start controlling until you get started, so let's do just that.

Chapter 17

Getting Started on the Right Track

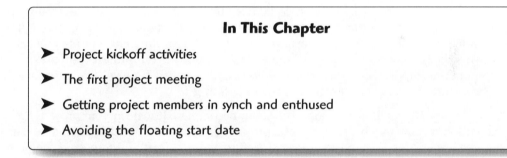

In This Chapter

➤ Project kickoff activities

➤ The first project meeting

➤ Getting project members in synch and enthused

➤ Avoiding the floating start date

At this point, you have an approved project plan in hand. You have identified most of the key team members, have sought permission to use them, and have established a budget and a source of funds to pay them. You're ready to get started. Or are you? How will anyone know what to do? What's the first step? Who's on first?

For most projects, these questions are answered at the project kickoff event and the first project meetings with the group and individuals. These activities are the first steps in the executing phase of any project. The big kickoff event (or at least a small one) serves to get everyone in synch with each other and to build a feeling of cama-raderie. The project kickoff is like the locker-room rally before a big game. It gets the juices flowing and reinforces the goals for the project. The first project meeting is like the initial huddle in the Super Bowl. This is where you actually agree on your first play in the project and get the team lined up to win the prize.

In this chapter, you'll learn how to hold a project kickoff that motivates the troops and gets everyone moving in the same direction—toward the project finish. You'll also see how to make the first project meetings part of the key strategy in your project game plan.

The Great Leap Forward

With the complete, approved project plan in hand, you are ready to get started on the actual work of the project. For small projects, getting started might involve simply sending a memo to the staff announcing the approved plan and reviewing key dates. This note and a few calls or personal visits to the team participants may be all that's necessary to get people started on their objectives. For larger projects, a project initiation or formal kickoff event is usually desirable. (We'll describe this in detail later in this chapter.)

If you're working on a really large project, you will have a cycle of execution phases in which plans, guidelines, and operating procedures are reestablished as each new milestone begins. This is because some large projects are really a succession of smaller projects linked together. In such large projects, you'll have a series of "first" meetings as each new milestone of the project gets underway.

Always Get Your Own Act Together First!

Before you have the kickoff event, you'll need to consider both your leadership style and your management tactics—the two are intertwined and are central to the implementation of projects. Your leadership skills and the appropriateness of the management tactics you adopt for each of the various people on your project team are of paramount importance in achieving project goals. The first time you get to try out these strategies and tactics will be at the kickoff event.

In Chapter 18, you'll learn a lot more about becoming a leader on your project. We mention it now only because, to get a project kicked off, you must be both a manager and a leader. You can use the project kickoff to gain the trust and respect of the project team so that people feel comfortable taking your direction. You can also use the kickoff to explain the reports and administrative procedures you'll use to help people get work done on time and within budget.

Are You Ready?

Before you schedule the project kickoff event, make sure you're comfortable with the plan's dates, the budget, and the resources available. It may be better to hold off on the official project kickoff until you are comfortable with all components and have all the round pegs in the round holes.

Of course, delaying the project kickoff is a double-edged sword. Jump in too fast, when all elements are not adequately quantified, and the project may unravel. Delay until everything is firmly in place, and the project window may elude you because you failed to beat the competition to market.

Do It Now and Do It Right

Once you've decided that you're really ready, you need to decide how to kick off your project. Whether handled formally or informally, the kickoff events of the project or subproject need to accomplish the following objectives:

➤ Communicate the goals of the project to all team members to ensure that everyone is crystal clear on their own objectives and responsibilities for the project.

➤ Attain the commitment you need for the project and get people enthusiastic about making things happen.

➤ Establish the leadership milieu for the project and get the team ready to follow you.

➤ Identify critical deadlines and phases of the project.

➤ Review the overall schedule and work plan with the appropriate team members.

➤ Explain basic operating procedures including required reports, meetings, and other ongoing communications necessary between you and other team members.

➤ Explicitly give the people responsible for the initial tasks the go-ahead to begin work on the project.

If you add all these objectives together, you'll see that the overall goal of the executing phase is to establish a set of conditions so work can get done. These conditions start with clear communications about the plan and other procedures associated with your project. The project kickoff is the first step in opening up the channels.

The Formal Kickoff

Although some projects don't require more than a small meeting and a memo to get started, when a formal project kickoff event is appropriate, the event should be both celebratory and informative. Some common formal kickoff events include:

➤ A slide show or multimedia presentation of the project in an auditorium with buffet lunch or snacks served afterward.

➤ A sit-down dinner with motivational speakers, formal introductions of key project personnel, and a spectacular multimedia display of project goals and objectives.

➤ A pizza and beer party at a local pub, where you talk enthusiastically about the project and introduce the various team members to each other. Here you'll also review the documents that describe the project.

➤ A meeting of all key project supervisors in the board room with coffee and a presentation on the overhead projector led by the project manager. A formal summary of the project plan is provided to all the attendees.

➤ In a distributed project with team members located all over the country or even the globe (these are becoming more common), you might want to use the opening of the project Web site as a kick off event and produce a project announcement video for viewing on the Web. You might even want to have a project chat session or video conference with the people involved.

The type of event will depend on the size, importance, organization, and budget for the project. Use your judgment. Look at the kinds of events given in your company for similar projects—and ask about the events that worked and the ones that didn't. If a customer is paying the bill, keep the event simple and economical.

It's a Go

Regardless of the sophistication or format of the kickoff event, the event should put team members on notice that the project is a "go." The event should emphasize that each individual's contribution is vital to the success of the project. The kickoff event can also help individuals relate their goals and work responsibilities within the overall project to the efforts of other team members. This is a first step in establishing a "team" spirit.

In most cases, a formal kickoff for a large project should include stakeholders, customers (if appropriate), managers, and most of the key team members, even if their contributions won't be required for weeks or months down the road.

The kickoff event should also establish the priorities, tone, and energy for the project. The kickoff should avoid too many individual details; leave those for the first project meetings and one-on-one sessions with key project players. These meetings should take place during the first week after the project kickoff event.

Words from the Wise

"[The project is] underfunded and doomed, but I've got inertia going and I'm setting up the Marketing Department to take the blame."

—Adapted from Dilbert by Scott Adams

Between Kickoff and Team Meeting: Use the Time Wisely

The time between the project kickoff and the first formal project meeting (usually three days to a week is recommended) gives team members time to reflect on their roles. Feedback after the kickoff event is invaluable to plugging up holes in the project plan. During the period before D-Day (the day of the first project meeting), you may have team members approaching you with questions or problems.

Based on the feedback, you can fine-tune your project plan and look into problems that team members throw at you. You can also run issues and problems by senior management to level out the small molehills before they turn into major mountains. Gathering feedback allows you to come to the project meeting prepared with answers to objections and explanations of issues that were inadequately addressed in the plan.

The First Project Meeting

After the kickoff event, you're finally underway! You'll need to schedule the first team meeting in about a week (or less for a small, short project). This meeting will be the first true test of your leadership skills as the project manager.

All working members of the project implementation team should be invited. (Customers and the executive management team should not be invited.) This is a meeting to get work started. The first team project review meeting should accomplish the following:

➤ Establish a model for future meetings.

1. Start on time.

2. Develop and distribute an agenda of objectives before the meeting.

3. Conduct one agenda item at a time and conclude it before moving on to the next item. (Avoid getting hung up on the order of topics.)

4. Encourage open communication; meetings give individuals a chance to express suppressed ideas.

5. Take notes.

6. Establish the time and place for the next project team review meeting.

7. Agree on and reiterate any follow-up activities or action items required. Be sure to assign people to these tasks and get their commitment to complete them.

8. End the meeting on time.

9. Distribute (brief) minutes to all attendees within two days of the meeting.

10. Make sure the action items and responsibilities are indicated in the minutes (so that people don't conveniently forget what they agreed to do in the meeting).

➤ Introduce the members of the team and their project roles.

➤ Review the first priorities for the project and repeat/reiterate briefly the other objectives and overall schedule.

➤ Review individual plans for getting work started.

➤ Discuss methods and tools to be used to manage, control, and operate the project.

➤ Deal with objections to the current project plan and work them out if possible.

➤ If decisions need to be made by the group, follow these steps:

1. Discuss the problems and seek opinions from all.

2. Don't allow one person to dominate the discussion.

3. Test for readiness to make a decision.

4. Make the decision.

5. Assign roles and responsibilities.

One-on-Ones: The Individual Starting Events

In addition to the kickoff and the first project meeting, you'll need to meet with key individuals at the beginning of the project to make sure they have all the information they need to get started. These initial meetings with new players may continue throughout the project as different aspects of the project get underway.

Formal meetings with project team members, known as *one-on-ones,* should be used to clarify priorities and to discuss schedules and plans. Many of the people will have worked with you on the project plan already, so you won't need to go over all the details with these folks. However, you will need to turn their focus away from planning and start delegating work to these people so things start happening.

One-on-ones with key players should also be scheduled on a regular basis throughout the project. For a short project, the one-on-ones might happen daily or weekly with key personnel. For a longer project with more players, the formal one-on-ones might be monthly or even less frequent depending on your other level of interactions.

Project Lingo

One-on-ones are meetings (often scheduled and formal) between two people involved in a project. These meetings are used to discuss priorities, to re-solve issues, and to communicate overall responsibilities to the project.

In the first one-on-one meetings, the following should be clarified and reviewed with each individual:

➤ Why he or she was selected

➤ Performance expectations

➤ Individual priorities, tasks, and milestones

➤ Administrative procedures and project management methods and tools in use

➤ Challenges and issues

➤ Processes for solving problems

➤ A schedule for future one-on-one meetings

➤ Action items for future meetings

Always take notes in these meetings. Suggest that the other participant do the same.

Step Up or Flub Up?

Your ability to organize and control the first team meetings will be a major step in establishing your leadership of the project team. If you do this well, the meetings will serve as a model for subsequent project meetings and will set a tone of open communication and professionalism that will make managing your project a lot easier. If you flub up the meetings, you'll not only waste the time used on the meetings, you'll also lose credibility as the project manager. Preparation, organization, and focus are critical to making the first team meetings a success.

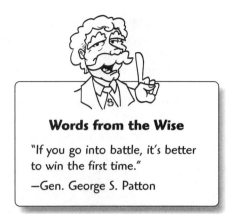

Words from the Wise

"If you go into battle, it's better to win the first time."

—Gen. George S. Patton

Information Everyone Needs to Get Started

The purpose of the kickoff and the initial meetings is to inform people and get them in synch with the project plan. From the beginning, people who work on the project need access to relevant information in the plan so they can do their jobs. Tasks and schedules should never be a secret (although budget and other financial information may be held confidential when people aren't responsible for the costs). The project plan should generally be an open book to help guide people to the promised land.

Provide every member of the team with a summary of the plan during the initial stages of the project. This can be done before the kickoff event, in a team meeting, or during a one-on-one at the very start of the project. For team members who will remain with the project from the beginning, we recommend presenting these documents prior to the kickoff event and then discussing them in the first project meeting and one-on-one sessions. As new team members join the project during later stages, you'll need to make sure they get the information as well.

Here are the pieces of information from the project plan that every team member needs in order to contribute appropriately to the project:

➤ A summary of the overall project goals. The project summary outlines and explains the purpose of the project, its goals, and the overall schedule.

➤ The team member's role and task assignments. The specific tasks and milestones for each team member (or subteam) should be laid out in writing. At the beginning, the milestones and task overview might be general with specific tasks being introduced by you or other supervisors and managers at a later date.

➤ A list of who's who on the project. The directory or list of key project team members should include a description of each team member, his or her role (and title) in the project, and contact information (telephone numbers, office location, and e-mail addresses).

In addition to information about the project plan, every team member needs to be informed of the administrative procedures that will affect his or her life: reports, forms, legal documents, and so on. Don't drown team members in paper. If your reports to them are crisp and timely, their reports will hopefully be on time and accurate. For a large project, you may want to provide a "Project Administration Handbook" that assembles examples of all the forms, reports, and other documents required from project personnel, along with other relevant documentation of the project plan. For small projects, a simple list and an example report will probably do the job.

Time Is Money

Always remember: What you don't know hurts you. And what your team doesn't know will also hurt you.

You should also let team members know that regular status reports are required. Explain why the reports are essential to tracking the project and keeping it on time and within budget. Set the report intervals for weekly, biweekly, or monthly intervals, depending on the nature of the project. Present people with sample reports and completed forms that set the expectations for their reports. (We offer more recommendations on reporting frequencies and formats in Chapter 21.)

If confidentiality or other legal agreements are required for your project, now is the time to get them signed. If your organization contracts with the military or other government agencies, rules may be more strict. Look into the proper forms of agreement and reporting that are required and make sure the appropriate team members understand the requirements at the beginning of the project.

Avoid the Floating Start Date

Getting a project started is key to finishing a project successfully. The right information in the right hands goes a long way to make things happen. A project with a floating start date, however, never goes anywhere. If you kick off a project and then fail to follow through with clear delegation of the work to get it started, you may have a good plan, but you won't have a project.

Never rev up your team to tackle mountains unless you're really ready to reach the summit. If a project fails to happen as announced, you'll likely find that the team has lost interest by the time you decide you're ready to begin work. Team members may even find something else to do that precludes their participation. Delays also mean adjusting the dates in your carefully honed project plan and getting things approved all over again.

The following is a list of information that every team member needs for every project:

➤ A summary of project objectives and milestones

➤ An organization chart of the project (large projects only)

➤ A description of key personnel on the project and their roles

➤ A personal task list

➤ Enough authority to do the job and an understanding of the limits of that authority

➤ The schedule

➤ Due dates for reports, meetings, and other recurring activities

➤ Samples of required reports, forms, and other documents

➤ Procedures for reporting problems and suggesting changes to the project

➤ Contact information for key project personnel and vendors

If you kick off the project, be sure to follow through with the next play. If you start as planned, you'll have a lot better chance of finishing as scheduled.

The Least You Need to Know

➤ Getting a project started right involves communication.

➤ All projects need starting events that clarify project goals, responsibilities, and operating procedures. These events can be simple or elaborate but should always be commensurate with the size and importance of the project.

➤ Prior to the first project team meeting, a review of the project by team members may point out holes in your plan that need patching.

➤ At the beginning, all (or at least most) major problems, whether financial or political, should be satisfied in the plan.

➤ Focused, productive, and informative team and individual meetings are the best way to get things started on the right track.

Chapter 18

Leadership and You: Taking the Bull by the Horns

In This Chapter

➤ Your role (and as James Thurber said, "Welcome to It")

➤ Establishing your role as leader and manager

➤ Management by walking around (MBWA)

➤ The leader in times of crisis

Since people will complete the work specified in the plan, you, as the project manager, must employ appropriate methods to motivate, coordinate, facilitate, and administer your project team. If you don't, the work may never get done. As a project manager, you must also identify and implement the appropriate leadership style for keeping the team motivated.

The Importance of Establishing Your Leadership

Whether managing the remodeling of the Empire State Building or the installation of a projection TV in a restaurant, you must take command to lead your project to success. You can use every technique in this book, but without assuming leadership of the project, you'll get nowhere. You must become the leader and manager of the project if you want to succeed.

As a leader, you will command authority and take responsibility for guiding the project. You will also be a trusted and reliable source of information on the project. As a leader, you will be expected by your team to be honest, competent, and inspirational.

As a manager, you will monitor and control the project through to completion using specific techniques and procedures that establish the framework and structure of the project. You'll review the plan, complete reports, balance the budget, update the plan, fix the schedule, update the plan again, report on the updates to the plan, and yes, update it again. You'll also do a lot of other administrative stuff that will drive you crazy. You'll continue to "manage upward" in keeping the key project stakeholders informed and involved about project decisions.

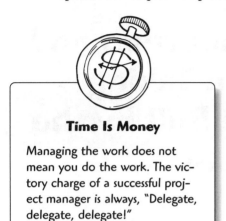

Time Is Money

Managing the work does not mean you do the work. The victory charge of a successful project manager is always, "Delegate, delegate, delegate!"

Some people get so caught up in management that they forget about leadership. It's possible to complete the management part of the project and not attain the status and influence of a leader. That's why we've written this chapter—to make sure all those project management traits get transformed into leadership skills as well.

Wearing the BIG Shoes

You must be a leader who provides strong guidance but at the same time offers a receptive ear to people with problems. Your team members may not always fill the big shoes you've offered them. The well-known Murphy's Law often ensures that anything can go wrong on projects from the tiniest to the most colossal.

As a leader, you should also know the plan inside and out and be able to talk to the team about priorities without sounding frustrated or rushed. If a team member has a problem that requires discussion, as a leader, you should always be seen as a resource to seek out rather than as an obstacle to avoid.

Also remember from Chapter 4 that, as a successful project manager, you must be both a manager and a leader. Managers go to meetings and complete paperwork. Leaders must gain the trust and respect of the project team. People must feel comfortable taking your directions; otherwise, they'll make up their own. Yes, as a manager, you must develop protocol and administrative procedures for ensuring that work is getting done on time and within budget. But establishing yourself as a leader is more important than any report or process.

Leadership style and your management tactics are intertwined and are central to the successful implementation of the project. Your skills and the appropriateness of the management tactics you adopt for each of the various people on your project team are of paramount importance in achieving project goals. There are lots of hard-nosed books on becoming a leader, but we favor a simple, soft approach involving only eight steps:

➤ Listen to the people.

➤ Ask lots of questions.

➤ Observe what is going on and take notes.

➤ Know enough to know that you don't know everything.

➤ Be available when people need you.

➤ Make decisions when called upon to make decisions, but also know when decisions should be deferred to other stakeholders with more authority.

➤ Delegate the work that needs to be delegated.

➤ Don't micromanage. You manage the project; they manage their work.

A Style That Gets the Job Done

Business writers have described a wide range of effective leadership styles that can be adapted to meet the needs of different people, organizations, and projects. You'll need to choose from three basic styles to lead your project:

➤ Task-oriented leadership emphasizes getting the job done and concentrating on methods for assigning and organizing work, making decisions, and evaluating performance.

➤ Employee-oriented or people-oriented leadership concentrates on open communication, the development of rapport with team members, and an ongoing direct concern for the needs of subordinates.

➤ Reward-based leadership ties positive feedback and other rewards directly to the work accomplished. The reward-based style assumes that a high level of performance will be maintained if work results in meaningful rewards that correlate directly with the quality of the person's efforts. Rewards include pay and promotion but also encompass support, encouragement, security, and respect from the project manager.

The approach of matching management style to the specific needs of a situation is often called situational management or contingency theory. Project managers must effectively apply the best style for the job—whether task-oriented, employee-oriented, or reward-oriented leadership—to meet the needs of individual team members.

As you try to implement a style, don't assume that, because you like something done a certain way, your team members will have the same preferences. Individuals differ from one another in experience and personality. Each person has a different conception of how the job should be done, who should get credit for the effort, and how each individual should be rewarded for his or her work. For these reasons, different leadership styles and management methods must be used to monitor and coordinate different projects.

How to Be a Leader

There are two components to project leadership: visibility and communication. First, you must be visible in the role as project manager. Second, you must communicate your intentions and the progress of the project to team members on a regular basis.

Taking the Reins Through Communication

Communication and leadership go hand in hand. The project managers who consistently succeed in bringing their projects in on time and within budget are those who effectively manage the interfaces and communications between people and organizations. The people working on your project, and other members of the project team, need to be comfortable with bringing issues to your attention. This goes for people who report directly to you, their managers, and your managers as well.

Three types of communications must occur for a project to be managed effectively:

1. **Vertical communications.** These are the up-and-down organizational communications based on the hierarchical relationships established on an organization chart.

2. **Horizontal communications.** Horizontal or lateral communications involve communicating and coordinating activities with peers.

3. **Diagonal communications.** The diagonal relationships are rarely shown on organization charts, but they are almost always important to the success of a project. Diagonal communications involve upward relationships with managers and officers from other areas and with subordinate groups in other departments. They also include downward diagonal communications with third parties such as contractors, suppliers, or consultants.

Words from the Wise

"The greatest mistake an executive can make is to be afraid of making a mistake."

—John Capozzi, *If You Want the Rainbow You Gotta Put Up with the Rain* (1997)

If you have established the requisite communications in all three dimensions before conflicts occur, when the inevitable conflicts do arise between organizations, styles, procedures, or priorities, there will be an established channel available for resolving issues. If you have established the basis for discussion before the conflicts arise, the resolution process will usually be easier.

Meeting regularly with team members, reporting to them on team accomplishments and success (or lack thereof) in meeting objectives, and becoming a resource of project knowledge, suggestions, and conflict resolution is what makes you the leader. Your team members will look to you as a central clearinghouse of knowledge and praise (and you should provide plenty of the latter).

This is not to say that some team members won't be uncooperative, but much of this eases once a project is underway and your—for lack of a better word—charm builds a cohesive team bent on meeting schedule dates and making you and them look good!

Good Communication from a Real Leader

If you want to be a really good communicator and a leader as well, here are some guidelines to follow:

➤ Hold regular meetings with team members—and don't cancel them. Effective meetings should start with the project kickoff (described in Chapter 17) and should continue throughout the life of the project.

➤ Meet both in groups and individually. Some things that won't be said in front of other team members in meetings may come out in one-on-one sessions. In groups, simmering conflicts, which won't be mentioned in private, may rear their heads.

➤ Provide your team with constant feedback on the project's status. Be available, friendly, and willing to discuss anything that team members are burdened with—from project problems to personal problems. Include outside vendors in relevant project conversations as you deem appropriate.

➤ Keep meetings short and to the point. Team members respect leaders who don't waste their time. Have meetings over lunch (you buy). That way, you have the benefit of a congenial conversation coupled with time required for the project. And everyone likes a free lunch.

Time Is Money

Projects are becoming increasingly virtual—staffed speedily by transient, dispersed teams. Achieving to potential under these conditions requires distributed project leadership using "virtual walking around" techniques via computer networks and the Internet. These techniques help people communicate, collaborate, and manage shared tasks in an integrated way.

➤ Save major parties and celebrations for important milestones and accomplishments. Members of your team, especially those with life commitments such as small children, may resent too much time spent on work-related dinners. Many people regard evening "get-togethers" as extensions to their workday.

➤ Use written messages like golden bullets. Written communications are important, but fire off very few and make them count.

Good leaders know how to prepare effective messages. Here are some guidelines to help your messages achieve your best intentions:

➤ Always think through the politics before you communicate. Before you send any message (oral or written), consider the potential effects the message may have after it is received.

➤ Be aware of all the people who will receive your message, even if they're not on the address line or at the meeting. Consider the people who will be copied, given the cover sheet, or told about the message over coffee in the cafeteria.

➤ Decide on both the format for the message (letter, e-mail, fax, telephone, face-to-face) and the timing. Writing is permanent and not soon forgotten, so always make written messages something you won't mind being brought up again. Oral messages can be misconstrued, so if absolute clarity over time is required, put it in writing as well.

➤ Make sure the content, tone, vocabulary, style, length, and grammar are exactly what you want to say.

➤ Always follow up on the message to see if it was received and understood. Note reactions and ramifications so you can do better next time—or change the approach if the message didn't accomplish what you expected.

➤ When in doubt, don't send the message.

➤ Keep written communication brief and to the point unless complex technical instructions are involved. No written communication should exceed one or two pages; otherwise, almost no one will plod through it.

Taking the Reins Through Visibility

The project manager's classic mistake is to climb into an ivory tower and effectively disappear. The disappearing act may be accidental as you get buried in a project problem, management dispute, paperwork, or just a lot of busy days. But the results are the same. When you're invisible, the project team assumes one or all of the following:

➤ You don't care about the project or them.

➤ The project is unimportant to the organization.

➤ You are an ineffective project manager/team leader who should be replaced.

Also note that, if team members perceive you to be invisible, they may feel free to make decisions and act on their own, sometimes to the detriment of the project. Worse, if you're invisible and team members perceive they are working on a doomed project, they may work actively to save their own reputations (and point fingers at you) instead of pulling together to make the project succeed.

For these reasons, you must become a Visible (with a capital V) member of the project team as well as a leader. Avoid the ivory tower routine and rendezvous regularly with the troops. Pitch in. When a body is needed for anything from draining the castle swamp to stapling 500 copies of the agenda for a frenzied user conference, be there if possible. Role up your sleeves and become an in-the-trench hard worker who inspires the team as well as leads it. You'll make friends, will make your workers appreciate you as a comrade, and will get a little project-related work done at the same time.

Use Management By Walking Around (MBWA)

Remember that the channels of communication are best opened by you being physically visible. When supervising a project, just walking around and chatting with the participants will improve both the quality and the timeliness of the work underway; it also will give you essential information on project progress. Building a 200-foot condo complex? On the phone, the foreman may claim progress on the tenth story. On-site, however, you may see that only nine stories are in place. By using MBWA, you get a real-life assessment of project progress, some exercise, and the chance to work out problems team members are experiencing. At the same time, you are building visibility as project leader, are establishing and strengthening communications channels, and are making sure that everyone knows you care about the project. It helps if you appear that you love working on it, too!

Leading a Technical Project When You Don't Have Expertise

You don't have to have technical knowledge to provide leadership to a technical project or to supervise engineers working in a discipline you know little or nothing about. Instead, you need to be an efficient project manager capable of listening intelligently and understanding and handling the human and business issues at hand. Yes, it's possible that technical people may try to "snow" you with jargon, but you can work around these efforts to stall the project.

Always talk regularly to each member of the technical team, insist on periodic updates, and ask (with genuine enthusiasm) to see results, no matter how small. At the same time, never allow a single team member to be the only repository of key project data. Instead, insist that more than one member of the technical team understand (or at least be involved in) key technical areas. Keep copies of work descriptions on paper or on backup tapes/disks and archive them regularly (off-site!) as additional backup and protection from acts of God (and disgruntled workers).

Being All Things to All People

As project manager, you change roles from day to day. One day, you may feel like a hands-on manager in charge of a group of productive, motivated employees. The next day, you may be relegated to a position that's really little more than that of petty bureaucrat, shuffling papers and dull appointments all day.

The role of project manager also changes as the project proceeds. At the beginning, during the initiation and planning phases, your role focuses on creating a vision for the project and working with stakeholders (managers, customers, and other project beneficiaries) to reach consensus on the goals and objectives of the project. Then, as the project proceeds into the executing phase, your role involves supporting, coaching, and otherwise guiding people to the promised land of project completion. You'll also have to spend time communicating the project status to the stakeholders to make sure they remain happy with the results you are achieving as the project proceeds.

In all these roles, you will be expected to excel. Obviously, you can't be all things to all people. But as a project manager who is also a leader, you better be—at the very least—a lot of the right things to most of the project team.

The Leader in Times of Crisis

To be the authority when things don't go right is the toughest challenge of all. You may have done 699 things right but blown it accidentally on number 700. Sadly, no one will look at the 699. Instead, they'll focus on—well, you can guess!

Avoiding problems is the obvious approach, but what can you do when 500 red bricks accidentally smash through your new glass ceiling? Before considering a long trip to Katmandu where no one can find you, consider these alternatives:

➤ Study the mishap, whether it's a failure to deliver or a public relations nightmare. Get a firm grasp on all aspects of the problem and focus on how it impacts project objectives, budget, and schedule.

➤ Call the team or team managers to an emergency meeting. Ask for suggestions and recommendations. Weigh each recommendation carefully and consider the cost and time for implementation.

➤ Adjourn to your office, home, or another quiet haven and pour over the suggestions to see which will cost the least and can be implemented the fastest with the least damage to project outcomes.

➤ Act to salvage the project. Be up-front and honest with management, customers, and team members. Quick response, decisive decisions, and team spirit must be used to pull the project out of the hole. If you need 24 hours to revise the project schedule, then have a couple of cups of coffee and do it. Most importantly, communicate the schedule fix and any new elements to bridge the gap causing the problem.

➤ Never let a project get the best of you. Eat well, get enough sleep, and work hard while taking care of your team members and yourself.

If you can do all the things we've talked about in this chapter and still keep your spirits up and your focus on the project goals, you'll become the leader the project needs to make it to the finish line.

The Least You Need to Know

➤ To lead any project, visibility and appropriate communications are essential.

➤ Your team members look to you for problem resolution, team management, and feedback both positive and negative. Make sure you give them what they need in appropriate doses.

➤ No project is an island. Your dedication is central to maintaining the schedule and controlling the budget to bring the project to successful fruition.

➤ Anyone with a good plan, dedication, and basic people skills can lead a project. The trick is really the people skills.

➤ A true leader can fix almost any project problem by adjusting objectives and realigning the project team and stakeholders.

Chapter 19

What an Organization!

In This Chapter

➤ Creating an organization that works

➤ Pointing team members in the same direction

➤ Considering various project structures

➤ Communicating, coordinating, and cooperating are the keys to teamwork

➤ Keeping focused on the end results

How can you know what the right organization is for your project team? How do you get people to move where you want them to go? Who should lead the work and who should follow orders? In this chapter, we look at some of the pros, cons, and alternatives so you can organize your players for maximum impact.

No Easy Task, but Someone Has to Organize These Guys

Creating a productive project organization is no easy task, even for a small project. Politics get in the way, people get sick, and your boxcar load of widgets from Mexico fails to materialize—and someone always gets blamed. As on *Jeopardy,* the answer is: "Build an adaptive structure coupled with personnel contingency plans." The question is: "How do I organize my project team correctly?"

These are the three C's in successful project organizations: Communication, Cooperation, and Coordination.

Making Sure Everyone Is on the Same Train

Structuring a project organization means more than just choosing team members and committing outside vendors to specific tasks. To function effectively, your project team members require clear reporting responsibilities and a roadmap to their location in the project. On top of this, your core team may require ancillary support such as administrative assistants, computer installers, technical help, and others who are trained, ready, available, and prepared for secondary but vital duties.

Turning all these people into a viable project team involves cementing relationships, making the right resources available in a timely manner to the right people, implementing reporting relationships, and establishing a schedule that works. Because people are involved, it sounds easier than it is.

The Human Drama—Personality, Politics, and Corporate Culture

To help you understand ways to organize the people in your project, you can compare your project team to the cast members in a play or a movie. You have the producers and backers of the project (managers and other stakeholders), the director (the project manager), the main actors (the workers who play a role throughout all or most of the project), the bit players (people who do one important task and then disappear from the scene), and the cameo players (the important people, such as consultants or advisors, who may add value to the project but don't necessarily stick around through the entire undertaking). You also have the special-effects folks and the production crew, who have special skills but aren't as visible as other members of the cast. You may have prima donnas and stars in your project team, and these people need special care and attention.

As you consider the organization of your cast, you'll need to develop a structure to get things done. Lead players, bit players, and cameo players might possibly be directed (supervised) by assistant directors (other managers), and the production crew might work for lead crew or assistant producers.

Sometimes, after you design your ideal project organization, you'll find that the first choice for a team member in a particular role is not even a possibility. For example, a person you would like to use in the project may not be available because of commitments to other, higher-priority projects. Or, you may ask to use one person from an organization and the manager

Words from the Wise

"There are two ways of being creative. One can sing and dance. Or one can create an environment in which singers and dancers flourish."

—Warren Bennis

from the group assigns a different person to your project. Thus, you may not get the experience you want and might have to adjust the schedule to accommodate for the slow learning curve.

If you say you need a person with a particular skill for your project and the line manager (middle manager) assigns a person to you, you usually must accept this person's judgment unless you can make a good case for someone you have more direct experience with. If you find out later that the assigned person lacks the required skills, you can negotiate or look at other alternatives.

Project managers often need to make these kinds of concessions to other managers to get people for a project. It's like signing up Sean Connery to star in your movie and then finding out that Eddie Murphy was assigned the role instead. Obviously, the script and direction will require some adaptations.

The Proud, the Few, the Project Team

When talented athletes play on a basketball team, they all share and support the same goal (to win the game). To this end, the team members generally follow the lead of the coach, and each player does his or her best to fulfill the specific role assigned in each play. Even the stars, like Michael Jordan, must follow the rules of the game. People on your project team need to play their positions in the same way.

For the people working on your project to become a real team, some specific things need to happen with your coaching and leadership as project manager. Project members need to:

1. Realize that they'll be working on tasks that involve more than one person. Therefore, they'll need to communicate and cooperate with each other to get things done.

2. Share common methods and tools for assessing and communicating the status of the project.

3. Identify and solve problems together—and then live with the results (together).

4. Accept the fact that, if one person messes up, the entire team suffers. Therefore, they need to help each other avoid as many mess-ups as possible.

5. Realize that new people will be joining and other people will be leaving the project as time goes on, but the overall team structure and project goals will remain the same until the project reaches fruition.

When other organizations or departments are involved, positive interaction between the project manager and these organizations is also critical to creating a good team. The relationships among line, staff, vendor, customer, and project personnel must be tempered with mutual trust.

On Becoming a Team—The Basic Ways to Organize People

Even though infinite possible combinations of people are involved, there are only a few basic ways you can structure the organization of a project. These include functional (or line) organizations, pure-project structures, matrix organizations, or mixed organizational structures. These structures may be distributed over multiple locations as well, making the organization more of a virtual team in cyberspace rather than a group of people in a defined location. And as you'd expect, each organization has its pros and cons.

High Water!

There are times when an individual has a unique technical skill and must be given a supervisory or leadership role regardless of how difficult this person is to work with. In this situation, you (and the rest of the team) just have to learn to work with the difficult personality to get the job done. This is one of the standard challenges project managers must handle with aplomb.

The Functional Project Organization

On a project that uses people from the same organization, the existing line organization can be used to manage the project. This organizational structure is appropriate when the project is clearly the responsibility of one department. Many small projects use the functional organization as the project organization. A functional project is assigned to the functional department or division in a company that has the most interest and technical ability to complete the project. Almost all tasks in a project organized as part of a functional organization will be completed within the one functional area. Existing managers in the department double as project managers.

The advantages of using a functional organization to complete a project include:

➤ **Familiarity of the team**   The team members are already familiar with each other, and the skill levels of the staff are clearly understood.

➤ **Established administrative systems**   The general administrative policies and procedures are already understood by the team and cost centers.

➤ **Staff availability**   The staff is readily available to the project because the line managers control the staff assignments. Thus, there are few, if any, interdepartmental conflicts over the use of resources.

➤ **Scheduling efficiency**   The scheduling of staff can be highly efficient. As a staff member is required, the person can immediately be assigned to a task and then return to routine work without serious logistical interruptions.

➤ **Clear authority**   The lines of authority and communication are understood. Thus, the conflicts between project authority and line authority are minimized.

The disadvantages of using a functional organization include:

➤ **Project isolation**   The project may be completed in isolation from other parts of the company and may fail to realize larger strategic goals as a result. However, if new collaboration, networking, and Web-based tools are employed, this isolation can be minimized.

➤ **Limited resources**   The project is limited to the technical resources within the department, which may not be adequate to complete the tasks required. Of course, outside vendors and consultants can be hired, but expertise within other departments of the company is not readily available. This may lead to inefficiencies or redundancies in the project organization.

➤ **Bureaucratic procedures**   There may be more levels of approval than really necessary for the project because of the established bureaucracy in the line organization. This may impede progress and slow decision-making.

➤ **Lack of project focus**   The project may lack focus or priority in a functional organization because it is not the only work being done. Thus, routine departmental work may interfere with project work. In addition, motivation for project work may suffer because the project is considered "additional" or "optional" work as opposed to being a clear responsibility.

➤ **Department orientation**   The project may suffer from "department-think." This occurs when the priorities of the department become the project priorities, regardless of the actual goals for the project. Work outside the department's normal concerns is given little attention, and the "finished" project may not be complete or may suffer quality problems as a result.

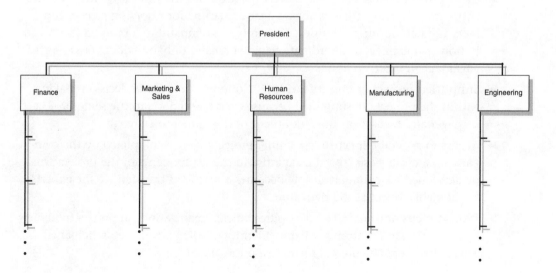

A functional organization.

The Pure-Project Organization

In a pure-project structure, a team or "task force" is put together to accomplish the project's goals. In such an organization, all the team members report to the project manager during the course of the project. The team members do not have responsibility to other managers or jobs during the course of their work on the project. When a team member's responsibility for the project is complete, the person returns to another job or is assigned to another project. Only one project and one job are assigned at a time.

In the direct version of the pure-project structure, every project team member reports directly to the project manager. This is appropriate for small projects with 15 or fewer people involved. In the indirect version of the pure-project structure (suitable for larger projects), the project manager may have assistant managers or supervisors to manage subprojects or functional areas within the project. As in an ordinary line organization, the supervisors and assistants report directly to the project manager, and the various functional teams within the project report to the second-level managers. Extremely large projects may have multiple management levels, just like a corporation.

Pure-project organizations are found in companies fulfilling large government projects or in some engineering-driven companies that produce predictable model updates for their products. Large construction projects often employ a pure-project organization as well. If work on a complex, priority project spans a year or more, a pure-project organization is often an advantage.

The advantages of the pure-project organization include:

➤ **Clear project authority**   The project manager has true line authority over the entire project. Thus, there is always a clear channel for resolving project conflicts and determining priorities. The unity of command in a pure-project organization results in each subordinate having one and only one direct boss—a clear advantage in most situations.

➤ **Simplified project communications**   Communication and decision-making within the project are simplified because everyone reports to the same project manager and focuses on the attainment of the same project goals.

➤ **Access to special expertise**   If similar projects will be completed by the company on a cyclic basis, specific expertise in the components of the project will be developed over time. It simply becomes a matter of transferring the experts to the right project at the right time.

➤ **Project focus and priority**   The pure-project organization supports a total view of the project and a strong, separate identity on the part of the participants. This helps keeps the project focused and integrated.

There are distinct disadvantages to the pure-project approach, however, including:

➤ **Duplication of efforts**   If a company has multiple projects with important goals in progress at the same time, some efforts may be duplicated, making the overall cost of the projects higher than necessary.

➤ **Unclear loyalties and motivations**   Project members form strong attachments to the project and each other, which is good. When the project is terminated, however, the team must be disbanded, and this leads to uncertainty and conflict. Team members fear layoffs or anticipate assignments in undesirable projects in the future. Thus, keeping technically qualified people happy over the long haul becomes a major challenge.

➤ **Intracompany rivalry**   Rivalry and competition may become strong between various projects in a company that uses pure-project organization for its major projects. This results in a company that competes with itself instead of with the competition—an ugly state of affairs.

➤ **Uncertain reintegration of resources**   Integrating a pure-project group back into the functional organization can be fraught with problems. People who were involved in the project may be considered "outsiders" when they return to their original jobs, or the jobs may have changed during the course of the project.

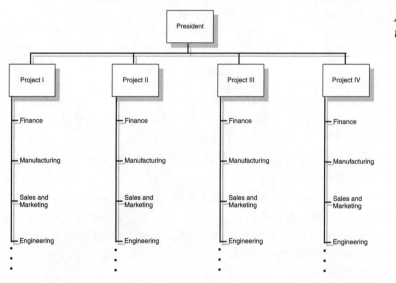

A pure-project organization.

The Matrix Organization

Implementing project management techniques sets in motion a significant change in the culture of an organization. One of the more common results of using project management in business is the introduction of "matrix management"—a situation in which people report to multiple managers. Matrix management involves coordinating a web of relationships that come about when people join the project team and are subject to the resulting multiple authority-responsibility-accountability relationships in the organization.

The matrix organization is an attempt to take advantage of the benefits of a pure-project organization while maintaining the advantages of the functional organization. It is rare to find pure-project or pure-functional organizations in business any more. Matrix organizations are typical today, even when other project management tools aren't involved.

In a matrix organization, a clear project team is established that crosses organizational boundaries. Thus, team members may come from various departments. A project manager for each project is clearly defined, and projects are managed as separate and focused activities. The project manager may report to a higher-level executive or to one of the functional managers with the most interest in the project. However, the specific team members still report to their functional departments and maintain responsibilities for routine departmental work in their functional areas. In addition, people may be assigned to multiple project teams with different responsibilities. The problem of coordination that plagues other project structures is minimized because the most important personnel for a project work together as a defined team within the matrix project structure.

The management responsibilities in these projects are temporary—a supervisor on one project may be a worker on another project, depending on the skills required. If project managers in a matrix situation do not have good relationships with line managers in the organization, conflicts may arise over authority over employees' work and priorities. Not everyone adapts well to the matrix structure for this and other related reasons.

The complexity that a matrix organization causes is clear: People have multiple managers, multiple priorities, and multiple role identities. Because of these complexities, before an organization enters into matrix organizational structures, at least two of the following criteria for the project or the enterprise should be met:

➤ A need to share scarce or unique resources that are required in more than one project or functional area

➤ A requirement for management to provide high levels of information processing and communication to complete the project

➤ Pressure from the outside by customers or agencies to have one person or group centralize control of the project even though the project may be carried out by other groups in the organization

In cases in which projects meet these criteria, the matrix organization has distinct advantages:

➤ **Clear project focus** The project has clear focus and priority because it has its own separate organization and management. Most of the planning and control advantages of a pure-project structure are realized in a matrix organization.

238

➤ **Flexible staffing**   Staffing is relatively flexible in matrix organizations because resources from various line organizations are available without job reassignment. Scarce technical resources are available to a wide range of projects in a company that regularly employs matrix-organized projects.

➤ **Adaptability to management needs and skills**   The authority of the project manager can be expansive or limited, depending on the priority of the project. If a project manager has strong authority, he or she has command authority over most of the project. If a project manager has weak authority, the line managers have a strong influence on project activities. Thus, the matrix organization can be adapted to a wide range of projects—some that need strong support from line managers and some that require independent management.

➤ **Staff development opportunities**   People can be given new challenges and responsibilities that are not as likely to be offered in a purely functional organization. People can gain exposure to new technical areas, develop management skills, and have new experiences that maintain their interest and motivation at work. Ultimately, these new experiences can lead to more effective employees with high degrees of independence and flexibility. And because people tend to be more responsible for the quality of their own work in project-oriented groups, overall corporate productivity can improve.

➤ **Adaptability to business changes**   Matrix organizations can adapt more quickly to changing technological and market conditions than traditional, purely functional organizations. This is largely because of the high people-to-people contact in these organizations. In addition, matrix-organized projects encourage entrepreneurship and creative thinking that crosses functional responsibilities.

The disadvantages and potential conflicts within a matrix organization must be understood and dealt with to take advantage of the benefits of matrix management. The more frequently reported problems in matrix managed organizations include:

➤ **Built-in conflicts**   Conflicts between line management priorities and project management priorities are inevitable. The question of who is in charge affects both the project and routine departmental work. The division of authority and responsibility relationships in matrix organizations is inherently complex. Matrix organizations are no place for intractable, autocratic managers with narrow views of organizational responsibilities.

➤ **Resistance to termination**   As in pure-project organizations, team members may prefer their project roles to their line responsibilities, creating interesting motivational challenges for managers. Because the team members have unique identities and relationships in their project roles, matrixed projects often resist termination.

➤ **Complex command and authority relationships** There is no unity of command in a matrix organization—a clear violation of traditional management principles. The team member is often caught between conflicting demands of the line manager and the project manager. The discomfort and uncertainty of having more than one boss at the same time cannot be adequately described to someone who has never experienced the situation. Of course, if the two bosses are adequately trained and are open in their communications, many of these difficulties can be resolved or eliminated.

➤ **Complex employee recognition systems** In a matrix organization, which manager should complete the employee's performance reviews or make recommendations for raises? If the reward responsibilities and authorities of the project manager and the line manager are not clearly identified, the employee may feel unrecognized. It is imperative that both line responsibilities and project responsibilities are accounted for in the employee's performance review process. Some form of reward system needs to be established for team members within the project—whether this is just public acknowledgment of a job well done or formal monetary rewards depends on the project and your budget.

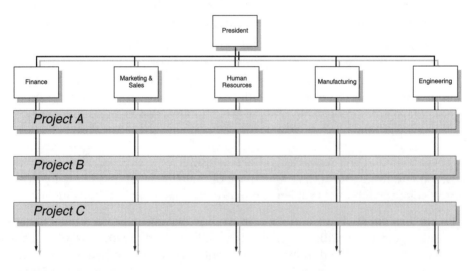

A matrix organization.

The Mixed Organization

Some companies employ a mixture of functional, matrix, and pure-project organizations to accomplish enterprise goals. In companies with a wide range of projects, a project office may be set up to help administer projects as well. The people in this office provide expertise and assistance in planning and tracking projects. In other companies, the project office may become a division in its own right with full-time project managers and staff responsible for project-oriented activities.

When a project has more than one purpose, mixed organizational structures are usually the norm. The space shuttle missions are a perfect example. Getting the astronauts ready for a flight is one project. Building and installing a new robot arm is another. Although someone is responsible for coordinating all the projects and making sure they get done at the same time so the launch can happen as planned, the people are organized on a subproject basis. The subprojects require a completely different set of team members and organizational structures.

Mixed organizations are not distinguishable from most matrix organizations because of the complexity of relationships, and most of the strengths and weaknesses of a matrix organization also apply to a mixed organizational structure. The unique problem in mixed organizations is one caused by the extreme flexibility in the way the organization adapts to project work. This leads to potential incompatibilities, confusion, conflicts, and duplications of effort if the managers are not adequately trained to deal with these complexities.

Which Structure Should You Use?

The organization you choose for most ordinary business projects will probably be an adaptation of a matrix or functional organization. If multiple departments must be involved and the project is outside normal functional responsibilities, then a matrix organization is appropriate. If the project is relatively simple and uses people from one primary department, then a functional organization can work.

Project size, project length, the experience of the team members, the location of the project, and factors unique to the project all have influence on the selection of a project organizational form. For example, on a small, short-term project for creating a newsletter, the organization of the project might be along functional lines that already exist with the involvement of a few outside resources and key vendors to complete specific tasks. On a larger project to design and build the prototypes for next year's luxury car model, however, a matrix organization might be more appropriate because of the wide range of involvement and ongoing communication required across departments of manufacturing, marketing, engineering, and services.

High Water!

Be aware that the combination of team players on a task always makes a difference. The combination will work either for you or against you. Both the personalities and the skills need to be complementary, especially on long project tasks in which people are in close proximity. It's important that the sum of the people should always equal more than the total of the individuals.

Because large organizations may be distributed over multiple locations, management authority is increasingly being wielded via virtual management tools such as e-mail, computer networks, team collaboration software, and the Web. This is a growing management challenge on large projects, but it's one that will likely continue to evolve to make project teams more virtual and easier to move among multiple project priorities. The trends toward virtual management and just-in-time employment almost dictate matrix-style organizations with local control of basic administrative services and reporting lines to the project managers for the working aspects of the jobs.

Working with the Outsiders

We've already discussed working with outside vendors of all sorts in Chapter 11. When assembling your organization, however, it's important to remember to tightly bind outsiders into the tangled web you weave for your project organization. Most key vendors should be included in the planning phases and should be updated regularly on the project's status. This will help you avoid bills for time not worked but committed to because your project ran late. Outside vendors should also clearly understand reporting relationships, invoicing requirements, and terms of payment. If your vendors are "hooked in" to information technologies, you can employ e-mail, the Web, and other e-business technologies, as well as face-to-face contact, to help you do this.

Managing Outside Resources

Don't forget that outside resources require careful tracking and management, even though the people you work with may be paid by other companies. You must ensure that the work is being completed on schedule and that your "outsiders" don't take on more than they can complete—whether it's your task, the company's workload, or client projects.

The Care and Feeding of the Off-Site Team

Many projects require resources available only off site. Whether essential personnel are working in the building next door or in manufacturing plants in Singapore, these groups require extra care. Without the MBWA (management by walking around, discussed in Chapter 17) technique at your disposal, its easy for project workers to assume that, if you're out of sight, the project is okay to put out of mind.

Obviously, you'll want to employ all the modern tools of intranetworking and electronic communication with these off-site people. A little human contact, however, is still a good idea for keeping team members in multiple locations on track. Make a few personal visits and phone calls to show your support and interest. If the locations are far removed, a trusted assistant project manager is often the answer. Teleconferencing and electronic mail (e-mail) are increasingly important tools in keeping long-distance, distributed projects in synch, but you should still make yourself or a surrogate manager available on-site on occasion to ensure that all is well and stays that way.

Focus on the Launch

As with the space shuttle missions, the complexities in project organization multiply as the project goals become more complicated. Whether your project is large or small, however, the team members need to know whom they work for, how to communicate project status, and where to go when there's a problem. As project manager, you must balance the workload, skills, and reporting structure of the organization to achieve its goals of on-time, within-budget delivery. If you do this, it really doesn't matter how you structure the team—as long as the people make it to the blast off at the same time.

The Least You Need to Know

➤ In addition to the right team members, the correct organizational structure (functional, project, matrix, or mixed) is key to managing a successful project.

➤ Smaller teams are usually more efficient, but sometimes this isn't an option. Therefore, organizing the team into smaller groups is often an option to make things manageable.

➤ As project manager, you're the coach for the team. If you don't make the rules clear and assign people to specific roles, the team won't know how to work together to win the game.

➤ The assignment of internal staff from other departments must be handled carefully to avoid political problems.

Chapter 20

Operating Guidelines: Setting Up to Get Things Done

In This Chapter

➤ The open-door policy and why it's a good idea

➤ Establishing administrative procedures

➤ The importance of a project diary

➤ Ordinary and fun things to keep people motivated

When you initiated the project with the stakeholders, you already established some basic rules for the project in the statement of work (refer to Chapter 7) including authorities and reporting requirements. Now it's time to extend those rules and expand the operating procedures for the entire project team.

The general operating procedures for your project should help you guide people to work on the right tasks at the right time. Operating procedures also help you stay abreast of the status of every activity and cost associated with your project. You need to delegate the work and gather information without demotivating the team with too much administration, paperwork, and redundant communications. In other words, your operating procedures should help you manage the project but not keep you from getting the project done.

Operating procedures should also allow you to gather the information necessary to make changes in a timely fashion, thereby maintaining control of the schedule, resources, and the costs—and ultimately guiding your project to completion on time and within budget.

The Things That Need to Get Done

Getting work done on the project should always be the first priority. To get the actual work started, you'll need to delegate all the work that isn't your own responsibility. You should do this in meetings, in written communications, and through reviewing the project plan with team members. As you start the project, however, you'll also need to develop a process or work schedule for the many activities that won't be found on the work plan or task list for the project. These required tasks include:

Time Is Money

The supervisory role may not appear to be a task, but project management is about managing projects, so you should treat the operations side of any project as a set of tasks and list them as such.

➤ Coordinating activities among groups and vendors involved in your project. Coordination is one of the major uses of a project manager's time in large projects. This involves managing the interfaces between people, vendors, managers, and clients who are involved with a project as well as controlling schedules.

➤ Monitoring progress on the project. Managers must compare the time, cost, and performance of the project to the budget, schedule, and tasks defined in the approved project plan. This must be done in an integrated manner at regular intervals, not in a haphazard, arbitrary way. Any significant departures from the budget and the schedule must be reported immediately because these anomalies affect the viability and success of the entire project.

➤ Adapting the project schedule, budget, and work plan as necessary to keep the project on track. As the project progresses, changes in the original plan may be required for a number of reasons. It is the project manager's responsibility to make sure that these changes are appropriate, valid, and approved.

➤ Documenting project progress and changes and communicating these to team members. The quality and level of detail of your reports and communications need to be consistent, reliable, and appropriate for each level of the project team.

To do all these things, you'll need operating procedures and policies. Necessary guidelines start with the general approach of working together as a team and go on to include formal and informal communications and procedures for doing the coordinating, tracking, adapting, and documenting necessary to keep the project pointed in the right direction.

Formal and Informal Ways to Tell What's Going On

Every project should have both formal and informal monitoring and reporting activities. The larger and more complex the project, the more monitoring and administration is required. Regardless of the type of administration, the goal is to keep your team working toward the final deadline, within the budget, and in line with the goals specified for the project.

Formal monitoring includes reports, audits, and project review meetings. Informal monitoring includes general conversations with the team, ongoing interactions with stakeholders, and observations during MBWA (management by walking around) sessions (discussed in Chapter 17). The size and complexity of the project, along with the culture of the organization, determine the extent and type of monitoring to use.

Keep in Touch

If any of your vendors or project participants are at a different location, a phone call now and then just to see how things are going is vital. This is also a good time to provide positive feedback about accomplishments to date.

Time Is Money

When distributing project status reports, make sure they are received, read, and understood by all team members. You may want to create two versions: one for people who need details and a summary or simple format for the less technical or less involved members of the team (such as customers or managers).

Never be a pest in your MBWA program—whether you're a physical presence or a virtual one in cyberspace. You want to be encouraging and motivating. If you are perceived as a spy, the results of your monitoring efforts will backfire. People don't want you standing over their shoulders, especially if they have creative or thought-intensive work to complete. Think how you would feel if your boss came over two or three times an hour and asked how you were doing. For best results, make the visits unpredictable, spontaneous, and sincere.

Start with the Open-Door Policy

Your operating and monitoring activities should start with informal guidelines, and the most important of these is the open door policy (ODP). The ODP should be the premise of everyday life on the project. Every organization claims to offer such a policy in which employees can discuss a difficult problem with their boss or boss's boss, but few people actually take advantage of this "opportunity" for fear of retribution. You must make sure that your team actually believes in the open door policy (even if your open door is really an e-mail address); otherwise, all the communications, tracking, and other procedures are of limited value. ODP is not just a "gripe line"; it's also a way to keep good ideas flowing and is a key aspect of identifying issues before they turn into problems. To repair project pitfalls quickly or to minimize their impact, you must be available to all team members regardless of rank, location, or job. The open door policy must be real.

The advantage of the ODP approach is simple. When people have little experience working together, communication can become a bottleneck, especially if someone tries to conceal a problem to save face. Team members who are aware of the problem must feel comfortable presenting the project manager with their concerns. That's where the open door policy comes in. If you are a trusted leader, you'll be told about predicaments before they become disasters.

If people know your door is usually open, they'll learn to respect the times when you need to close it for private meetings or intensive work sessions. Sometimes you may want to use a closed door as a filter for trivia. The occasional closed door informs people to make minor decisions on their own that day and invites them to depend on themselves to answer ordinary questions. When the closed door is used with sensitivity and in contrast to the ODP, it can be a powerful tool for getting things done.

Establish an Environment of Motivation

Beyond the ODP, you need to cultivate an environment of motivation around your project. People often refer to the work environment as the "culture" of the organization, and you want your policies and actions to establish a positive culture for getting things done. Here are some things you can do as project manager to ensure that the culture you nurture is one of motivation (as opposed to frustration):

➤ Lead by example. Arrive at work on time and work hard. Get things done as promised, be respectful of others' time, be knowledgeable about the project, and ask good questions when you don't have answers.

➤ Adopt a positive attitude and others will do the same.

➤ Respect your leaders and the staff will respect you. Never criticize management in public. Be considerate of others, even if you disagree with them.

➤ Never make promises that you know can't be kept.

➤ Don't be secretive about the project. Let people see the things they need to see such as reports, customer requests, and letters of appreciation.

➤ Don't try to conceal problems when you encounter them. Instead, seek advice from more senior or experienced people.

➤ Give people the attention they require. Initiate MBWA from day one and schedule (and keep) one-on-one meetings on a regular basis.

➤ Offer assignments that provide challenges, but don't challenge people to the point of exhaustion.

➤ Clearly define performance expectations before people start their tasks.

➤ Make all team members aware that their efforts are important and have a direct impact on the outcome of the project.

As the project progresses, remember to always acknowledge work well done but never reward mediocrity; otherwise, you'll end up with a mediocre project. We discourage monetary bonuses and exclusively individual awards. The results of such "incentives" are often counterproductive. Instead, offer public acknowledgment of good work at meetings or in status reports and provide group rewards for meeting milestones in the form of group events or tokens of appreciation that everyone on the team gets at the same time.

It is also important to have some fun on projects. This is an important part of creating a motivated team and a positive project culture. Here are some ideas to get you started:

➤ Use jokes (sparingly) to loosen up tense situations. Sometimes a bit of humor can break the ice so people can get on with solving the problem.

➤ Circulate cartoons that relate to projects. The Dilbert strip is a rich source, but there are others. Encourage team members to do the same.

➤ Copy articles about project disasters and circulate them. These usually are educational and can help team members see that their own problems pale by comparison.

➤ Have pizza parties for team successes (or for solving problems). A little bribery never hurts, especially if you need to ask people to stay overtime or work weekends.

Informal Meetings and One-on-Ones

Not all operations, reports, and meetings need to be formal and planned to be effective. Just inviting a team member or a few people who are working on the project to your office to sit and chat over coffee may be appropriate. Another useful technique is to schedule regular one-on-one meetings with staff members so they can go over their own concerns, not just yours. Giving team members an opportunity to tell you about the project from their point of view can be very enlightening. People will often let you know about particular problems and concerns in a one-on-one situation that they would never reveal in a meeting or report.

Administrative Procedures That Won't Hurt

Eventually, in spite of your good attitude and informal chats with people, you'll have to ask people to do administrative tasks like writing reports and reconciling expenses. Most people won't like it, but if you have a positive culture, they'll comply with your guidelines (most of the time and as long as you make the requirements clear in advance).

249

As you develop administrative procedures, be sure to collect only the information you'll use. At the beginning, you may collect more information in the form of reports and updates than you really need. As you realize you're gathering too much data, make sure you give the troops a break and tell them to simplify or shorten their reports. For the data you really need, make sure the information is stored for ready access and is easy to retrieve when you need to analyze it.

If your project is one of many similar projects in your organization, there probably are established operating and administrative procedures already in place to help you complete your ongoing responsibilities to the project. These include report formats, time frames for project review, and other tracking procedures.

If review procedures and administrative reports are not already well-established in your organization, you need to develop basic administrative procedures before you begin work on your project. To establish what you'll need, you must answer all of the following questions:

➤ How will you assign the work? If team members are already clear on "who is going to do what" because of their involvement in the planning process, how will you coordinate these efforts?

➤ How will you measure the project's progress? Will you ask for formal updates, just walk around, or both?

➤ What kind of information do you need to assess progress? Make sure you let people know exactly what you need, or they won't give it to you.

Time Is Money

Document each project-day's events as they come and go. Putting it off "for a few days" may find you at the end of a project without enough data or notes to write a report or to defend yourself should something beyond your control go astray. Your project diary will have little value if it's incomplete.

➤ What standards will be used for evaluating the quality of project deliverables? People like to know these things in advance, as do customers paying for the project. People will try to achieve standards they know about—they will do what they think is best, but sometimes that isn't as good as you'd like.

➤ How many project meetings will you have? Which people need to attend? Be specific, put it in writing, and don't have too many meetings; otherwise, you'll never get any work done.

➤ How often will you update the project plan? We recommend that you do it as often as necessary, and that means every time a major change is made to objectives, the schedule, the budget, or sequences. And don't forget to date the plans so you know which plan is current and which should be sent to the archives.

➤ How will you determine what has been spent on the project? How will you verify the accuracy of these amounts? Maintaining control over expenditures is key to project success. Know how to get financial information before any money has been spent, and don't forget to have the accounting folks send copies of the invoices to you to review before outside vendors are paid.

➤ How often will reports on the project be made and to whom? The number, frequency, and detail of the reports and procedures you use will depend on the management requirements for your project, your manager's preferences, and your own need for ongoing information about the project. At a minimum, a formal status report should be distributed once a month for a long project and weekly for a shorter project.

ACTION	DAILY	WEEKLY	MONTHLY	QUARTERLY
Informal Discussions with Team	S	L		
Staff Meetings with Managers		B		
Project Review Meeting with Team		S	L	
Status Report		S	L	
Project Audit (optional)				L
Team Building Activity			B	
Report to Management			B	

Reports & Administrative Guidelines for Small and Large Projects

S = Small Project
L = Large Project
B = Both Small and Large Projects

Action items for different size projects.

There's always an excuse to produce too many paper and e-mail messages. Like advertising, too many "communications" degrades their impact. (Ever notice how, on the most boring freeway journey, you tune out the billboards after the first 20?) This means that your vital project status report gets the same attention as a project newsletter you never saw prior to publication. Since the newsletter has several strawberry jam recipes that aren't germane to the project, your report is ignored. That's why the paper trail must be carefully controlled.

The Reports You May Need

Your team, stakeholders, managers, and customers deserve informed communication about the project on a timely basis. In addition to a regular status report—which contains information on current progress, schedule changes, and budgets—other reports may be required to both inform and motivate team members. On large projects, there may be cost-variance reports, load-leveling reports, supply inventories, and other formal documentation to track specific aspects of the project.

In addition to general status reports, a daily or weekly update report on large projects may be a good idea. The update report is a document distributed to all team members to emphasize important priorities, issues, or deadlines. The purpose of the update report is to convey information that might otherwise fall through the cracks. (If a major snag crops up, the update form provides information to keep troops focused on their own work while you deal with the problem.)

Simple Forms to Create Useful Reports

Reports allow your team to follow the project "roadmap" and stay on track, but the reports need to be easy to produce. We suggest using a good project management program (see Chapter 30) or simple forms for gathering regular report information. Here are some forms we often use on our projects that may be useful for yours.

Schedule update forms   You will need to update the schedule as the project progresses and evolves. Team members should be notified each time the "map" changes, for whatever reason, so they can review the master chart and adjust their duties to match.

Supply and equipment request forms   Team members will require supplies and possibly equipment you haven't considered. Give them a simple worksheet to complete so they can tell you what they need before they need it.

Status reporting forms   If you don't use a groupware reporting system on a computer network that reminds people about status reports and other administrative requirements, paper systems can accomplish the same goals. Simply give each team member a stack of forms for reporting their weekly and monthly progress. Add a section specifically for them to report problems and roadblocks getting in their way. You're more likely to get completed status updates when you provide the blank forms in advance and have an assigned person go around to pick them up at a specified date or time. The status forms should include blanks for providing the following kinds of information that should be included on every formal status report:

➤ Tasks completed since the last status report with dates completed

➤ Tasks in progress with forecasted completion dates

➤ Tasks planned with expected completion dates

➤ Budget expenditures

➤ Issues that need attention

➤ Recommendations for project improvements or changes

➤ Questions or items that require other people's approval or input

When everyone uses the same forms, it becomes easier to summarize, synthesize, and analyze the status information for the formal status report you'll write as the project manager.

Every Report Needs a Purpose

For each report (or form) you choose to use on your project, the following should be documented:

➤ How often is the report produced? Some reports are produced weekly. Others are submitted monthly or quarterly.

➤ What is contained in the report?

➤ Who is responsible for producing the report?

➤ What is the objective of the report?

➤ Who will follow up on action items identified in the report?

➤ Who is the intended audience for the report? For example, there are three potential audiences for status reports: team members on the project, company management, and customers or stakeholders (if there are any involved). The report to management and customers is typically more formal, but less detailed, than the report made to the team members. The reports that team members send to you (as project manager) probably have the most information; some of this information is for your eyes only, however, so you need to filter what you summarize for other staff and managers.

Writing status reports for various audiences allows you to synthesize the formal and informal monitoring you've been doing. It allows you to relate your progress to the original project plan and to understand any risks to meeting your planned goals.

Ask One Final Question Before You Start

Before any report or procedure becomes part of the bureaucratic process associated with your project, ask yourself the following questions:

Is this report or procedure the best way to communicate this information?

Is there some other form of communication or action that would be more expedient and just as useful?

Read Chapter 21 before you answer these questions.

Overdoing It

It's common to be too structured in organizing a project. While this sounds improbable at first, when you look at all the tasks and people that need coordinating, watch for the following problems as you proceed with the project to see if you're going overboard with paperwork and control:

➤ Do you feel isolated from the rest of the team because you always have reports due? If so, you probably have too many reports or other administrative procedures to do. Try simplifying and combining reports to keep the volume under control.

➤ Are the team members complaining of being micromanaged? You must achieve a balance between task assignments and task management. Some team members will need more structure than others. You must decide which approach best suits individual personalities and the project. Err on the side of trust and loose control as you begin the project. You can usually tighten things up later (unless the schedule is a cruncher).

➤ Are status reports always late from your team members? Either they don't regard them as important (which you can resolve by talking to them) or perhaps your report is too complex or detailed. Remember that every hour spent on forms and reports is an hour taken away from getting project tasks completed. Again, simplify and consolidate to keep administration in balance.

Dear Diary—Do You Need One?

In addition to taking notes at meetings, gathering information from project participants, and making general reports, a prudent project manager makes a personal project diary part of standard operating procedure. The daily diary should include notes on progress, problems, and any issues that impact the project in a positive or negative light. Unlike a young girl's "Dear Diary" entries, this notebook resembles a captain's log from a ship. Entries are to the point, are dated (by page), and contain as much or as little information as required to document project progress and issues.

Use a computer if it's convenient, but back up your entries so this vital document doesn't suffer from disk or power failure.

The diary should contain information about the outcome of key meetings, accomplishments, conflicts, and extraordinary events affecting the project's health and well-being (not to mention your own).

The purpose of the project diary is four-fold:

Time Is Money

Document each project-day's events as they come and go. Putting it off "for a few days" may find you at the end of a project without enough data or notes to write a report or to defend yourself should something beyond your control go astray. Your project diary will have little value if it's incomplete.

1. It tracks your progress and can be inspected by all parties concerned with project status. The diary may pinpoint project sinkholes that are hard to identify by reading a pile of status reports. Long-term problems, such as a failing team member, become easily visible as you flip through the book. Unloading the team member is easier when you can document his or her nonperformance through the written record.

2. Future project managers can use your experiences to better understand their role as project managers and the ins and outs of the organization.

3. If management complains about a problem such as budget overages or tardy delivery, your meticulously kept diary serves as the perfect memory of what really happened so you can explain the situation.

4. Your diary is an excellent tool for doing a better job next time. Review it occasionally to see what worked and what failed last time. Employ the positive and reject the negative. A good project is fuel for laughs years down the road.

Before heading home for the night, always update your project diary. This process gives swirling thoughts and worries a place to rest and acts as the formal termination of your workday. The diary also keeps the "fossil" record intact for later review and for writing the final report. With your work done, reports completed, and diary done, you can go home and watch *Gilligan's Island* without a pinch of guilt.

Keeping People Up to Date

One of the most important operating procedures you need to develop is a way to make progress visible to team members as work progresses on the project. Seeing movement toward the finish line of the project is vital to maintain morale and to keep people focused on their contributions to the project. Here are some things you can do to make project progress visible from the onset:

➤ Display a large map of the project-network diagram and post it where everyone can see it. Fill in the shapes or highlight the activities on the list as they are completed. If remote sites participate, each site should have a chart so they can see what the other sites are doing.

➤ Use a whiteboard or another display to show current tasks and to schedule assignments. (This puts pressure on lagging team members to get with the program.)

➤ Display samples (where appropriate) of the team's progress. This might include brochures printed for a product launch, a sample of a new product or its prototype, or anything tangible that represents team progress. Change this display frequently to keep people interested and motivated.

➤ Regularly publish a project newsletter. This is a good communication tool if the contents are relevant. Articles can be used to describe team accomplishments. Include a list and photos of team members who contributed to the accomplishments if possible and relevant. Be careful not to leave anyone out. Focus the articles on group accomplishments. (If you don't intend to keep the newsletter going, however, don't start one.)

➤ If your project has a Web site or an intranet (most large projects should in this day and age), you can gather information via Web-based reporting tools. You can also put all the shared reports, news items, and updates on the Web—even pictures and voices of the people working on the project around the world. This really helps develop a "reality" for the team aspect of a distributed venture.

Remember, recognition rewards don't have to be large to be effective, but they do have to be part of the operating procedures if you want to create an environment of motivation. A laser-printed (but signed) certificate congratulating team members on special-project success or work above and beyond the call of duty can make a big difference in making people feel appreciated. A coupon for a pleasant dinner out for two makes these awards more fun. Be careful not to overlook unsung team members located at a remote site or those who work quietly with little day-to-day visibility to the rest of the team.

The Bottom Line

In implementing all the operating aspects and creating the administrative guidelines for your project, you should remember that it's the management and leadership of the project that make the difference in your success, not the forms or the paperwork. You must act as a manager and a leader, not just as an administrator. With this in mind, we're ready to attack some of the best ways to keep all the "adminis-trivia" under control and to make communications more effective.

The Least You Need to Know

➤ Every project needs administrative procedures to delegate work, track progress, and report status, but no project needs long-winded reports with irrelevant details or meetings without objectives.

➤ Recognition for work done well and open communications are the two most important operating procedures any project manager can initiate.

➤ Leading a project by example and keeping a project diary are things that every project manager should do as a matter of policy.

➤ Leadership is always more important than paperwork in getting any project done, but paperwork gets noticed, so you'll need to do it anyway.

➤ The Web (or company intranet) is a powerful tool for communicating with team members on large, distributed projects. Web-based technologies also can be used for many of the tracking and reporting requirements on a project.

Chapter 21

Making Your Communications Count

Consider the United States government paperwork-reduction act in which an additional piece of paper is printed to explain the paper reduction. Projects typically generate too much paper and too little information. Even using computer technology, the plans, status reports, and action item lists (to name just a few) use significant cellulose-related resources. Fortunately, most of this paper is recyclable, and large project management firms regularly recover significant sums of money from the piles of paper they recycle. They even lock down their dumpsters so no one steals the bulk of recyclables. It's a good thing, too, since reusing the paper saves both trees and money!

We noted in Chapter 20 that good administration is central to a project, but that doesn't mean you have to have lots of paperwork. Yes, in theory, you can use a computer and a whiteboard (for communication purposes), but all too often, people opt for the paper-only approach to cover their posteriors. We think this is a bad idea for most project managers.

In the modern world, there are many alternatives to the traditional memo and written report. You can communicate in person, both formally and informally. You can use the telephone for long conversations or leave short messages via voice mail. When you choose to use the written form for your messages, you can write casual notes by hand, send e-mail, transmit a fax, or when necessary, publish a formal document or dazzle people with a multimedia presentation.

In this chapter, we look at some techniques to make your project communications more effective (whether written, e-mailed, faxed, or phoned). These tips should help you improve your overall control of the project as well as the impact of your communications.

The Advantages and Disadvantages of Various Communications

By considering the format of your message, the time of day, and the job of the recipients, you can predict with a fair degree of accuracy whether a message will reach the intended receiver. Before you deliver any message, however, always consider the impact if it gets into the wrong hands—because it might.

To paraphrase Marshall McLuhan's wisdom: On projects, the medium is often as important as the message. In other words, the means of communication can have a greater influence on people than the information you're sending. With that in mind, the following tables present some general advantages and disadvantages of using various kinds of communication formats.

Telephone Calls

Advantages:

➤ The telephone is good for short, focused communications that need a personal touch or should not be put into the permanent, written record.

➤ It's possible to combine a personal approach while reaching people in remote locations at a relatively low cost.

Disadvantages:

➤ It's possible to play phone tag for days. The chance of actually reaching someone on first call is about 25 percent.

➤ It can be disruptive to the receiver if the call is not expected in advance.

Voice Mail

Advantages:

➤ Voice mail is great for getting short messages that aren't sensitive or personal in nature.

➤ It's a quick way to contact people in remote locations.

Disadvantages:

➤ Long messages can be lost, scrambled, or deleted without the receiver knowing there is a problem.

➤ People may not pick up their messages on a regular basis.

Electronic Mail (E-Mail)

Advantages:

➤ It provides a written record without sending paper, and it allows you to attach other documents to your message.

➤ It's a quick way to send messages to people in distributed locations.

➤ Most of the time, you can find out if the mail has been read.

➤ It provides high credibility because people perceive it as being written by the sender (not an administrative assistant).

➤ It's good for precise details that can be conveyed in one screen.

➤ Messages can be forwarded to other people who need to know.

Disadvantages:

➤ People may forget to save important messages or may fail to realize that other materials are attached to the e-mail.

➤ It can seem impersonal if not worded properly. It's also not good for sensitive issues because it's easy to forward messages to others without thinking about the long-term ramifications.

➤ People may not read their e-mail messages on a regular basis.

➤ It requires a good, precise title so that people take the messages seriously and read them.

➤ Long messages are considered bad form and may alienate the reader.

➤ They can be risky because of the permanence of the message and the lack of privacy. (It can be forwarded to almost anyone.)

Handwritten, Short Notes

Advantages:

➤ Short notes are great for kudos and thanks. They're a personal approach that contrasts positively with computerized communications.

➤ They're quick, simple, friendly, and cheap.

Disadvantages:

➤ They might be overlooked if the note is small.

➤ They're limited to short, concise messages, and they work best when people are in the same general location.

Informal Visits and Management by Walking Around

Advantages:

➤ This is a great way to see things in action.

➤ It gives you a real impression of the tone and productivity of the team.

➤ You can discuss a wide range of topics and issues in detail.

Disadvantages:

➤ You might be perceived as nosy or disruptive if you aren't genuine in your interest or if you visit too often.

➤ Discussions can be forgotten or misinterpreted at a later date.

➤ You must keep the discussions focused to avoid wasting the team's time.

Formal Meetings

Advantages:

➤ Formal meetings enable multiple people to express opinions and issues.

➤ You can discuss and resolve a wide range of topics and issues in detail.

Disadvantages:

➤ These meetings can degrade into time-wasting and confrontations if not managed effectively.

➤ Some people may feel uncomfortable offering their opinions in public.

Formal Reports and Memos

Advantages:

➤ If used sparingly, these are good for communicating updates and important procedures.

➤ They provide a permanent record.

Disadvantages:

➤ They can be easily misunderstood, especially if the message is negative.

➤ They can't be taken back and aren't easily forgotten if the message is poorly conveyed.

Faxed Messages

Advantages:

➤ Faxes are good for getting reports and messages to people in diverse locations.

➤ They provide a quick way to get important written documents to people.

Disadvantages:

➤ They are too easily seen by others, so this is not a good idea for sensitive messages.

➤ If no one is expecting your fax or if the fax machine is not regularly checked, your fax can languish, defeating the purpose of a fax.

Formal Presentations

Advantages:

➤ These presentations are great for presenting complex status reports to audiences of various sizes.

➤ They allow effective use of graphics and other display methods.

➤ If done professionally, they can have a lasting positive impression on the audience.

Disadvantages:

➤ These presentations require considerable planning and skill to achieve a positive impression.

➤ They are time-consuming for production and attendance and are an expensive alternative.

➤ Poorly presented material can negatively affect attitudes toward an otherwise successful project.

Other Media

There are other media you can use as well. Many people have pagers and beepers, although contacting people through these devices is generally annoying unless you really have an emergency to convey. You can use groupware (software that lets people talk together through a computer network) for keeping status reports and general

263

project information up-to-date. You can create a project Web site for a really large project to keep people informed of objectives, accomplishments, and project plans.

Regardless of the medium you choose, you need to employ common sense. You can never ignore the unexpected impact of your messages. You need to select the medium wisely and with intention. Even a casual disparaging remark to a team member can come back to haunt you later in the project.

Words from the Wise

"Speak less... No one ever put their foot in their mouth when they were not speaking. Worse, if you are speaking, you can't be listening, and we always learn much more from listening."

—Mark H. McCormack

Words from the Wise

"You know, sometimes, when they say you're ahead of your time, it's just a polite way of saying you have a real bad sense of timing."

—George McGovern

Selecting the Best Medium for Your Message

To help you select the best medium for delivering your project information, consider these guidelines that we've come to appreciate through trial and error. You can avoid many of our mistakes if you take these truisms to heart.

➤ When you have real issues to resolve, have the discussions in person. People are reluctant to commit their opinions about controversial issues in writing.

➤ Never use meetings to berate people or make personal attacks. If you must discuss performance problems, limit the meetings to the people involved and keep the discussions confidential.

➤ Use e-mail for routine messages and day-to-day work on the project, but limit the number of messages. Don't send everything to everybody. Too much e-mail can actually waste time and can distract people from more important project issues.

➤ Let people know through fax, voice mail, or e-mail that a long report or other formal document is coming. This will improve the likelihood that the document will actually be read and taken seriously if you announce it in advance.

➤ Limit your formal meetings to those that are absolutely necessary. Have clear agendas for meetings or don't bother to have them. Limit the attendees to the people who really need to be there. Distribute minutes of the meeting when other people need to know what was discussed.

➤ Consider the culture of your team. For a number of reasons, some teams require more communication than others. Some teams are simply more or less cohesive than others. Some team members have only limited contact with each other. Other team members may have established relationships. Less cohesive groups need more ongoing communication and support from the project manager. More cohesive groups will generally be more self-directed and will require less direct communications from you. Consider the individual and group issues as you choose and construct each communication.

Developing Effective Messages

Communicating on a project is an art. The better you get at it, the smoother your project will flow from beginning to end. You must provide enough information to keep team members informed without boring them out of their socks or stockings. Every word counts. What you send, whom you send it to, and when you send it are always issues. If in doubt about a message, always wait. When you decide you need to say something, however, here are some guidelines to help you decide exactly what you want to say (regardless of the medium you choose):

Words from the Wise

On Writing: "The aim, if reached or not, makes great the life: Try to be Shakespeare, leave the rest to fate!"

—Robert Browning

➤ Always outline the message before you deliver it. This will help when you feel the urge to send something nasty and negative. If you wait, you'll probably realize that sending such a message is a bad idea.

➤ Think about the audience expectation for the message, any actions required as a result of the message, and your expectations after the message is delivered.

➤ Justify your choice of delivery medium for the message and the timing of the message.

➤ Start the message with an introduction that identifies the issue, context, or opportunity of interest.

➤ Make any required actions clear and specific in the message.

➤ Be as concise as possible without seeming insensitive or rude.

Listening Is Part of Communicating

In addition to the ability to construct powerful, appropriate messages, the ability to listen is one of the most important communication skills a project manager can possess. Only through listening can you determine whether your messages are understood. Focused listening also helps keep you abreast of project progress better than

any status report. Observant listening can also help you foresee political issues before they start bogging down the project.

Here are some hints to make you a better listener:

➤ Stop talking and let others tell you what they want to say.

➤ Let people finish what they are saying. Try not to interrupt because you'll never hear the complete intent of the person if you do. If there is a brief pause in the discussion, don't jump in prematurely. Make sure the other person has finished before you take your turn.

➤ Eliminate distractions such as telephone calls or people coming in and out of the office. Give the person your full attention.

Words from the Wise

" ... Just as a wise man can say a foolish thing, a fool can say something wise once in a while."

—John Capozzi, *If You Want the Rainbow You Gotta Put Up with the Rain* (1997)

➤ Listen with purpose and intent. Try to hear between the words for the underlying meaning of the message. Notice body language and facial expressions as people talk. These are often the clues to dissatisfaction or issues that are not being addressed. If you see something wrong in the person's face, ask some probing questions to get at the real concerns.

➤ Restate what you heard people say to make sure you got the message right. You must receive and understand the message for communication to occur.

Along the Critical Path

Remember that all members of the implementation team have four basic communications needs for which you're responsible: information about their respective responsibilities, information to help them work together efficiently, status information to help them identify problems and plan their own priorities, and information about decisions made by management, the customer, and other stakeholders that may affect the business environment of the project (and possibly their own work assignments).

You Are Responsible for What Other People Hear

If you really listen and find out that a message doesn't accomplish its goals or causes problems you didn't have before the message was sent, you've failed as a communicator. The reasons for most message failures are simple:

➤ The message was misinterpreted. This means your tone, vocabulary, medium, or timing (or any combination of these) was deficient.

➤ The message was considered unimportant or was ignored.

➤ The message arrived too late to be effective.

➤ The message ended up in the hands (or ears) of the wrong person.

Regardless of the reason for your message's failure, you need to take responsibility for the problem and work harder to improve your communications. We always recommend being hard on yourself and being forgiving to others. You must constantly strive to become a better communicator and to make better interpretations of the ways in which receivers will interpret and act on your messages. Once you learn to deliver messages that get noticed in the right way, you'll have achieved one of the most important skills in leading your project to a successful conclusion—the skill of effective communication.

The Least You Need to Know

➤ Because you're in charge, everything you say or write counts toward helping or hindering your project.

➤ Never underestimate the importance of personal communications or the risk of putting things in writing.

➤ Carefully plan, assess, and construct every formal communication you make.

➤ Only through careful, focused, sensitive listening will you find out what's really going on.

➤ Never send a message that has more negative than positive potential to motivate people.

Part 5

The Controlling Processes

Like any good driver, to maintain your lead over the project, you need to exercise control. As a project manager, you need to adjust your speed on the curves and compensate for the condition of the road. Control of a project starts with a detailed plan, good communication, and clear administrative procedures you've developed for the project. To actually have some control, however, you need to deal with change, problems, and unexpected circumstances. You need to compare the time, cost, and performance of your project at every stage—and then make adjustments to the activities, resources, and plan to keep things on track. Sometimes you may need to slam on the brakes or slow things down to avoid catastrophe. Other times, you'll need to step on the accelerator to keep pace with the traffic.

Learning how to use information to keep the project under control is the theme of this section. Just focus on the plan and keep your eyes on the prize, and you'll reach the project finish in first place.

Status Report

Cool!
Fair
Yuk!

Chapter 22

Monitoring and Control: Keeping on Top of Schedules and Expenses

---

In This Chapter

➤ Why control is a good thing

➤ The criteria for establishing positive control over the project

➤ How to use status information to help control the objectives, schedule, and budget

➤ Keeping the plan up-to-date to help keep the project on track

---

Once a project is underway and you establish the operating procedures and start working on perfecting your leadership style, your key responsibility is to keep things going on time and within budget. After meticulously planning your project, you might assume that team members will simply stick to your plan and get things done as specified. Unfortunately, this almost never happens. Like using the autopilot on a modern airliner, when faced with an uncharted mountain, you need the intervention of a real person who can take the controls and guide the project safely to its destination.

In this chapter, you're going to learn about the basic control techniques that can help you.

Taking Charge and Getting Control

Once a project is underway, it takes on a life of its own. You know the company's future depends on getting the projects done on time and within budget. Your job and your reputation are on the line. You may feel out of control. How can you keep it together? How will you know if people are doing what they promised to do? How can you meet your objectives and still get everything else done? It's all too overwhelming.

High Water!

Never make the mistake of confusing activity with progress.

Words from the Wise

"Trouble has no necessary connection with discouragement—discouragement has a germ of its own, as different from trouble as arthritis is different from a stiff joint."

—F. Scott Fitzgerald

Don't give up yet. You've just started. Getting a handle on your project isn't really that hard. You have a plan, and now is the time to use it. Your plan is your main tool for maintaining control of the project through its lifetime. This requires careful management of both the plan and its resources—including the people—to move forward and keep everything in gear and well-lubricated. Although change is an inevitable consequence of moving through time (see Chapter 24, "Changes, Changes, and More Changes"), you must measure and manage its effects. Otherwise, you won't meet the goals established at the project's outset. The schedule, budget, and procedures you've put together to this point provide you with the structure you need to evaluate where you are at any time.

Control Is a Good Thing

The word "control" may have a pejorative connotation to you. Control can imply domination, headstrong authority, or excessive power. Because of these negative connotations, people new to project management may be reluctant to implement project control. The controlling phase is not about domination, however—it's about gathering information so you can measure, monitor, and adjust progress toward your project goals. That's a good thing because, otherwise, you'll never know if your project is on the right course.

Success Criteria for Project Control

How you use your reports and communications (from the preceding chapter) to control your project will directly affect the end results your project will achieve. Here are some guidelines for using reports and communications that can help you achieve positive control of your project:

➤ Use the project plan as the primary guide for coordinating your project. A major portion of this book is devoted to preparation of the plan because of its centrality in the project management discipline. If you diligently follow the steps laid out in previous chapters, your plan is likely a good one—and thus is something worth following.

➤ Consistently monitor and update the plan and the other control documents including the statement of work, the requirement specification, the blueprints, and the functional specifications (if these documents are used for your project). A plan or supporting specification that stays in the top drawer of your desk will not help you guide your project to a successful conclusion. Instead, it must be updated regularly to be useful. It must also reflect the current status of the project and any changes that become necessary because of new information, budget constraints, or schedule or product modifications.

➤ Remember that quality communication is a key to control. Never provide too much information. Never offer too little. Every person on your project org chart requires ongoing communication at various levels of detail. Higher-level management requires summary reports on the project. Operational members of the team require more detailed information. Some communication will be formal, and some will be informal. The objective of communication is to keep people informed, on track, and involved in the project.

➤ Monitor the progress of the project against the plan on a regular basis. Managers must compare the time, cost, and performance of the project to the budget, schedule, and tasks defined in the approved project plan. This should be done in an integrated manner at regular intervals, not in a haphazard, arbitrary way. Any significant departures from the budget and the schedule must be reported immediately because these anomalies affect the viability and success of the entire project.

➤ Get involved. You won't have time to sit in your ivory tower waiting for results and accolades from the big boss. Instead, you'll need to roll up your sleeves and get down in the trenches with the team. That way, you not only have a finger on the project's pulse, you actually contribute to a workload that may otherwise weigh heavily on team members' shoulders.

High Water!

Be sure to gather status information from all members of the project team, even from people low on the totem pole who don't report directly to you. More-senior team members may whitewash or deliberately misrepresent problems in a misguided effort to present themselves in the best possible light.

➤ Adapt the project schedule, budget, and work plan as necessary to keep the project on track. As the project progresses, changes in the original plan may be required for several reasons. It is the project manager's responsibility to make sure these changes are appropriate, valid, and approved.

➤ Document project progress and changes and communicate them to team members. The quality and level of detail of your reports and communications need to be consistent, reliable, and appropriate for each level of the project team.

What Should You Monitor?

To keep things running smoothly, the following must be monitored for every project, regardless of size or complexity:

➤ The status of work being performed as compared to the plan

➤ The volume of work being completed

➤ The quality of work being performed

➤ The costs and expenditures as compared to the plan

➤ The attitudes of people working on the project or involved with the project including customers and management

➤ The cohesiveness and cooperation of team members

Note that there is more to be monitored than just the tasks, the schedule, and the budget. The level of communication and cooperation between team members and the quality of the work being performed are also obviously important aspects of the project. In addition, you must monitor the use and availability of equipment and machinery. For example, you may be responsible for the usage of computer equipment or heavy machinery on a large project. You also want to make sure the equipment doesn't "walk out the door," so to speak.

On a large, complex project, the effort required for monitoring and control may take more time than you actually spend working on the project. This is okay. It is your job as project manager to guide the project to a successful conclusion. Of course, on smaller projects, the degree of monitoring and control should be much less time-consuming.

One thing that helps minimize the time spent monitoring activities on both small and large projects is the use of simple reporting formats. Keeping reports clear and succinct is more important than getting hundreds of pages of narrative on each aspect of the project. In addition, the use of appropriate project management

Time Is Money

Here are three things you can do to make communications better: (1) Be sympathetic to others' problems; (2) Always make an extra effort to remember names and titles; (3) Make it easy for people to talk to you by being available and friendly.

software that is adapted to your project needs can help reduce the time required to understand the impact of current activities and changes in the project plan. (See Chapter 30, "Software for All Projects Great and Small," for more information on choosing an appropriate software program to help you track progress.)

What Monitoring Should Accomplish

The tasks, milestones, and budget you documented in the plan for your project are the starting point for project coordination and control. These tasks and milestones form the checkpoints to be used to monitor progress. Whether formal or informal, project monitoring should serve one or more of the following basic functions:

➤ Communicating project status and changes to other project team members

➤ Informing management (and clients or customers) about the status of the project

➤ Providing the justification for making project adjustments

➤ Documenting current project plans compared to the original project plan

Consistency is very important in the monitoring and control process. The project must be monitored from start to finish because problems can occur anywhere along the way.

Inexperienced project managers may start out full of energy and monitor everything during the first few weeks. Then, when things seem to be going okay, the monitoring falls off. These managers often end up with a big mess at the end of the project because they've failed to keep track of progress and problems. Don't let this happen to you! Maintain your zeal throughout the project.

Getting a Handle on Project Status

Controlling a project takes time and effort, but it's not that difficult if you keep up with things. In the following sections, we'll give you some tips to help you keep on top of the work flow.

Make Status Reports Useful

Status reports are more than nice documents that fill your filing cabinets—they are a fundamental monitoring tool to identify progress and problems.

You should encourage your team members to take status reports seriously and should help them learn to write and interpret them. Whether you require formal or informal status reports, status updates

High Water!

Project managers fall into three basic categories: those who watch what happens, those who make things happen, and those who wonder what happened.

should be completed by each team member (or supervisor) and then should be compiled and summarized by you, the project manager. You should add your own comments to the summary report, draw conclusions based on the data you've received from others, and make recommendations for actions and changes before you send your report on to other managers, executives, or customers who need to be kept apprised of project status.

By reviewing status reports and personal communications, you'll discover the discrepancies between where you are and where the plan says you should be. These discrepancies are always there because no plan can predict the exact sequence you'll follow in getting from idea to finished project. But isn't it better to know about the discrepancies sooner rather than later? That's what project control is all about—being able to take action sooner so the project will still come in on time and within budget.

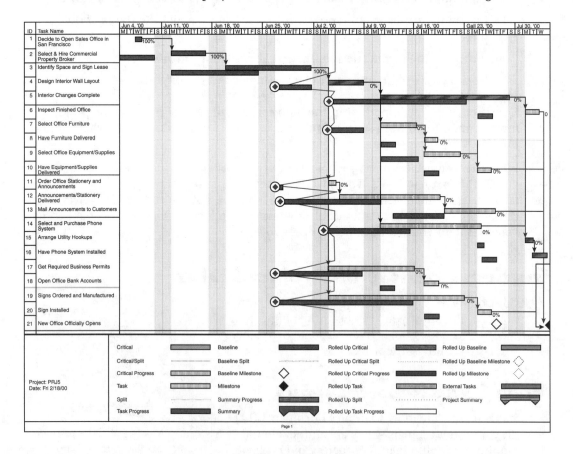

Computerized project management tools can help you compare the current status of the project with the planned or baseline status of the project. Here you see a Gantt chart produced in Microsoft Project 98 that compares the approved plan to the current status of the project.

Compare, Compare, Compare

An easy way to monitor status is to use two columns to compare the current schedule and expenditures with the original project plan. The comparison allows you to understand the most immediate issues regarding your plan, and it can help prioritize your needs to adapt the plan or to make further inquiries regarding the problem areas. Always keep in mind that monitoring is used to establish the project's current position compared to the planned position. You need to make this goal clear to your team; otherwise, they'll perceive your scrutiny of budget and schedule as actions of a Gestapo sergeant with an insidious, covert mission.

The Project Review Meeting as a Control Process

Analyzing reports from your office chair will never be enough to help you guide your project to fruition. Resolving conflicts, problems, and staffing issues is almost impossible using just reports, so meetings with people are always a necessary component of project control.

The project review meeting is an opportunity for key team members, not just managers and supervisors, to get together to resolve issues. It's also a time to discuss current project status and to review performance toward meeting objectives. Project review meetings are often held at the completion of a major milestone or before or after a key phase of the project. Some project review meetings are held on a periodic basis in place of formal reports. For example, a short newsletter project is best handled with brief reports and regular meetings because the project is of a short duration. A project to build a new sales office will have less frequent meetings until the end of the project when more coordination is required.

Time Is Money

When working with outside vendors, suppliers, and agencies, strike up friendships with their support personnel. That way, if things start running off the rails for any reason, your friends can tip you off before your project skips the tracks.

If a project meeting is necessary to resolve issues, have one now, not later. It's best to take action as soon as you are aware of a problem instead of waiting for a regularly scheduled meeting. Make the meeting short and focused. Long, drawn-out meetings with no clear focus can dampen enthusiasm and obfuscate the problem. At the end of three hours, no one cares anymore.

The Project Audit

The most formal type of project monitoring (and the process most feared by project managers) is the audit. Sometimes audits are required as a point of contract; sometimes they are necessary because the project is really off track and the source of the problem remains a mystery. The goal of a project audit is to get an accurate picture of the quality of work, current expenditures, and the schedule of the project. (These are the goals of all monitoring activities, so the audit is really no different from putting together a big status report.)

Audits are commonly performed on large government projects, projects involving multiple companies and big budgets, and projects involving customers who need outside assurance that work on the project is proceeding as planned. Audits may be initiated both during and at the end of a project. Internal audits also can be performed by project managers and team members at key milestones in a large project.

In most cases, an audit is performed by (supposedly) objective outsiders who review progress, costs, and current plans. After discussions with team members, reviews of reports, and direct observations, the objective auditors (who usually work for the customer or the government) then report their conclusions on the current status of the project based on their audit to the project manager or to executive management. They often make strong recommendations about better ways things should be done to keep a large project under control.

If your projects ever get audited, you'll be okay if you've followed all the tips for monitoring and tracking progress that we've given you in this chapter. If you've done a good job of communicating and monitoring, the audit shouldn't reveal any surprises—but if it does, take them to heart and take action. Just because you didn't discover the problem is no reason to ignore the solution.

Monitoring and Controlling the Budget

Reports and meetings are great for tracking schedules and performance, but budgets and cash outlays require special monitoring techniques. The way the budget tracking is set up depends on the accounting systems already in place in your company. As you make expenditures or sign contracts with vendors, you need to establish a formal tracking method to measure your actual commitments.

To help control expenditures, you should initiate review procedures for any expenditures not in the original plan. Even if expenditures are in the plan, you may want to have approval or review of any purchases that exceed a certain amount (say, any expenditures that exceed $1,000).

In most companies, if you rely on expenditure reports from the accounting department to provide the financial status of your project, you will likely go over budget or think you have more money than you actually have. Money is often "spent" in the form of contracts or agreements long before it is accounted for in the billing and invoice cycles of the corporation. Accounting reports typically report on invoices that have been "paid to date." Unfortunately, they don't usually report on invoices that have not been paid or have yet to be billed.

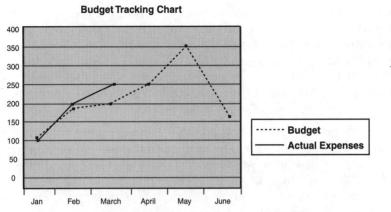

Budget Tracking Chart

Graphs like this one are useful in projecting current expenditures as compared to those planned for the project.

For this reason, you must track actual expenditures to date in addition to reviewing the accounting reports. Ultimately, your expenditures and the accounting department documentation should match, but it might take as long as 90 days for the two systems to be reconciled.

You (and each person on your project team who will be making financial commitments to vendors or suppliers) must account for all monetary commitments as they occur. At a minimum, all expenditures should appear on the formal status reports.

A simple way to keep track of the money is to have each person provide a photocopy of each contract, agreement, or order for your project as it is approved. These go into your "project expenditures file." The total of these expenditures then becomes part of the actual expenses committed to your project. As vendors specify new prices or change their bids, these must be put into the file as well, and budget figures must be adjusted accordingly for the next status report and plan review.

When you get reports from accounting that do not match your budget file, you will have the documentation necessary to reconcile the differences. If you don't have such a file, you'll be at the mercy of your accountant or finance officer (not a desirable condition).

Why Status Reports Don't Tell the Whole Story

Never rely on written reports alone to assess progress on your project. People often leave problems out of reports because they don't want to put them in writing. They also may fail to report schedule slips in meetings because they think time can be made up later. People often don't want to expose a problem in front of others for fear of reprisal or embarrassment.

Words from the Wise

"So much of what we call management consists in making it difficult for people to work."

—Peter Drucker

For example, John, the customer support manager, was late on writing the articles for the newsletter project. Still, in the weekly report, he stated that the articles were "on schedule" even though they hadn't been started. John reported this way in good faith, fully believing he would be able to make up the time next week. Unfortunately, this kind of reporting causes many problems, especially if the person never does find the time to get back on schedule. If Sue, the project manager, fails to realize the problem until it is documented or reported, the entire newsletter project could be in jeopardy.

The quality of performance on a project is also subjective. Performance reported as outstanding by one group may be substandard to another. In the sales office project, the contractors assembling the new office walls reported that everything was completed "to specifications." It wasn't until Roger, who was responsible for the project, actually visited the site that he realized two of the offices had doors in the wrong place, and the baseboards in the conference room were missing altogether.

For reasons like this, you need to informally review progress on the project on your own through direct observation and direct communication with the team members. Informal monitoring can be completed by simply listening, observing, and communicating on an ongoing basis. The goal is to spot problems before they become unmanageable.

Using Information from the Project Team

The project team is your best source of ideas for keeping the project on track. The more you allow people to adjust their own work and schedules to meet project goals, the easier it will be to keep the project on track. Thus, everyone on your project should be part of project control. People can do more than just tell you what they're up to; they can also provide ideas for speeding project progress or saving money. (Evaluate these ideas as you would any change to the plan.) In general, the best ideas come from informal sessions with the team member, not from written status reports or scheduled meetings.

While visiting team members, not only do you get to observe people at work, they should have materials on hand to explain their progress and ideas. A similar meeting held in your space may find a team member without the requisite documentation, demonstration, or explanation on hand. By all means, take these opportunities to show your appreciation for a job well done, assuming it was.

Information from Other Sources

As part of your ear-to-the-rail approach to collecting information, other sources can provide useful information as well. Vendors involved in your project provide important feedback on the performance of the team member(s) they work with. Other managers may have thoughts or opinions on project progress, especially if yours is a high-visibility project. Take outsiders' comments, at least initially, with a grain of salt until you have a chance to weigh them. At the very least, document them in your project diary for future reference.

Employing a Guru for Guidance

We've already touched on the sensibility of using a project guru to help in the planning stages. You can also use such a person—either an experienced project manager or a person with technical knowledge you lack—to help control the project. This person does not replace your authority as project manager; instead, he or she steps in on occasion to verify project progress and to provide advice for making project adjustments. Your guru can be another manager who works for free or an outside consultant "rented" for the occasion.

Words from the Wise

From listening comes wisdom, from speaking repentance.

—Italian proverb

Choose your project guru wisely. It must be someone you can work with who won't step on your toes. The person must be affordable if you have to pay for his or her services and be truly experienced. Before hiring someone, check references and ask for specific evidence of past results. Otherwise, your guru may lead you down the primrose path instead of the path to enlightenment!

What's Really Going On?

Beyond gathering data about schedules, budgets, and outcomes, you must consider the emotional status of your team to control a project effectively. All projects involve a mix of people with different emotional requirements. Some are highly dedicated and committed; others aren't. Even though your team was carefully selected—whether by you, a previous manager, or senior management—once underway, a number of "strangers" may emerge where team members used to be. This is especially true when the pressure of missed dates puts a strain on personalities. Here are some of the folks you may encounter:

➤ The overly ambitious team member who aims to please but still doesn't get much done. (The person's skill levels may vary.)

➤ The middle-of-the-roader who does competent work on time but has recently developed a thirst for project blood.

➤ The procrastinator who promises results but delays progress by piddling. This person may do excellent work but deliver it late. He or she may also claim progress in expectation of completing the task later without you knowing about the inflated claims.

➤ The industrialist who puts more effort and time into a task than it requires or deserves because he thinks you're wrong in specifying a lower quality for the outcome.

As you can see, each of these "new" employees requires a different management style to handle. While the ambitious team member may be hurt if you aren't overwhelmed by his or her progress, the procrastinator may require micromanagement to keep moving. Eventually, all four employees may produce equal results, assuming their experience is also equal, but you'll get them to that point with different types of control. Some require kid gloves, others a kick in the pants.

Quality and Goal Assessment

When you're up to your rear in alligators, it's hard to remember that the objective was to drain the swamp. As project manager, you will be constantly barraged with input, problem resolution, nonperforming vendors, and other issues. It's easy to get buried in day-to-day operations and forget about your real goals—to meet the project's goals with appropriate quality.

For that reason, you must make an ongoing review of project goals part of your project assessment and control activities. If the project is to repaint the Golden Gate Bridge, the project is a failure if the painters can only meet their dates if they use green paint instead of red. (For those of you who have never seen this monument, it's always been red, never gold.)

It may take a trained eye to see problems early in the project. On a technical project, you may need to bring in outside experts to make sure quality, as well as timeliness and careful budget management, is in place. Otherwise, at the end of the project cycle, you may end up with egg on your face when you were expecting to pop corks from champagne bottles.

Putting It All Together

Once you have complete input from your team, you can analyze project status and decide on new actions to take (if any) to keep the project moving toward a successful conclusion. This includes two steps. The first step involves updating the project plan to reflect the current status. The second step is a review with the stakeholders and team to gain consensus on the revisions to the plan. We'll discuss this second step in detail in Chapter 24.

Updating the Project Plan and Other Control Documents

Your plan documents, including the SOW, product specifications, blueprints, budget, and schedule, are the most important control tools you can use. They allow you to present the work that's been agreed to and to communicate necessary changes.

Words from the Wise

"There are many limits to authority; so project managers should learn how to wield influence."

—Milton D. Rosenau Jr.

If you're comfortable with your cross-checking of project tasks, schedules, and budgets after gathering data on the current status of the project, it's time to compare reality with the approved plan and other project documents as appropriate (such as comparing the SOW and product specifications to better predict what's going to happen from here on out). For large projects, this is most easily done with computerized tools (see Chapter 30). Plugging in the status data may predict required changes to the schedule, budget, and critical path. (Computerized project management tools allow you to see comparisons of the old versus the new by highlighting changed paths, dates, tasks, and budget variances.)

Once the new data has been used to forecast a new schedule and budget, you can look for the problems causing the variances. If your critical path suddenly goes late, you can follow the lines back to see what tasks are late and who or what is responsible. If the critical path changes, it may or may not be a major flag. Again, study the flow to see what went wrong.

Tracking the budget is a matter of having good accounting practices in place that can give you timely figures on the committed costs and expenditures of the project. The process of comparing current to planned expenditures is similar to matching work completed to the planned task network. Graphs and spreadsheets are useful for demonstrating cost variances and projections. Good project management programs will offer a number of graphing techniques to allow you to visualize the budget through time. If the bottom line suddenly jumps $100,000 in your new projections, follow the money trail back to the point of discrepancy. Look for an overall change such as the carpenters' union getting a 35 percent pay raise. Such an event may mean cutting back on the project, asking for more money, or hopping a rusty steamer to Mandalay to look for another job. (Leave no forwarding address!)

High Water!

If your managers feel that your project is doomed or is seriously in jeopardy, they may take resources, including staff, from your project to work on other projects. The best way to avoid this problem is to keep everyone informed of positive results and to keep the project on track through careful monitoring and control.

The People Side of Things

Once you are comfortable with the plan and the necessary changes, it's time to look at the people side of things. Who is performing well? Who is almost burned out because a task has taken longer than expected and there's no extra time? This is an opportunity to review your notes from the on-site meetings to see how you can help your staff. A trip to the resource-leveling chart may be required to study how to change task assignments.

If a task handled by a project team seems to be constantly late, study your notes to look for personality conflicts, procrastinators, work overload, lack of experience, or lousy equipment. You may find a mix of all five as team members struggle first with too much work, second with inadequate equipment, and third taking it out on each other. No wonder they're slow! Most people try to work hard—so never blame the people until you understand the issues.

Clue 'Em In ...

The central tenet in controlling your temporary fiefdom is through monitoring and adjusting the plan. As schedules, tasks, or other assignments change, let the team members know as soon as possible—better yet, let them be part of the decision to change the plan in the first place. Then, as Jean-Luc Picard implores, "Make it so!"

The Least You Need to Know

➤ Control requires knowledge of the project status. Since the status is constantly changing, you'll need to monitor the project and compare it to the plan in some way every day.

➤ If you keep the plan and other key project documentation up-to-date to reflect changes and adjustments, your status can be more accurately determined.

➤ Reports are good tools for synthesizing information, but informal discussions often reveal a more accurate picture of the project.

➤ Always ask the team to offer suggestions when things are off track.

➤ If your project is in serious trouble, ask for expert advice before it's too late.

Chapter 23

Conflicts: Resolving and Benefiting from Them

In This Chapter

➤ Conflicts are inevitable but not always bad.

➤ People are the source of most conflicts.

➤ Conflicts are usually strongest at project initiation.

➤ Not all conflicts have a negative impact.

➤ There are five basic ways to resolve conflicts.

Conflicts are a way of life in projects. Just like families, all projects have them. Sometimes project managers are even described as conflict managers. But conflicts don't have to bring your project to a halt. If you know something is going to happen, you can plan for dealing with it—and that's the way you should handle conflicts.

Recognizing the difference between negative and meaningful conflicts is vital. (Yes, some conflicts are a good thing because they bring ideas and energy to a project.) Getting control of the negative variety, however, is necessary to reach your project goals.

It's possible for just two people to bog down a project through a clash of personality, ideas, or opinions. (Don't believe it? Consider the venerable institution of marriage!) In this chapter, you will learn what causes conflicts, what kinds of problems manifest themselves at what point in a project, and how to resolve them.

Most conflicts, short of reconciling the Russians and the Chinese, can be resolved, but not all conflicts are worth the effort to eliminate them. Some interpersonal problems are unlikely to be fixed. Some conflicts require more effort (and time) than a repair merits. Instead, a little creative thinking to invent a way to work around the problem to neutralize the conflict may be just what the doctor ordered. In this chapter, you'll learn where and when to draw this line.

Questions to Ask to Scope Out the Issue

As you read this chapter, especially if you're looking for advice on resolving an immediate *project conflict,* ask yourself the following questions:

1. Do I have enough information to understand the true source of the conflict?
2. Do I have the diplomatic skills to resolve it?
3. Will the conflict work itself out with a meeting between members?
4. Is it self-terminating? (Amazingly, some conflicts work themselves out or burn themselves up without your intervention.)

If the answer to the first two questions is "no," whom can you tap for the task? It must be someone with enough authority for the job without overshadowing you in your role.

Conflicts Are Inevitable in Projects

As a project progresses, people conflicts enter into the picture. Properly identified in a timely manner, these *project conflicts* can be mitigated without affecting the project's schedule. What causes conflicts? Essentially, any project, no matter how mundane it looks (digging a trough for a new phone cable, for example), is a creative project of sorts. Ideas may come from multiple players for planning the project. Once underway, better ways to accomplish the same objectives may appear. Team members may become out of synchronization with one another.

Project Lingo

Sounding like something worked out via fisticuffs, a **project conflict** is one in which something—people, priorities, or problems ("the three Ps")—begins to interfere with completing a project on time and within budget.

There are two schools of thought as to why personnel or group conflicts occur. One is considered increasingly old-fashioned but plays a role in many conflicts: failure or lack of leadership on the part of the management team. The other, considered more important today, recognizes conflicts as part of the project process. Surprisingly, they can be beneficial, as you'll see later in the chapter in the section "Conflicts Aren't Always Negative."

In a commonplace project such as laying a phone cable, team members may disagree on the start date due to weather, how to route the cable, or how long the project will take. Once underway, the route may become perilous due to an old concrete sewer main blocking the original plan. Part of the team may want to route the cable differently, while the other part may want to add time to the schedule and remove the offending concrete. This second option also requires approval from the sewer department. Further, the dig crew may be late because they must work by hand near a gas main rather than rely on a backhoe, and the wiring specialists may appear two days before they can actually start work. You may still have to pay them. Or worse, they may not be available to handle the wiring by the day you need it done.

The Four Kinds of People Conflicts

Conflicts involving project team members manifest themselves in a number of ways:

1. **Intrapersonnel.** A team member feels he or she isn't living up to expectations or is frustrated with something on the project.

2. **Interpersonal.** Two team members don't get along, or one member may not get along with the rest of the team.

3. **Intragroup.** Internal feuding and bickering occurs among people working on the same part of the project.

4. **Intergroup.** Hostilities, rivalries, or competitions appear between two different groups working on the project.

Any of these conflicts can have negative or positive consequences. Positive conflicts foster harder work, new ideas, or positive competition to excel at getting things done. Negative conflicts result in poor morale, decreased productivity, or even work stoppage.

Negative conflicts are resolvable but in different fashions. Before you can resolve a conflict, you must know what led to the conflict in the first place. Keep in mind that more than one source of conflict may be at hand, and it takes careful evaluation to decide which one(s) you are dealing with. The general sources of conflict are covered in the following sections.

Words from the Wise

"There's trouble ... right here in River City! ... and that starts with T and rhymes with P and that stands for project ..."

—Adapted from lyrics for "Ya Got Trouble" from *The Music Man*

Time Is Money

According to conventional wisdom, no one is irreplaceable. But just try losing a couple of key team members in the middle of a project and see just how untrue this idea really is!

Goal Incompatibility

It's possible that not everyone in the organization is functioning on the same wavelength regarding the project's goals. From a simple misunderstanding of the project's intended outcome to differences between the project manager's goals and team members' goals, conflict can arise. There might be a difference in perception or erroneous assumptions, or others might disagree on the precedence of tasks, dates, and performance criteria.

Lack of Task Focus

Tasks must be specific. You must provide detailed instructions instead of relying on brevity. For example, as part of an office-remodeling project, you may plan to move the office cubicles in a department to lay new carpet. An ambitious facilities manager and his laborers may assume, lacking specific instructions, that the entire 10,000 square foot building is involved and may knock down everyone's cubicles over the weekend.

Administrative Procedures

As mentioned in Chapter 19, "What an Organization!" conflict can arise in a project with regard to the number of reports, their kinds, and who should receive what. On a project involving sensitive or even classified information, team members experience conflict at all levels. High-level personnel want to keep as much information secret as possible. Low-level members complain, "How can I complete my tasks correctly with so little information at hand?"

Role Uncertainty

A common kind of conflict is one in which people are not sure what they should be working on. Every team member, manager, and even the project management staff (if there are others in addition to yourself) must have a clear understanding of their roles. Not having this understanding is especially problematic if your project is structured using a matrix management approach. (See Chapter 19 for information on project organizations.)

Technical Uncertainty

If new technology is being developed, uncertainty and conflict are sure to arise. What's the best way to do it? What steps must we take to complete the project faster? Will it work at all? The Boeing 747 required an entirely new engine to actually get the monster off the ground. One team demanded the choice of manufacturer A's new engine. The other demanded engines from company B. Company B finally won out. Good thing, too, because when A's engines were completed for sale to other companies, they did not provide nearly enough power for the 747!

Staffing and Resource Allocation

Staffing is a major source of conflict—from who will have to give up staff for use on a project to people perceived as having the fun tasks versus those doing dull tasks or menial labor. Even within a multi-team project, managers can act like kids assembling a baseball team. Insist on getting the choice members for your team at the expense of the other team. Plenty of controversy is common, and even when a project is well underway, staff members may attempt to move up the ranks or undermine other team members for a variety of unpleasant reasons.

Budgets and Costs

Another point of conflict in every project is its budget. Conflict begins when the people footing the bill for the project fail to allocate adequate funds. Then the project manager must allocate funds with team members or groups squawking for a bigger piece of an already too-small pie. Even more conflict is generated if a group is seen as spending too freely at the expense of other less-well-endowed groups. The process repeats itself if and when the project runs out of money and the project manager must go back to the well for more.

Schedules

The schedule is usually the main focus of conflicts. People never think they have enough time to do the work right. One team may want more time than the next in line perceives as necessary. Squabbles over scheduling lead to conflict. When upriver, the project may start late, and those downstream are often squeezed to make up for lost time. Anxiety and conflict result.

In resolving schedule or task difficulties, we've had good results by dragging the entire master plan into a conference room (or auditorium, if that's what it takes). We then work through the network diagram and break down the structure with the staff to see where the plan has misstated the actual work requirements. As we adjust the tasks, we work through the schedule.

By comparing the work being done to the work that was projected in the plan, you'll eventually get the team to understand why the schedule or the objectives are derailed—and hopefully, you'll get some insights about what can be done to get back on track.

Personality Clashes

Personality clashes are almost inevitable when many people work together. People with superior roles, training, and experience may look down their noses at team members perceived as less important. Sometimes people seem caustic or have different values about work and quality. Sometimes it's just a chemistry thing that can't be explained. You can minimize the negative affects of personality conflicts by building open communication and trust among the team members, but sometimes you'll just have to mediate to keep things on track.

Conflicts Are Strongest at Project Initiation

Problems such as personality conflicts can pop up any time in the project cycle, but some conflicts are more common at specific times. During the project initiation phase, conflicts tend to swirl around goals, priorities, authority, and responsibility. At the beginning of the executing phase, conflicts over administrative procedures emerge but soon fade as people get used to project operations. As the project gets into full swing, conflicts move from goals to schedules and technical issues. As the project phases out, conflicts continue to involve the schedule but may also have growing personality-related issues. Of course, this sequence of conflicts is not true of all projects, but it's predictable enough to help you plan for your resolutions before the problems emerge.

Words from the Wise

"When you add power, self-esteem, motivations, and status to the equation, you'll likely see fireworks where the project team used to be."

—Sunny Baker, *On Time and Within Budget* (1992)

Ignore It or Solve It? What Should You Do?

Conflict resolution requires careful consideration. The conflicting parties may both have legitimate grievances. As project manager, your task is to sort out the real problems that may be buried in the hubris of personalities. On the other hand, the clash may be the problem itself. We recommend the time-honored technique of interviewing each person or team separately and taking careful notes. It helps to have a witness with you in case legal issues come up later. (This is unlikely but not unheard of.) Then, after a period of time to reflect on the issues and a solution, present your resolution to both sides, either individually or together. Usually there is no perfect solution, but adjustments and compromise may mend the breach, at least until the project is complete.

Resolving Conflicts: The Five Options

Many people have studied conflicts and how managers resolve them. In general, these studies have identified five general ways that conflicts are resolved—and all of them are appropriate at one time or another:

1. **Withdrawing** means that the manager retreats (withdraws) from the disagreement. This is often an option if the conflict is petty, of inconsequential impact to the project, and not worth spending time to figure out.

2. **Smoothing** is used to emphasize areas of agreement to help minimize or avoid areas of disagreement. This is the preferred method when people can identify areas of agreement and the conflict is relatively unimportant. However, this is a weak approach; chances are, the conflict will flare up again even though sparring parties shake hands and make up. Use it to get the project moving until a better solution can be found.

3. **Compromising** involves creating a negotiated solution that brings some source of satisfaction to each party in the conflict. Compromises are best made after each side has had time to cool down (if the conflict has escalated to the anger and hostility stage). The best compromise makes each party feel as though he or she "won." A well-constructed compromise will hold the project together. A poor or weak one will come apart in the future, and you should be ready for it. The solution to a collapsed compromise is usually another compromise. This works best when people have a give-and-take attitude and a shared focus on the priorities of the project. (The delicate art of negotiation is described in Chapter 25, "When Push Comes to Shove, You Can Always Negotiate.")

4. **Forcing** is used when someone exerts his or her position of power to resolve a conflict. This is usually done at the expense of someone else, and it is not recommended unless all other methods failed to resolve the conflict.

5. **Confronting** is not quite as strong as forcing, but it is the most used form of conflict resolution. The goal of a confrontation (if handled professionally) is to get people to face their conflicts directly, thereby resolving the problem by working through the issues in the spirit of problem solving.

Time Is Money

When you have difficulties to communicate, the best way to do it is with a presentation of facts. The sooner the problem is truthfully acknowledged, the easier it will be to solve. Bad news that is covered up only grows larger over time—and damages your credibility in direct proportion to the length of time you waited to let people know about it.

Decide on the Best Approach

Almost any conflict can be ironed out, although resolution may impact the budget and schedule if the problem is complex or has been allowed to fester too long. Analyze the situation and choose the method of conflict resolution that makes the most sense and has the most chance of success. Of course, if you are trying to reconcile the Russians and the Chinese, the five methods of conflict resolution may be of little use. Instead, you'll just have to work around the conflict to get things done.

Provide What's Needed

Attempt to provide what each party wants if possible. We once saw a conflict over computer floppy disks (still expensive then) that brought a major software development project to a halt. One team thought another was taking more than its share of disks. Buying separate supplies of disks resolved this incredibly stupid source of hostilities in minutes!

Work It Out

Best saved for personality conflicts, getting the unhappy parties together in a room with you as a mediator can work. From a mix of yelling and tears, a new friendship can often grow like a phoenix rising from the ashes. Beforehand, have each side prepare a list of grievances so that nothing is forgotten that can smolder later. Two meetings might be required to work out a complex problem. If the problem is a highly technical one on a topic in which you are not well versed, bring a third-party expert whose impeccable credentials are unassailable by either party.

Know When to Ignore It

Some problems fix themselves. A problem team member might realize that he or she doesn't fit in and find another job or flee the country. This approach is only applicable to projects in which the schedule is loose and the problem isn't vital to the project's success. On the other hand, mature teams or team members may work things out themselves without your intervention. Finally, if a conflict is tangential and doesn't affect the project, it can also be ignored, at least until it does affect the project.

Employ Brute Force

As a last resort, use the chain of command to order warring parties back to work, with or without compromise. This approach is best saved for situations in which the schedule is so tight that there's no time for forging a compromise. It can also be used when one side is adamant in its position and refuses to accept a compromise solution.

The toughest problem is one you can't fix—a fundamental weakness in the project that you can't easily remedy such as an impossible schedule or a lack of resources, whether it's cash, personnel, equipment, or facilities. The only solution is either an ingenious workaround (more common in movies than in real life) or going to management, fingers crossed, and explaining the quandary and what is required to solve it.

Conflicts Aren't Always Negative

What does the conflict mean in the scheme of the universe? As project manager, you probably look at any conflict as troublesome. It slows the project, costs budget dollars, and reflects poorly on your abilities as team leader. But not all conflicts are negative in their impact. A conflict can point to real problems, can lead to better ideas for the project, or can serve as an attack on the entrenched thinking of the citadel.

When studying a conflict situation, look underneath the obvious motives to see whether there may be a better way to accomplish a task, a method for producing a better end product, or an imaginative team member constrained and confined to a lowly role. Stop, look, and listen. You may find something useful or important to the future of the project underlying any kind of conflict.

The Least You Need to Know

➤ Most conflicts can be resolved, but you may need to bring in an outside project expert to resolve a sticky conflict.

➤ To successfully resolve a conflict, you need to choose the right action for the job: withdrawing, smoothing, compromising, forcing, confronting, or, as a last resort, using brute force.

➤ Conflicts are particularly common during the project initiation phase, and the schedule is almost always a candidate for conflict at any stage of the project.

➤ Not all conflicts are negative if you know how to manage them for positive impact on the project.

Chapter 24

Changes, Changes, and More Changes

In This Chapter

➤ Making changes to keep on track

➤ Accommodating the unexpected

➤ Understanding the trade-offs and the options for change

➤ Handling resistance to necessary changes

You can't predict everything, and since noted psychic Jeanne Dixon died, you're out of luck if you want to see into the future as a way to eliminate changes to your project plan. Because you can't always predict changes, we recommend that you rely on on-going monitoring, open communications, and careful analysis as ways to deal with unforeseen changes. Of course, there are always tarot cards and tea leaves if you want to guess your way through the project.

Managing Change Is Part of Control

Some projects get completed exactly as planned—but not many. Projects often change direction, shape, or size. Goals. Budget. Schedule. Work plan. Priorities. Personnel. Any or all of these can change during the life of a project.

Some changes are under your control. For example, you might be able to shorten a schedule because you learn faster ways to do things as you proceed through the steps of the work plan. On the other hand, if it rains on the day you were going to pour cement, you'll have to change the schedule, like it or not. In both cases, you'll have to anticipate the impact of the change and adjust your project plan accordingly. Because change is inevitable, managing the impact of change is a key aspect in controlling your project.

The Battle Cry of Change: Flexibility

Yes, there are project managers, often former military officers, who will tell you that the quickest way from Point A to Point B is a straight line. But after managing a multitude of projects of all sizes, we've learned that only a flexible project manager can actually complete a project on time and within budget—and that often means taking a longer or more circuitous route to get things done. If you insist on the rigid attitude of getting things done exactly as planned, you'll only frustrate yourself and your project team. Remember, plans are guidelines, not bibles. Your project plan is a living document that should be designed to be changed.

The Marriage of Review and Change

Managing change and reviewing the project go hand in hand. As you monitor your project over time, you'll get feedback on the general issues, problems, and other factors that may be affecting your progress (positively or negatively) in completing the project. Lots of things enter the picture as the project proceeds; some are desirable, others are unpredictable, and once in a while, a disastrous event occurs. The good ideas and the unpredictable problems will all result in the same thing: the need to change the project plan in some way.

High Water!

When managing a project, you need to constantly monitor it. Today's purring project can become tomorrow's glitch-filled problem if you don't stay on top of things. Ongoing monitoring is always your first defense against the undesirable impacts of a changing world.

Through project review, new ideas and new ways of doing things become apparent. The realities of what can and cannot be accomplished shift tasks and goals. Then there are the changes handed down from senior management or the customers.

All these things require that you update your plan (including the SOW) for the project, and updating the plan means making changes to the goals, tasks, workflow, schedule, budget, or people and getting them approved by the appropriate stakeholders. Be prepared for change. It's not a question of what to do *if* there is an issue; it's what to do *when* there is an issue.

The Rules of Change

Now that you've accepted the inevitability of change, here are five rules that will help you anticipate changes on your projects:

1. The longer the project runs, the more likely it is that changes will occur and the more shifts in direction the project will undergo.

2. Projects that lack firm political roots in your organization are the most likely to be extensively modified or done away with completely.

3. The project manager must negotiate, be assigned, or have the authority to make appropriate operational project adjustments. The PM also needs authority to control outside interference that's ill-advised. If the project manager lacks these basic authorities, uninformed changes made by people outside the project are more likely, and eventually, the inability of the project manager to control change will doom the project.

4. The project manager must involve the key stakeholders (especially functional management and the customer) in all decisions that involve changes to the project costs, the delivery date, or project objectives.

5. Change is necessitated by external factors as well as by poor planning. Weather, a shortage of materials and equipment, legal complications, labor stoppages, process failure, and many other factors can run any project off both the schedule and budget tracks. The trick to employing the risk management process (learned in Chapter 8) is to minimize the changes due to incompetence and to reduce the impact of changes beyond the control of mortals.

High Water!

Meddlers beware! There's always someone associated with your project who "knows" how to do things better than you're doing them. Sometimes you need to put your foot down and pinion these meddlers to keep them from getting in your way. Establish a clear process for suggesting and reviewing changes so that people offer constructive advice instead of bothersome chatter. And if you fail at a project because of outside meddling, guess who will get the blame? We bet it won't be the meddler with all those "good" ideas.

Communicate with Everyone!

Yes, you've heard it before. When dealing with change, it's vital to get input from everyone on the team. Comments should also be solicited from other managers, senior management, and customers (when appropriate). Multiple inputs provide perspectives you may not have considered in your plan of change.

For example, if you make a task, resource, or schedule change, make sure the whole team is involved in understanding the need for new roles or task assignments. Have alternative activities identified if primary activities are stopped. You'll also need to ensure that all resources are aware of new job responsibilities and schedule implications.

Change and Conflict Go Hand in Hand

In Chapter 23, we looked at ways to deal with conflicts. Many of the forces that cause conflict have to do with project changes. New ideas enter the project. Change is required. Schedules slip. Change is required. Jane and Joe are acting like children. Change is required. When a task proves impossible as originally defined, you guessed it. Change is required again.

The list of potential change sources is a long one. Some changes you can see coming, and you can make a preemptive strike to minimize their impact. Others occur without warning. Project changes also vary in their impact on your project. Some are little more than a blip easily accommodated within the project flow. Others radically alter the budget, schedule, and scope of the project. Hope for the former but prepare for the latter.

Here are some of the "typical" changes we've seen in our experience as project managers:

Time Is Money

The best way to deal with a runaway project is to get involved as soon as you suspect a problem. The longer you wait, the less you will be able to salvage of your schedule and budget. Before you jump in, however, ask what's really wrong. Determine what precipitated the problem so you don't end up in the same place next time.

➤ The organizational priorities are realigned, and the priority of the project comes into question. Sometimes you can salvage the project through careful planning, justification of the project, and skillful renegotiation; sometimes you just end up on the wrong side of the corporate priorities and have to look for another project to manage. Once a project has lost the support of the stakeholders, resign yourself to the inevitable and don't try to salvage it.

➤ A company's restructuring or reorganization moves staff around, possibly depleting you of key team members. Again, the first step is negotiation to get whom you need. If that doesn't work, there are always outside vendors. And don't forget to consider staff development for the people you have left.

➤ An organization announces sweeping cuts in operational budgets. This can have a profound impact on a project with a budget that's already on the slim side. Go back to your plan and look for ways to cut back on expenses. Make sure everyone knows that the results will likely be cut back along with the budget (which is almost never a good idea or a good choice).

➤ A competitor announces a product that is similar to yours. You must get to market first, budget be damned. Now is the time to pull out all the stops and redraft the plan to get to market faster. You'll need more money as well as other resources, so expect to make a presentation to management that justifies your scheme.

➤ The team committed to something impossible—like making a cow jump over the moon—and needs to put some reality into the plan. As soon as you realize that your cow can't jump that high, you'll have to ask for more resources, scale back the project, or go back to the drawing table and draft a new plan. Should you accept an impossible mission even after you realize the goal is impossible, you and your Impossible Missions Force are simply doomed to failure. You'll need to negotiate another goal—or start updating your resumé. The choice is yours.

Darwin and the Origin of Species

Charles Darwin had a brilliant theory of change that explained how species adapt over time to evolving circumstances. Fish developed legs (of sorts) to trek from the seas to sing blibbit in the swamps. Polar bears developed long necks to haul 400-pound seals over the ice to their family get-togethers.

Darwin's ideas apply to projects, too. Projects also evolve. If the project manager is in charge, the project evolves to be more adaptive to outside changes. The project survives. If the project manager lets people and things go on their own, things still evolve. The difference is in the animal you end up with.

Understanding and Estimating the Impact of Changes

If you want to stay in control and help your project evolve in the right direction, a well-documented project plan is your first line of defense in managing change. If you want the results you expect as opposed to the consequences that just happen, you need to keep your plan up-to-date. Period. With a plan in hand, you can quickly assess the impact a change will have on the project's budget, schedule, and resources. You can also use the plan and your current status analysis to show why a new or different user requirement may have a negative impact on the final results of your project.

As you review your plan, you'll see that there are really only five major components in any project that can be changed. They are the same components that were used to create your project plan in the first place. Here they are again (in case you've forgotten):

1. Goals and specifications for the end results of the project
2. The people who work on the project
3. The money (budget) you have to spend on the project
4. The material and technical resources you have available to support your project
5. The time you have available to complete the project

Any change in your project plan will affect one or more of these project components. Most changes will affect all five in some way. If you want to keep changes under control, you'll need to address the impact of changes by updating your project plan and communicating the changes to everyone involved.

Sometimes you'll need to replan, reapprove, and replan again. That's why we drew the planning, executing, and controlling processes of the project management cycle in a circle. (Refer to the diagram in Chapter 2.) As you execute your project, things change. You control these things by adjusting the plan. As you execute the new plan, things change again. You repeat the cycle until the project is declared finished—and that means (finally) moving on to the closing phase.

This type of change is called "balancing the project." As you find that the project is running out of time, costing too much, or short of resources—you must balance the cost, schedule, and results (goals) of the project to keep things on track. This will require involvement of all the stakeholders on the project.

The Balancing Act

Balancing a project can take place at three levels of authority in a project, depending on the severity or immediacy of the change needed:

➤ Project-level balancing involves making adjustments to keep the project within its approved cost, schedule, and quality outcomes. The project manager and core team members should have enough authority to make these decisions.

➤ Business-case balancing is necessary when a project cannot achieve its approved cost, schedule, and quality goals. When this becomes obvious through project monitoring, the business case for the project must be reevaluated. Maybe the project will be useless if it doesn't come in on time. Maybe there isn't enough money (or profit) left in the project to make it worthwhile. Business case changes are beyond the scope of the project manager's authority alone and must involve the review and approval team of stakeholders. Most of all, the customer must agree to any changes that affect the cost, schedule, final features, or end results of the project.

➤ Enterprise-level balancing is required when a firm has to choose from various projects to spread limited resources out. This could result in a project being cancelled (terminated) or postponed. This is primarily a business management decision that is well beyond the scope of the project team, although the key team members will likely be involved in the process. The enterprise responsibility for this type of decision could lie with the customer, a government agency, or the corporation as a whole.

The Steps for Measuring and Accommodating Change

The best approach for accommodating change in a project starts with apprising your team members (or team leaders in a larger project) of the need for change and then asking their opinions on ways to implement the changes. This "town hall meeting" approach is vital because changes always impact people's work on a project. Occasionally, an inventive team member may even introduce a solution that accommodates the change with no hard feelings or frustrations. This is rare—but it happens.

Beyond this, you should follow these steps to make sure the changes have the desired impact on the project:

➤ Establish how changes will take place before you need to make any. This should be done as a formal part of the project administrative procedures. On a large project, the change management process will likely include detailed, written steps for submitting and reviewing project changes. It may also include the formation of a change management team (also called a change board) comprising a subset of stakeholders from all relevant areas of the project. This team will review and recommend changes for approval at various levels.

➤ Clearly define the expectations for the change. You are not making changes for fun but to improve something or to fix a problem. Be sure you determine how you'll measure whether the desired effect on the project is achieved. How will you know if the change is successful?

> **Time Is Money**
>
> Instead of wasting time fighting a change dictated by your boss, ask questions and try to understand the rationale involved (*if any*). Then run the numbers to see what, if any, impact the change will have on your project. Communicate this impact clearly before you begin implementing the change. Chances are, the imperative for the new idea will change if the numbers don't look too good.

➤ Document requests for changes from team members as part of the change management process. If these changes meet criteria of importance or urgency, the recommendations should then be reviewed for further action.

➤ Plug the proposed changes into the project plan to see what happens to schedule, budget, and resource requirements. Never commit to a set of changes before assessing their impact on the project. Violators of this rule might find themselves with a failed project on their hands. Team review of the impact is vital. Others may spot an impossible task dependency that you missed, and the technical folks may have knowledge of dependencies for tasks you don't understand.

➤ Always look for alternatives before you, the change management team, or other stakeholders make a decision to change a major component of the plan. One more time, consider the budget, the staff skills, and the ability to meet the scheduled dates. Keep in mind that there is more than one way to accomplish almost anything.

➤ Have the changes reviewed and eventually accepted by the appropriate group of stakeholders.

➤ Once the changes are determined, document changes on the original plan, date them, and communicate them as you would a new project plan. On large projects, the documentation of the changes is often called *configuration management,* and it can require a full-time staff in the "project office" responsible for controlling the different versions of the project plan.

It's important to always get formal approval for revisions from the powers that be. Even if the disruption is minimal, managers and stakeholders should be fully cognizant of changes. For changes that impact delivery dates or the budget, written correspondence should accompany your request. Remember, if they're not in writing, agreements are easily forgotten.

➤ After the new plan is approved, inform all team members of the changes to their tasks and delivery dates. Make sure all team members are aware of exactly what will be expected of them and how the changes will impact the project. You'll also need to let team members know how the effect of the changes will be measured so that things don't end up going on just like before. This should be done through ongoing monitoring, reports, and communication. (And yes, you might need to change some of your project reports or procedures to make sure you get the new information you need.)

Along the Critical Path

Always remember that using more people doesn't always mean more work gets done. Yes, naive managers often solve problems by throwing more resources (usually people) onto the project. But adding more people doesn't always improve productivity—especially when creative people are involved. Adding additional writers, designers, architects, or engineers may actually slow a project down.

The Basic Changes You Can Make

In balancing a project that's missing its time, cost, or quality objectives, here are the basic things you can do:

1. **Reestimate the project.** This means double-checking things to make sure the estimates are really valid. Don't just give in to management to reduce the cost or schedule estimates; instead, look for opportunities to do things better or differently to achieve the same goals. For example, you may be able to take advantage of the float in the schedule to resequence noncritical tasks. If you do the review of the project correctly, your new estimates should provide an even firmer foundation for meeting project expectations.

2. **Add more people to the project.** Beware of this simple-sounding solution, however; as you add more personalities, people can lock horns in what is called a "creative conflict." This can bring work to a standstill until the mess sorts itself out or a creative team member stomps off for good in self-righteous disgust. This is sad but common. Only add people if people will actually help get things done faster. Look for other means to improve productivity. If you scoped out the work and selected a good team in the first place, you may need to change objectives instead of the team.

3. **Reduce the scope of the tasks.** Sometimes the best way to get a project done is to scratch some of the work from the list. This can turn an impossible list of tasks into a doable (and scoped down) project. Before promising to do less as a way of dealing with change, however, make sure the downsized project is really worth doing. Also make sure the stakeholders agree to the downsizing. If not, you'll need to negotiate what you really need—more time or resources or a bigger budget—to get the project done right.

Time Is Money

Keep in mind that people get frustrated with endless rounds of picky changes. To avoid this frustration, limit the self-induced changes to those that are truly necessary and important.

High Water!

There's a dimension in many projects that you might call the twilight zone—the unreality between the actual time and resources available and the demands by the customer or senior managers in your company. Try to avoid entering the twilight zone by being firm and honest with people who attempt to pressure you into unrealistic goals, schedules, or budgets. Otherwise, say "Hi" to Rod Serling for us ....

4. **Increase productivity by using in-house experts.** Some people are simply more productive than others. By reassigning people, you may still be able to meet your original cost and schedule performance. Sometimes this is a good solution for the project but a bad one for the company, however. For example, it's not always a good idea to put all the best engineers on one project; the other projects may suffer as a result. Some of these engineers might end up doing work for productivity's sake that's well below their capabilities. Be sure there isn't a better way to make the staff more productive such as training people or prudently using new technologies.

5. **Use outside resources.** Assign part of the project to an external firm that can manage and complete it within your original guidelines. (This is called outsourcing.) This moves the work to outside experts who will hopefully be more productive. However, this may create more risks in terms of lost in-house control and the gamble that the outside experts will actually be able to do what they say they can.

6. **Use overtime.** Use it prudently, however. It can backfire in lost productivity and morale problems if this option becomes the default action. If you're using hourly employees as opposed to salaried ones, it can end up pushing the budget out of control.

7. **Shift some of the work to the customer.** If a project is high on cost or short on people resources, this can be a good choice—if the customer agrees to it. You and the customer should identify tasks that the customer's staff can perform. This only works if the customer agrees with the plan and has adequate resources to take on the tasks. It can also create political problems between your project organization and that of the customer. Be careful when you consider this option; it needs to be done in a way that preserves the integrity of the project and your authority as project manager.

8. **Crash the schedule.** This involves compressing the tasks on the critical path to reduce the time required to meet the desired finish date. You'll need to produce a cost/schedule/trade-off analysis, which can help analyze the cost of reducing the schedule. Sometimes the increases in cost to get things done faster will outweigh the need for speed.

9. **Adjust the profit requirements for the project.** A reduced profit margin can free up cash for needed resources. If the project won't bring in enough money for the company to survive, however, this is a bad idea. A decision to reduce profit is clearly the territory of the company executives—not the project manager.

10. **Adjust the project goals.** This is like playing on thin ice. Although it may be appropriate to reduce some of the functionality or scope of the project end results, it's not usually a good idea to reduce the performance characteristics (quality) of the project. Remove some of the functionality only when it doesn't affect the performance of the product overall. Performance cuts may initially

save time, but these cuts result in cost increases in the long run due to reworking broken or deficient parts or damaging the reputation of your firm. Remember that quality is never free.

Comparing Changes with Trade–Off Analysis

Trade-off analysis is one method of dealing with change that lets you evaluate the impact of various alternatives. "We can do this if we skip that. Which is more important?" Analyzing trade-offs is also a way to understand the pressure change is placing on the project. Understanding trade-offs clarifies the changes that affect later tasks and milestones. Here are some considerations for understanding the impact of various options (or trade-offs) when implementing a change to a project:

1. Determine the underlying rationale for the change. Are the changes motivated by rational thinking or a political agenda? Does the change really make sense?

2. Are the project goals still appropriate? Will the change also affect the eventual outcome of the project? Imagine if God set out to make the eagle but, due to project changes, created the dodo bird instead. Make sure your dodo will still be a desirable species—or figure out how to make the eagle you really wanted.

3. Do the options affect the likelihood of completing the project successfully? You should have already reviewed how the various options impact schedules, budgets, and team member availability. When changes increase the risk of failure, this needs to be carefully analyzed and then clearly communicated to all involved. Sometimes the risk is for good reasons, but sometimes it's just a plain mistake. Make sure you know which it is before you choose one change over another.

4. Analyze the options at all levels. Try to hold the budget and objectives constant and then evaluate how you can accommodate the changes. Look for alternatives, tasks that can be deleted or shortened, or dollars that can be moved around in the project. This is usually a team exercise. Be patient when trying to come up with alternatives. Don't always jump on the first ideas. It's often at 11:00 p.m. over a seventh cup of coffee that a team member suggests the perfect compromise that hadn't occurred to you during the first review of the problem. Only after looking at all options should you ask for more money or more time.

Use the Zero-Based Budget Approach

Sometimes you need to prioritize what really needs to be done in order to understand the things that should be changed on a project. If you're building a hot new computer system with many new multimedia features, for example, maybe some of the features could be released in next year's model. To make this kind of decision, we often use the zero-based budget (ZBB) approach to establish the priorities and the bottom line for a changing project. ZBB is an approach that separates the must-do from the would-like-to-do work. (This is different than a trade-off analysis, which looks at one option for change compared to another.)

Assembling a ZBB is simple. Make a list of all the elements you would like to see done at completion (see the following chart). Then rewrite the list according to priority. List the most important must-do tasks or goals at the top and work your way down to the less important tasks toward the bottom.

A zero-based budget is a simple tool for understanding and simplifying priorities based on the cost of getting things done.

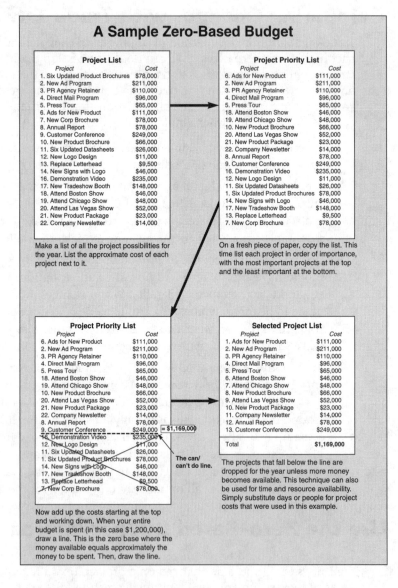

A Sample Zero-Based Budget

Project List

Project	Cost
1. Six Updated Product Brochures	$78,000
2. New Ad Program	$211,000
3. PR Agency Retainer	$110,000
4. Direct Mail Program	$96,000
5. Press Tour	$65,000
6. Ads for New Product	$111,000
7. New Corp Brochure	$78,000
8. Annual Report	$78,000
9. Customer Conference	$249,000
10. New Product Brochure	$66,000
11. Six Updated Datasheets	$26,000
12. New Logo Design	$11,000
13. Replace Letterhead	$9,500
14. New Signs with Logo	$46,000
16. Demonstration Video	$235,000
17. New Tradeshow Booth	$148,000
18. Attend Boston Show	$46,000
19. Attend Chicago Show	$48,000
20. Attend Las Vegas Show	$52,000
21. New Product Package	$23,000
22. Company Newsletter	$14,000

Make a list of all the project possibilities for the year. List the approximate cost of each project next to it.

Project Priority List

Project	Cost
6. Ads for New Product	$111,000
2. New Ad Program	$211,000
3. PR Agency Retainer	$110,000
4. Direct Mail Program	$96,000
5. Press Tour	$65,000
18. Attend Boston Show	$46,000
19. Attend Chicago Show	$48,000
10. New Product Brochure	$66,000
20. Attend Las Vegas Show	$52,000
21. New Product Package	$23,000
22. Company Newsletter	$14,000
8. Annual Report	$78,000
9. Customer Conference	$249,000
16. Demonstration Video	$235,000
12. New Logo Design	$11,000
11. Six Updated Datasheets	$26,000
1. Six Updated Product Brochures	$78,000
14. New Signs with Logo	$46,000
17. New Tradeshow Booth	$148,000
13. Replace Letterhead	$9,500
7. New Corp Brochure	$78,000

On a fresh piece of paper, copy the list. This time list each project in order of importance, with the most important projects at the top and the least important at the bottom.

Project Priority List

Project	Cost
6. Ads for New Product	$111,000
2. New Ad Program	$211,000
3. PR Agency Retainer	$110,000
4. Direct Mail Program	$96,000
5. Press Tour	$65,000
18. Attend Boston Show	$46,000
19. Attend Chicago Show	$48,000
10. New Product Brochure	$66,000
20. Attend Las Vegas Show	$52,000
21. New Product Package	$23,000
22. Company Newsletter	$14,000
8. Annual Report	$78,000
9. Customer Conference	$249,000	= $1,169,000
16. Demonstration Video	$235,000
12. New Logo Design	$11,000
11. Six Updated Datasheets	$26,000
1. Six Updated Product Brochures	$78,000
14. New Signs with Logo	$46,000
17. New Tradeshow Booth	$148,000
13. Replace Letterhead	$9,500
7. New Corp Brochure	$78,000

The can/ can't do line.

Now add up the costs starting at the top and working down. When your entire budget is spent (in this case $1,200,000), draw a line. This is the zero base where the money available equals approximately the money to be spent. Then, draw the line.

Selected Project List

Project	Cost
1. Ads for New Product	$111,000
2. New Ad Program	$211,000
3. PR Agency Retainer	$110,000
4. Direct Mail Program	$96,000
5. Press Tour	$65,000
6. Attend Boston Show	$46,000
7. Attend Chicago Show	$48,000
8. New Product Brochure	$66,000
9. Attend Las Vegas Show	$52,000
10. New Product Package	$23,000
11. Company Newsletter	$14,000
12. Annual Report	$78,000
13. Customer Conference	$249,000
Total	$1,169,000

The projects that fall below the line are dropped for the year unless more money becomes available. This technique can also be used for time and resource availability. Simply substitute days or people for project costs that were used in this example.

Next, review your list. Rewrite it if you've made lots of notes, erasures, or arrows to move things around. When you have a prioritized list, starting from the top, write down the costs and schedule significance of each goal or task and weigh the time and budget required. As you work down the list, when you run out of resources, draw a line under the last goal or task you can accomplish within your budget (or schedule).

Items above the line can be done. Items below the line should be scrubbed since the resources required to complete them successfully are not currently available.

Haul your entire network diagram and schedule into a boardroom and lay it across the table. Your convincing arguments to senior management may persuade them that the change is not a good idea when you review the impact on the plan in detail. Often, simply telling them how much extra cash the change requires is a very persuasive tactic in managing expectations and change.

Sometimes Quitting Is the Only Choice

In spite of looking for reasonable options to keep your project on track, there are some changes that force only undesirable options. We're sorry we don't have better news. As frustrating as such unforeseen problems are, sometimes no amount of planning or management will fix the problem. You'll just have to start over or quit the project. That's why it's always a good idea to have a contingency plan when opening a new business or bringing out a new product—along with some extra income sources in the background—just in case Murphy's Law prevails.

People Predictably Resist Change

Change has predictable effects on the project team. Even changes for good reasons can have bad effects among the people on a project. Motivation-sapping resentment may build against the new bodies, management, schedules, or the project itself.

People may perceive that changes invalidate the work of team members. Imagine working 16 months to develop an engineering process and then having your work swept under the rug in less than a day when the changes to a project make the process unnecessary in the new plan!

If you anticipate that people will resist change, you'll have a better chance of getting their support—eventually. Never lie or pretend it's business as usual. Just tell it like it is, and then try to communicate the need for the changes. Take their concerns seriously and listen to their ideas. Don't let the project unravel.

In the following sections, we'll present some tactics for handling the effects that changes have on projects and project personnel. You should put these into your "change management" arsenal. You may need to combine two or more of them for particularly sticky situations.

Frank and Open Discussion

When you know changes will involve people's jobs, talk to them now instead of waiting until the last minute. Even people forced into lesser or nonexistent roles will appreciate your empathy and

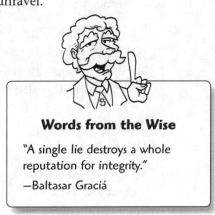

Words from the Wise

"A single lie destroys a whole reputation for integrity."

—Baltasar Graciá

candor. The earlier you let people know they'll have to go, the more time they'll have to look for another position inside or outside the organization.

Dwell on the Positive, But Don't Cover Up the Negative

Focus people on the positive aspects of the changes being made. (This is easier if there really are positive aspects!) If the news is bad, for example, and cutbacks are at hand, be honest and forthright in explaining why they are happening. Above all, don't make team members feel like it's their fault, even if it really is.

Spell Out the Details

Clearly define or explain any new expectations, new organization charts (if there are any), new schedules, or new goals. Put changes in writing for distribution after your discussion so that everyone is in sync with the changes, even if they don't remember everything you said. According to current management wisdom, if major and negative changes are imminent, schedule the big announcement for Monday. That way people can adapt without a weekend of inaction.

Assure Team Members of Your Support

Make sure team members know you are fully supportive of the changes and are putting your weight behind them. Don't allow individual team members to foment discontent that spreads like the flu among other workers. If people won't get with the program, spend one-on-one time with them discussing the issues. If that fails, dump them from the project before they do more damage to the morale. It's a last resort, but sometimes you have no choice.

The Least You Need to Know

➤ Changes are a natural and expected aspect of any project, but changes made through a defined process will be easier to control.

➤ Change is not a negative word; many changes on projects are made for positive reasons.

➤ The end result of changes affects the budget, schedule, and goal outcomes. This means the plan must be updated on a regular basis to reflect the impact of changes.

➤ Change should be resisted when unnecessary, frivolous, or obviously detrimental to the successful completion of the project.

➤ Changes should be communicated openly to team members at the earliest possible date.

Chapter 25

All right, you've convinced me...

When Push Comes to Shove, You Can Always Negotiate

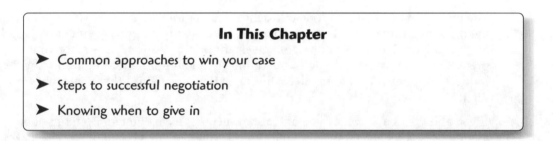

In This Chapter

➤ Common approaches to win your case

➤ Steps to successful negotiation

➤ Knowing when to give in

Negotiating skills are central to managing any project: How much will it cost? How much will you pay or will the other side charge? How many hours will it take? Can you do it in less time for less money? Do we need you? Do you need us? Asking yourself these and other questions is part of setting up and running all aspects of a project. Almost every resolution to every problem in your project takes negotiating prowess to keep your project as close to its original plan as possible.

You will be faced with negotiable issues throughout the project as problems and differences of opinion affect the budget, schedule, and even the team's morale. Unless you're approaching the negotiating table with a white flag in hand like the losers on a battlefield, each party (you and the other side) will have something of value to put on the negotiating table. Even if the value is not totally equitable, terms can be worked out. Negotiating is much like playing poker. When you're holding four aces, you can take a lot more risk than when you've got a hand with a four of hearts, a seven of diamonds, and a five, a three, and a deuce of clubs.

The Three Sides of the Negotiating Table

What makes negotiating in project management different is the three sides of the theoretical negotiating table. On one side is the customer being pitched to (your manager, for example) who may be trying to unrealistically limit expense and hours. On the second side are team members—whether they're inside your organization or outside vendors. On the third and toughest side of the table is the middleman—that's you. Being a good, patient negotiator is a skill that takes time to develop. You as the pitchman of sorts must work on the budget, the schedule, and convincing would-be team members to sign on, work on the schedule, and accept a realistic salary. You also must explain why you can't afford to send them to Aruba just for joining up.

The initial elements of negotiation happen long before the letters, discussions, meetings, and possible lawsuits. Before you negotiate, you must establish what you have to bring to the negotiating table.

What Will You Negotiate For?

The process of negotiating is one of reaching a compromise. Your goals in the negotiation for your project will be to establish realistic pricing, prompt payment, appropriate resources, extended deadlines, or agreement on the terms of success for your project. Your positive spirit, high level of integrity, and fulfillment of promises will motivate team members to say to each other, "Hey, I really like that approach! Let's do it!"

If you and your customer or you and a staff member have different opinions about any measure, task, or resource in your project, you need to negotiate. You also negotiate up front before hiring a team member or consultant, signing a lease for equipment, or buying a 20,000-square-foot prefab tilt-up building that arrives as a "kit" on several tractor trailers.

Here are several examples of things you'll be asked to do as a project manager. You'll need to negotiate a compromise if you can't give everything that's asked of you.

High Water!

Never say, "I have someone who will do it for half that price ..." when the other side knows that no one else in town can do the job. Not only will you lose credibility, you may also jeopardize the ability to get the project done at all.

➤ **Reduce the cost.** Your compromise will involve changing the specifications of the project or coming up with less expensive staff to get things done.

➤ **Deliver things faster.** Your compromise will involve changing product specifications, extending the budget, or coming up with new sequences of tasks.

➤ **Add or change people on your team.** Your team is the central component (aside from you) in making the project a success. As project manager, the big boss may approach you with a list of people or vendors to use. You want the best team possible, and negotiating may involve taking people obviously lacking skills, stamina, and cooperation off your team; revising their dictated roles; or (hopefully) getting better talent. Remember: If you get lesser skills than desired, you'll probably have to compromise on the schedule, the quality of the project, or both.

➤ **Deliver a different quality or product than the one originally specified.** Stakeholders often change their mind about what they want in the middle of the project. You can negotiate to provide more or less quality—depending on your side of the table—but you'll also have to compromise on the budget, the schedule, and a lot of other things. Make sure this is what the customer really wants before you do anything to reduce the quality; this should be your last option.

➤ **Accept the budget without looking at the details.** Stakeholders will try approaches like "I'll sign a contract right now if you can do it for $25,000 instead of $40,000." Don't be swayed until you understand the compromises you'll need to make if you take less than you asked for.

Negotiations of All Sizes

There are many kinds of negotiations that involve a careful mix of power, money, skill, and prestige. Each negotiation for your project will have a different tone and priority. As you consider each situation, you should think about the approach to use during the negotiation to maximize your potential of getting the agreement you need to proceed. You may want to read up on negotiation in more depth than we present here (see *The Complete Idiot's Guide to Negotiation*), but here are some basic tactics to choose from in your negotiations:

Time Is Money

When working out a schedule, you can negotiate too diligently for that better deal. A desperate employee, consultant, or vendor may cave and offer the sky at a reduced rate. You'll end up paying for overtime, project problems (or failure), and a lot of unhappy employees—all because, when push came to shove, you squeezed a little too hard.

➤ **Stressing mutual self-interest.** You need a specific team member because you need a team. He wants your project's name on his resumé, and it adds to his credentials. You both get something you want and need.

➤ **The appeal.** An employee about to be let go or a vendor in need of a contract would probably be very willing to join your project. In fact, he or she may outperform the rest of the staff just to have a job or to stay in business. But if the person is simply desperate, he or she may be the wrong party for the project.

➤ **A power play.** You can exert pressure on a lower-level employee or on a vendor who does a lot of business with you to join your team. This unhappy tactic makes for employees who don't perform and won't act with team spirit, but it's done every day in business. Use it as a last resort.

➤ **A *win-win* situation.** In this scenario, compromises are made so each side gets something it needs and wants.

Centering

If you don't know what you really want—and what you can really do without—you'll never get what you really need. Before beginning even the first sparring steps in a negotiation for specific services or resources—whether it's for 12,000 pink pencil erasers, 10 temporary employees to support a telemarketing promotion, or the cheap carpet you need for the new cloakroom—you must nail down (in writing) exactly what you're looking for.

After understanding what you need, want, and would like in a negotiation, you need to understand the alternatives that would be bad, good, and better. This is a Zen-like process in which you must look at the negotiation from all known angles and decide on the most likely outcomes. After listing the alternatives, choose the five that are acceptable and also feasible. This doesn't mean you'll get the ones you want, but at least you have a center from which to begin negotiations.

If you find in this analysis that you're completely lost, you may need to bring in expert outsiders to help you assess value, to isolate and analyze options, and to study what the other side will likely bring to the table.

The Other Side

While you are studying what you have to offer, you must also consider the other side. What have they got to "sell?" It could be a hot new technology effectively shielded by 2,000 patents and 5,000 attorneys. Or, it may really be worth next to nothing as you further examine it under a financially equipped microscope.

Who Has What?

Build a chart of what you bring to the table and what the other side offers. Carefully analyze each contribution. If possible, assess value. (Unfortunately, this is easier said than done for many items.) How much is an expert scientist going to cost? How much is he or she really worth? What about someone who answers the phone or a vendor that offers services at a rate so much lower than the competition that it scares you? (It should! See Chapter 15 on budgeting.)

You'll want to create a chart of your own. You'll need one with enough room to accommodate your project's needs, your way of working, or your computer's formats and compatibility. Create your form with enough space to address the number of issues you will deal with. Then add about 50 percent more space for the alternatives you forgot.

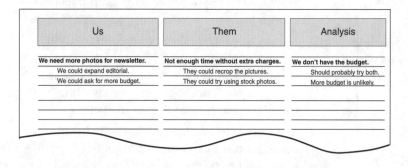

Looking at who has what for negotiating purposes.

For example, when hiring a new employee for your project, you may have only a couple of items in your "must-have" columns such as salary level and specific skill requirements, but the person you want (the other side) may have many more requirements for you if you want to put him or her on the team. That's the purpose of the chart. Are you hiring a certain well-known Mr. Einstein or someone lacking skills who is in need of a job and is looking for (and therefore lacking) experience? How much compensation is required? For an in-house "hire," is this a project that will benefit the employee or a major compromise that will jeopardize the project in the name of the budget?

In a supplier negotiation, you always try to get the most for the least—but without compromising quality or bankrupting the vendor. This is not always an easy negotiation because what you get may not match your needs. It may turn out to be an apples-to-oranges discussion in which you ordered apples but the supplier delivered oranges or even potatoes for that matter.

What to Do

To negotiate successfully, we recommend some standard steps outlined in the following section. Always let time be on your side. Go slowly and accommodate your people and suppliers, but don't pay too much or look rushed because this almost always affects your ability to work out an equitable arrangement. Try using that poker face you've been secretly rehearsing in the bathroom mirror.

Negotiating Step-By-Step

Here are some basic steps to get you started negotiating with potential employees, contractors, or vendors:

1. Know your adversaries (and your allies). Find out as much as you can about their credentials, reputation, and ability to contribute to your project. This will also help you determine their worth if you have to pay them as an internal employee from your budget or as an outside vendor.

2. Always be pleasant and avoid confrontation. Listen to the other person, consider all arguments, and encourage discussion. Emphasize how you can work together. The last thing you want is to put him or her on the defensive.

3. Make plans to "do lunch." Breaking bread in a neutral, nonthreatening environment is an ideal place to begin a working relationship.

4. Be clear on your situation and status. Everyone involved in the negotiation must be fully up to speed on the project and what your negotiation is about.

5. Slow down if things go awry in early talks. If the other side is particularly confrontational or completely impossible, try working it out, choosing someone else, or structuring the negotiation so that you can do it in writing. If someone's demands or attitude is outrageous, offer him or her the bottom line and show the person to the door if that fails. If you must have that person because he or she possesses skills not available elsewhere, you may have to meet his or her terms.

6. Don't be forced into anything. Take time to understand the ramifications of each proposal—but don't take too much time. You should have an idea about each alternative before you get into negotiating mode.

7. Get back to the person. Your proposition will mean a lot more to someone who needs money or employment after two weeks of not hearing from you while you are both busy and studying possible alternatives.

8. Accept only acceptable alternatives. If this sounds obvious, just wait for your first project in which an employee fails to perform or a vendor delivers something useless and bills at the same time. The process of project management is fraught with people turning in work that's late, unsuitable, unacceptable, or

simply incompetent. Occasionally, it can also be too late to use. Avoid this problem by refusing substandard work and contributions. Why? Once you accept any kind of work, you have legally accepted it. (Ask an attorney for your state/provincial regulations.) Once "accepted," your bargaining power is limited—all you can do is withhold payment. (But this tactic gets noticed surprisingly fast.)

Get It in Writing!

Obviously, all workable agreements need to be written, but you can also handle initial negotiations this way. Your people can provide potential contributors with a request for a proposal (RFP), or potential contributors may offer a proposal drafted from scratch without much input from your end. Regardless of who initiates the proposal, you will still need to negotiate the final document unless the purchase is inexpensive or you're experienced and trusting of the provider.

Time Is Money

On a project that's costing a lot of money, you need experts familiar with the field to look over the contracts, work with you on the terms, and generally grease the skids to make things work. If the people funding the project won't pay for mandatory assistance and expertise, then the project won't come to fruition anyway.

Sometimes the proposal is simply a jumping-off point for price negotiations and hammering out terms. Read such documents carefully to understand their terms fully. If things go wrong, the document could be used against your organization. That's why you want to provide a written response acknowledging terms and changes you agree on.

A Room with a View

Choosing the right place to negotiate facilitates fruitful negotiations. Unfortunately, you may not be able to use the comfortable confines of your well-furnished office or a similar environment. Instead, you may negotiate in a crowded room of the seller and be surrounded by managers from both sides. Or worse (at least until video phones actually happen), you may find yourself conducting a faceless interview over the phone with someone you've never laid eyes on. Here's an approach for each scenario, although a comfortable environment for everyone involved is superior to a 90-degree conference room packed with self-important people and noisy phones:

➤ **In your office:** Hold all calls—quiet should prevail. Relax and treat your guest to coffee, a snack, a cigar—whatever it takes to keep things calm. Work in Phoenix with the sun pouring in? Lower the blinds somewhat and keep the

315

temperature as close to 70 degrees as possible. Too hot or cold anyway? Take your guest elsewhere such as a conference room or even a meal out on your tab.

➤ **In a conference room with assorted managers from either or both sides:** Have an agenda to pass out so you stick to the topics. Set up a starting and an ending time. If you can't reach consensus in an hour or two, these may be the wrong people to work with. The exception would be a highly technical project, but laying groundwork before this critical agreement meeting saves time and frayed nerves on both sides.

The Least You Need to Know

➤ Negotiation is a skill you'll develop over time. We suggest reading a lot of books on the topic and watching the pros at work.

➤ You can negotiate for almost anything in a project including better team members, lower prices, and a more realistic schedule.

➤ Know the needs and motivations of your opponent before opening any negotiation.

➤ Getting to a win-win compromise is always preferable to beating your opponent into the ground.

➤ Take a step back in any negotiation before committing to something you don't totally understand.

Chapter 26

Common Project Problems: Get Them Before They Get You

> ## In This Chapter
>
> ➤ How to recognize the urgency of the problem before you take action
>
> ➤ A dozen or so common problems to expect on any project of any size
>
> ➤ Signs for identifying problems in the making before they undermine project objectives, schedules, or budgets
>
> ➤ Strategies to help you solve or avoid the most common project problems

Okay, you've read every chapter so far, and as hard as you try, some of your projects aren't getting done better. They're taking too long. They're not reaping results. Your team doesn't seem interested in meeting the deadlines. Your boss keeps asking for changes. The customers want more results. Even Dogbert's advice and Dilbert's humor don't seem to help when deadlines are slipping and expenses are skyrocketing.

If you think that project management techniques will eliminate all your problems in getting things done on time and within budget, forget it. All projects have problems. In some ways, project management success depends on problem-solving techniques more than any other processes.

Recognizing All Problems, Large and Small

The successful project manager is able to maintain a perspective that allows honest, objective evaluation of each issue as it comes up. Not all problems require immediate action, and some don't require any action at all. They just need to be monitored to make sure they don't get out of hand.

Most large or urgent problems require immediate attention and effective action before the project can continue. Small and nonurgent problems may require minimal resources and, in some cases, may become nonproblems as the project moves forward. Safety problems may be associated with the potential for loss of life. These must be analyzed and resolved immediately.

Large problems typically have multiple owners and involve several resources or significant amounts of money with jeopardy to budget, schedule, and specification. These frequently take a great deal of time to resolve.

On the other hand, small problems may be solved quickly and with the help of only one or two resources. Nonurgent problems are those that can be deferred until later without impact to the project, the customer, or the organization. In fact, a great many of these become nonproblems as time passes.

The good news is that most project problems, whether large or small, are predictable. To help you anticipate problems in your projects and thus minimize their impact, we'll describe some of the common project problems in this chapter. Like a Boy Scout, expect to encounter them and be prepared to minimize their impact.

The Floating Start Date

Some projects just never seem to get off the ground because other priorities keep getting in the way. Unfortunately, even though a project may start late, everyone expects it to finish on the original schedule. If you find that your project never gets started, consider these strategies for solving the problem:

➤ Reanalyze the priority for the project. Maybe the project really isn't that important after all.

➤ If the project really needs to be completed as scheduled, communicate the problem to management and get someone else to start the project or adjust your own work habits to make time for it.

➤ If the project starts late, communicate (in writing as well as verbally) the new finish date to management and the project team. If you need to keep the original date, complete a trade-off analysis of project changes as described in Chapter 24, "Changes, Changes and More Changes."

High Water!

Never assume that people will be available when dates slip. If you don't ask about the new schedule and people's availability, you may be the last to find out that you don't have who you need to get things done.

➤ Analyze your daily activities and determine whether you are wasting time on less important tasks. If you need time-management training, get some. There are many good books that offer guidelines for identifying the time traps in day-to-day work—get one and implement its advice.

There's Not Enough Time for Everything

Things always seem to take longer than we anticipate, and there are always more things than we have time to do. In a search for solutions to the ubiquitous problem of finding more time for the project, look into the following alternatives:

➤ If the team is falling behind, don't try to catch up all on your own. Delegate more of the activities and involve other people in the prioritization and assignment of work.

➤ Eliminate work that is not really necessary. Always question the necessity of each task on a project. Skip tasks that don't count.

➤ Learn to politely say "No" (or if this isn't possible, at least say, "I'll think about it") when someone asks you to add tasks that may interfere with more important project priorities.

➤ Change the priorities for the work. Some things may get done later than originally planned, but this is better than nothing getting done. Of course, you must communicate this change to the other people working on the project.

➤ Work longer hours when this is an option, but don't overdo it for too long; otherwise, you and your team will become less productive and less motivated. All work and no play are ingredients for disgruntled project teams and poorly executed projects.

Too Many Reports and Not Enough Communication

Reports are not a substitute for one-on-one communication with your project team. Too many reports also bog projects down in unnecessary paperwork, and this affects quality, schedules, and motivation. To ensure that reports are not substituting for communication, do the following:

➤ Make a list of all the reports being produced for the project, the people responsible, and the content of each report. Then critically review each report and make sure it is really necessary. Also make sure that the reports are as simple as possible while still conveying the required information.

➤ Create a card file, or tickler file, reminding you to visit key team members on a regular basis. Note the last date you spoke with each person. Write a note to yourself in your calendar or organizer to talk to specific team members each week or day as appropriate.

➤ Take people to lunch when you have time and ask them how things are going. Informal get-togethers often result in more open communications and more honest updates on progress.

➤ Keep your door open unless you're really in a private meeting. There is nothing more intimidating than a project manager who is always locked behind a closed door.

Time Is Money

You can avoid many costly problems by simply using the MBWA (management by walking around) technique you learned about in Chapter 18 to keep in touch with project progress and team attitudes. Remember to be casual and interested, not threatening, as you cruise the cubicles, offices, and hallways to find out what's really going on.

They Always Need It Faster

Shortening the schedule is a frequent request because of predictable business demands, especially competitive pressures to get products out faster or to generate the revenue anticipated from the completion of a project. It's always good to consider faster alternatives for completing a project. However, implementing a "crash" schedule may cause your team to "crash and burn." You must consider the trade-offs in terms of other business priorities, the use of resources, and the costs of getting things done faster. The ways to do this were explained in Chapter 24.

The 90-Percent-Done Syndrome

Many people are optimistic about their ability to make up for lost time. Others simply attempt to look good on paper. For these reasons, whenever we see the phrase "90 percent done" on a project status report, we know there's a big problem.

What is hiding behind that unfinished 10 percent that no one wants to admit? Why does it seem that 90 percent of the effort only takes 30 percent of the time, and the last 10 percent takes 200 percent of the original schedule?

If you see that 90 percent or some other large percentage of a complex task is completed very quickly, but then the work only inches up to 91 and 92 percent over the next couple of status reports, you need to figure out what is really going on by talking to the staff in an environment of support and understanding.

Here are some guidelines for getting to the root of the 90-Percent-Done Syndrome:

➤ Investigate the scope of the remaining work through meetings or one-on-one sessions with key project members. Are there technical difficulties that the team doesn't want anyone to know about? Should the task be broken down into smaller, more measurable tasks?

➤ Consider whether the remaining 10 percent of the work is really predictable. Creative tasks, such as inventions or coming up with ideas, are often difficult to schedule. In the development of a new technology and in other high-creativity situations, the breakthrough that is required to complete a project may not happen as scheduled. Creative tasks need to be more realistically assessed. You can't schedule spontaneity, so don't try. Just be honest about the creative blocks and document the schedule changes accordingly.

➤ Help the team be honest in its assessment of project status by encouraging open communication and by pointing out the problems with being too optimistic about risky endeavors. Team members may be giving you the estimates they think you want to see—not the real ones. Reward yourself and the team for honesty and effort rather than false statements of accomplishment or unrealistic commitments to impossible dreams.

Moving Target Objectives

Changes in project plans are valid for many reasons, as we discussed in Chapter 24. However, sometimes the changes in project goals and objectives seem to occur every time your manager walks into the office. Because there isn't time to plan and adjust for these daily or hourly changes, you might not bother to update the current plan. This is a bad idea.

Not adjusting the plan is just about the easiest way we know of to end up with a project disaster. When changes are requested frequently and arbitrarily on a project, it is an indication of a lack of consensus regarding the original plan or some other political problem between your manager, the project, the stakeholders, and the organization. Here are some ways to save yourself in this situation:

➤ Make sure the authority for making project changes is clearly documented in the project plan.

➤ Don't start a project until the plan is approved by all appropriate levels of management and other appropriate stakeholders (customer or client).

➤ Don't promise to implement changes in a project until you have time to analyze and document the impact of the changes. Follow all the other rules for making project changes that are discussed in Chapter 24.

The Key Person Always Quits

Many projects depend on the special skills of a single person. If this person leaves, the project could be doomed. However, there are a few basic ways to keep the departure of a key person from becoming a catastrophe:

➤ Keep the key person happy in the first place. Listen. Be aware of problems in advance. Most people don't just walk out; it takes time for them to become disgruntled. If there is a reason for the dissatisfaction, try to find it and fix it.

➤ Cross-train people as work proceeds on the project. This training can minimize the impact of losing a key person on the team because others will be familiar with the project.

➤ Make sure the key person is also part of the team. Try to have someone work with this person to document his or her work. If the key person works in isolation, the impact of this person's absence could be disastrous. On the other hand, if the work is documented, you can usually hire someone else to take over where the other person left off.

Costs Spiral Out of Control

Budget and cost-control problems occur for many reasons including lack of skill or discipline in estimating costs in the original plan, inadequate detail in the plan that results in vague or inaccurate budget allotments, schedule delays that cause more resources to be used than planned, unforeseen technical problems, changes in material or service costs that weren't anticipated, and changes in the scope of a project that are not reflected in the updates to the budgets—along with a myriad of other "justifiable" events.

In spite of excuses to the contrary, there is only one way to control costs: Keep on top of expenses through regular monitoring and appropriate accounting controls. There simply isn't any other solution.

Cost overruns don't just happen. Costs increase because of poor communications, lack of control, inaccurate reporting, or inadequate documentation of project changes. Through diligent monitoring of expenditures during the project, money problems can be dealt with when budget problems first appear—before the costs get out of control.

The Staff Has More Enthusiasm Than Talent

Unfortunately, the most likable people are not always the most competent. If you choose people for their personalities alone and not their skills, you can end up in a situation in which a congenial team just doesn't get the work done.

What should you do when you have a great group of fun people working on the project, but they just don't seem to deliver what you need? Here are some guidelines to help you decide:

➤ Develop an objective skills appraisal system to select team members at the beginning of the project. This can help keep friendly but unskilled people off the team.

➤ Watch the team to see if too much time is being spent in social activities. Sometimes the problem isn't a lack of competence at all; instead, the schedule suffers because of too much socializing during work hours. Usually, a simple meeting to reemphasize the priorities of the project can solve this problem.

➤ If a congenial but unskilled person (or group) is willing to be trained and has potential, additional education is sometimes a solution. However, getting people up to speed is only an option if the schedule can absorb the time required for training.

➤ If competence is the root of the problem, a consultant or outside vendor can sometimes make up the difference in skills, allowing the friendly person in question to remain on your team in a lesser capacity.

Ultimately, you may need to tell your "friends" that they aren't making the grade. Give people every opportunity to do the job, but if everything else fails, you'll have to find someone else for the team. When this is necessary, cut the ties earlier rather than later. Getting rid of dead wood on the team is one task that most managers dread and put off. In business, if the goals for the project are important, the project must take priority—no matter how much you like the person (or the group).

Words from the Wise

"I always figured that I've learned the most about projects from the ones that fell apart. It's a lot like taking the rings off a partly rotten onion. You can't tell what's worthy inside until you see the whole thing. Then you become a project leader: like it or not."

—A project manager with 30+ years experience

The Impossible Remains Impossible

In an attempt to look good, novice project managers often commit to more work than is possible. Even worse, they commit to projects that are impossible from the start. The budget and schedule may be so unrealistic that there is no possibility for completing the work as specified.

Here are some examples of impossible projects:

➤ Projects that stem from poor plans or lack of support. Any enterprise that begins a project must have a commitment to complete it. Sadly, some projects never reach completion, and you may become the scapegoat for a failure for which you are not wholly responsible.

➤ Projects already in the works that have no hope of completion. If you're assigned a project that's already in progress, make sure you interview the team to ensure you aren't being handed a loaf of day-old bread.

➤ Projects with no staff and no budget to hire a staff. Don't laugh. Lots of people get handed objectives with no commitment of resources and no support from the stakeholders.

➤ Projects that have been underway for more than six months with no perceptible progress. If this happens to you, you need to evaluate the reasons. It may be that people are trying to do the impossible or have no idea what they're supposed to be doing. Either way, the project won't get done.

➤ Projects that assume you will bring in the money on your own to keep the project rolling. Common among modern corporations and a long-time standard among not-for-profit organizations, you become a fundraiser as well as a project manager. No one person can do both roles, and it's unfair of the organization to demand that you bring in $2 million in capital to fund your $75,000 salary.

➤ Projects in which a senior manager is fighting with others in upper management to cancel or significantly modify the project. This type of project needs some concerted effort in the "stakeholder management" arena.

➤ Projects with impossible or unfocused goals (more common than you would think). Here's an example: "Develop a cure for the HIV virus while using the same team to build a suspension bridge like San Francisco's Golden Gate Bridge capable of linking England's south coast to that of Calais, France."

It is difficult for project mangers to admit defeat, but often the best solution is to realize that some things just won't happen as planned. Like walking on water, some projects are outside the realm of possibility for ordinary people.

The best way to avoid an impossible project is to never start it in the first place. Document the risks before the project is approved. Let everyone know in advance that the project may be impossible. If you still find yourself caught in an impossible situation in spite of your realistic communications, the best way to get out is as quickly as possible. As soon as you know the project is impossible, try to convince the powers that be to stop it and quit spending the money. Prolonging the agony makes the problem worse and has brought many a company (and project manager) down in the process.

Politics, Politics, and More Politics

Politics in human endeavors is unavoidable because people always have different opinions and motivations. If the political attitudes are annoying but don't affect the end results of your project, ignore them. It's only when *political* agendas start undermining project goals that they pose a problem. When this happens, treat the politics as any other conflict and resolve the situation by following the conflict resolution options covered in Chapter 23, "Conflicts: Resolving and Benefiting from Them."

Dopey Fads Mandated by the Boss

Senior management may push one of many ineffective, concocted-over-cocktails ideas on your team. Gently agree to consider the idea no matter how stupid or insufferably dopey the book or seminar from which the idea came. Then, if forced into management-by-fad, put the process into practice but complement it with the basics of good project management, inspired leadership, and common sense to make sure you actually get things done.

Basic work and organizational concepts, like the scientific method, have been honed, refined, and repaired since the dawn of time. The proof of their timeless truth is the many large projects, such as the Golden Gate Bridge (1937), that have worked thanks to astute project management and good planning. Imagine if The Watermelon Workplace or another equally shallow fad had been used instead. We'd still be taking the ferry from San Francisco to Sausalito and points north.

Project Lingo

A **political** situation can be described as two people in a room trying to get something done.

Taking Care of Yourself to Remain Sane

Does your family treat you like a boarder because they never see you? Does aspirin seem like candy in relief of your headaches? If this sounds familiar, it's time to get a life.

Sometimes the best way to handle problems is to take care of yourself first. Stop everything! Get a handle on the problems that are causing you to live at work and then use your leadership to fix the problems. Or, choose to scale back or step down from the project. Your life is worth more than any project—even if your boss may express other sentiments.

After gaining some perspective, pick up the pieces (if possible), ramp the project back up in phases to maintain control, and eliminate the snarls that dogged it previously. And the project workers? If they're freelancers, as little fun as it is, furlough them. If they're employees, either put them back on their regular jobs or ask for their help analyzing and reconstituting the project. Listen closely to their complaints. This might be the source of the problem—and your exhaustion!

A Parable of Last Resort

As project manager, you'll be faced with pressure from both above and below in the organization. Things often seem impossible when you have too many roles and too much to do. When you feel that way, consider the following story, which according to a computer industry wag, probably originated at IBM. The story goes something like this:

A new project manager proudly walks into her new office. She arrives just as her predecessor is walking out the door in disgrace. The departing manager tells her that he has left three envelopes numbered 1 through 3 in the top desk drawer. The departing manager instructs the new manager to open an envelope and follow the instructions only when an impossible-to-rectify problem occurs.

Several weeks go by and the project problems seem overwhelming to the new project manager. Everything is behind schedule, and the new manager must explain the failures to the executive committee in a review meeting. Not knowing what to do, the project manager decides to open the first envelope before going to the meeting. The note inside instructs, "Blame it on the last manager." The new manager decides this is a way off the hook. In the meeting she points her finger to the last manager's inept handling of the project. The committee agrees and reluctantly approves more time and money to complete the project.

Time goes by and the project once again becomes mired in the murk. Stalled and without a clue as to how to handle the problems, the manager must approach the executive committee for more project moola. Opening envelope number 2, she is advised to blame the problem on the inept project team. Again, this tactic proves successful, and the grumbling committee caves in and offers the project more time and more money. Upon leaving the meeting, the committee admonishes the project manager with, "This better not happen again!"

Six months fly by with winter changing to spring. Again overwhelmed with problems, the project manager feels trapped and helpless. The project is late again, is way over budget, and is probably doomed to failure. She pauses, takes a deep breath and then opens the third and final envelope. The instructions are simple: "Prepare three envelopes ...."

You should remember this story when faced with the fatalism that infects some projects. Before you give in and write your envelopes, remember that almost anything can be fixed—but not if you blame the wrong source for the problems. You, as the leader, must use what you know about project management to pull the rabbit out of the hat that others are assuming won't appear. If you do your work to plan and scope the project at the beginning and keep track of things as they go along while always keeping communications open, you'll probably never need the three envelopes. Yes, you'll have problems, but they will probably be solvable—or at least not fatal.

The Least You Need to Know

➤ Ask questions, listen, observe, and communicate with candor and clarity. If you do these four things, you'll reduce the impact of almost every project problem.

➤ Remember that problems and change go hand in hand. Change may cause new problems, but change handled well can often be the best solution to keeping a project on track.

➤ Always be honest (but not brutal) in your assessment of project problems and make sure to support your honest appraisals with documentation.

➤ Tell your boss or customer as soon as you know something is wrong. Waiting will only delay the inevitable and make the problem worse.

Part 6
The Closing Processes

Whether it's a summer vacation or a visit to the smiling Dr. Kevorkian, there comes a time when all things good (or bad) must come to an end. The swan song. The last breath. Finish. Fin. That's all, folks! Likewise, your project must undergo the closing phase so you can wrap up the details, pay the bills, and move on to the next project with a sense of satisfaction—or at least without regret. That's what this short section is all about—the steps to bring a project to a proper conclusion so life can go on.

Chapter 27

Will the Last One Out Please Turn Off the Lights ...

In This Chapter

➤ The steps for closing a project

➤ Moving team members from the project into other roles

➤ Projects that have taken on a life of their own

➤ Deciding whether to fix a project or end it now

If you've successfully completed your project, the closing phase is a time of celebration and accomplishment. But not all projects end gracefully. Without a proper closing, some projects ramble on forever like a rickety truck on a bumpy road.

In this chapter, you'll learn how to close down any project including those that finish successfully, those that must die a natural death, and the more annoying ones in which team members never seem to leave. Closure is important because it is the point at which, while wiping your sweaty brow with relief, you say to yourself, "It's over." (And regardless of the outcome, break out the chilled champagne! You deserve it.)

Is There Life After Project Termination?

When the end is near, project members get nervous. What will their next assignment consist of? Will there be a next assignment at all? Unfortunately, this morale problem occurs with the worst possible timing—when a project is almost complete. The problem runs deeper than just the risk of unemployment or a new assignment in Siberia.

It means the end of budding friendships, interesting after-hours at the tavern playing poker for pennies, and the other good times that accompany a well-run project. Your people will miss it. You will too ... really.

Why Is a Closing Phase Necessary?

People need to be acknowledged for goals that are achieved and to feel like the work is complete. Because project managers need to evolve their skills for managing projects, the techniques, processes, and procedures used on one project should be analyzed so they can be adapted and improved in the future. These are the most fundamental and underlying reasons to formally close a project. You may want to hold similar closing, acknowledgement, and review meetings at the close of major milestones or phases in a larger project as well.

The Final Shutdown

The following tasks are part of the final termination process for most projects and are necessary to bring them to final closure:

➤ Meet with stakeholders to get their final approval of the project. They are the reason for the project existing in the first place. Their approval signals the project's completion.

➤ Finalize all contractual commitments to vendors, suppliers, and customers. This may include reports or final payments. It may also include letters thanking vendors for a job well done when appropriate.

➤ Transfer responsibilities to other people if required. For example, the end results of some projects are inputs for new projects to be managed by other people. Consider a project to design a new product, for example. Once the product is designed, the responsibility for it is transferred to the manufacturing department, where the product will be produced and distributed. The development of the ongoing production system for the product becomes another project. To make this transfer, there are reports, drawings, and documentation that must be completed before manufacturing can begin. These activities are all part of the final termination of the product design project.

➤ Reassign people in the project and redirect efforts to other priorities or projects. People may be returned to their functional areas, assigned new projects, or both.

➤ Release resources, such as equipment and materials, so they can be disposed of or used for other work. Some construction and manufacturing projects also require cleanup tasks to prepare the facilities for new activities.

➤ Complete the final accounting of the project. This includes totaling the costs, paying all the bills, and closing the books on the project.

➤ Document the results of the project and make recommendations for the future. More information on the final reports and documentation required for a project can be found later in this chapter. The amount and detail of final documentation will vary based on the size, importance, and issues associated with each project.

Like a living entity, projects grow, mature, and finally become memories after the work is complete. And like the Energizer Bunny, some projects just won't quit.

Projects that aren't closed formally may continue to consume resources required elsewhere. Most projects should end as soon as either the goals have been achieved or you recognize that there's no hope for success.

Closing a Small Project

For small projects, the formal closing (also called a termination by some project managers) can be a simple matter of having a meeting with the team and the stakeholders to acknowledge attainment of the project goals and writing a brief final report on the project. The closing meeting should focus only on the accomplishments of the completed project so that people feel satisfied with the work performed.

Closing a Large Project

For large projects, the closing phase can be a time of stress and anxiety. Team members may have friendships and a sense of family. Some team members will be going their separate ways, adding to the anxiety. Termination of a long project with a close-knit team is always difficult, and it can be complicated. However, the frustration can be reduced if the team members are acknowledged for their current accomplishments and then given new assignments and challenges as soon as possible.

Because some people fear leaving the security of an established project team or changing roles after the project is complete, it is often difficult to get the final details of a large project completed. People may continue to work on insignificant tasks related to the project.

As a project manager, it is your responsibility to see that the project ends. The project manager should help the people involved move forward into new challenges and opportunities. To reduce the stress associated with project termination, remind your team members of the overall goals that have been achieved and that the stakeholders consider the project completed. Emphasize the importance of the project to the business and their contribution in meeting the project objectives. Then remind them of the new goals and objectives they have yet to achieve on other projects and assignments.

In addition to having a formal meeting or even a party to acknowledge project completion, many projects involve other formal termination tasks, some of which were mentioned earlier: reassigning personnel, auditing the final expenses and closing the books on the project, archiving any drawings or other project materials, passing the end results of the project on to another organization (for example, setting up a product for manufacturing or installing the final product at a customer's site), informing other departments (including purchasing, finance, manufacturing, or whoever needs to know) that the project is done, and completing other miscellaneous documentation of the project. And, of course, there will be an extensive final report.

The closing tasks for a large project are not always clear-cut. When such a project is almost complete, there may be some small details that need to be resolved. The project manager must decide when a project is "finished" so it can move into the termination phase. Don't drag the close-out phase and clean-up details to keep the project alive. This is a common problem in large projects. Get on with it because there are always more projects—and the next one will offer new relationships and new challenges.

When major goals for a project are complete, begin the closing phase of the project. Because of loose ends, the termination of a large project may be a mini-project in its own right, demanding schedules, priorities, and budgets. Identify the major steps in the project close-out and implement them as quickly as possible. Follow all the steps and methods for managing any other project.

For many projects, large or small, a checklist is useful in determining the requirements for termination. An example of a termination checklist for a complex product development project is provided later in the chapter to demonstrate the kinds of tasks that might be required to terminate a large project. Of course, the checklist you develop may include entirely different elements that require shutdown, but our example should give you the basic idea of what to consider.

Under the Microscope, Again ...

Closure is also the point at which management evaluates your success in meeting the goals and your skills as a project manager. Not all projects glide to success like a 747 touching down softly; some come to a crashing halt like the ill-fated Hindenburg. Termination replaces closure for such a monster, but the steps to closure are the same as for any project. Big success? Dismal failure? The termination process is essentially identical except that the smiles may be replaced with frowns.

Project Shutdown

The cleanest closure of a project comes when all work is done and team members already have other work or have returned to their permanent jobs. The easiest project to close down is the small one in which tangible (visible) results demonstrate completion to one and all. For example, closing down a newsletter development project is relatively easy. Once it reaches print and is distributed, everyone can hold the tangible results in their hands. At least until the next issue!

On the other hand, closing down the project of building the twin World Trade Center towers in New York is much more complex. Not only are there multiple subplans, but for the uninitiated project manager, reaching the state of completion may seem impossible. Yes, the steel skeleton is in place, but what about electrical wiring, plumbing, elevators, and interior walls? In addition, some work may linger on. After completion, repairs may be on the project manager's shoulders as necessary. In a sense, the project continues rather than winding down in a planned and predictable process. Although 99.8 percent of the work is complete, that other .2 percent must be addressed by the remnants of the team, or outsiders must be hired at higher rates if former team members are no longer available.

The most frustrating kind of shutdown is rightfully called *project murder*. (Yes, that's the real term used to describe the cancellation of a project.) You won't read about such murders in the newspaper (usually), but it does materially affect the lives of the project team and its leader. In this kind of termination, work may be suddenly halted even though the project is proceeding on schedule and within its allocated budget. Then we can only watch dumbstruck as the guillotine blade softly falls ….

To shut down a project, steps should be taken toward an orderly closure. Not all of these procedures will be popular with team members (or you) when a windfall paycheck suddenly disappears like teardrops in the rain. On a large project, shutdown may occur in phases. One major component of the project may be completed earlier than others as projected in the project plan. Shutdown of each facet should be treated similarly to the termination of the entire project. After all, each of these facets amounts to a project unto itself and deserves the celebration that accompanies completion of any project. The steps to project termination are as follows:

Project Lingo

Project murder may sound like the plot from an Agatha Christie novel, but it's really the sudden termination of a project for reasons that range from rational to absurd. An attempt on a project's life may take place during economic downturns, acquisition of the parent organization, or the unexpected death of a company's visionary founder.

Time Is Money

The formal ending of a project takes you off the hook for the budget, so everyone concerned must be fully aware that the deed is done. Otherwise, miscellaneous charges may pop up and be assigned to your now-closed project accounts. Should bills be unavailable upon termination of a project, ask whoever handles finances to build separate accounts for each one with your review before payment.

1. **Decision to terminate.** Careful scrutiny of the project tasks discloses that the project is (or should be) complete. Visual inspection must accompany this conclusion. It's always possible that a loose end remains or that a part of the team has been feeding you overly optimistic information of its progress. See the section "Use MBWA (Management By Walking Around)" in Chapter 18, "Leadership and You: Taking the Bull by the Horns."

The steps for an orderly closing phase for your project.

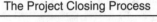

The Project Closing Process

2. **Task list.** Make a list of small tasks that need to be accomplished and get them taken care of. For example, if the project requires user documentation and it's not fully "user ready," this must be done now!

3. **Consensus.** You, the team, and management agree that the project has satisfactorily met its goals. If termination is for other reasons, such as failure or budget depletion, consensus is limited to an agreement to shut down the project before more money is tossed over the cliff.

4. **Meetings.** Hold individual meetings with team members and team managers who reported to you. Thank them for their contribution, even if they did a lousy job. (They're someone else's problem now.) Take notes on what they thought of the project's highlights and lowlights, your leadership (take a deep breath first), and what they would like to do in the future if you don't already know their intentions.

5. **Communication.** All team personnel must be instructed in writing when the project will end. This puts pressure on the stragglers who need a little more time to complete their role. If you suspect that more time is needed, set the end date several weeks into the future with weekly reminders of the drop-dead date. For real problem people, visit them daily to assess their progress and remind them of the date.

6. **More communication.** Outside suppliers and vendors must be notified that the project will cease to exist in X number of days, weeks, or months. Since the project is ending, bills not received within 30 days of the termination date will not be accepted. (Be flexible on this one. It's really a tactic to get the bills coming in the door from vendors with tardy billing practices.) It also saves you interest charges, and really prompt payment may knock a percentage off the bill. If possible, check purchase orders to see what's outstanding.

DESCRIPTION	NEEDED? YES	NEEDED? NO	REQUIRED DATE	RESPONSIBLE PERSON	NOTES
Checklist for Closing a Large Project					
Identify Remaining Work	☐	☐			
Closing/Termination Plan	☐	☐			
Personal Evaluations	☐	☐			
Close-Out Work Orders	☐	☐			
Audit Final Changes	☐	☐			
Pay All Vendors	☐	☐			
Close-Out Books/Audit	☐	☐			
Final Delivery Instructions	☐	☐			
Customer Training	☐	☐			
Notify Purchasing of Completion	☐	☐			
Equipment Redeployed	☐	☐			
Materials Returned to Inventory	☐	☐			
Staff Reassigned	☐	☐			
Close-Down Procedures	☐	☐			
Engineering Documentation	☐	☐			
Final Staff Meeting(s)	☐	☐			
Final Report and Review Meeting	☐	☐			

A checklist for terminating a project.

7. **Even more communication.** Let managers of "borrowed" employees, temporary agencies, and contractors know—in writing—that the project's termination date is near. This provides the managers time to find other opportunities for these people or to move them back into their usual job responsibilities.

8. **The books are closed.** Assuming you are working with a finance department, once a project is complete, finance must close the books so that wayward bills aren't charged against a nonexistent budget. Most companies assign code numbers to accounts for projects. Assuming your project receives one or more codes, have finance render the codes invalid. That way, you can review any invoices that pop up for legitimacy prior to payment or rejection.

9. **The celebration.** Once a project is (successfully) completed, a beer-and-pizza-type event should be held. Awards may be in order for team members who performed above and beyond the line of duty. This event is not only fun, it marks the official end of the project in everyone's mind. If the project was a flop but not because of team failure, such an event should still be held, even if the occasion is somewhat more subdued. If you or the team failed, save the pizza money.

Along the Critical Path

There is evidence, albeit limited, that something besides blueprints was used to build some of Egypt's most important monuments. It's unlikely computerized PERT technology was at work since even the Apple II was two millennia away, but several surviving documents and carvings appear to be a list of steps to be taken, the name of the responsible party (probably a slave overseer), and some kind of obscure timing/dating system. Or, it could have been misinterpreted by archaeologists. Maybe it's an order for take-out lunch from the local deli.

10. **Dispersal of resources.** An inventory is taken of current supplies and equipment. Borrowed and rented equipment is returned, unused supplies are sent back for credit where possible, and unrecyclable trash is hauled off to the landfill. If the project was large and ends up owning a lot of surplus equipment, an auction can be the ticket to parting with 12 table saws or 48 slightly dated computers. Money from such an event can go into the organization's general fund, be distributed to team members in the form of profit sharing, or be donated.

11. **The new kids.** The transition team is brought in and trained. These are the people who will staff your project if it's one of that nature.

12. **Handing over the keys.** A transfer of responsibilities takes place if new staff must be brought in to man the completed project. (The people who built the Aswan High Dam aren't the same ones who manage its power generation and floodgates. Instead, a new, specially trained crew was employed for this task to replace those whose expertise focused on pouring concrete.)

Three Ways to Deep-Six a Workforce

Al Capone's mob might have had other ideas, but there are three ways to terminate a project that are standard in the project management biz: inclusion, integration, or extinction. You need to choose the right method for your project, or you'll have lots of unhappy campers with nowhere to go.

Inclusion

Inclusion is a happy ending of sorts. Your project proved successful, and upon nearing completion, it was absorbed into the organization. Again, it may become a part of the company or be run as a separate organization. In the happiest scenario, many of the original team members keep their jobs and continue to contribute. However, it may be that all staff members are replaced because they are deemed unsuitable for the post-completion phase of the project. Some team members may choose to leave anyway because, while they found the project phase exciting, the thought of running day-to-day operations makes them yawn. You may find yourself the head of a hot new company or updating your resumé and looking for another project.

Integration

Integration is the most common technique for dissolving a project workforce. Team members are reintegrated into the organization from which they were borrowed. On a long project, integration becomes complex because management may have been forced to fill slots held by the team members. A new position must be found for the returning team member that is satisfactory to the employee and the headcount. Often new skills acquired by the project member open the door to new job responsibilities.

Extinction

The dinosaur route—outright extinction of a project and everything related to it—is an all-too-common route to unload personnel. Once a project is closed down, the people are simply let go. (There's a theory that a large meteorite striking the earth off the Yucatan invented this kind of staff reduction.)

Time Is Money

Leave good documentation for your successors. When you consider the project to bring water from upstate New York to the Big Apple, you'll understand why this is a good idea. Scheduled completion is around 2007. Given current job tenure across the nation, it's entirely possible that at least 3 different people will run the project over the next 10 years.

Give It Up!

At the end of a project, especially a major one that has absorbed six or more months of your life (some take decades), there's a come-down period for which you should be ready. It's like postpartum blues. You've spent nine months devoting your energies to a specific project (a baby). You've been so focused on that one goal that, once it is successfully achieved, you feel lost, directionless, and sad. You feel these emotions even though you know what your next project will be (raising the baby). Think how much more difficult it would be to cope if you didn't have the prospect of a new project and had to adjust to your former everyday routine.

High Water!

Changing from a role in a fast-paced project to the drudgery of answering piles of monotonous memos and megabytes of energy-sapping e-mail takes time. Most people adjust within a few days, but if feelings of anxiety persist for more than a few weeks, consider seeing your doctor about an evaluation. Or, maybe you just need a long-deserved vacation.

Suddenly, you are no longer the head honcho of a project with team members constantly seeking your advice and decisions. Instead, you return to civilian life with your normal job duties and responsibilities. There may be a period of letdown in which the project stays on your mind. You may keep thinking of improved ways to accomplish some tasks, or ideas may come to you that might have better met the project's goals. Your "symptoms" may indeed be real. But if it's your skill and desire, freelance project managers do well and make good incomes depending on their experience and success. This could be you! Be encouraged: There's always another project to manage somewhere.

Right now you should have a celebration. Your project is done (except for the final report, which you'll learn how to write in the next chapter. You didn't think you'd get away without another report, did you?).

Get your team together. Revel in your accomplishments. Then move on to the next project.

The Least You Need to Know

➤ Dissolving a project takes time and deliberate effort on your part.

➤ All projects must come to an end. Period.

➤ Closing down a project is a process that follows a predetermined series of steps.

➤ You need to find a place for the displaced workers if they came from within your organization.

➤ A journal and a final report will help others learn from your successes and mistakes. Update the journal each day before you forget things.

Chapter 28

The Final Evaluation: The Short and Long of It

Now that your project is shut down, you may think you're finally done. But there's one more important step—the final project evaluation. The purpose of this step is to appraise your actions: what you did well and what you could have done better. Only through a final project evaluation will you learn how to better manage your next project.

Through an effective postmortem, lessons learned from this project can be effectively applied to the next one. The final evaluation should happen whether the project achieved its goals or evolved into a dismal failure.

Small leftover tasks, such as installing the built-in office coffeemaker or screwing in light bulbs, shouldn't delay the final evaluation from going forward. Large leftover tasks indicate a project that's incomplete, however, making it too early to analyze results—even if the scheduled completion date has come and gone.

There are three components to the final evaluation: project assessment, a final written report, and team member performance reviews. A final meeting of the core team is often in order as well because this will assist you in evaluating the project and producing input for the report. The team's technical expertise and experiences may provide data that you hadn't previously considered.

Understanding Why Some Projects Succeed and Others Flop

It may seem at this point that project management is a lot of work without a lot of guaranteed benefits. The chances of a project succeeding or failing vary according to the nature of the industry, the project's complexity, the personalities involved, and the culture of the company. A fast-moving project that would fly through an aggressive startup company might stumble quickly in the bureaucracy of a large public utility, a stuffy corporation, or another sluggish organization.

In Chapter 1, "Projects, Projects Everywhere," we listed several general factors that contribute to the success of projects and project managers alike. That list probably makes more sense now that you have gone through the entire process and methodology on your own.

As you consider your own project experiences, remember these factors and determine whether your project and your skills as a project manager measure up.

Projects that don't meet the majority of their objectives should be studied closely to understand what went wrong, but successful projects also deserve inspection and evaluation. There are lessons to be learned from every project.

By the way, a project that is terminated for unforeseen changes in the environment is not a failed project; it is just a project that was not brought to fruition. Projects that fail due to unforeseen circumstances or changes in the organization's requirements, culture, or direction are not true project failures either, although you may have trouble convincing the person paying the bills otherwise. Projects that are extremely late, come in over budget, use too many resources, or leave participants and clients unhappy are projects that were not properly managed. Depending on how much the problems impacted the budget and schedule, give yourself credit for completing the beast. At least it got done.

Why Projects Don't Meet Their Goals

There are several basic reasons why projects fail to meet their goals relating to cost, performance, and schedules. Predictably, these reasons are the opposite of the reasons why projects succeed. Here are some common reasons why projects don't live up to expectations:

➤ Your plan is too simple, too complex, or unrealistic.

➤ Major conflicts are not ironed out and waste time and resources.

➤ Your leadership or that of managers under you is unskilled or inappropriate in style.

➤ The initial goals and objectives were not completely agreed upon, and no resolution was forthcoming.

➤ Inadequate monitoring and controls keep problems from being anticipated or dealt with immediately upon recognition.

➤ Staffing is inappropriate or insufficient.

➤ Required tasks and resources are overlooked and must be forced into the project later, if that's even possible.

➤ Weak communication between team members, the project manager, and senior management slows decision-making.

➤ The wheel is reinvented. Rather than studying other similar projects and their fate, an inexperienced project manager jumps in headfirst, taking his or her team down the primrose path.

Why Projects Succeed

The whole reason you read this book is to learn how to make projects succeed. If you follow the processes presented here, we bet you'll have a better chance than most. We believe projects succeed for the following reasons:

➤ A realistic plan has been built and agreed upon with stakeholders through careful analysis of the requirements involved.

➤ Conflict is quickly accelerated to the project manager's office for resolution.

➤ You, as project manager, are a strong leader and click with both team members and senior management.

➤ Goals and objectives are clear and concise. Team members fully understand them.

➤ Careful reporting and monitoring are in place for tracking the project from start to finish.

➤ The right people in the right number are available at the right time to handle each and every task.

➤ Ninety-eight percent of task and resource requirements were successfully identified and budgeted for before the project start date.

➤ The manager participates routinely with team members to help out, to listen to their problems, and to see firsthand what needs to be done to address them.

➤ Similar projects are studied to learn what problems to expect and how to handle them.

➤ Most importantly, the stakeholders are kept satisfied throughout the project, and at the end, they agree that the project met their expectations (even if it came out a little later or a bit more expensive than originally planned).

Your Evaluation of the Project

Before you formally evaluate your completed or closed-down project, you need input from your core team. Ask for a brief written report or provide a simple questionnaire to complete. Then schedule an informal meeting with key players and ask them their opinions about the project and what they would do better next time. Take notes so you remember comments and confirm that you value their input.

The first question when evaluating a project is whether the desired results were accomplished. Then consider the stages from start to finish to understand what worked and what didn't. Look closely at problems and how you and your team coped with them. Picking up the pieces and successfully gluing them back together is an art. Consider when you did this well and when you could have done better.

Sit Down with Pen in Hand

There are no hard-and-fast rules for project evaluation. Essentially, you match your achievements to the project's goals. If what you produce lines up clearly with well-defined goals, chances are you've succeeded. If you have met the goals only part way, your project may be considered a success by some and a failure by others. The toughest evaluation is one in which the goals were fuzzy to begin with.

To evaluate your project's success (or lack of success), make a list of the project's accomplishments and place it next to the goals page(s). Study each list, checking off goals as you consider your list of accomplishments. This is the best way to evaluate your project.

It's a Wrap! Time Now for the Final Report

With the exception of the smallest projects (and sometimes even for those), a final report is mandated by management at the close of the project. The final report for a megaproject is more formal and obviously longer than for a small, simple project. As previously mentioned, reports are necessary for both successfully completed projects and those that are canceled. On a successful project, the final report may precipitate bonuses for the team members and their mentor (you). If the project went belly-up, the report serves to document the problems and to help others avoid the quicksand you and your team slipped into. The report can also document why a project problem wasn't your fault.

The Final Report

The final report is both a history of the project and a final evaluation of performance. While the final report for a small project may be no more than a two-page memo, the report for a large project may be 10 or 20 pages in length. If you kept a project diary (refer to Chapter 20), producing the final report will be relatively easy.

All of the topics covered in the project report for a simple project should be included in the final report for a large project, but they should be covered in more detail. These are the main things to include in the final report:

➤ An overview of the project including revisions to the original project plan

➤ A summary of major accomplishments

➤ Analysis of achievements compared to original goals for the project

➤ Final financial accounting and an explanation of variances from the budget

➤ An evaluation of administrative and management performance

➤ The team's performance (this section should be confidential when it applies to specific individuals and their performance)

➤ Issues or tasks that require further investigation

➤ Recommendations for future projects of this type

➤ Special acknowledgments to team members

In addition, the following elements are appropriate to include in the final reports for more complex projects:

➤ A summary of performance issues, conflicts, and resolutions

➤ The results of each phase of the project including actual versus forecast dates and the budget versus actual expenses (budget use, additions, and so on, require thorough documentation)

➤ A description of ongoing project-related activities that will require further team member participation (if any)

➤ Recommendations for changes to future projects so they will run more smoothly and be more compatible with the sponsoring organization

➤ In-depth analysis of reporting procedures and recommendations for improvements

➤ Analysis of the project management process as a whole

In each section of a final report for a project, the procedures used in the project should be analyzed. Things that worked should be acknowledged. Things that didn't work should be explained. Recommendations for improvements in future implementations of the project methodology should be made, and there should be clear examples and rationales for the changes. All key team members should either contribute to the report or review its contents for accuracy before the report is finalized. You can have others write and submit their relevant portions of the final report and then, after editing, add your own two cents' worth as an overview to cement the document.

Packaging Options for the Report

Your final report should be reviewed by everyone involved in the project from your management to the project stakeholders to the administrative assistant who makes the copies. You may want to break it into five sections, as outlined in the following sections.

The Executive Summary

This one- to two-page document summarizes the report's content for people who need a quick briefing and don't have time or are unable to digest the entire document.

The Report, Part A

This section contains information that can be disseminated to all team members, managers, and other interested parties. It includes a detailed review of the project and a goal-by-goal assessment of the project's success in meeting each one.

The Report, Part B

This section includes information for management only or that may be confidential in nature. (See the section "Confidential Reports" later in this chapter.) It can contain information not appropriate for team members' eyes, such as salaries, team-member performance, and recommendations for using the results of the project. It can also include the financial reports for the project.

The Project Plan

The project's overall plan should be included along with copies of the goal information. If it fits and makes you look good, include the original plan and the final plan so that readers can see how you met the scheduled dates.

Miscellaneous Components

If tangible proof of a project's success is possible, such as the opening of a new store or the discovery of life on another planet, photos can be included in this section and referenced from report parts A and B.

Confidential Reports

Confidential reports are the most difficult to manage. Consisting of anything from a new product kept away from competitors to government and military material, it may be that your own boss isn't authorized to read it. All such documents must be kept under lock and key, whether in a locking desk drawer or a sealed document repository much like a large bank vault. In James Bond terms, a portion of a report may be "for your eyes only" while the rest is available for distribution. If you find yourself in the awkward situation of not knowing what to release, get advice from someone who is privy to the report's contents anyway.

The Political Impact of Final Reports

In a politically sensitive organization, a negative report can cause problems. Before you state emphatically that ol' so-and-so was the major roadblock to successfully completing the project, you had better be in line for another job or an unemployment check.

As was strongly (if wrongly) suspected of the Warren report on the slaying of President Kennedy, for political reasons there were two versions of the report: one for the public and another for high-level government officials and operatives. You may want to consider this tactic for presenting complete information to your managers while, in a second brief report, withholding proprietary or personal information from rank-and-file team members.

In the building of the atomic bomb for World War II, a few senior government officials knew what was being developed. Thousands of project team members, however, learned only about the part, system, or explosive components they were personally responsible for designing and building. It wasn't until months after the surrender of Japan that some of these people put the pieces together, so to speak.

Who Accomplished What and How Well?

If your project involved people, you'll likely be called on to evaluate the performance of each team member. This may be limited to core team members, or it may apply to all team members and even outside vendors, consultants, and suppliers. The evaluations can be used for anything ranging from promotions to new assignments to lay-offs. In a project in which a team member's contribution is made before the project terminates, a review should be held when the team member departs rather than waiting for project closure. Why? Because on a really large project, completion and the review might be years away.

Many companies have standard evaluation procedures that must be followed, and the personnel department will insert itself into the evaluation process. Chances are, personnel will provide standard evaluation forms for both you and the employee to fill out. In a matrixed project organization (refer to Chapter 19), other managers who work with the team member may contribute to the written evaluations as well.

The basic criteria for appraising team member performance include the following:

➤ Quality of work

➤ Cost consciousness

➤ Timeliness

➤ Creativity

➤ Administrative performance

➤ Ability to work as part of a team

➤ Attitude

➤ Communication skills

➤ Technical ability

➤ Recommendations for improvement

➤ Consistency in meeting deadlines

Words from the Wise

"I'll need everyone's help on this project. I hope you can overlook the cloud of doom that hovers nearby."

—Dilbert, from the strip by Scott Adams

When giving a performance review in person, try for a relaxed atmosphere away from other team members. For stellar performers, this is a good time to hand out any bonus checks, with the agreement that the team member will keep it quiet so as not to make other members unhappy.

The Bottom Line and You

In addition to the formal review of a project, every project manager needs to do some personal soul-searching to understand why a particular project went well or why it went poorly. After the project has been completed for a while and the emotion is gone, stand back and look at the project and your own management skills as objectively and dispassionately as possible. What did you do well? What could you have done better? What do you still need to learn? These are the observations, if acted on and taken seriously, that will help you prosper, develop, and improve as a project manager.

At this point, you have been exposed to the complete process of project management. You have learned how to complete project management calculations and develop diagrams, reports, and communications that will help you plan, monitor, and control your project to a successful conclusion. Congratulations—and good luck in your role as project manager!

But wait! Don't forget about the last section of this book. There you'll learn how entire organizations are realigning their operations to improve project productivity, and you'll discover the wealth of new software tools available to help you in your project management ventures.

The Least You Need to Know

➤ After a project ends, take stock of what went right and what went wrong.

➤ On most projects, a final report is required to inform all participants and stakeholders of the project's results.

➤ Not all report information should be available to team members and outsiders.

➤ Performance should be formally or informally (depending on the organization) reviewed when team members depart the project or when the project is completed.

Part 7

The Organization and Tools to Make Project Management Prosper

In this section, you'll learn how to put the discipline of project management to work throughout your organization. We start by looking at ways a company can use lessons learned in the project management paradigm at the organizational level. In the final chapter, you'll learn how an empowered project-oriented organization can benefit from using new project management software to help implement the planning, control, administration, and communication aspects of project management with less effort and more consistency. And you'll discover how new Internet-enabled collaboration tools can assist in facilitating the interactions and work among team members, even if the people are separated by international borders.

Chapter 29

The Project-Enabled Organization

In This Chapter

➤ Focusing your business culture on project success

➤ Adapting your organization to focus on projects

➤ Establishing a portfolio management strategy

➤ Creating the "project office" for supporting projects

Project management offers many opportunities for creating consistency in meeting goals that can be applied to entire organizations. If a department or even an entire corporation can institutionalize the factors that lead to project management success, the entire organization should be able to achieve successes consistently.

Firms that have adopted zero-defect strategies now view project management as one of the necessary components for achieving dependable, quality results. They have discovered that the consistent, defined processes of project management are a foundation for improving not only quality but productivity and profitability as well.

In this chapter, we'll look at some of the steps an organization can take to move from ad-hoc project control to becoming an efficient, projectized organization. Projectized is the term used by the Project Management Institute (PMI) to describe an organization in which most of the resources are focused on project work.

Understanding the Benefits of Formalizing Project Management

In Chapter 1, "Projects, projects Everywhere," we listed several general factors that contribute to the success of projects and project managers alike. Here's that list again; consider how it applies to the work in your organization:

1. Agreement among the stakeholders on the goals of the project
2. A plan that describes a clear path and unambiguous responsibilities that can be used as a baseline for measuring progress as the project proceeds through time
3. Effective, consistent, quality communication between the stakeholders involved in the project
4. A scope that is both controlled and understood by project stakeholders
5. Support for the project priorities and resources required

Is Your Organization Ready for Projectization?

If projects are becoming a larger and more important aspect of the work in your organization, project management offers potential for increased quality and efficiency. To determine the degree to which your organization can benefit from consistent employment of the project management discipline, you need to ask yourself some tough questions about your current organization:

➤ What's your organizational style now and should you change it to better match your priorities? The organizational models presented in Chapter 19 (functional, pure-project, matrix, and mixed) can include a wide range of organizational styles. Every company has projects and ongoing operations. In most cases, favoring one comes at the expense of the other.

➤ How much of the budget is spent on projects now? If you spend the majority of your cash (or earn most of your money) on projects, then a project-oriented structure makes sense.

➤ Do your projects include multiple functions such as an accounting staff, engineering personnel, and marketing experts? Do you have to borrow these resources from the functional departments? If so, the cost of communicating and coordinating with these functional areas (if you work in a functional organization) is increased. The more frequently you need to depend on the functional areas for support, the more a project-oriented style will improve efficiency.

➤ How large are the projects in your organization? The larger the projects, the more sense it makes to organize around them. Size is measured in terms of duration (projects of a year or more are considered large), level of resource utilization (if most of the team members are employed by the project on a full-time basis, then it's a major project), the size of the project team (any project with more than 50 team members is a large project), and the size of the budget in proportion to your organization's budget. Obviously, when a project consumes a large portion of an organization's budget, it demands more focus. (In all of these examples, an organization could be a department, a division, or an entire company. Project size is always relative to the size of the organization you're considering for projectization.)

➤ How similar are the projects in your organization? Projects are always unique, as you've learned already, but in some firms, there is a great deal of similarity among projects. The more similarities there are, the greater the opportunity to manage projects as ongoing operations. The more projects produce unrelated or dissimilar results, the more the project-oriented structure makes sense. Product-focused organizations are a good example; software companies often organize and focus their groups on one specific product in their portfolio.

➤ How complex is the work and how important is knowledge transfer from one project to another? This is an especially important question in engineering-oriented organizations. The complexity and size of major engineering endeavors often favor projectized organizations. However, in functional organizations, people organize their careers and expand their expertise within that function; the knowledge is maintained within the company. In a project-oriented structure, knowledge transfer from one project to the next requires conscious effort. If this isn't done (and it often isn't), technical innovations or special skills may be lost when the project is over. Thus, the short-term benefits of a projectized organization can result in losing valuable institutional knowledge—unless a structure and process is designed within the larger organization to prevent this from happening.

As you consider your own project experiences and forthcoming endeavors, remember these factors and determine whether your own organization should become more or less project-oriented. The size and complexity of modern corporations defy a definitive recommendation for an organizational style. Any organizational format has strengths and weaknesses. The key is to adapt the organization of projects at the right level and in the right way for the organization in question.

Define the Organizational Boundaries First

The first decision in projectization is defining the organizational boundaries for the change. Should projectization occur at the project, department, division, or corporate level? In your analysis of organizational change, you can use the risk management techniques you learned. Ask yourself how much risk there would be of losing the information gained from one program to the next if each were being managed as an independent project organization. What is the risk of losing quality and productivity if you don't organize in a project-oriented manner?

We've provided three examples of projectized organizations to demonstrate how different organizations can incorporate the project-oriented approach at different levels.

In business, when catering to fast-changing markets, each division may be largely autonomous with complete start-to-finish control of a product. This way, a separate division of the company such as manufacturing won't slow throughput as it copes with other orders.

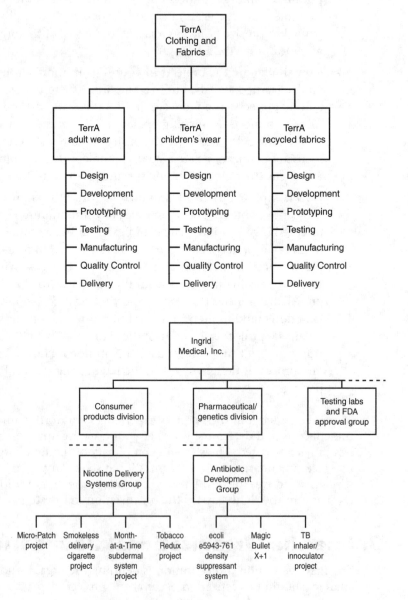

Not all organizations can use the "top-down" project development management scheme. There may be too much expense to completely duplicate all functions. Instead, one or more elements—here, the testing and FDA components—are shared. This reduces expenses but also creates a potential bottleneck for all parties if not properly implemented.

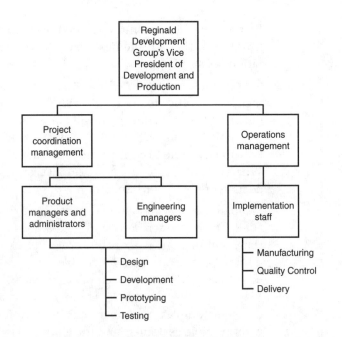

Now Come the Standards

Once you've decided that the projectization of all or part of your organization is a good idea, you'll need to work on developing consistent procedures for implementing project management. This book can help you do that, but be forewarned. You can't buy *standard* practices for your organization in an off-the-shelf format; you need to adapt the standards to your own projects and organizational preferences.

As you develop the procedures for your own organization, here are some of the procedures and support tools you'll need to consider:

➤ Common project roles including authority levels and responsibilities for the project manager and other key players. Who will have the authority to approve a project or cancel it? Who will be able to assign people (or remove them) from a project? To whom does the project manager report? What responsibilities do the functional managers have if any? What exactly is the sponsor's role and responsibility to the project? Don't

Project Lingo

Standards often begin as guidelines that describe a preferred approach. As these standards enjoy widespread adoption, they become *de facto* regulations. Regulations, on the other hand, are rules for which compliance is mandated (usually by a government agency or corporate management). It's important in discussing requirements for projects to differentiate between standards (which enjoy some flexibility in implementation) and regulations (which are dictated and absolute).

High Water!

Don't weigh your projects down with excessive amounts of bu-reaucracy. Guidelines that are appropriate for a project to build a new Mars research probe would be inappropriate for a project to reorganize the sales force. Standards are important, but make them flexible enough to accommodate the differences in projects of various sizes.

be vague in these definitions. Don't leave authorities and responsibilities subject to interpretations.

➤ Support staff for projects. Will you have a formal project office to assist with administrative duties and coordination? Or, will you have a full-time staff for each project? Maybe you'll borrow staff time from the functional areas. Whatever is appropriate, make sure it's clearly documented in your standards.

➤ Standard formats and criteria for project deliverables. This will often consist of templates for the statement of work, work plans, project plans, status reports, and other deliverables; there might be multiple sets of templates required for projects of different sizes. For example, the standards for complex projects in multiple locations with multiple customers and the employment of outside resources would require more standardization than small, internal projects.

➤ Approval processes for projects (sometimes different processes will be required for projects of different scopes) and criteria for making approvals.

Establish a Lifecycle Standard

You likely remember the discussion of project lifecycles in Chapter 2, "The Processes That Work." All efforts at improving project management start with the definition of a consistent lifecycle. This lifecycle definition can help you define consistent project management practices for each phase in a project. Once again, you might have two or three different lifecycle definitions for different types of projects in your organization.

Probably the most commonly used lifecycle is four phases, usually defined as the definition, planning, execution, and closing phases. In this model, each phase emphasizes a certain type of activity, and each phase requires approval from the key stakeholders to move to the next phase.

You can also have a lifecycle with as few as three phases, which might be defined as initiate, implement, and close-out. A single approval and the initiate phase might be appropriate for this project because of its small size and the need for rapid development.

Then again, you might want a lifecycle with five, six, or even seven phases that require more approvals at each lifecycle phase to help reduce risk in a complex project or to add time to hire project staff.

We've provided a diagram of different types of lifecycles used in different industries to give you an idea of the type of lifecycle that might make sense for your projects.

Six phase lifecycle

| Preplanning | Budgeting | Work | Planning | Execution | Closing |

Five phase lifecycle

| Initiate | Planning | Staff | Implement | Terminate |

Three phase lifecycle

| Planning | Executing | Closing |

Three lifecycle possibilities with common project deliverables by phase.

Standard Deliverables and Approvals Required

Be sure that your lifecycle is more than just words on paper. The lifecycle should include a clear definition of deliverables, stakeholder roles, and approvals required at each phase. In your lifecycle definitions, create a document that answers questions like these: What must you achieve to move to the next level? Who will approve your movement into the next phase? What criteria will the stakeholders use to make this approval?

Where Do the Standards Come From?

Ideas for project standardization can come from reading a number of books including this one. The best source for standards, however, are the project histories from your own organization and those from expert project managers who may be called upon to help you as you projectize your organization.

People who have been project managers in your organization in the past can help you define the success factors and problem areas in past projects. That's why the documentation in the closing phase of the project is so important: It provides key information for improving processes in the future. By addressing both success factors and problem areas in your standards, you'll be able to emphasize the processes that will lead to triumph within the culture of your company.

Manage Projects Like an Investment in Your Future

A major institutional step in developing a consistent project management framework is to begin managing projects as a portfolio, just like you'd manage a portfolio of investments. This means that you'll need to develop a systematic approach for choosing, monitoring, and canceling projects. To do this, accurate information is required from every project that is submitted in consistent formats from one project to another.

Managing your projects as a portfolio also requires clear authority for a group of people, often called the steering committee or project board, who have been granted authority to manage the portfolio (including initiating, reviewing, canceling, and continuing projects).

Furthermore, project portfolio management requires clear operational and strategic goals for evaluating projects and a disciplined process that requires regular review of projects and clear guidelines for proposing, reviewing, and approving them.

Portfolio management also depends on the use of a quality project reporting system or enterprise resource management system. (You'll learn more about project management software for this purpose in the next chapter.) In defining the right type of information systems to support the portfolio management process, you'll need to ask questions like these:

➤ Who needs the information and for what purpose?

➤ What information is needed?

➤ Where does the information come from?

➤ How often is the information needed?

➤ Does the information exist already or does it need to be created?

Without a portfolio management system in place, these simple questions are almost impossible to answer.

Putting a Project Office in Place to Support the System

Without visible and ongoing support for project management, it's likely that standards and policies will degrade and return to their previous, unproductive state. One common way to prevent this from happening is to employ a group for continuous development and support of the standards, practices, and information systems that define project management. This group is often known as the project office.

The project office is called by many different names including the Program Management Center, the Center of Excellence, the Project Support Office, and so on. In general, these offices are responsible for various levels of planning, budgeting, scheduling, and hiring assistance. The objective is to help people put good project management practices in place.

The project office can be assigned various levels of authority for a project from basic guidance to complete authority. In some cases, project offices are temporary—they exist only during the development of a long program. In other cases, project offices are at the top of the authority structure and oversee all the cross-functional projects in an organization.

The responsibilities of the project office (regardless of what it is called) will vary based on the degree to which the organizational structure favors projects and embraces project management processes. Here are some of the responsibilities that a project office can assume:

➤ Maintaining project management standards

➤ Providing training on project management

➤ Consulting on technical and procedural issues

➤ Scheduling assistance

➤ Creating and tracking budgets

➤ Providing staff, including project managers, for the organization

➤ Providing enterprise-level project information

➤ Supervising project managers

➤ Procuring resources

➤ Participating in project portfolio management

➤ Making project management decisions

The most successful project offices will provide expertise in the discipline of project management and enthusiasm for its value in getting things done on time and within budget. The simple presence of a project office, in any form, helps breathe life into the organization's commitment to project management principles.

In the End, It's Leadership That Makes It Work

It's critical that you understand the nature of your organization's projects to organize project management. It's even more important, however, that the changes required to reap the benefits are supported by management for the long haul.

Change won't happen overnight. There are few higher risk projects in business than consciously attempting to change the cultural and operational practices of an organization. It will take both discipline and commitment. If you make the standards optional, that's exactly what you'll get: optional project management and optional results. But if you provide authority and funding to the endeavor, you'll win cynical employees over to your side.

Words from the Wise

"There are two things to be considered with regard to any scheme. In the first place, 'Is it good in itself?' In the second, 'Can it be easily put into practice?'"

—Jean-Jacques Rousseau

People will take project management standards seriously if the authority of the project managers and the project office is taken seriously. This means the organization must grant enough authority to the project managers to be taken seriously. While this might sound obvious, it's not easy. Project managers must have a career path that's well-defined and well-rewarded. Nothing speaks louder about management commitment than what's rewarded.

Even enthusiastic supporters of the organizational changes may be bogged down as things proceed. Learning a new process can be tedious, especially when ordinary work must get done in the process. To eliminate this frustration, break the projectization process into phases—just like any other project—so the work is doable. People also need to be supplied with appropriate training and support. Let people experiment with the new ideas in a classroom setting so they won't be embarrassed when using the new skills on actual projects.

Changing the organization to embrace project management can entail significant risk if people aren't convinced of the need to use the processes. Thus, your critical task in this endeavor is to win those people to your side through leadership, training, and persistent communication. (Sounds a lot like project management work, doesn't it?)

The Least You Need to Know

➤ Reorganizing for project management requires planning, management support, assigned authorities, training, and time for implementation.

➤ Projectized organizations employ consistent standards to help guide their projects to success.

➤ The structure of a project-oriented organization will vary based on the products produced, the size and frequency of the projects, and the culture of the organization.

➤ The forms and names for project offices may be different, but the support functions, in terms of planning, budgeting, and staffing assistance, are similar.

➤ The authority level of the project office will vary depending on the degree of projectization of the organization.

➤ Without management support for the processes, a projectized organization is doomed to return to older, less efficient ways of getting things done.

Software for All Projects Great and Small

Creating a detailed project plan and keeping it up-to-date for most nontrivial projects can be a very time-consuming process if completed manually. The complexity of figuring in vacations, holidays, weekends, early-starts, and other factors can be overwhelming to someone inexperienced in project management techniques or short on pencils. The details involved in producing networks and work breakdown structures seem daunting, and assembling a budget can be tedious.

Just producing the plan is a lot of work for a project. And, as you've hopefully concluded by now, project management entails more than just creating a good plan. Producing the reports, updating the charts, and incorporating changes to a project plan along the way add complexity and more paperwork. Of course, if you need to manage multiple projects at the same time, the calculations, graphs, and reports can seem impossible.

In this chapter, you'll learn about software that can help you keep it all straight. And because the programs are easy to use, you won't have any excuses for not keeping your plans up-to-date.

Software That Simplifies the Details

All the graphing, changing, and reporting in project management can drive you crazy. Some naive managers simply reject project management methods because of the reports involved. Instead, they choose to manage projects with intuition and guesswork (and much of the time they guess wrong). The benefits of project management methods are too important to ignore just because the charts and graphs take time to produce. Today, thanks to the rise of the personal computer and the World Wide Web, there are solutions that enable everyone to benefit from using project management methods. There are easy-to-use project management programs such as Microsoft Project that anyone can master in a few hours. There are also highly sophisticated systems that can integrate projects across the organization and can help teams collaborate on their efforts from around the world.

With the right project management program or information system, you can concentrate on the management of the project, leaving you more time for thinking and planning. You can let the computer provide tactical support in the form of charts, graphs, schedules, resource allocations, and virtual communication capabilities.

This chapter covers the basics of selecting and using computerized project management programs so you won't give up on project management before you get started.

What Can Project Management Programs Do?

Project management programs range in capabilities from simple scheduling programs that produce Gantt charts to prodigious mainframe applications that are integrated with the corporation's budgeting, marketing, manufacturing, personnel, and other management information systems.

The underlying methods supported by most project management programs are similar to those presented in this book. Depending on the capabilities of the program, you enter task sequences, resources, dates, and costs, just as described in this book, and the computer calculates or modifies the schedules, budget, or resource utilization for you. Most programs even draw the networks or can convert one network format into another. Most of the time, you'll enter your project data into a form that looks like a spreadsheet with columns and rows; this allows you to define WBS levels and to describe tasks, precedence, resource requirements, and almost anything else that's relevant—including resource calendars, labor costs, and overhead allocations.

In addition to helping you calculate schedules and costs, project management programs produce a wide variety of reports from simple to comprehensive. If you have a special project management requirement, such as a custom report or chart, there is probably a program out there with the capability to produce the output you need.

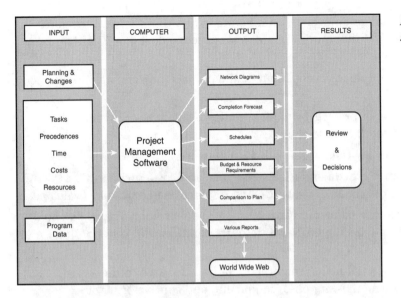

How project management software works.

Not even the most sophisticated software package is a substitute for competent leadership and skilled decision-making, and by itself, it can't correct any task-related problems or human-centered conflicts. Project management software can, however, be a terrific boon to the project manager tracking interrelated variables, schedules, resources, costs, and tasks that come into play. New project management tools can enhance communications among team members and can facilitate collaborative problem solving. Although not all programs do everything, most of them can help you do some or all of the following:

➤ Graph costs, schedules, and resource utilization using Gantt charts, histograms, line diagrams, and a variety of other charts.

➤ Create standard and custom reports including standard accounting and tracking. Some programs will even produce special report formats required by government agencies such as the Department of Defense (DOD).

➤ Maintain resource and project calendars that record the availability of staff and equipment. These internal program calendars are used to create optimum schedules. This feature allows the project manager to establish workweeks based on actual workdays and to specify nonwork periods such as weekends, holidays, and vacations. The project calendar can be printed out in detail or in a summary format.

➤ Make schedule changes based on a variety of resource-leveling parameters (for example, no overtime!) and priority scheduling attributes.

➤ Maintain skills inventories that match resources to task requirements.

➤ Track and schedule multiple projects at the same time. Some packages feature a single, comprehensive database that enables cross-project analysis and reporting.

363

Cost and schedule modules share common data files that allow integration among projects and that minimize problems of schedule inconsistencies and re-dundancies.

➤ Allow multiple people to access, input, and report on project data at the same time.

➤ Collapse the view of projects by work breakdown structure or organization structure, subproject, or milestone.

➤ Calculate and display the critical path for a network.

➤ Display alternative schedules, task assignments, and cost criteria so that the im-mediate impact of schedule, sequence, and resource changes can be evaluated.

➤ Assign early-warning parameters that let the program inform you of potential trouble including schedule problems, resource conflicts with other projects, and cost overruns.

➤ Integrate with material management, purchasing, and accounting systems to as-sist in ordering materials, supplies, equipment, and contractor services.

➤ Produce presentation-quality graphics for making reports to management and customers about the plans and status of a project.

➤ Display actual and planned data simultaneously.

➤ Summarize data in a variety of ways including expenditures, timing, and activ-ity data.

➤ Complete cost analyses, cost accounting, and variance analyses.

➤ Create free-format reports with an integrated word processor or other report generator for incorporating personalized project annotations.

➤ Display relevant information on the Web or corporate intranet so that project team members can view the status and schedule of the project and their own as-signed tasks.

➤ Communicate and collaborate with the project team across project locations. (This is called virtual communication.)

The Virtual World of the Project Needs Virtual Tools

A virtual project is a collaborative effort towards a specific goal or accomplishment that is based on "collective yet remote" performance. Some experts have called this "working together, apart." This increasingly common mode of work needs informa-tion management tools that enable communication and coordination at a distance.

You may recall from Chapter 20 that management by walking around (MBWA) is one of the most effective methods of tracking work and motivating people. The trouble is, today's "teams" often have team members scattered across the city, state, or continent. The solution is to visit project resources virtually rather than physically, a variation that might be called management by Web surfing—and you need not leave your office to do it.

Virtual project management (VPM) is the Information Age equivalent of management by walking around. The rise to dominance within organizations of Internet-based collaboration tools offers new possibilities for group-based and Web-based project management. Virtual project management requires several layers of information system support:

➤ *Multimedia communication* incorporates e-mail, phone calls, memoranda (hopefully as e-mail attachments but possibly as paper), and other media.

➤ *Collaboration* goes beyond basic messaging to sharing information. This is often done using the collaboration capabilities of the World Wide Web.

➤ *Tracking and leveling of resources* are functions performed by traditional project management products that must be shared across spatial boundaries in virtual project management systems.

➤ *Access to project-related information systems* such as computer-aided design and corporate information databases is advantageous. For complex projects, this project information may reside in specialized repositories such as CAD programs, CASE tools, simulation software, and data warehouses in addition to the information contained in project management software.

➤ Some organizations are required by regulation or self-imposed standards to use a specific methodology (such as ISO 9000) to maintain complete configuration control over project deliverables. A pharmaceutical firm, for instance, might need to store not only the final specification for a new drug but all alternatives and iterations leading up to it. In such cases, the dimension of *process management* can consume as many resources as the projects themselves. The new virtual tools should also help with maintaining this ongoing documentation.

The Power of Networking

Drug manufacturers and bridge builders weren't exactly on hold until the advent of distributed computing. All of the activities mentioned so far have been handled for years with pencil and paper and human ingenuity. How do electronic information systems change this? How do Web-based applications in particular add value? The answer is in the power of networking and the Internet.

Because of networking, e-mail allows ideas to flow asynchronously (that is, without parties online at the same time), enabling work to flow across time zones. E-mail doesn't require incremental labor and provides a searchable audit trail; this is key to many formal project processes.

365

Networking also enables remote collaboration. The ability to "work together, apart" is hardly possible without shared storage and concurrency control—problems solved because of modern client/server database technology. There are a growing number of client/server collaboration products coming to market that allow multiple contributors to share and add content to project information. Some of these products allow project members to collaborate directly from a Web-based browser.

Increasingly, corporate Web sites are becoming project infrastructure. Not until recently, however, with the rise of new Web application technologies, have project teams had access to integrated environments that bridge project domains and applications. The goal of integrated process management through a suite of cooperating tools is becoming the new standard in large-scale project management.

So What's in It for Me?

One of the most powerful benefits of using software to assist in the implementation of project management methodology is the what-if analysis capabilities facilitated by interactive software products. Even the products that aren't Web-enabled allow you to do this. Changes to the time estimates of individual tasks can be made, and a new schedule is immediately displayed for review. The sequence in tasks can be changed and then put back the way it was almost instantaneously. The same thing can be done with costs and resources. Imagine trying to do that with a pencil and eraser. It would take hours. With a computer, it takes seconds!

To facilitate what-if analyses, many programs establish a separate, duplicate project database before changes are entered. The software then performs a comparative analysis and displays the new against the old project plan in tabular or graphical form. This makes it fast and easy for managers to review the impact of changes and come to better, more-informed conclusions.

Simple Versus Complex Projects and the Software They Need

If you manage your projects using manual techniques, you will probably limit yourself to Gantt charts and simple precedence or PERT networks. Early project management programs were also limited to these simple displays because they used "character-based" graphics. The imprecise resolution of character-based project management graphics makes it hard to build projects and more difficult to view results.

For a project management software program to be considered for general business use today, it must facilitate interactive changes and support high-quality graphics. And, by modern standards, it probably should have the ability to use collaborative capabilities provided by networks and the World Wide Web.

Traditionally, project-driven organizations preferred mainframe software. Today, the companies that offer mainframe programs also offer desktop versions that can be integrated into a corporate-level project management system. Organizations that were less project-driven looked for less expensive, personal-computer software that was either networked or not, depending on the size and consistency desired in project management procedures.

The Types of Project Management

For purposes of easy classification, project management software products can be divided into four categories based on the functions and features they provide. These include scheduling programs, single-project programs, corporate-level programs, and mega-project programs. Let's take a closer look at each of these.

Scheduling Programs

Scheduling programs are relatively simple software products that typically are designed for people who manage small projects with only a few team members. These programs usually produce Gantt charts and work in a fashion similar to spreadsheet programs like Microsoft Excel. A large number of these programs are available for most common personal computers. They typically cost less than $200 and offer little, if any, ability to report on resources or budgets. These programs are usually limited to producing a small number of charts and reports. Some of the programs allow you to enter actual data to be displayed simultaneously with planned data; others do not.

Choose a scheduling program if your projects are very schedule-intensive but require minimal control of costs and resources. If your reporting requirements are simple and your projects are small, one of these programs can be very useful. The good ones are easy to learn, provide color display capabilities, and offer a variety of Gantt-charting symbols.

Single-Project Programs

Full-featured software packages designed for managing single projects are a step up in sophistication from scheduling programs. These products are still relatively simple and easy to use, and their output is easy to understand. Most of them provide the ability to produce Gantt charts in a variety of formats, network diagrams (either PERT or precedence), and a number of standard reports. These programs sometimes offer simple resource management and cost control capabilities.

Single-project programs are best for projects with fewer than 200 tasks. They provide only a limited analysis of the data, and since programs at this level often fail to provide automatic rescheduling based on specific resource changes, they are not useful for projects that require extensive staffing changes and what-if analyses. Programs in this category cost as little as $200 and are almost always less than $500.

Corporate-Level Programs

There are many programs in this category. Some of them are produced by well-known personal computer software companies such as Microsoft, Computer Associates, Software Publishing, and Symantec. Others are produced by companies such as Time Line, SMG, and Scitor that specialize in project management programs. (Some companies and their Web sites are listed in Appendix B; you can contact them for more information.)

Words from the Wise

"The installation is successful. I have 128 kilobytes of access to the Internet. As tradition requires, I do the engineer's victory dance."

—Dilbert, from the strip by Scott Adams

These corporate-level programs extend the features already discussed for the other two categories of software, and many run on personal computers. Others run on servers, and their manufacturers often provide a personal-computer version for smaller projects. These programs typically allow sophisticated cost accounting, resource leveling, charting, and what-if analyses. Most provide some sort of Web-based reporting. The specific features vary considerably as do their ease-of-use, flexibility, and reporting capabilities.

If you intend to regularly manage projects with 100 or more tasks or if you coordinate multiple projects, you need to start looking at software in this category. Some corporate-level programs offer a beginner's and an expert's mode that allow you to start out simple and add functions and capabilities as your project management skills develop.

Corporate-level programs range in price from $400 to over $3,000 for a single user. Network, multiuser, or minicomputer versions, when available, can be considerably more expensive. The most sophisticated programs in this category may offer add-on modules for contract control or specialized reporting functions that rival the capabilities of the mega-project programs.

Mega-project Programs

Mega-project programs, which may or may not have more features than the most sophisticated desktop computer programs, are typically designed for use on servers or mainframe computers. There may be a personal-computer version available that can share data with the mainframe program, but these PC-based versions are often difficult to use and lack the graphics sophistication of programs designed specifically for a personal computer.

Mega-project programs can handle thousands of tasks and hundreds of resources. They almost always have sophisticated cost-accounting modules and resource-leveling functions. They are sometimes difficult to use and can certainly be difficult to install, but they offer advantages in processing speed and information exchange including advanced collaboration capabilities. Most importantly, their success depends on a commitment from management to standardize the program and use it consistently across projects.

Mega-project packages (with sophisticated accounting and cost-analysis modules) are priced from $50,000 to $150,000—and that doesn't count the equipment, training, and other implementation costs for a complex system. Some of these programs come as modules for different functions so you can buy just the modules you need or add more as you learn to use the first ones.

If your project management requirements include the management of thousands of tasks or complex multiple projects with shared resources, adherence to government contract specifications, and integration with corporate accounting and information systems, then one of these mega-programs may be necessary.

How Do You Choose?

After you determine the category of software you need for your project management efforts, you should consider several critical factors for evaluating software before you make a purchase decision. Complete the following worksheet and then consider the factors in the following sections.

Cost/Feature Analysis

Prices for project management software vary greatly. Depending on the kinds of projects you intend to manage, study the features of products under consideration to match your requirements. The most expensive products are not always the most capable. On the other hand, unless your budget is heavily constrained, rule out programs that skimp on features just to save a few dollars. A product that lacks basic functionality results in frustration because it won't do what you need it to. After a couple of poorly managed projects, you'll once again be out shopping for software.

As you evaluate different products, add features to your requirements list that you hadn't considered before studying the software options. Don't make the mistake of selecting a package simply because it has more features at its price than any other package. Consider the other factors discussed later in this section, but make sure there are enough features for your current needs and those in the foreseeable future.

If you have the opportunity to evaluate products before purchase (either at a dealer's showroom or through a demo disk or the company's Web site), try using the package to assemble the plan for a small project. That way, you can test the package's reliability and see how it performs. Also check the program's speed when saving to disk, its recalculation after new tasks are added, and its printing efficiency. A program with a strong features set that takes all day to print a network diagram is probably not the one for you.

An example requirements checklist.

Requirements Checklist for Project Management Software

Scheduling Programs
- [ ] Schedules
- [ ] Gantt Charts
- [ ] Presentation

Single-Projects Programs
- [ ] Network Diagrams
- [ ] Simple Resource Tracking
- [ ] Actual versus Planned Reports

Corporate-Level Programs

[ ] Tracks Multiple Projects	[ ] Email/Group/Network Communications
[ ] Internet/World Wide Web Publishing	[ ] Multiple Budget Types
[ ] When-If Analysis	[ ] Reporting by Resource
[ ] Task Splitting	[ ] Reporting by Milestone
[ ] Sub-Project Tracking	[ ] Multiple Calendars
[ ] Variance Reports	[ ] PERT-Least to Most Likely Projections
[ ] More then 200 Tasks per Project	[ ] Integration with General Applications
[ ] More then 50 Resources per Project	[ ] Resource Leveling
[ ] Multiple Operating Systems	[ ] Audit Trails

Mega-Project Programs
- [ ] Integration with Corporate Mainframe Programs
- [ ] Over 2,000 Tasks to Be Coordinated
- [ ] Government Requirements for a specific Program or Report
- [ ] Advanced Cost and resource Accounting

If you check boxes at more than one level, choose a product in the highest category checked.

Once you select what appears to be the right product, try to purchase it from a source that gives you a 30-day money-back guarantee. That way, if the product performs poorly or ultimately doesn't fill the bill, you can return it and try something else. If you purchase software through mail order, use a credit card. You'll have more leverage returning the product because your credit card company may take your side.

When considering the cost of the software, don't forget the other system configuration requirements. Will the program work on your existing system or do you need to buy new hardware?

Ease of Use and Consistency of the Interface

One of the most important aspects of choosing software for managing projects is to select a package that's easy to use and that responds consistently throughout its interface. The easier the product is to use, the more likely it is you'll keep using it.

For example, if you choose the most feature-laden package, you may get a product with a number of menus, commands, dialog boxes, and cryptic functions that not only get in your way but actively interfere with laying out and managing projects.

Project Management Software Selection Worksheet

Product Name _____ Date _____

Price: List Price $_____ Street Price $_____

Dealer Name and Address _____

Rate each product from 1 to 10 with 10 being the highest rating:

Features [ ]   Ease of Use [ ]   Flexibility [ ]

Compatibility [ ]   Documentation [ ]

Reputation of the Manufacturer [ ]

Experience of Others with the Product [ ]

Technical Support [ ]   Training Availability [ ]

_____

Overall Rating [ ]

Comments:
_____
_____
_____
_____
_____
_____

Use this project management software selection worksheet to compare products and to make the best choice for your needs.

Although these may be important functions for a professional project manager, unless you have four months to learn the package, it may get shelved and never used. Such a package forces you into overmanaging even comparatively simple projects, thereby negating its usefulness.

Flexibility to Adapt to Various Projects

Because projects in business vary from small to large and from simple to complex, you want a package that's flexible in how it adapts to various project requirements.

Compatibility with Other Programs

In many cases, you will want to take network diagrams and other project-oriented charts and combine them with documents such as reports and presentation materials. If this is important to you, look for a package that can save or export images in a format compatible with the word processing, page layout, or presentation software you own or plan to acquire.

Documentation and Support for the Program

When learning how to use a product, your first point of reference when looking for a solution to a problem is the manual (whether it's online or printed in a book). Check the documentation and help menus carefully before purchase.

Study the documentation carefully. The information should be well-organized, have a detailed index, and offer plenty of screen shots showing how the product works. A lengthy troubleshooting section doesn't hurt either. Keyboard templates, quick-reference cards, and disk-based sample projects are also useful. Complex products with skimpy manuals should be avoided at all costs. Also, make sure the company offers training options for the program that are commensurate with the complexity of the software.

The detailed Gantt charts produced by modern project management software let you see how your whole project will unfold. You can also change dates and let the computer do the hard scheduling and tracking for you.

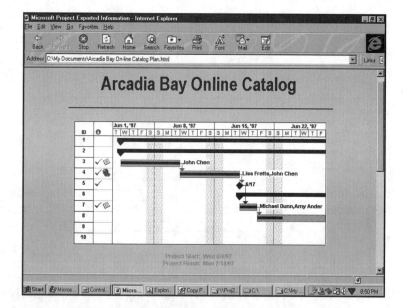

Reputation of the Product Manufacturer

If you are purchasing an expensive product that will get considerable day-to-day use, check up on the company that designed the product. If the company discontinues the product or closes its doors, you'll be on your own with the software. Look for a stable company with a strong track record of designing useful software and providing regular updates and bug fixes. Once a product becomes incompatible with the current version of your computer's operating system, project plans that could have been re-vamped for future use become unavailable if the software is not updated.

Word of Mouth Experiences

Talk to other users of a particular package to get feedback on how well the product performs with real-world projects. The users you query should use the package for projects similar in scope to the ones you plan to carry out. If calling references provided by the manufacturer, take anything less than a glowing tribute to mean that the product performs less adequately than expected.

Technical Support

When considering any software product, evaluate the technical support provided by the manufacturer. Find out if it's free or if you must pay an annual fee after 90 days or a per-use fee after a certain number of calls. Do they provide a toll-free number? Must you listen to an automatic telephone system recite a long list of options before connecting you to a technician at your expense? Dial the number and see what happens. Check out the technical support information on the company's Web site. If you're fortunate enough to have other users to ask for recommendations, query them on the quality of technical support.

Software makes creating network diagrams and schedules a breeze. You also can easily update precedence and task relationships as the project proceeds. Here you see a project that's sending information to a corporate database.

So which computerized tool is best for you? The one that meets your feature requirements with the most flexibility, with an acceptable learning curve, from a reliable and supportive vendor, and at a price you can afford. (This is pretty much the standard formula for choosing any software or computer product, not just project management software.)

Things Project Management Software Can't Do

As powerful and efficient as project management programs are, many aspects of the project management process are not within the computer's realm. Using computer-assisted project management streamlines administration, reporting, analysis, and even communication, but the following are things the computer can't and shouldn't be allowed to do:

➤ Project management software can't gather data. You'll have to decide how much and what type of information you need to manage the project. You or members of your team will still need to gather data regarding the project status, as described in Chapter 22. The computer only helps compute and display the information after it is gathered and entered.

➤ Project management software can't make decisions. The computer can make it easier and faster to look at alternatives, but it is ultimately you and your project team who will have to make the choice between the alternatives and take responsibility for the decisions.

➤ Project management software can't solve problems that require subjective judgments. Sometimes human intuition is the most important ingredient in project management, especially when dealing with people. People require understanding. Software is programmed and is not intuitive. It only reports back what you put into it. You still have to manage the conflicts, solve the problems, and use your own judgment.

➤ Project management software can't find the errors in your input. If you put biased, incomplete, or erroneous data into the project management program, it will output biased, incomplete, and erroneous project reports. Don't blame the computer for human error. The best way to eliminate this problem is to check the reports and entries a couple of times before they are distributed.

➤ Project management software can't communicate for you. Software is great at producing reports that look good and contain a wealth of detailed information, but there is more to reporting on a project than sending out the report. You still need to communicate with people face to face, build interfaces between people and departments, and listen to what is going on around you.

➤ Project management software won't save money by reducing the need for project personnel. Automation almost never really reduces the personnel costs on a project. The software can make you more efficient and make decision-making more effective because the information is better, but project management software will not significantly reduce the need for project management people. In fact, in a large projectized organization, you'll probably need to add a person or two just to help keep the computerized project definitions and Web site up-to-date and the project personnel supported when they have questions.

Go Get Yourself Some!

Now you have been introduced to the features for selecting project management software for your needs. Start talking to store personnel, reading computer magazines, and asking friends and colleagues about the programs they use. Then go out, select a program, and get started in computer-assisted project management. Follow the step-by-step guidelines for implementing the project management process you have read about. As your projects come in on time and within budget, you will have achieved membership in the league of successful project managers, and the opportunities available to you and your company will take on new perspective. With each success, you will contribute to the business, the economy, and your own career—no mean feat for just learning a few project management skills. Go for it!

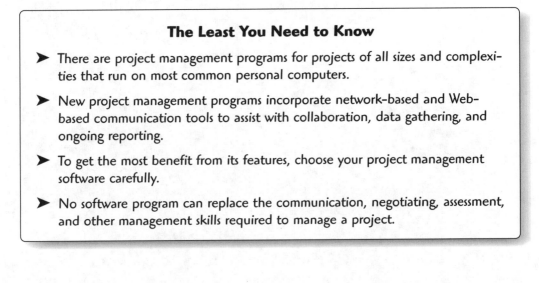

The Least You Need to Know

➤ There are project management programs for projects of all sizes and complexities that run on most common personal computers.

➤ New project management programs incorporate network-based and Web-based communication tools to assist with collaboration, data gathering, and ongoing reporting.

➤ To get the most benefit from its features, choose your project management software carefully.

➤ No software program can replace the communication, negotiating, assessment, and other management skills required to manage a project.

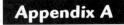

Project Lingo—A Glossary of Project Terms

action plan   A plan that describes what needs to be done and when it needs to be completed. Project plans are action plans.

activity   A specific project task that requires resources and time to complete.

activity-on-node (AON)   The two ways of documenting and drawing a network: placing the activities on the arcs or on the nodes.

answer-back diagram   If a process is highly technical, involves creative effort, or is large or complex in scale, an answer-back diagram can help. In an answer-back diagram, the vendor takes your specs and builds a simple model that demonstrates (or doesn't) a clear understanding of your project specifications.

arc   The line connecting two nodes or representing precedence in a PERT or CPM network.

audit   A formal and detailed examination of the progress, costs, operations, results, or some other aspect of a project or system.

baseline plan   The initial approved plan to which deviations will be compared as the project proceeds.

bill of materials   The formal documentation of the complete set of physical elements required to build a product. This is used by the project manager or purchasing department to order any material or supplies required.

budget decrement   A reduction in the amount of money available for a project task or activity.

buying the job   When a vendor bids at a loss to blow away the competition and get the work. An unusually low quote amidst a pile of higher but nearly identical quotes is either a "bought" job or the effort of a vendor who doesn't know what he's doing. Before you accept the low bid, make sure you know which it is.

champion   A person who takes on personal responsibility (though not usually day-to-day management) for the successful completion of a "visionary project" or creative change in an organization. It may involve a product launch, an innovation in process, or any type of project.

confidence level   A level of confidence, stated as a percentage, for a budget or schedule estimate. The higher the confidence level, the lower the risk.

conflict   Sounding like something worked out via fisticuffs, a project conflict is one in which people, priorities, or problems (the three "P's") begin to interfere with completing a project on time and within budget.

consultant   Here's the old joke that defines consultants (and it's more true than it should be): A consultant is an unemployed person who has a watch and a briefcase. Make sure the consultants on your project have better credentials than this.

contingency plan   An alternative for action if things don't go as planned or if an expected result fails to materialize. See *padding*.

control   A process for ensuring that reality or actual performance meets expectations or plans. Control often involves the process of keeping actions within limits by making adjustments to a plan to ensure that certain outcomes will happen.

cost-benefit analysis   An analysis, often stated as a ratio, used to evaluate a proposed course of action.

crash   Conducting a task at an abnormally accelerated pace to meet a deadline. Crashing is completed at a greater cost than a normally paced task or project.

critical activity   An activity or event that, if delayed, will delay some other important event, commonly the completion of a project or a major milestone in a project.

critical path   The sequence of tasks that determines the minimum schedule for a project. If one task on the critical path is delayed, the schedule will be late.

Critical Path Method (CPM)   One of the two most common forms of networking systems. CPM uses a one-time estimate for creating a project schedule. See *Project Evaluation and Review Technique (PERT)*.

critical ratio   A ratio that measures an important characteristic. This ratio is often plotted or tracked in some way to determine priorities among items or events.

cross-check   One of the best tests of completion, whether referring to doors on an airliner or the workability of a project plan, is to cross-check it. To cross-check a plan, one person lists a procedure and another verifies it. With two independent bodies carefully verifying the plan, chances for error are much smaller.

Decision Support System (DSS)   A sophisticated computer program to assist managers in making decisions. It may include simulation programs, mathematical programming routines, and decision rules.

deliverables   The clearly defined results, goods, or services produced during the project or at its outcome. Deliverables and goals are often synonymous. Deliverables, like goals, may include organizational attributes, reports, and plans, as well as physical products or objects.

dependency diagram   Another name for a network or precedence diagram that shows the dependencies (precedence) among tasks.

duration   The period of time over which a task takes place, in contrast to effort, which is the amount of labor hours a task requires. Duration establishes the schedule for a project. Effort establishes the labor costs. Each task in a project has a duration, usually specified in workdays or portions of workdays, that may or may not be different than the amount of effort (or labor) required to complete the task.

early warning system   A monitoring system that provides advance notification or indication of potential problems in a project. Many computerized project management systems incorporate early warning functions.

effectiveness   A measure of the quality of attainment in meeting objectives. This should be distinguished from efficiency, which is measured by the volume of output achieved for the input used.

effort   The amount of work or labor (in hours or workdays) required to complete a task. Effort is used to establish the labor costs associated with a project. Effort is in contrast to duration, which is the span of time over which the effort takes place. (See *duration* for more information.)

element   See *subtask*.

evaluate   To appraise or determine the value of information, resources, or options being provided to you as a project manager.

event   In CPM and PERT networks, the end state for one or more activities that occurs at a specific point in time.

extinction   The end of all activity on a project, usually before meeting its stated objectives. The end results of a project terminated by extinction are terminated by neither inclusion nor integration.

facilitator   A person who makes it easier for other people to accomplish objectives by offering advice and assistance in solving problems either with technical issues or with other people. Project managers are often referred to as facilitators.

float   The amount of time for a task to be freely scheduled without affecting other tasks in a project. Also, the difference between the duration available for a task and the duration required to complete it. Float is also known as *slack* or *slack time*.

functional management   The standard departments of a business organization that represent individual disciplines such as engineering, marketing, purchasing, and accounting.

Gantt chart   A chart that uses timelines and other symbols to illustrate multiple, time-based activities or projects on a horizontal time scale.

go/no-go indicator   A level of measurement that quickly tells a reviewer if an object's dimension is within certain limits. In the case of project management, this can be any monitoring or observation that allows a manager to decide whether to change, terminate, or continue an activity or a project.

hierarchical planning   A planning approach in which each managerial level breaks planning tasks down into the activities that must be done at that level. Typically, upper-level planning establishes the objectives for the next-lower-level manager's planning.

inclusion   A way of terminating a project by incorporating the project operations and team into the organization as an ongoing entity. The project work still exists, but the project is no longer separate from the business operations.

integration   A way of terminating a project by bringing project team members back into the organization and distributing project results and outcomes among existing functions. The project as an entity no longer exists after integration.

interface management   Managing the problems that often occur between people, departments, and disciplines, rather than within the project team itself.

interfaces   The formal and informal boundaries and relationships between people, departments, organizations, or functions.

lag   The amount of time after one task is started or finished before the next task can be started or finished.

lateral communication   When information exchange occurs across lines of equivalent authority or between managers at the same level in an organization's hierarchy.

lead   The amount of time that precedes the start of work on another task.

Leveling   The process of shifting the use of resources to even out the workload of team members and equipment. If, in your ideal plan, Joe is required to work 86 hours a week on the project, you'll need to find other resources that can take on part of Joe's workload and adjust the schedule accordingly. Computer programs can help do this for you. Be aware, however, that resource leveling will likely cause changes in the network diagram, budget, or timing of a project.

Loading   The amount of time individual resources (people, vendors, and so on) have committed to a project. A team member or other resource who has a large block of time committed to the project can't work on other projects. If the load exceeds his or her work week, you'll have to pay overtime or add resources.

Material Requirements Planning (MRP)   An approach for material planning and ordering based on known or forecast demand requirements, lead times for obtaining each item, and existing inventories of all items.

matrix organization   An organizational structure that uses functional supervisors as well as project supervisors to manage the same people, depending on the assignment. A strong matrix is similar to a pure project organization, while a weak matrix operates more like a functional organization.

milestone   A clearly identifiable point in a project that summarizes the completion of a related or important set of tasks. Milestones are commonly used to summarize the important events in a project for managers and stakeholders who don't want or need to see the details in a project plan.

mixed organization   This organizational structure includes functional groups, pure project groups, and perhaps a matrixed group in its hierarchy. It is similar to a matrix organization.

model   A way of looking at reality, usually for the purpose of abstracting and simplifying it to make it understandable in a particular context. A plan is a type of model used to describe how a project will be completed.

negative float   The state at which all the float in a project is used up and any imposed or approved schedule dates are impossible to meet. In essence, a project with negative float is another description for a project that will come in late.

network diagram   The logical representation of tasks that defines the sequence of work in a project. Networks are usually drawn from left to right with lines drawn between tasks to indicate the precedence among tasks. On a large project, several network diagrams may exist: one for the overall project based on the project milestones and one for each subproject that represents the completion of a milestone.

one-on-ones   Meetings (often scheduled and formal) between two people involved in a project. These meetings are used to discuss priorities, to resolve issues, and to communicate overall responsibilities and statuses on a project.

padding   A standard project management tactic used to add a little extra time or money to estimates to cover for the uncertainty and risk in trying to see into the future. Also a type of contingency planning. Too much padding can get you into trouble. Padding of 15 to 25 percent is probably the most you should ever use. If you need more than this to feel comfortable with your plan, you need help with the estimates from experts or more experienced managers.

path   A sequence of lines and nodes in a project network.

political situation   Two or more people in a room trying to get something done. This means projects always have a political dimension.

portfolio   A group of projects or other items that are being worked on at the same time or that have been completed and are used as an indicator of ability.

precedence   When one task must be completed before another task can be started, the first task is said to have precedence over the second.

product development lifecycle   The specific set of phases and steps to bring a product to market within an industry or company. Most product development lifecycles comprise multiple projects as well as ongoing operations.

pro forma   Projected or anticipated. This term usually is applied to financial data such as balance sheets and income statements.

project   A sequence of tasks with a beginning and an end that uses time and resources to produce specific results. A project has a specific, desired outcome, a deadline or target date when the project must be done, and a budget that limits the amount of people, supplies, and money that can be used to complete the project.

project duration   The time it takes to complete an entire project from starting the first task to finishing the last task.

Project Evaluation and Review Technique (PERT)   One of the two most common forms of networking systems. PERT uses three time estimates to determine the most probable project completion time. See *Critical Path Method (CPM)*.

project management   The combination of systems, techniques, and people required to successfully complete a project on time and within budget.

Project Management Information System (PMIS)   A system used to chart activities and data and to track progress and information flow in a project. It is most frequently computerized but not always.

Project Management Institute (PMI)   A professional organization that studies and promotes project management techniques. If you want to join PMI to learn more about project management, contact information is provided in Appendix B.

project management process   The five phases of initiating, planning, executing, controlling, and closing that can help people bring projects in on time and within budget.

project manager   Any person who takes overall responsibility for coordinating a project, regardless of size, to make sure the desired end result comes in on time and within budget.

project murder   The sudden termination of a project for reasons that range from rational to absurd. An attempt on a project's life may take place during economic downturns, acquisition of the parent organization, or something entirely unexpected. In the case of a well-known computer map-making program, the unexpected death of its visionary founder sunk a hot new project the next day. A knife in a project's back may lead to not only angry team members, but possible lawsuits.

risk analysis   An evaluation of the feasibility or probability that the outcome of a project or policy will be the desired one. Usually conducted to compare two or more alternative scenarios, action plans, or policies.

rush charges   Charges that are applied by outside vendors when you, well, rush them. If at all possible, avoid incurring rush charges through the techniques described in this book.

scope   The magnitude of the effort required to complete a project. As you would rightly assume, the project scope for bringing a new toy airplane to market is much smaller than the project scope for designing a new attack jet.

scope creep   The process of adding work to a project, little by little, until the original schedule and cost estimates are completely meaningless. Always make sure that any "creep" in the statement of work (SOW) or project plan is agreed to in writing along with the schedule and budget changes.

situational management   The approach of matching management style to the specific needs of a situation. Project managers must effectively apply the best management style for the job—whether task-oriented, employee-oriented, or reward-oriented leadership—to meet the needs of individual team members.

slack   See *float*.

split   Dividing a task into two or more tasks.

stakeholders   People who have a personal or enterprise interest in the end results of a project. Not all stakeholders are involved in completing the actual work on a project. Common stakeholders include customers, managers, corporate executives, and representatives of government agencies.

standard task unit   An agreed-upon description and amount of effort for a common task used in multiple projects.

statement of work (SOW)   An integrated set of task descriptions, goal descriptions, risks, and assumptions that accompany the evolving master project plan during its development. When completed, the SOW will detail the work to be completed on a project and the contingencies for dealing with known risk factors.

subcontract   Delegating tasks or subprojects to contractors or other organizations.

suboptimization   The optimization of one component of a system or project, such as task sequence or schedule, often to the detriment of the overall plan or project.

subproject   A portion of the whole project that can be viewed as a project in its own right. An example would be building the new Trip to Jupiter ride (a subproject) within the project of building a new Disneyland theme park in Africa.

subtask   A portion of the complete task. For example, the task might be to write the articles for a newsletter, while a subtask might be to write the lead article for the newsletter.

systems approach   A wide-ranging method for addressing problems that considers multiple and interacting relationships. This approach is often contrasted with the analytic approach. Project management is a systems approach to managing projects.

task   A cohesive unit of work on a project—one that's not too big or too small to be tracked. A task may include several steps (or subtasks) that are conceptually related.

task description   A description that defines all the work required to accomplish a project activity including inputs, outputs, and quality specifications.

termination team   A project team responsible for wrapping up the administrative details of a project.

trade-off   Allowing one aspect of a project to change, usually for the worse, in return for another aspect of the project getting better.

win-win negotiation   When both parties are better off after a negotiation has been completed.

work breakdown structure (WBS)   A basic project diagram or listing that documents and describes all the work that must be done to complete the project. The WBS forms the basis for costing, scheduling, network diagramming, and work assignments.

Resources for Project Managers

This part of the book provides information on software products and organizations that can assist you in your project management endeavors.

Software Products for Project Management

The following companies sell or distribute project management software. This is by no means a comprehensive list. There are many other companies and products out there, and more are added every day. The companies listed here offer either products we have worked with or products that have been recently reviewed in computer literature. A listing in this book should not be considered a testimonial for the functionality or suitability of any of these products—it is only provided to get you started in your search for project management software. Many of the products listed are corporate-level programs that include Web-based collaboration capabilities. Some are easy-to-use programs for the occasional project manager. Note that all product and company names are trademarks and registered trademarks of the respective companies.

Company	Project Management Products
AEC Software, Inc. 22611-113 Markey Ct. Sterling, VA 20166 Phone: 703-450-1980 Fax: 703-450-9786 Toll-free: 1-800-346-9413 Web site: www.aecsoft.com	Fast Track

continues

continued

Company	Project Management Products
Artemis Management Systems 6260 Lookout Rd. Boulder, CO 80301 Phone: 1-800-477-6648 (U.S. and Canada) International: 303-531-3145 Fax: 303-531-3140 Web site: www.artemispm.com	Views, Artemis, and KnowledgePlan
Ballantine & Company, Inc. P.O. Box 805 Carlisle, MA 01741 Phone: 508-369-1772 Fax: 508-369-9179 Web site: www.ballantine-inc.com	QuickGantt
IMSI Turboproject IMSI Corporate Headquarters 75 Rowland Way Novato, CA 94945 Phone: 415-878-4000 Fax: 415-897-2544 Web site: www.turboproject.com/	Turboproject
Mesa Systems Guild, Inc. 60 Quaker Ln. Warwick, RI 02886-0114 Phone: 401-828-8500 Toll-free: 1-888-MESASYS (1-888-637-2797) Fax: 401-828-9550 Web site: www.mesasystems.com	Mesa Systems Product Line
Microsoft Corporation One Microsoft Way Redmond, WA 98052-6399 Phone: 206-882-8080 Web site: www.microsoft.com	Microsoft Project
Netmosphere Inc. 2225 E. Bayshore Rd., Ste. 100A Palo Alto, CA 94303 Phone: 650-855-0430 Fax: 650-855-0467 Web site: www.netmosphere.com/	Project Home Page and Action Plan, among others

Company	Project Management Products
Primavera Systems Inc. Two Bala Plaza Bala Cynwyd, PA 19004 Phone: 610-667-8600 Fax: 610-667-7894 Toll-free: 1-800-423-0245 Web site: www.primavera.com	Primavera Project Planner and others
Scitor Corporation Business Solutions Group 256 Gibraltar Dr. Sunnyvale, CA 94089 Phone: 408-745-8300 Fax: 408-745-8301 Web site: www.scitor.com	Project Scheduler and others
SME Corporation 1038 Redwood Highway B7 Mill Valley, CA 94941 Phone: 1-888-763-3555 Fax: 415-381-9673 Web site: www.smecorporation.com	Project Invision
Time Line Solutions Corporation 7599 Redwood Blvd. Suite 209 Novato, CA 94945 Phone: 415-898-1919 Fax: 415-898-1919 Web site: www.tlsolutions.com	On Target, Time Line, and others
Web Project, Inc. 1900 South Norfolk St. Suite 100 San Mateo, CA 94403 Phone: 650-574-0578 Web site: www.wproj.com	WebProject

More Resources

The following World Wide Web resources provide general information about project management or offer special training programs for project managers.

Project Management Institute
130 South State Rd.
Upper Darby, PA 19082
Web site: www.pmi.org

Project Management Institute (PMI) is a not-for-profit organization dedicated to the advancement of project management methodology and the training of project managers. The quarterly *Project Mangement Journal,* published by PMI, includes timely articles about project management procedures, experiences, and techniques. The institute holds regular seminars and meetings for members. PMI also offers a certification program for people who want to verify and document their project management expertise. As of this writing, the membership fee is $80 per year. A subscription to *Project Management Journal* and *PM Network* is included as part of the membership fee.

Project Management International
Web site: www.infoser.com/infocons/pmi/

This site provides information on project management activities and standards around the world.

PM-Project Manager: The Industrial Project Management Site
Web site: www.project-manager.com/

This site provides links to a wide range of industrial project management resources.

The SMG PM IQnet
Web site: phl.smginc.com/smginc/marketing/pmiqnet/demo/

The demo of the PM IQnet from SMG (Strategic Management Group) illustrates the training, consulting, and other resources available from SMG to help develop project management skills within the corporation.

Online Project Management Course through UC Berkeley
Web site: learn.berkeley.edu.

Sunny Baker (one of the authors of this book) offers an online project management course (Management X.470) through the University of California, Extension. You can find out more information about this open enrollment course on the site.

Index

C

D

F

facilities constraints, 83
failure of projects, 26
faxes (communication tool), 263
  advantages, 263
  disadvantages, 263
final evaluation, 340-342
  confidential reports, 345
  final report, 342-344
    Executive Summary, 344
    miscellaneous components, 344
    Part A, 344
    Part B, 344
    political impact, 345
    Project Plan, 344
  individual team member performance, 345-346
  listing accomplishments, 342
  personal evaluation, 346
  why projects fail to meet goals, 340-341
  why projects succeed, 341-342
final reports, 342-344
  Executive Summary, 344
  miscellaneous components, 344
  Part A, 344
  Part B, 344
  political impact, 345
  Project Plan, 344
final shutdown tasks, 330-331
finish dates, setting goals, 68
first project meeting (implementing the plan), 215-217
  avoiding floating start dates, 218-219
  getting members of the team in synch, 217-218
  one-on-ones, 216
flexibility
  as rule of success, 32
  managing change, 296
  software, 371
float time, 168
  calculating with critical path worksheets, 170-172
  negative float, 179
floating start dates, 318
focus on project end, project managers, 38

forcing (conflict resolution option), 291
formal
  kickoff events, 213-214
  meetings (communication tool), 262
  monitoring activities, 247
    establishing environment of motivation, 248-249
    meetings and one-on-ones, 249
    ODP (open door policy), 247-248
  presentations (communication tool), 263
  proposals, estimate negotiations, 126
  reports (communication tool), 262
forms for reports
  schedule update, 252
  status reporting, 252
  supply and equipment request, 252
functional
  management, as role of stakeholder, 50
  project organization, 234-235

G

Gnatt charts, 116, 156-159
  schedule-charting formats, 156-159
goal incompatibility (people conflict), 288
goals
  assessment, monitoring and control, 282
  consensus, 68
  document, 70
  establishing scope, 70-72
  finish dates, 68
  identifiable responsibilities, 69
  limiting, 69-70
  measurability, 68
  neccesity, 64-65
  primary goals common to all projects, 66
  realistic, 67
  setting appropriate goals, 65
  specificity, 67

golden rules of project management success, 26
  accommodation of people's needs and priorities, 30-31
  appropriate scope, 30
  building the best team, 28
  communication, 32
  consensus on project outcomes, 27
  detailed project plan, 28-29
  flexibility, 32
  leadership, 32-33
  management and stakeholder's approval, 31
  minimizing failure, 33
  realistic schedule, 29-30
  sufficient resources, 29
  willingness to adapt, 31
Goldratt, Dr. Eliyahu M., Theory of Constraints (TOC), 168
groupware (communication tool), 263

H-I

handwritten notes (communication tool), 261
hiring staff, selecting the implementation team, 136-137
histograms (resource utilization), 177
horizontal communcations, 224

identifiable responsibilities, setting goals, 69
identifying
  constraints, 79
  risks, 84
  stakeholders, 47
implementation team, 129-143
  as role of stakeholder, 51
  assigning people and skills to a job description, 137
    compromise, 142-143
    contacts and suppliers, 141
    creating a skills inventory, 138-139
    matching people to jobs, 139
    narrowing choices, 142
    political ramifications, 140
    replacements, 142
    training, 140-141

N

W–X–Y–Z